EMPIRE OF THE ELITE

Inside Condé Nast,
the Media Dynasty That
Reshaped America

MICHAEL M. GRYNBAUM

SIMON & SCHUSTER
New York Amsterdam/Antwerp London
Toronto Sydney/Melbourne New Delhi

Simon & Schuster
1230 Avenue of the Americas
New York, NY 10020

For more than 100 years, Simon & Schuster has championed authors and the stories they create. By respecting the copyright of an author's intellectual property, you enable Simon & Schuster and the author to continue publishing exceptional books for years to come. We thank you for supporting the author's copyright by purchasing an authorized edition of this book.

No amount of this book may be reproduced or stored in any format, nor may it be uploaded to any website, database, language-learning model, or other repository, retrieval, or artificial intelligence system without express permission. All rights reserved. Inquiries may be directed to Simon & Schuster, 1230 Avenue of the Americas, New York, NY 10020 or permissions@simonandschuster.com.

Copyright © 2025 by Michael M. Grynbaum

All rights reserved, including the right to reproduce this book or portions thereof in any form whatsoever. For information, address Simon & Schuster Subsidiary Rights Department, 1230 Avenue of the Americas, New York, NY 10020.

First Simon & Schuster hardcover edition July 2025

SIMON & SCHUSTER and colophon are registered trademarks of Simon & Schuster, LLC

Simon & Schuster strongly believes in freedom of expression and stands against censorship in all its forms. For more information, visit BooksBelong.com.

For information about special discounts for bulk purchases, please contact Simon & Schuster Special Sales at 1-866-506-1949 or business@simonandschuster.com.

The Simon & Schuster Speakers Bureau can bring authors to your live event. For more information or to book an event, contact the Simon & Schuster Speakers Bureau at 1-866-248-3049 or visit our website at www.simonspeakers.com.

Interior design by Kyle Kabel

Manufactured in the United States of America

1 3 5 7 9 10 8 6 4 2

Library of Congress Cataloging-in-Publication Data has been applied for.

ISBN 978-1-6680-0391-6
ISBN 978-1-6680-0393-0 (ebook)

For Juli, my favorite

"This effect of certain of the manifestations of wealth in New York is, so far as I know, unique: nowhere else does pecuniary power so beat its wings in the void, and so look round it for the charity of some hint as to the possible awkwardness or possible grace of its motion, some sign of whether it be flying, for good taste, too high or too low."

—Henry James, *The American Scene*

"I wish I was the editor of a magazine, and I could tell everybody what to do and think."

—Courtney Love

Contents

Introduction   Perfect Bound xi

Chapter 1   Class, Not Mass. 1

Chapter 2   Mitzi's Boy 17

Chapter 3   The Silver Fox 27

Chapter 4   Si Finds His *Self* 39

Chapter 5   British Invader. 53

Chapter 6   Enter Anna 73

Chapter 7   A Man's World 95

Chapter 8   The Ballad of Donald and Si 109

Chapter 9   Philistine at the Gate 121

Chapter 10   Eustace Tina 135

Chapter 11   Lapses of Taste 151

Chapter 12   Life as a Party 169

Chapter 13   Age of Empire. 187

CONTENTS

Chapter 14 "Do It All Grandly!" 203

Chapter 15 Up Is Up 227

Chapter 16 A House Divided 243

Chapter 17 Technical Difficulties 251

Chapter 18 The Elephant 263

Chapter 19 The Back of the Book 281

Acknowledgments 293

Notes 297

Index 327

Introduction

Perfect Bound

For decades, one company in Manhattan told the world what to buy, what to value, what to wear, what to eat, even what to think. Before Instagram, before TikTok, there was the Condé Nast Publications, merchant of fantasies and supreme arbiter of sophistication. *Vogue* chose the designers whose clothes would be worn by millions around the world, and the models who became global icons of sex and femininity. *Vanity Fair* determined which moguls we envied and movie stars we worshiped. *GQ* made it okay for straight guys to care about clothes, *Architectural Digest* pioneered real estate porn, and *The New Yorker* elevated tabloid fare like the O. J. Simpson murder trial to the realm of serious journalism. Our contemporary Instagram culture—airbrushed, brand-name-laden, and full of FOMO, where pretty people do pretty things in pretty places without you—is a DIY replication of the universe that the celebrity editors of Condé Nast carefully created month after month, year after year.

At the peak of its powers, Condé Nast cultivated a mystique that captivated tens of millions of subscribers across four continents, with brands that became international symbols of class and glamour. Editors such as Tina Brown and Anna Wintour were venerated, celebrated, and feared, with unrivaled sway in determining who and what was elite, who was "in" and who was "out." Their magazines were glossy manuals to the good life, defining our modern notions of class, consumerism, politics, lifestyle, and taste. To be featured by Condé Nast meant that one had arrived—as an actor, author, designer, thinker, or socialite. *Condé Nast*—even the name announced itself with a continental flair, that exotic accent above the *e* so redolent of fine living and superior judgment.

Never before had so much cultural influence been concentrated under one roof—and it never will happen again.

Now, Condé is a husk of its former self, its clout diminished, its magazines closed or riddled by layoffs. Staff uproars over race and class have punctured its once-impenetrable aura. *Bon Appétit*'s editor resigned in 2020 amid complaints of racial insensitivity and bias, and in 2021, unionized *New Yorker* employees, vexed by low wages, picketed Anna Wintour's town house in Greenwich Village, chanting "Bosses wear Prada, workers get nada." Condé's chief architect and feared billionaire boss S. I. Newhouse Jr. is dead. Young people may vaguely know Condé Nast as the real-life inspiration for *The Devil Wears Prada*: the imperious bosses, obscene expense accounts, and ubiquitous town cars. Or they may not know of Condé Nast at all. While brand names such as *Vanity Fair* and *Vogue* persevere, the fundamental idea that a monthly package of pulp and ink, delivered via trucks and postal workers, could wield such influence is alien to anyone under the age of thirty.

And yet we still live in the world that Condé bequeathed to us: the world of the *Vanity Fair* Oscar party and *Vogue*'s Met Gala, *Allure*'s industry-standard Best of Beauty prizes and *Condé Nast Traveler*'s Readers' Choice Awards, a world obsessed with status and celebrity and consumption—a world that has persisted even as old-line notions of "elitism" have become increasingly passé, and the only gatekeepers we can credit or blame for our present-day culture are ourselves.

How Condé Nast amassed so much power and influence—and why, at the height of its culture-shaping savvy, it failed to foresee the digital revolution that would devour it—is a saga of self-invention and raw ambition, clashing egos and a ruthless pursuit of excellence. It is a tale of outsiders who longed to be insiders, and eventually conquered the rarefied spheres they once yearned to join. It is the story of how one company defined a nation's ideal image of itself.

WHEN AN AWKWARD SCION named Samuel Irving ("Si") Newhouse Jr. inherited his father's magazine business in 1979, Condé Nast was a faded Jazz Age icon, a second-tier publisher of women's titles, already seven decades old, that clung like Miss Havisham to its past glories. *Vogue* was read by fashionistas, but had little impact on the zeitgeist. *House & Garden* was losing ground to a splashier, wealthier West Coast rival, *Architectural Digest* (not yet part of the Condé stable). Si had money, but little status; at around five foot six, he was diminutive, physically and socially. "So incredibly shy and inarticulate," as one longtime Condé editor recalled. "So inarticulate it was shocking." The Newhouse name was an afterthought in the power centers of Wall Street, Washington, and Hollywood, where the rival Time Inc. magazine empire held greater sway. And Si's younger brother, Donald, controlled the real moneymaker of the family's empire: the newspapers.

But Si viewed the Condé Nast magazines as vessels for his own fantasies of status and class, his backdoor entry into the establishment whose rituals he had studied through the social equivalent of a two-way mirror. Unlike other publishers, who were happy to attack the power elite, Si wanted to celebrate it. Or better yet: become it. His timing happened to be excellent. Si was taking over Condé Nast right on the cusp of the Reagan eighties, when the desultory post-Watergate seventies were yielding to an era of exuberant excess. A new generation of strivers had awoken to the pleasures of consumerism. If the pre-eighties East Coast establishment prized discretion, thrift, and subtlety—threadbare Shetland sweaters, shabby station wagons—the new elite was all about the flaunt. And Condé Nast, which itself had been founded in the era that spawned the term "conspicuous consumption," was perfectly situated to supply the user manuals the *nouveau* needed.

To create this world, Si turned to strivers whose own yearnings for success and social dominance reflected the cult of aspiration their magazines fetishized. Americans' idea of what it meant to be elite had long been shaped by the fantasies of outsiders: the splendid penthouses and tuxedoed balls of 1930s Hollywood movies were made by Jewish immigrant studio heads who were forced to build their industry on the other side of the country after the Eastern elite rejected them. The mythmakers of Condé Nast similarly willed their world into existence. *Vanity Fair*'s Graydon Carter was raised middle-class in Ottawa and worked as a lineman on rural railways. Art Cooper, who took *GQ* from fashion trade rag to a global byword for the dapper male lifestyle, grew up a chubby Jewish kid in Pennsylvania coal country. Paige Rense, the mastermind of *Architectural Digest*, was born into abject Midwestern poverty. *The New Yorker*'s David Remnick was a New Jersey dentist's son. And there was Alexander Liberman, Condé's longtime editorial director, an unrepentant aesthete and spendthrift who tutored Si in all things tasteful, but, as a refugee from Bolshevik Russia, was always outrunning his own tragic past.

Si empowered his editors to fuel his new American fantasyland, urging experimentation and extravagance that competing publishers balked at and could not compete with. Not content to merely chronicle the establishment, Si insisted that the leading players of his empire emulate the lives of those they profiled. Hence the no-interest loans for West Village town houses and Long Island country retreats, and Wall Street–level perks like chauffeured town cars and fat expense accounts. The excess was legendary. For years, there simply were no budgets: Si's billions funded an operation where sizzle and status often mattered more than breaking even. Feasts from gourmet provisioner Fauchon were trucked in to fashion shoots; editors zipped back and forth to Europe on the Concorde. Outsiders who scoffed at such profligacy misunderstood the rationale behind Si's masquerade: for Tina Brown or Anna Wintour to earn the respect of the rich, they had to live like the rich. To shape taste, one had to embody taste. Condé Nast editors were the original influencers, their lives a top-to-bottom marketing campaign for the company that hired them.

Before individuals could amass millions of followers on Twitter or Instagram, Condé was the chief arbiter of the elite, its editors' whims and signals relentlessly covered, dissected, and mimicked. Tina perfected the practice of hyping her magazine's upcoming articles to outlets like *The New York Times* and the network morning shows, turning *Vanity Fair* stories into meta events—news in themselves. Her high/low sensibility—opulent, celebrity-centric, insiderish, buzzy—reshaped American journalism, demolishing cultural guardrails. Her editorial DNA eventually found its way into journalistic bastions such as *The New York Times*, which created its Styles section in 1992 in part to compete with Condé's lifestyle content. Anna Wintour's *Vogue* became the most powerful force in global fashion, championing upstarts like John Galliano and Alexander McQueen and helping them secure funding to start their own labels. Graydon's guest list for the annual *Vanity Fair* Oscar party elevated movie stars to the A-list.

And the Condé empire played a key role in the fateful rise of a real estate developer named Donald J. Trump, who was a provincial curiosity before *GQ* featured him on its cover and Si Newhouse personally dreamed up *The Art of the Deal*, the book that launched Trump's national stardom (and was published by a Newhouse-owned press). Trump, along with two of his three wives, later graced the covers of *Vanity Fair* and *Vogue*, and he proposed to Melania, the future First Lady, at Anna Wintour's Met Gala, taking advantage of the enormous publicity surrounding the event. Indeed, Condé parties were covered relentlessly by other media outlets, with seating charts presented as a taxonomy of influence. This was especially remarkable given that these extravaganzas were, at heart, simple branding exercises meant to dazzle advertisers and advance the commercial prospects of Condé Nast magazines. No other publisher's events approached this level of renown: Americans were not talking about a gala thrown by Hearst.

Inside Condé, editors jockeyed for the approval of Si, the "Sun King" whose court was the site of feuds, fiefs, and beheadings. Grace Mirabella, longtime editor of *Vogue*, learned from a five o'clock local news report that she had been replaced by Anna Wintour: the leading editor in American fashion undone in an instant. Si's ouster of William Shawn from *The New Yorker* prompted one of the great literary revolts of the twentieth century. Ron Galotti, an ad honcho who inspired *Sex and the City*'s Mr. Big, was hired, fired, and rehired by Si in quick succession;

Steve Florio, Condé's chief executive, forced his own brother out of a job. A mercurial Medici who could be maddeningly opaque about his views, Si kept his talent nervous about where they stood. Editors compared the bottles of wine they received from Si at Christmas—who had gotten the more expensive cru? Decades of service could be swept aside the instant the publisher sensed that a title was losing too much money or generating too little buzz. Si so adored this internal competition that when he purchased *Women's Wear Daily* in 1999, he asked its editor to gather gossip on Condé Nast—the better to keep tabs on his empire.

In 1999, the company moved to a sleek new skyscraper, 4 Times Square, that not only helped revive Midtown Manhattan's fortunes—Condé's influence even extended to urban planning—but also evoked the mid-century power of the Time & Life Building, perhaps the last time a magazine company had so flagrantly expressed its power and arrogance in expensive corporate architecture. The building's centerpiece was a space-age cafeteria designed by Frank Gehry, which quickly became the most scrutinized corporate canteen on earth; an architectural review in *The New York Times* ran under the headline "Tray Chic." By the time it opened, 4 Times Square was the flagship of an international empire, with outposts on multiple continents. In the new millennium, *Vogue* has expanded into Dubai, Mumbai, and Beijing—Condé colonization.

FOR SUBURBAN KIDS LIKE ME who grew up at the turn of the twenty-first century, Condé's magazines were emissaries from a cosmopolitan world that shimmered just beyond our horizon: a monthly or weekly spectacle of temptations, refinement, sensual possibilities, and intellectual sophistication that set my imagination ablaze. The name Si Newhouse meant nothing to me, but *Vogue, Vanity Fair*, and *The New Yorker*—and the writers, artists, and photographers whose work filled their pages—represented a world I yearned to join. Condé publications carried the promise that writing and journalism could be a glamorous trade, that nerdy kids like me could combine smarts with style, facts with flair. My parents may not have been rich or socially prominent, but they subscribed to *The New Yorker* and *Architectural Digest*, an economical way to demonstrate appreciation for superior taste. By age eleven, I'd started a magazine for my fifth-grade class—my own elementary-school version of *Vanity Fair*—commissioning articles from friends and distributing copies at the local library. When I finally made it to Manhattan—I could not wait to get to Manhattan—I met my future wife while she was writing at *Vanity Fair*. Fetching her for dates from the lobby of 4 Times Square, I watched *Vogue*'s coiffed gazelles and *The New Yorker*'s tweedy editors greet the purring town cars provided by their employer. These glimpses of Condé's inner workings only intrigued me further. How had this company become so glamorous and influential—and why was it declining so fast? What would become of the fantasy realm it had loosed upon the world?

BY THE LATE 2000s, Si Newhouse's notion of the elite had been shaping dreams and desires for nearly three decades. In 2007, when Condé launched *Portfolio* magazine—a celebration of swashbuckling corporate culture that promised to do for business journalism what *Vanity Fair* had done for covering Hollywood—Si reportedly committed more than $100 million to the project; Tom Wolfe was commissioned to write at a rumored twelve dollars a word. "We are the top-end publisher and it has served us well and I believe it will stand the test," the company's CEO, Charles Townsend, said in 2008.

It didn't.

The internet demolished the notion of authority in American life—and the animating spirit of Condé Nast. Power has swung from institutions to the individual; what we covet is no longer beamed outward from a Manhattan office tower, but forged across a million digital byways on Instagram, TikTok, Pinterest, Snapchat, Twitter, and Facebook. *Portfolio* collapsed in 2009, barely two years after its debut. Condé Nast had thrived by showing Americans how to cultivate artistic, graceful, stylish lives. Now the internet had birthed a Warholian utopia where anyone can be famous and commune with the famous. The cultural elites who ran movie studios, programmed TV networks, and controlled FM radio playlists—the symbiotic stars of the Condé universe—not only lost relevance, but were refashioned into the villains of a populist revolution against yesterday's cultural gatekeepers. Upstart bloggers such as Tavi Gevinson were among the first to prove that teenagers can dictate trends from their bedrooms without the infrastructure (or overhead) of a traditional media company behind them. Readers who grew up absorbing the company's glamorous imagery—the product of lavish photo shoots and hundreds of hours of styling, editing, and design—can now reproduce a version of it on their Instagram and TikTok accounts in minutes.

And as American institutions came under increased scrutiny, Condé Nast faced its own internal reckoning over class and race. In June 2020, in the wake of George Floyd's murder, Anna Wintour apologized for publishing "hurtful or intolerant" material and acknowledged that "*Vogue* has not found enough ways to elevate and give space to Black editors, writers, photographers, designers and other creators." Bracing testimonials emerged from former Black staff members who critiqued the magazine's culture of exclusivity and its elevation of Eurocentric notions of beauty—the very editorial model that had, until then, generated decades of success.

Si Newhouse died in 2017 at age eighty-nine, leaving behind descendants who did not share his infinite patience with financial losses. Budgets were tightened, titles shuttered, and staffers laid off. *Vanity Fair*'s Oscar party was pronounced "past its prime" by *The New York Times*. The Newhouses installed a new chief executive, Roger Lynch, from the digital music streamer Pandora, who had no experience in the magazine industry; he then pushed out the editors of *Vogue* editions in Brazil, China, France, Germany, India, and Spain. Today, Condé is in retrograde, even as the company's apogee remains an object of fascination: a reminder of more vibrant days when the America it symbolized was the envy of the world. As Graydon Carter told me, reflecting on his career, "I miss the black-and-whiteness of the twentieth century."

But the choices of Condé's editors can still resonate. The gloss and voyeurism of Instagram is an updated version of the wealth porn epitomized by Condé Nast; our digital obsession with house tours and opulent lifestyles has its roots in *Vanity Fair*, *Vogue*, and *Architectural Digest*. Even the old-fashioned printed product makes an occasional splash: a *Vogue* cover of Kamala Harris, dressed casually in sneakers and a jacket, caused an uproar shortly before she was sworn in as the first female vice president. The chattering class still cared about how Condé Nast depicted its stars.

I did not set out to write an exhaustive encyclopedia of the company; inevitably, I have had to leave out the stories of certain people, and in some cases entire titles, that played significant roles across its 116-year history. This book is intended as an assessment of Condé Nast's profound impact on American life. The Newhouses—many of them, anyway—were not receptive to my inquiries, and Condé Nast itself did not cooperate beyond confirming the corporate titles of three of its executives. Dozens of writers, editors, artists, publishers, and photographers—some of whom are still employed at Condé Nast—did help, and I am deeply grateful for their generosity. It's been nearly fifty years since Si Newhouse began building his mythology of American power, desire, and exceptionalism. Consider this a guided tour through the dream life that he sowed.

1

Class, Not Mass

Condé Montrose Nast was born in 1873 in New York City, a grandson of a strident Methodist preacher and the third child of a father who abandoned his wife and children when Nast was three. The family moved to St. Louis, where Nast attended public schools; when he went to college at Georgetown, he avoided trips home for want of train fare. After graduation, he returned to Missouri to pursue a law degree, and a career as a Midwestern lawyer beckoned. Then a fortuitous friendship changed his life. His college classmate Robert Collier, a wealthy publishing heir, offered Nast a job at his family's magazine, *Collier's Weekly*. In 1897, the preacher's grandson headed back to where his life had started: the burgeoning secular cathedral of New York.

Over the next decade, Nast helped turn *Collier's* into one of the country's leading publications, attracting star writers like Upton Sinclair and Jack London. He lured the illustrator Charles Dana Gibson away from rivals by doubling his pay in exchange for an exclusive contract. The job also led to Nast's initiation into the higher echelons of Gilded Age New York. Robert Collier had married into the family of Caroline Schermerhorn Astor, the society doyenne whose list of Manhattan's "Four Hundred" most prominent citizens was the final word in America's still-nascent social caste system. When Nast met Clarisse Coudert, an eligible daughter of a Four Hundred family, she was impressed by his friendship with Collier. They married in 1902, and Clarisse bestowed on her husband a rather apt kind of dowry: his inclusion in the *Social Register*. Overnight, Nast had entered the ranks of the American aristocracy; now he wanted to rise to its zenith. And he soon identified the perfect vessel for his ambitions: *Vogue*, a sleepy society gazette, barely solvent and barely read beyond a handful of drawing rooms on Fifth Avenue.

Founded in 1892 by a clique of old-money scions, *Vogue* attended to leisure-class concerns like golf, bridge, country club etiquette, and the passenger manifest on John Jacob Astor's yacht. The publisher, a wealthy typography enthusiast named Arthur Turnure, once forgot to send an issue's cover to the printers. With a select audience of fourteen thousand subscribers—forty times fewer than the readership of *Collier's*—the magazine regularly expressed revulsion toward the encroaching hordes of the nouveau riche. Even a cataclysm like the Spanish-American War was an opportunity to provide readers with a lesson on understatement. "Don't be so violently, alarmingly and visibly patriotic as to wear the tri-colors on everything," *Vogue* instructed in 1898. "Bad taste never yet helped a good cause." Above all, the magazine affected a tone of unerring authority, fueled by the egos of its founders and their credo, expressed in the earliest editorial meetings, that what "'*Vogue* says' was to be final."

Nast was certain that *Vogue*'s potential was woefully untapped. In a rapidly changing nation, where mass industrialization had generated unprecedented new wealth and the term "conspicuous consumption" had recently been coined, Nast recognized that social aspiration was itself a commodity that could be harnessed for influence and, with shrewd marketing, lucratively exploited. He set about finding investors to help him purchase the magazine, using his own journey of upward mobility as the inspiration for his business plan. Nast was a social climber par excellence, exacting in his appearance—even as a young man, he adopted an old-fashioned pince-nez as his signature look—and a devoted reader of fashion magazines from London and Paris. To meld with the Newport crowd, he arranged for a camera to film his golf swing so he could improve his form at the tee.

In his pitch to investors, Nast had argued that the market for a guide to good living was surely there. And because *Vogue* would be aimed not just at the affluent, but also those who yearned to be, it could charge advertisers higher-than-average rates in exchange for access to the nation's "wealthiest and most discriminating individuals." At the time, most major magazine publishers simply strived for the biggest possible audience. Nast's alternative model—"class, not mass"—was deeply counterintuitive: leaning into *Vogue*'s air of exclusivity could, paradoxically, broaden its appeal to readers and advertisers alike. As one *Vogue* editor put it: "He didn't want a big circulation. He wanted a good one." It was the motto from which all of Condé Nast's future success flowed.

Nast won control of *Vogue* in 1909. He introduced color photography, raised newsstand prices to create a greater perception of luxury, and paid large sums for the services of star photographers like Edward Steichen and Cecil Beaton, just as decades later his company would secure Richard Avedon and Annie Leibovitz to exclusive contracts. To appear more cosmopolitan, Nast included dispatches on European society, drawing on his and his wife's socialite friends as correspondents. Rumors began to circulate that Nast was descended from the Condé branch of France's royal House of Bourbon, or perhaps related to the political cartoonist Thomas Nast. Neither was true—Condé was a family name—but Nast didn't mind the gossip, because it buttressed his reputation.

Crucially, Nast also sought to make middle-class readers—those who might be curious about Parisian fashions but couldn't afford a Cunard crossing—feel included. He mailed free copies of *Vogue* to Midwestern department stores and Junior Leagues, to lure audiences outside of New York. *Vogue* included retailers' names in fashion spreads so readers would know where to buy the clothes, a primordial step toward democratized luxury; until then, chic dress shops like Henri Bendel kept their inventories secret to all but the most "proper" upper-crust customers. "It is the avowed mission of *Vogue* to appeal not merely to women of great wealth, but more fundamentally, to women of taste," Nast wrote. "A certain proportion of these readers will be found, necessarily, among the less well-to-do cousins of the rich." His strategy of inclusive exclusivity was a moneymaker. In 1910, *Ladies' Home Journal* was read by forty-three times more Americans than *Vogue*—but *Vogue* was carrying 44 percent more pages of advertising.

One event did more than anything to prove that Condé Nast, in the eyes of high society, had arrived. In 1914, *Vogue* threw a fashion show at the Ritz-Carlton ballroom featuring American designers, a radical idea at the time. Chic Americans considered domestic designs a poor substitute for French couture, but as Europe descended into conflict, it had become increasingly difficult to obtain the latest fashions. Debutantes were out of luck, and so was *Vogue*: with fewer clothes to feature, advertising revenue sagged. *Vogue*'s editor in chief, Edna Woolman Chase, pitched Nast on the idea of a fashion contest to boost the American garment industry. To ensure high society's blessing, Chase trekked to the Hudson Highlands mansion of Mrs. Stuyvesant Fish, who had succeeded Mrs. Astor as a key social arbiter, to ask if she would be a patron of the event. Mrs. Fish was about to rebuff Chase's offer . . . until her secretary mentioned to Chase that her son was an aspiring illustrator, and how wonderful would it be if his drawings were to appear in *Vogue*? A deal was struck, and Mrs. Fish was persuaded to get onboard. The Fashion Fête, as it was known, was presented as a charitable event for Great War widows and orphans. It was the Met Gala before the Met Gala—a magazine marketing stunt turned public sensation—and it made headlines around the world. In a few short years, Nast had transformed insular *Vogue* into a global tastemaker. *British Vogue* was introduced in 1916; *Vogue Paris* followed in 1920. By 1926, American *Vogue* touted the second-highest advertising volume of any magazine in the country.

Having landed on a profitable model, Nast set out to conquer new subsets of elite audiences. In 1911, he had invested in *House & Garden*, an obscure architectural publication in Philadelphia. As with *Vogue*, Nast intuited that the magazine could appeal to a broader audience: America's growing population of newly affluent homeowners eager to signal their status through decor. His next acquisition further advanced the sophisticated image accruing to the Condé Nast brand. He bought a men's magazine called *Dress*, which he considered a prospective rival to *Vogue*, and revamped it as a lively compendium of wit and commentary on the arts, society, and current affairs. He changed the name to *Dress & Vanity Fair* and hired a new editor, Frank Crowninshield, who dropped the *Dress*.

Unlike Nast, "Crownie" was no outsider. A Boston Brahmin born in Paris and educated in Rome, he was an aesthete and bon vivant who co-organized the famed Armory Show in 1913, now considered the dawn of American modernism. At *Vanity Fair*, Crownie published art by Picasso, Matisse, and Gauguin and writing by Gertrude Stein, Aldous Huxley, and Noël Coward. He also liked humor writing, and he spotted a potential talent in a young woman named Dorothy Parker (then Rothschild) who was toiling on the *Vogue* copy desk. Crownie hired her to write theater criticism, for which she showed an affinity: years later, at *The New Yorker*, she panned a production with a nine-word summary: "*The House Beautiful* is, for me, the play lousy."

Nast had no inkling that, in the far-off world of the 1980s, a resuscitated *Vanity Fair* under the editor Tina Brown would spark a revival of the company that bore his name. In the 1920s, he was just happy to count another success. Actors, artists, and writers clamored to be in the pages of *Vanity Fair*, which became a monthly chart of who was in and who was out in Jazz Age society. In a precursor to the celebrity-soaked *Vanity Fair* Oscar party, Nast began hosting all-night soirees at the palatial Park Avenue penthouse where he moved in 1925. Vanderbilts mingled with Marx Brothers and French nobility flirted with Hollywood moguls. Guests like George Gershwin, Fred Astaire, Samuel Goldwyn, and Edna St. Vincent Millay ascended to Nast's thirty-room spread, which featured a seventy-five-foot-long, glass-covered outdoor terrace filled with chrysanthemums. The opulent interiors, with Louis XV furniture and Savonnerie rugs, were designed by the society decorator Elsie de Wolfe. Diana Vreeland, a regular attendee who boogied one night with Josephine Baker, recalled, "Everybody who was invited to a Condé Nast party stood for something."

The name Condé Nast had meant nothing when he moved to Manhattan at the turn of the century. Now an invitation to his apartment meant the height of social success. Mr. Nast had become the new Mrs. Astor, and the thousands of copies of his magazines that landed on the nation's doorsteps and newsstands had become monuments to his cultural authority. Still, Nast hoped for something more permanent. After he took over a printing plant in Greenwich, Connecticut, in 1921, he erected a pair of enormous obelisks, engraved with titles rendered Roman-style: "VOGVE", "HOVSE & GARDEN", "CONDÉ NAST PVBLICATIONS." The pillars doubled as a monument to his own ego and as a billboard: they were installed astride the Boston Post Road, the preferred motoring route for Manhattanites and Fairfield County residents taking their progeny to New England prep schools. (Long after Nast died, and the printing plant was replaced by a Hyatt, the obelisks sustained his legacy: Lauren Santo Domingo, who later became a *Vogue* editor and significant tastemaker, drove by them every day growing up in Greenwich. "Probably why I became obsessed with working at Condé Nast one day," she joked.)

Nast's upward passage halted abruptly in 1929, when Wall Street collapsed. Condé Nast stock fell from ninety-three dollars a share to two dollars. The crash not only annihilated the fortunes of wealthy Americans; it also cratered the advertiser and reader base of the magazines that catered to them. For Nast, the crash was devastating: he lost a significant portion of his personal wealth. A man who built his life on illusions, Nast now tried to carry on the act. He continued throwing parties even as he relied on wealthy friends to keep him afloat. In 1933, a British media baron, Lord Camrose, quietly purchased a controlling stake in Condé Nast. Nast's name was still on the executive suite, but his control over his eponymous empire was gone. In March 1936, *Vanity Fair* was folded into *Vogue*. Nast had a final success with *Glamour of Hollywood*, a celebrity-focused magazine started in 1939. By then, he was in his mid-sixties, twice divorced, on the verge of serious heart trouble, and millions of dollars in debt; the prospect of restoring past glories was fading. In 1942, a bank took his Long Island country house, and he suffered a second heart attack. Nast died that September in his Park Avenue aerie, overlooking a city whose splendor and ferment he had done so much to package and sell to the world. His prized penthouse furnishings were sold for cheap at a disappointing auction.

But in death, the myth of Condé Nast bloomed. "Does the young woman in Fort Smith, or San Antonio, or Birmingham, or Topeka dress somewhat better than her ancestors, and does she have a surer appreciation of the world of manners and decorum and what might be called the art of gracious living? Then much of the credit must go to Condé Nast," wrote the *New York Herald Tribune. Time* eulogized him as the man from whom millions of people "got most of their ideas, directly or indirectly, about the desirable American standard of living." Condé Nast, the mortal—the child abandoned by his father who once struggled to decipher the codes of the rich—had evanesced into Condé Nast, the brand: global icon of sophistication, unimpeachable arbiter of the best that life had to offer.

The magazines, however, were being read by fewer and fewer people, their influence ebbing against competitors like *Harper's Bazaar*, *Life*, and *Esquire*. Nast, master of the mores of the Gilded Age, now seemed poised to share the lukewarm legacy of that era, remembered with a hazy nostalgia and unmistakable whiff of must. The indignity must have seemed total in 1958, when the ailing Condé Nast Publications were sold to the parent company of Britain's working-class *Daily Mirror*, a gauche fate for once-glittering *Vogue*. Within six months, the company changed hands again. The new owner was a diminutive Jewish publisher of mid-market newspapers with little public profile, a child of immigrants born into poverty who concentrated his business in second-tier cities like Cleveland, Ohio, and Syracuse, New York, whose parvenu wife happened to like reading the fashion pages. The transaction merited little mention in the press.

No one imagined that the most glorious, most profitable, and most powerful years of Condé Nast were still to come.

NAST HAD BEEN DEAD for nearly seventeen years when Samuel I. Newhouse, the wealthy but obscure owner of a national newspaper chain, purchased the tattered remains of the Nast magazine empire in 1959. It was effectively a fire sale. On the cusp of the 1960s, Condé's magazines felt more retro than cutting-edge, their pages preoccupied with cotillions and fedoras just as the world of debutantes and formal dressing was being swept away.

So, the Condé kingdom needed a savior. But who was this newcomer Newhouse? "A 5-3, kinky-haired, thick-lipped, friendly-eyed, flat-nosed dynamic insomniac who likes to buy publications," clucked *Women's Wear Daily*, the institutional voice of the fashion elite. "He went to work at 12 because he *needed* the money." *Collier's* compared his rumpled appearance to that of "a not-too-successful salesman, or perhaps a dealer in antiques." On the rare occasions he granted interviews, Sam Newhouse emphasized that he was a workaholic who didn't get out much; he even declined to respond to questions from the society roster *Who's Who*. To the Condé snobs, the idea that this unfashionable man could take charge of the most fashionable of American magazines was absurd. Newhouse was rich—his newspapers made a mint—but it was the wrong kind of rich, the slightly embarrassing fortune of a crass salesman. His company, Advance Publications, was based in, of all places, Staten Island. And then there was his wife, Mitzi Newhouse, who purported to have "a sixth sense about fashion." *Vogue*, it seemed, had been reduced to a naïf's bauble.

"It was a toy for Mitzi," one editor griped to *Women's Wear*, "like Marie Antoinette getting her farm."

Newhouse, who had been underestimated his entire life, shrugged it off. What the society wags failed to notice was that Sam and Nast had several things in common. Both men were born to mediocre fathers and moved to Manhattan determined to succeed. Both applied a shrewd financial acumen to the chancy business of magazines. And both eventually celebrated their success by acquiring grand residences on Park Avenue, just fifteen blocks apart. In their overlapping lifetimes, Nast and Newhouse traversed distinct but parallel pathways of the American dream. But first, Nast had to escape Missouri, and Sam had to escape his past.

Solomon Neuhaus was born on May 24, 1895, inside a five-story tenement building at 53 Orchard Street on the Lower East Side, a world away from the Gilded Age aristocracy that held sway a few miles to the north. He was the oldest child of Meier Neuhaus, a rabbi's son who had endured an odyssey of his own. Meier was born in a tiny village near Vitebsk in Russia, trekked to Western Europe by caravan, and then crossed the Atlantic in steerage in 1890. He spoke no English. Meier married Rose Arenfeldt, an immigrant raised on an Austrian farm, and then found work as a machinist in the garment industry. When Solomon was around one, the family moved to New Jersey, settling near Bayonne with other Russian Jews who toiled as laborers. In 1902, Meier restyled himself "Meyer" and changed the spelling of his surname to Newhouse, perhaps an effort to improve the prospects of a new business manufacturing suspenders. Solomon became Sam, or "Sammy" to his family. The suspenders venture failed, and the Newhouses fell into poverty. Meyer, who suffered from severe asthma, left the family for long stretches to convalesce in rural settings. To support her eight children, Rose sold sundries door to door to neighbors, trudging to Manhattan on the ferry to pick up linens and dry goods and hauling them back to Bayonne.

The deprivations of his early years still gnawed at Sam decades later. When he appeared on the cover of *Time* in 1962, Newhouse told the magazine that his middle initial, *I*, stood for nothing at all. He later tried to bolster his father's reputation, insisting that Meyer Newhouse's failures were the fault of a swindling business partner; Meyer, in fact, had lost his company all by himself. In a privately published memoir, intended for the Newhouse family, Sam confessed to experiencing "a certain shame" about his origins, although he also drew a direct link between his childhood penury and the ambition that drove his climb up the American ladder. "I was small, young and poor, and I learned as I grew," Sam wrote. "I could no more stop forging ahead than a blade of grass could turn away from the light."

Anointing himself his family's breadwinner at thirteen, Sam left school after eighth grade and enrolled in a typing and bookkeeping course, but struggled to find work. One prospective employer burst into laughter when Sam came to his office for an interview. "I can't hire you!" the man said. "Your head doesn't even come to the top of the desk!" Eventually, Sam found a mentor in Hyman Lazarus, a political fixer and godfather type to Bayonne's Jewish families, whose law office sat above the newsroom of the failing *Bayonne Times*. Lazarus hired

Sam to manage the books, and when he purchased the *Times*, he put sixteen-year-old Sam in charge; within a year, the newspaper had turned a profit. Like Nast, Sam had considered a career in the law, but decided he showed more of a knack for publishing. Also like Nast, he quickly set his sights on expansion. The *Staten Island Advance*, a stalwart of New York City's then-rural outer borough, was struggling to stay afloat, and in 1922, with Lazarus as a partner, Sam took a majority stake.

Not long afterward, Sam met the woman who would play an improbably large role in the destiny of Condé Nast. Mitzi Epstein was a chatty four-foot, eight-inch brunette, a fashion student at what later became known as the Parsons School of Design. Mitzi's parents, Sam and Judith, ran a prosperous women's clothing company that imported scarves from France; they enjoyed foreign films and retained an in-house Hungarian cook at their Upper West Side apartment. This sophisticated lifestyle impressed the tenement-bred Sam, who also appreciated that Mitzi was the first woman he'd dated who was shorter than he was. The Epsteins, however, were skeptical. Staten Island, Bayonne, and a life of little-known newspapers was not the bright future they had envisioned for their daughter. Judith Epstein even encouraged Mitzi to date one of Sam's taller friends; in his memoir, Sam noted with satisfaction that "the other fellow went into bankruptcy." Eventually, the Epsteins yielded, and on May 8, 1924, Sam and Mitzi were married at the Commodore Hotel in Manhattan, where guests took home cake slices wrapped in white satin boxes.

The couple settled into a handsome Tudor house in the Staten Island neighborhood of Ward Hill, on a bluff with sweeping views of the harbor. Mitzi was the lead decorator, but Sam, buoyed by success, insisted on one detail: the railing of the home's primary staircase was bent into the shape of his initials. Sam descended to breakfast each morning along a row of *S*'s bisected with *I*'s, a strip of wrought-iron dollar signs. The family soon expanded: a son, S. I. Jr., was born by cesarean section on November 8, 1927; in what was perhaps a sign of the family's assimilationism, the baby was named after its father, in defiance of Jewish custom that discouraged such a practice. Another child, Donald, arrived two years later.

Ward Hill was a symbol of how far Solomon Neuhaus had traveled from Orchard Street. After taking over the *Advance*, Sam bought up more struggling papers in Long Island, Newark, and Syracuse and turned them into profit centers; his holding company, Advance Publications, eventually included lucrative outposts in Alabama, Louisiana, Michigan, Missouri, Ohio, and Oregon. But Mitzi, tempted by the Manhattan tableau out their window, yearned for more. She read smart fashion magazines like *Vogue* and considered herself an aesthete; she also held strong opinions on how an upwardly mobile New York family ought to live. The couple's Saturdays soon revolved around a short drive to the ferry terminal and then a windswept ride across the water, the city's bouquet of skyscrapers growing large on the horizon. In Manhattan's gilded canyons, the Newhouses absorbed art, design, and opera, and Mitzi perused fashionable boutiques. A different sort of life beckoned.

By May 1940, the Newhouses were wealthy enough to rent a thirteen-room duplex apartment at 730 Park Avenue, in one of America's most desirable neighborhoods. This was no Ward Hill. 730 Park encased gracious apartments with marble staircases and East River views. The Newhouses' unit, on the seventh and eighth floors, included a formal library and four maid's rooms; among their new neighbors was the composer Richard Rodgers, of Rodgers and Hammerstein. Mitzi commissioned an expensive renovation in antique French style from a decorator who said he had done work for the du Ponts; a foot pedal at the dining table summoned a servant. Thus the Newhouses settled on Park Avenue—but not *Park Avenue*, meaning the insular WASP society of boarding schools, men's clubs, and Ivy League signet rings that represented membership in America's financial and social elite. Despite their ample residence and household help, the Newhouses were still marked by the stigma that New York's chattering classes affixed to Sam's generation of Eastern European Jewish immigrant stock. (In fact, the Newhouses' building was one of the few Park Avenue addresses at the time that allowed Jewish tenants.) The family took annual trips to Europe, wintered in Florida and Acapulco, and later bought a sprawling estate in New Jersey with a tennis court and five-car garage. But Sam

Newhouse was too blatant a striver to be welcomed by a Manhattan society where sangfroid, not sweat, was prized. Reporters often called Sam "restless," "hustling," and "indefatigable"—dirty words for the *Vogue* set that preferred a studied ease.

It wasn't just the WASPs who looked askance. Sam was also rebuffed by the city's "Our Crowd" circle of wealthy old-line Jewish families, the mainly Germanic banking and merchant dynasties of Lehmans and Loebs and Kuhns who had amassed fortunes well before the arrival of poor Jewish refugees in the late nineteenth and early twentieth centuries. Sometimes referred to as the "One Hundred," a cheeky variation on the old Four Hundred list, these elite Jews policed their ranks and rejected arrivistes as firmly as old Mrs. Astor.* This narcissism of small differences underscored just how difficult it would prove for Sam to transcend his lowly background, even as his fortunes grew.

On top of these indignities was the low opinion of Newhouse within his own profession. Sam once offered to buy *The New York Times* from its "Our Crowd" owners, the Sulzbergers, but the family did not seriously consider his proposal. Sam's reaction underscored the separation between himself and the city's more established Jews: "They'd never sell to a kike like me." When *Newsweek* went up for sale in 1960, Sam submitted a bid significantly higher than the market value of the magazine, which was controlled by the family of Vincent Astor, one of America's wealthiest men. Condé Montrose Nast, despite his prosaic origins, had few problems wooing Vincent's grandmother Mrs. Astor, but in 1960, Sam's entreaties received a cooler reception. Vincent's widow, Brooke Astor, insisted that *Newsweek* would never fall into his hands; *Newsweek* was available, it seemed, but it was not available to a Newhouse. While it's hard to pinpoint the reason for Brooke Astor's opposition, it's likely she and her advisers were channeling the dim view of Sam that prevailed among their fellow sophisticates. When Sam tried to buy *The Washington Post* in 1963, his solicitations so repelled Katharine

---

* Their circle was so fiercely guarded that a minor scandal brewed when one Our Crowd scion, Gerald Warburg, had the temerity to marry a Nast—Natica Nast, Condé's daughter, who had been raised Catholic.

Graham, the *Post*'s high-born publisher, that she complained about it in her memoir years later, marveling that the "ever-eager" Newhouse would not take no for an answer.

This sneering view of the family was best summarized by A. J. Liebling, the great wit of *The New Yorker* and mainstay of its "Wayward Press" column of media criticism, who dismissed Sam as a pretender who had purchased second-class newspapers through the disreputable practice of preying on more upstanding owners and exploiting family feuds. Liebling's own father, like Sam's, was a Jewish immigrant who had arrived in America penniless. But the Lieblings prospered in the fur trade, and A. J. grew up in comfort on the Upper East Side. As a second-generation American Jew, Liebling could have evinced some sympathy for Sam's difficult path, a recognition that the difference between his father's success and Meyer Newhouse's failure may have boiled down to circumstance and luck. That Liebling forged ahead with his ridicule makes all the crueler the French slur that he later assigned to Sam, a sobriquet that rankled the publisher for the rest of his life. In Liebling's phrasing, Sam was a "journalist *chiffonier*"—a ragpicker.

IT WOULD BE TEMPTING to assert that Sam's subsequent decision to purchase Condé Nast was a straightforward example of social aspiration, an outsider seizing a plum opportunity to buy his way into the long-sought graces of the upper class. Here, in a slightly bruised condition ripe for the taking, was all the prestige of *Vogue*, its historic ties to the Four Hundred, its taste-making editors whose opinions mattered to all the snobs who so casually and callously disdained the Newhouse name. In one anecdote, repeated so often that some otherwise authoritative accounts of Condé Nast have accepted it as fact, Sam claimed that he bought *Vogue* as a thirty-fifth-anniversary present for his wife. One version of the story went that Mitzi asked Sam to go out and buy her *Vogue*—that is, an issue from the newsstand—and he instead came back owning the company.

If there is any truth there, it lies in Mitzi's very real fixation on status and class. A woman besotted by clothes, socialites, and celebrities, she relished the company of boldfaced names and all outward signs of social rank. She also adopted a conspicuous and, at times, crass kind of snobbery, to which her family was not immune. When her son Si and his first wife, Jane Franke, moved into a sprawling co-op at Park Avenue and East Ninety-third Street—in a luxury building complete with an interior courtyard, Gothic limestone entryway, and porte cochere—Mitzi declared herself less than impressed.

"My god," she exclaimed to her son. "You're practically in Harlem!"

So, yes, *Vogue* made sense as a vessel to advance Mitzi's social ambitions. But while Sam was generally happy to bankroll his wife's indulgent lifestyle, he also felt conflicted about the world of affluence she adored. Mitzi "wanted a Park Avenue life," recalled Sam's granddaughter, Pamela Mensch. "I'm sure my grandfather would have happily lived the rest of his life in Staten Island." For Jews like Sam who had clawed their way out of poverty, the uptown world of the wealthy was often viewed with indifference, and perhaps some contempt. "I got the idea that eating at Sardi's or living at 730 Park Avenue was the sort of thing that Sam thought, or somebody had persuaded him to think, that somebody in his position *ought* to do, rather than something that was natural to him," said Calvin Trillin, the longtime *New Yorker* writer who, as a young correspondent at *Time*, trailed Sam for a cover story on the Newhouse empire. Sam was uneasy about the publicity, Trillin recalled, and irritated about having to answer so many questions from a journalist. After a day of interviews, Trillin hopped out of Sam's limousine and was nearly hit by a passing car.

"Be careful," Sam warned him. "I wouldn't want to go through this again."

In reality, when Condé Nast was presented to Sam as an acquisition target in 1959, his interest was more straightforward and hard-nosed: Was it undervalued, and could he wring a profit? For all of its residual glitz, Condé Nast appealed to Sam because it was his favorite kind of distressed asset. The company had lost $534,528 in 1958 ($5.6 million in today's dollars). *Vogue* was making less money than its Hearst-owned rival, *Harper's Bazaar*, and Nast's Greenwich printing press had become a woeful money pit. Plus, Sam, who had previously tried and failed to buy *The Saturday Evening Post*, had been looking to break into the magazine business—not for the glamour, but for the lucrative advertising.

There was, however, a younger Newhouse who sensed more potential in the family's newest asset. Sam Newhouse was happy for his status-conscious wife to enjoy the perks of owning *Vogue*, granting Mitzi the illusion that she had been accepted by the elite. His eldest son, S. I. Newhouse Jr., had little use for illusions. Like Condé Montrose Nast, Si wanted to *be* elite—to choose, rather than be chosen—and by the early 1960s he was beginning to grasp the social possibilities uniquely available to him as the freshly minted heir to *Vogue*. It was Si who believed that the mystique of Condé Nast, and the refinement of its readership, could be the key to something more profitable, influential, and exciting than, say, a regional newspaper in Oregon. Si had grown up all too conscious of the fine gradations of New York society, the invisible old-world barriers and codes that had kept him, by all appearances a wealthy scion, still stuck on the outside looking in. And he knew exactly how his father, and by extension all of the Newhouses, was perceived. When Sam died, in 1979, at age eighty-four after a long decline, his *New York Times* obituary quoted him referring to himself as a "shrimp" and repeated Liebling's insult. In death, Sam Newhouse had made the front page—but he was still the chiffonier.

And so Si bided his time. His vengeance would come slowly, and then all at once.

2

Mitzi's Boy

In the spring of 1966, *The New York Times* devoted nearly a page of its weekly features supplement to the phenomenon of upscale bachelor living in Manhattan. "An interesting city apartment," the paper reported, "apparently doesn't require a woman's touch." The lavishly photographed spread touted the exquisite decorating skills of single men and their tastes for Flemish tapestry, Chippendale ice buckets, and wraparound terraces. Conspicuous among these conspicuous consumers was one bachelor, pictured on a cushy sofa as a bow-tied servant poured him a cup of tea. A cigarette dangled from his fingers, and his feet were nestled in black espadrilles.

His duplex apartment, S. I. "Si" Newhouse Jr. explained to the paper, is "very much me at the moment."

Shy old Sam Newhouse was so allergic to press coverage that he almost refused to cooperate with his own *Time* cover story. Now, his thirty-eight-year-old son was musing in public about the joys of a fox-fur bed throw, felt-covered walls, and a rug sewn from fifty jackal skins imported from Greece. Si gushed to the *Times* about his famed decorator, Billy Baldwin, and the domestic ministrations of his Filipino "houseboy," Pedro, whom he deemed "one of the great luxuries of the world." Abstract art and a stack of tasteful fashion magazines rounded out the image of a wealthy scion at rest.

Bragging about one's living space is de rigueur among today's celebrities and influencers, thanks in part to the massive popularity of *Architectural Digest*, published by Condé Nast. For Si's tenement-bred father, who believed in the immigrant's ethic of modesty and hard work, the *Times* feature would have been a massive embarrassment: his son and namesake in the paper of record sounding like a distracted prince, delighted by his own idleness. The *Times* article even raised the subject of Si's recent divorce, a source of shame for the tradition-minded Sam, who was increasingly alarmed by his son's playboy habits. The decorating story would prove to be among Si's last major interviews in a publication outside of his family's control. Looking back, the episode stands as an inflection point in the transformation of the Newhouse family, its uneasy passage from the privations of immigrant life to the trappings of newfound wealth, and the tensions between a sometimes austere patriarch and his prodigal son.

In fact, by the mid-1960s, Sam Newhouse had already started to lose interest in the glossy magazines under his control, which had proved less profitable than he'd hoped. He was refocused on his lucrative syndicate of mid-tier newspapers, while preparing his favored son—Si's younger, steadier brother, Donald—to take over the family business. At the time, it would never have occurred to Sam that the spirit of self-gratification he so lamented in his firstborn son would prove to be the guiding light of Condé Nast's future success. Si's love of material pleasures drove him to mold the family's magazines into global arbiters of taste, to revive moribund titles like *Vanity Fair* and *GQ*, and to extend the Condé Nast brand around the world. It was also the fuel that lifted the Newhouse name out of the regional newspaper trade and into the highest levels of social repute.

ONE EVENING IN THE 1950s, years before he would be featured in the *Times*, Si and his first wife, Jane, were due to attend an upscale cocktail party in Manhattan. (They had married in 1951, when Si was twenty-three.) Si, working a day job in the bowels of his father's newspaper empire, was coming directly from a business appointment, so Jane got dressed alone and traversed the twenty-two blocks to her in-laws' place at 730 Park. When Jane stepped off the elevator and into the exquisitely decorated duplex—the home her husband had grown up in, the nerve center of the Newhouse universe—her mother-in-law, Mitzi, approached.

"Go home," Mitzi told her. "You look terrible."

"I got a cab, went home, and I changed my dress," Jane recalled decades later. "And I went back and joined them." She laughed. "Can you imagine? That I did that? I cannot believe that I would have accepted that criticism and done that."

It is difficult to understand the idiosyncrasies, indulgences, and ambitions of Si Newhouse—and the hugely successful magazines he came to control—without understanding the woman who raised him. Mitzi Newhouse weighed less than eighty pounds, yet she held enormous sway over Si for much of his life. She was acquisitive and anxious, snobbish and judgmental, as obsessed with fashion trends and party invitations and knowing the right people as any Edith Wharton antiheroine. She was invariably draped in Givenchy and Dior; at Si's wedding to Jane, she carried a handbag that spelled out "Mitzi" in diamonds. When Mitzi attended a ball in 1962 at Blenheim Palace, the sprawling Oxford country estate of the Duke of Marlborough, she grew impatient when her chauffeured Rolls-Royce was forced to wait in a line of cars. Princess Margaret had just arrived and was being greeted by the hostess when Mitzi, fed up, barreled out of the Rolls. Her escort, the fashion designer Arnold Scaasi, attempted to explain that it was customary for a royal to be allowed to enter first.

"I'm going in *now!*" Mitzi shouted, sprinting up the steps to the entrance, where she was presented to the princess without delay.

It's notable that the other man accompanying Mitzi that evening was not her husband, but her oldest son. Si, who was thirty-four years old at the time, "seemed very young" to Scaasi, who got the impression of a man still very much in thrall to his mother. Before the ball, Scaasi was dressing for dinner when Mitzi called: "Arnold, Arnold, do you know how to tie a bow tie? We are having the most terrible trouble." The designer hurried to the Newhouse suite and discovered Mitzi, in a dressing gown, beside a shoeless, trouser-less Si, looking bewildered in an unbuttoned tuxedo shirt, his legs poking out in long black stockings. Scaasi assisted Si with his shirt studs and then tied his white bow tie.

"I thought they would send me a tie that was already made and would just clip on," Si explained. It was like something out of a *New Yorker* cartoon about the hapless rich.

Mitzi's squiring Si to aristocratic dinners in Europe was in keeping with a closeness between mother and son that dated to Si's childhood. Sam's idea of quality time with his young sons was bringing them to his office on the weekends, a routine that started when Si was barely five years old. Mitzi tutored Si in softer matters, imparting her enthusiasms for art, design, and the finer things in life. In the fall of 1939, when Si was eleven, the Newhouses enrolled him at the private Horace Mann School for Boys in the Bronx. The Our Crowd Jews had their own favored institutions—the Sachs School, which later became Dwight, educated Herbert Lehman, Henry Morgenthau Jr., and other sons of prominent German-Jewish families—so Horace Mann became the preferred choice for a newer generation of Jewish aspirants. Si was a managing editor of the student paper, *The Record*, and served as president of a "Speakers Club" that arranged visits by prominent public figures. But his extracurricular contributions were less meaningful than the friendships he forged with a pair of ambitious boys who went on to prominence. One was Allard K. Lowenstein, who became a liberal civil rights activist and served a term in the US Congress. The other was Roy Cohn.

It can still come as a shock that the maestro of Condé Nast—whose magazines advanced the careers of so many gay and progressive writers, artists, editors, and photographers—was also a lifelong confidant of Cohn, the notoriously savage lawyer and conservative political fixer who abetted Senator Joseph McCarthy's communist witch hunt, played Aristotle to Donald Trump's Alexander, and was immortalized in Tony Kushner's 1991 play *Angels in America* as a closeted gay man who denied having AIDS up until he died from the disease. Yet Si and Roy were close for their entire lives, often speaking by telephone at least once a day. Roy grew up at 1165 Park Avenue, a mile north of Si's place, and the boys often carpooled together to class. As a teenager, Roy—who, like Si, had an overbearing mother—had already found his knack as a behind-the-scenes player, engineering the election of friends to the Horace Mann student government.

Si was awed by Roy's silver tongue and easy confidence, traits that Si would come to deeply admire in others, perhaps because he lacked them. Si was awkward in every way: moody and sullen, prone to shyness and melancholy, the sort of depressive, navel-gazing tendencies that his father, forced to start work at age thirteen to provide for his impoverished family, never had much patience for. In high school and college, Si sometimes felt so dejected that he confided to Lowenstein, his close friend from Horace Mann, that he had entertained thoughts of suicide; Lowenstein was once so alarmed by Si's late-night phone calls that he traveled from Westchester to the Newhouse home to console his friend.

Si's doldrums may be explained by the pressures he was facing at home. Sam Newhouse had long gravitated toward Si's younger brother, Donald, who embraced the family's nose-to-the-grindstone work ethic and rarely rebelled. Si, meanwhile, fought with his father over everything from his grades at Horace Mann to his subscription to *PM*, a left-wing pro-labor newspaper published in New York City that Sam, an ardent capitalist, worried would corrupt his son. In letters to Lowenstein, written when he was sixteen years old, Si repeatedly describes his efforts to free himself of Sam's expectations, writing at one point, "S.I.N. Hopes Once and For All To Rid Self of Family Influence." (Si used his monogram, "S.I.N.," to refer to himself.) Si, who throughout his life could be opaque to the point of obscurity, expressed himself in these letters using a format he knew well: each missive is designed like the front page of a newspaper, complete with headlines. "WAR DECLARED," reads one, referring to a titanic fight between Si and Sam. "Mother, Father Intent on Crushing Newfound Liberalism and '*PM* Influence' . . . 'Social Position Too High,' They Say! S.I.N., Shocked, Will Fight Back." According to the letters, Sam blamed Lowenstein for Si's middling marks in class and demanded that his son cut off the friendship, calling Lowenstein a "leftist" who had led Si "onto evil ways." Si, who wrote that he fought "violently" with his father over the matter, described Sam as "stupid, stubborn, malicious and mean." It isn't clear if Sam recognized just how much the friendship meant to his son, who ended at least one of his lengthy notes to Lowenstein with the sign-off, "Love, Si."

Lowenstein, like Cohn, was a closeted gay man, and it has not been lost on observers that several of Si's closest adolescent friends were gay. (Another was Sanford Friedman, who became a novelist whose books contained explicitly gay themes.) Si's sexuality has been a matter of some speculation over the years. Those who suspected he was gay often cited his enthusiasm for art and design, straying into the realm of ugly stereotypes. It is true that, given the time period and the socially conservative family he grew up in, Si may have been disposed to suppress any stirrings of same-sex attraction. But in my research, I found no evidence that Si ever pursued a gay liaison or expressed interest in one. Graydon Carter recalled that Patricia McCallum, who later married the actor Michael York, dated Si when she was single in the 1960s. Graydon asked Pat, "How was Si in bed?" Her reply: "Fantastic."

In 1945, with college on the horizon, Si was hopeful for the academic and social validation of an Ivy League acceptance, setting his sights on Harvard. But his academic performance at Horace Mann was middling, and he was rejected not only by Harvard, but Cornell, too. It was yet another moment that showcased the limits of the Newhouses' privilege: at the time, Cornell was considered such a safe bet for wealthy private-school boys that Si had prematurely shared his plans to go there in his Horace Mann yearbook. The rejection left him reeling. Spurned by these elite institutions, Si instead matriculated at Syracuse University in upstate New York, a second-tier college in a town where his father owned two newspapers and a radio station.* As

---

* Syracuse may have been a disappointing outcome for Si, but the school certainly benefited: the Newhouses have gone on to gift more than $100 million to the university, which is home to the S. I. Newhouse School of Public Communications, one of the country's leading journalism programs. Horace Mann has barely received any money from the family.

an undergraduate, Si wrote for the campus paper under the nom de plume of "Si Mason." But he did not relish his time at Syracuse, and he eventually asked his father if he could abandon his studies and go work at the family's newspapers. When Sam relented, Si left without a degree. He did, however, leave with the prospects of a wife.

SI FIRST SPOTTED JANE FRANKE across the room at a Syracuse frat party. She was laughing in a friendly, uninhibited manner, and sitting on another man's lap. "I didn't feel the least bit embarrassed," Jane recalled decades later, "and that appealed to him." They were soon going steady, watching foreign films together and attending nights at the opera. "I felt as if I were Bette Davis' boyfriend," Si wrote to Jane after one date in 1948, signing off with "Love." By the end of 1950, they were engaged.

Jane was a middle-class girl from Westchester County, where her father, Chester Frankenstein, ran an auto parts dealership. According to Jane, Mitzi avoided telling friends about her daughter-in-law's maiden name "because it was so shocking." (Jane shortened it to "Franke" at the suggestion of a school guidance counselor.) The couple married at the Waldorf-Astoria in March 1951; a rabbi performed the ceremony, though Jane accessorized with an ivory-bound Bible covered in clusters of white orchids, perhaps a nod to the family's assimilationist aspirations. Si and Jane later sent out a holiday card: "To Mommie + Father," it read. "Merry Christmas."

The couple moved around as Si apprenticed at his father's newspapers, including stints in Portland, Oregon, and Harrisburg, Pennsylvania, before settling at 1185 Park Avenue, the luxurious address Mitzi had deemed "practically in Harlem." Three children—Sam III, Wynn, and Pamela—were born in quick succession. Si, however, was growing restless. Jane was happy to stay home with the kids, but Si liked the nightlife; soon, they were regulars at the 21 Club, El Morocco, and the Copacabana, dining alongside Broadway stars and gossip columnists like Walter Winchell. Around this time, Si reconnected with Roy Cohn, who, after the disgrace of the Army-McCarthy hearings, had made his way back into New York power circles. Roy and Si began going on double dates, sometimes with Roy's on-again, off-again girlfriend, Barbara Walters; on family vacations in Florida, the Newhouse kids played cards with "Uncle Roy." But Cohn was also subtly driving a wedge between Si and Jane, suggesting to Si that, given his family fortune, he could aim higher for a spouse.

The end of the marriage came abruptly—in a manner that foreshadowed Si's notorious style of firing editors at Condé Nast. Jane, by her recollection, had traveled with friends to the 1958 Brussels World's Fair, but Si declined to accompany her. When Jane returned to her hotel one night, there was a cable waiting from her husband: he wanted to split up. Jane was stunned. She flew back and the two briefly reconciled, but Si eventually hired a divorce lawyer: Roy Cohn. "We weren't meant to be together," Jane told me, as we chatted in the sprawling apartment at 1185 Park where she and Si once lived. (Jane kept the apartment in the divorce and never moved out.) She showed no signs of bitterness, even noting that Si became a more doting father after their split, playing with their children most days after work. But Jane partially attributed the marriage's collapse to Cohn, for encouraging her husband to seek out a glitzier lifestyle than the one she preferred. Si, she recalled, "wanted to squeeze everything into his life." The couple were no longer living together in 1959 when the Newhouses purchased Condé Nast, but she recalled feeling happy for Si when she heard the news.

"He loved magazines," Jane said. "That's where he got his thrills."

CONDÉ NAST TURNED OUT to be the greatest gift that Sam could have bought for his wayward son.

Si had been visiting Newhouse newspapers since he was a child, but in his first forays into the workforce, he showed little acumen for the job. Colleagues viewed him as ineffective and uninterested in daily journalism; he alienated the blue-collar staff of the *Newark Star-Ledger* by wearing monogrammed shirts. The daughter of a longtime Newhouse executive remembered that Si would shut his office door and chat on the phone with Mitzi for hours; when Si was urged to focus on his work, he'd reply, "I have to finish with my mother." His brother,

Donald, meanwhile, married a woman whom Sam and Mitzi adored, and moved into the apartment at 730 Park directly below his parents. "If I asked Donald to jump off a bridge for me, he would do it," Sam once told a colleague. "If I asked Si to do it, he'd turn away from me." One evening, when the family was dining together at 730 Park, Si insisted on being served a different entrée from the rest of his relatives. From the head of the table, Sam uttered wryly, "Si gets whatever he wants."

"Mitzi gave him better treatment than she gave her own husband," recalled Jane, who witnessed the exchange. "He was a little bit jealous. It was a little bit sad."

Si's spending habits became a source of family tension. In 1962, Sam rebuked his son for the sin of charging eleven dollars' worth of shaving cream ($115 in today's dollars) to his expense account. When Si asked his father for a Jaguar sports car, Sam was so frustrated that he dispatched a deputy to tell his son to buy a cheaper American vehicle instead. "When you grow up with a mother like that who is so focused on you, you're bound to pick up her taste and her preoccupations," Si's daughter, Pamela Mensch, told me. "Early on, he got very dependent on having an affluent sort of life."

Indeed, Si came by his snobbery honestly. For years, Mitzi employed a personal assistant she referred to as Alice "Hee-*gahnz*," pronounced with a continental flourish. Her grandchildren assumed that Alice was European, maybe German or French. They only discovered later that the woman was an American and her name was Alice Higgins—a mundane moniker that Mitzi evidently demanded she elevate for appearances. This obsession with status only accelerated after Sam purchased Condé Nast. In June 1964, Mitzi reached the pinnacle: *Vogue*'s "People Are Talking About . . ." column, a regular feature that purported to keep readers abreast of society trends. That week's readers were greeted with a formal Cecil Beaton photograph of Mrs. Samuel I. Newhouse, "a woman of astonishing energies . . . with a feeling for the amenities of life." *Vogue* depicted Mitzi as a philanthropist with passions for French furniture and Dixieland jazz; nowhere did it mention that she was married to the owner.

Nineteen sixty-four was also the year that a different Newhouse found his place at Condé Nast. In a mix of pragmatism and desperation,

Sam appointed Si as *Vogue*'s publisher. Sam had always relied on his relatives to oversee many of his media properties; at one point, dozens of Newhouses were employed across different components of the company. Somebody had to take care of the magazines, and Sam figured it made sense for Si, given his Mitzi-like interest in art and design, to start learning that side of the business. In reality, Sam considered the *Vogue* job beneath the rank of his eldest son. *Vogue* was supposed to be a waystation for Si before he applied himself to more important matters, like the family newspapers—a respite for a stubborn child who had gotten lost in life and was grasping for purpose.

But Si was besotted by the world of *Vogue* and the fascinating characters who inhabited it. It was the first time that he had found a role in his father's empire that he relished, where he did not feel woefully out of place. The cover of *Vogue*'s October 15, 1964, issue featured an Irving Penn photograph of a pouty model, her head encased in a satin bonnet studded with glittered flowers. The headlines touted features on "Balenciaga: The Big Excitement" and "7 Top Diets Explored and Rated by Vogue." Inside, next to the table of contents, an almost imperceptible change had been made to the masthead. In tiny type, the words "Publisher: S. I. Newhouse, Jr." appeared for the first time.

Si's ascent had begun.

3

The Silver Fox

For all the tectonic change sweeping American society in the 1960s, it was a relatively quiescent time at Condé Nast, which had the atmosphere of a women's finishing school when Si Newhouse began working there. The well-heeled and well-coiffed women who populated the halls often referred to the place as "the Eighth Sister," a nod to the elite all-female Seven Sisters colleges that routinely sent their graduates into the company's lower ranks. Inside the Deco-style Graybar Building, Condé's Midtown Manhattan headquarters astride Grand Central Terminal, it was common to see *Vogue* editors in white gloves and silk veils wielding Cartier cigarette holders at their desks, where the typewriters were customized with an acute accent key so that memos and letters could spell "Condé" with the correct French flair.

Characters like Baron Nicolas de Gunzburg, the reed-thin, exquisitely clothed Parisian fashion editor who may or may not have squandered a family fortune (no one quite knew where the money was from, or had gone), spent afternoons leafing through imported copies of *Le Monde*. Cecil Beaton might wander by holding a bird in a cage. Conversations in Russian and French floated through the hallway and junior editors regularly retreated to the swimming pool at the nearby Shelton Hotel for a lunchtime dip. *Vogue* was edited by, and primarily for, an insular class of socialites and fashion industry professionals. Compared to behemoths like *Life* and *Newsweek*, its reach was small—by design. At one point, the magazine quashed an effort to attract new readers, reasoning that if circulation expanded, so too would production costs, and then niche retailers like Harry Winston might not be able to afford to buy ads.

Si changed all this. Within twenty-five years of his arrival, Condé Nast would be transformed from a clubby little business to the imperious steward of global brands like *Vanity Fair*, *GQ*, *Architectural Digest*, and *Allure*. Si founded powerful new magazines and, taking a cue from his father, purchased and revived struggling rivals, including *The New Yorker*. He recruited Tina Brown and Anna Wintour and hired hyper-aggressive salesmen to corner the market in luxury advertising. Condé went from a publishing laggard to the center of the culture-making industry. And Si remade himself from a feckless scion into an esteemed patron, splashing out millions to hire the country's finest writers and photographers and filling his town house with blue-chip works by Johns, Rauschenberg, and Rothko.

He did not do it alone. One enigmatic and exotic figure was the driving force behind this personal and professional metamorphosis, the Rasputin to Si's princeling: Alexander Semeonovitch Liberman, Condé Nast's powerful editorial director. Silver-haired and darkly handsome, with a silky patrician accent that evoked his pan-European upbringing, Alex (as he was invariably known) was the embodiment of Condé panache: a snob, spendthrift, and sensualist. For decades, he personally reviewed every layout, headline, caption, and photo that appeared in a Condé Nast publication, impressing his style and artistic instincts on the entire oeuvre. He was also a cunning careerist. When Si arrived, Alex took him under his wing, tutoring the young heir in the ins and outs of superior taste. The notion of a partnership between diffident Si and sophisticated Alex struck many of their colleagues as far-fetched. But for all their differences in pedigree and personality, Si and Alex were two Jewish outsiders with something to prove. Their close collaboration would revolutionize American journalism, fashion, and design. For Si, it also represented something deeper—he would later describe their relationship as no less than "the most meaningful experience of my life."

THEY MET ONE DAY in 1961 in the offices of *Glamour*, *Vogue*'s kid-sister publication that was aimed at a younger and more middle-class readership. Si had just started at Condé Nast, working as an assistant in the promotions department. He wanted to understand how a publication emitted from a New York skyscraper could conjure that intangible aura of class that had eluded his striving mother, bored his workaholic father, and fascinated Si himself. To his sophisticated new colleagues, Si had less in common with the editors of *Vogue* than with its striving subscribers, a group described that year by Gay Talese as "those thousands of female Walter Mittys who, under the hair dryer each week, can flip through the gossamer pages and perchance dream that *they* are the Countess Crespi lolling on Niarchos' three-masted schooner, *they* are at Monaco being sketched by René Bouché, *they* are flying their own Beechcraft toward some exotic spot far, far from Oshkosh . . . far, far from the Bronx." Or, in Si's case, far, far from the *Newark Star-Ledger*, his last workplace before Samuel Newhouse agreed that Si could begin learning the magazine business.

Si had also just purchased his bachelor pad and had no idea how to decorate it, so he called on Alex, a painter and sculptor in his spare time, for advice. Alex was keenly aware of Si's importance to the future of the company, and by extension, his own career. He quickly befriended the young heir, escorting him on lunch breaks to Leo Castelli's Upper East Side gallery, and drew on his copious connections to make crucial introductions. Alex arranged for Si to meet Barnett Newman for lunch at Barney Greengrass; before long, Si was an important Newman collector. Most weeks, Si and Alex met at the Grill Room at the Four Seasons, where Alex came prepared with the latest art world gossip. Si, who was still learning to tell his Rauschenberg from his Rothko, began bursting into Alex's office, brandishing auction catalogues and demanding Alex's opinion on the pieces he wanted to buy.

It is not hard to see what entranced Si about Alex. Raised by a father who eschewed glamour and a mother who crassly galloped toward it, he had never met anyone as singularly refined and well connected as this curious new friend. With his bespoke suits and neatly trimmed mustache (he was often said to resemble the British actor David Niven), Alex evinced the manner of a pre-Revolution Russian aristocrat. In fact, he was born in Kyiv, Ukraine, the only child of a successful Jewish lumber merchant. His father, Semeon, served the czar's family until 1917, after which he pivoted to an advisory position with Vladimir Lenin. Their life was relatively comfortable but scarred by upheaval; by the early 1920s, his parents had joined the exodus of White Russians who escaped Bolshevik rule for the uncertainties of a new life in Western Europe. Alex attended elite schools in Britain and France and eventually became a designer at *Vu*, a trendsetting Parisian weekly whose large-format photographs directly inspired Henry Luce's *Life* magazine. (In a neat bit of proto-Condé nepotism, Alex was hired thanks to his mother, Henriette, who was a doyenne of Paris's artistic émigrés and carrying on an affair with *Vu*'s publisher, Lucien Vogel.) Alex built a reputation as an avant-garde designer, but his life was upended again after the Nazis invaded France, forcing him and his wife-to-be, Tatiana du Plessix, to flee. They arrived in New York in 1941; within weeks, Alex had secured a job in the *Vogue* art department thanks to Vogel, who by then was employed at Condé Nast.

One day, Alex made a fateful doodle. Pondering a photograph by Horst P. Horst of a swimsuit model balancing an oversized red beach ball on her toes, Alex's pencil arced across the page. In an elegant cursive, he spelled out V O G U E—with the ball taking the place of the 'O.' Frank Crowninshield, the former editor of *Vanity Fair*, wandered by and spotted Alex's design; he took the drawing to Nast himself and declared that a genius was in their midst. (The drawing, which ran on May 15, 1941, remains one of *Vogue*'s most famous covers.) By 1943, Alex had been promoted to *Vogue*'s art director; by 1944, he was overseeing art at every Condé magazine.

Alex's contributions in the years that followed were legion. He discovered Irving Penn, then an aspiring painter, when Penn was laboring in the art department at Saks Fifth Avenue. Alex later hired Penn as his assistant at *Vogue*, and urged him to refocus on photography. In 1945, Alex persuaded Edna Woolman Chase to publish Lee Miller's photographs of cadavers at Buchenwald in *Vogue*, among the first depictions of the Holocaust in an American publication. Alex integrated artwork by Mondrian into *Vogue* layouts and posed models in front of Jackson Pollock drip paintings, his way of exposing readers to contemporary art under the auspices of fashion. In 1942, he asked Marcel Duchamp to design a *Vogue* cover that conveyed "some sense of Americana"; Duchamp's submission—a portrait of George Washington's head covered in bloodstained medical gauze, as if an assassination had just occurred—was politely rejected.

In the Condé offices, his authority became absolute: Alex's impeccable manners and exacting standards set the template for a *Devil Wears Prada* office culture that was elegant and cutthroat all at once. In his courtly way, Alex addressed nearly everyone as "my dear" and rarely flashed a temper, even as he found subtly savage ways to assert power: generations of Condé editors learned that even a raised eyebrow meant Alex had sized up their work and silently deemed it trash. "When I took layouts or story ideas up to Alex, he would always begin his judgments with 'Friend' or 'Dear friend,'" recalled Gabé Doppelt, an editor in chief of *Mademoiselle* which joined the Condé Nast stable in 1959. "I learned early on that they were not the same. 'Friend' was just that, a term of endearment, but 'Dear friend' was a warning shot across the bows. It let me know that what would follow was a harsh evisceration of what he'd just looked at. I would be crushed, and the mere mention of the 'dear' before the 'friend' sent shivers down my spine." His behavior eventually earned him a nickname: the Silver Fox.

Alex also cared deeply about status—particularly his own. He raised snobbery to an art, slicing the gradations of caste gossamer-thin: he might instruct a friend headed to the Ritz Paris to stay on the quieter Rue Cambon side of the hotel, never the grander suites overlooking the Place Vendôme. (Coco Chanel preferred the Cambon entrance, Alex explained, adding that the Vendôme side was vulgar.) Alex's stepdaughter, the novelist Francine du Plessix Gray, later wrote that "power and publicity were the two motivations that had inspired much of his life."

He and Tatiana, by then a celebrated hat designer at Saks, established their East Seventieth Street town house as a center of postwar New York social life. Guests at their parties might include haute Europeans like Marlene Dietrich and Christian Dior, or artists like Salvador Dalí and René Bouché. Like many of the stars who passed in and out of Condé Nast over the decades, Alex was a chameleon, an outsider who masqueraded as an insider—and sometimes prized that masquerade to a fault. When Princess Margaret and her husband, the photographer Lord Snowdon—whose own career had been advanced by Alex's decision to publish him in *Vogue*—visited New York in 1967, they arranged to stay at the Libermans' home. Alex was so eager to flaunt his association with the royal couple that he evicted his stepdaughter and son-in-law from their bedroom so Margaret would have more space.

This was a world quite alien to Si Newhouse, and it thrilled him. Alex brought Si along to photo shoots, explained his theories of magazine design, and instructed him on what set an Irving Penn or Cecil Beaton photograph apart from the pack. "If Si Newhouse knows anything about how to pick up a fork, look at a picture, or have a conversation, it was taught to him by Alex Liberman," said the art critic Barbara Rose, who knew both men well.

For Alex, this was an act of corporate survivalism above all else. Unbeknownst to Si, Alex was struggling with his own prospects at Condé Nast. He had recently fallen out with his chief rival, another dashing Russian émigré named Iva Patcévitch, who had run the company since Nast's death in 1942 and orchestrated the sale to the Newhouses. "Mr. Pat," as he was known, had been friends with Alex for nearly two decades, but their relationship cooled dramatically in the aftermath of the company's sale in 1959. Alex had encountered anti-Semitism before, but he was taken aback by Pat's private contempt toward the Newhouses; Pat's wife referred to Sam and Mitzi as "the little heebs." If Pat was going to ice out the Newhouses, Alex reasoned, he would welcome them in from the cold. A multigenerational seduction ensued. After an afternoon with Alex at the galleries, Si would go to dinner at Sam and Mitzi's Park Avenue place and discover Alex and Tatiana at the table, regaling his parents with anecdotes about their glory days in Paris. Tatiana arranged lunches for Mitzi with her socialite friends; Sam began turning to Alex for advice on the magazine business. In a matter of months, Alex had become consigliere to the Newhouse family. At the end of 1962, Sam promoted him to "editorial director" of Condé Nast, the omnipotent role Alex would retain for thirty-two years.

Those who knew Si in those years believe that Alex came to occupy the role of a stand-in father, given all the tensions Si had suffered with Sam earlier in his life. At times, Si resisted the comparison, but when Alex turned eighty, Si wrote a letter describing Alex as "associate, friend, brother, father . . . there have been elements of all these in our relationship with none of the tensions there might have been." He added: "I hope we continue forever—in a deep sense we will."

Where Si wilted under the glare of Sam's disappointment, he found Alex patient, encouraging, tolerant of missteps. Si still struggled with the social graces that came naturally to the Condé set. "He didn't really move with the 'right' crowd," recalled Grace Mirabella, who later edited *Vogue*. "He hadn't had the 'right' sort of first wife. Or the right clothes. Or manners." Alex was appalled when Si invited him to see the latest decorations in his Condé Nast office: framed comic strips, a collection that later included original cels from *Krazy Kat*. (In an example of Alex's politesse, he later claimed to his biographers that this choice was in fact an endearing trait of Si's that demonstrated the publisher's omnivorous taste.) *Vogue* was a particularly tough nut to crack. When Si worked in the magazine's promotions department, he encouraged the magazine to accept ads from lower-tier companies to raise revenue. "Si couldn't resist, say, a toilet paper promotion or God knows what," the *Vogue* editor Babs Simpson recalled. It was up to Alex to swoop in, suggesting to Si that toilet paper ads may not be quite right for *Vogue*.

Si's love life was a mess, too. He was an heir to an enormous fortune, and yet several women he pursued in those days recalled their fathers sternly warning them off any potential romance. One ex-girlfriend recalled his "weenie boyness." At this deeply awkward time in Si's life,

Alex became a role model for how to be more courtly, more urbane. He was "very at ease with himself in the world," Francine du Plessix Gray said of her stepfather, "and I think it may be that ease in the world which Si needed the most."

All this time, Alex was subtly indoctrinating Si to his firm belief that Condé Nast stood for something more than mere commerce: "a certain dignity, a certain decency, a sense of quality, a chance for people to be creative." For Alex, the haute European, *Vogue* represented a beacon of high-mindedness in an otherwise crass American culture: "We were part of a crusade, an ideal, of communicating civilization, communicating culture, communicating thought." Before *Vogue*, he argued, "there was no concept, frankly, of a real American life." This corporate noblesse oblige inevitably blended with Alex's own ego and his belief that Condé Nast's success rested solely on his shoulders. As he told his biographers about the company, "I just, frankly, feel, to a certain extent, I own it."

In darker moments, away from the luminosity he projected in public, Alex harbored a refugee's fear of his world evaporating overnight. He had seen firsthand how the beaux mondes of czarist Moscow and interwar Paris were shredded by war and violence. Condé Nast had been his life raft. How many of his and Tatiana's friends came to their parties, sent gifts, and bought her hats, because entrée to Alex meant entrée to *Vogue*? The company footed the bill for his and Tatiana's vacations in Italy and France; it had even secured the mortgage on his house. And while Condé art directors might cower at the sound of Alex's footsteps or simper as he tore apart their layouts, there was one person whose opinion mattered to him above all else: his wife. Alex was in thrall to Tatiana, who had once been married to a French viscount, and she relied on Alex to provide the first-class, jet-setting lifestyle she expected. It was no mystery whose favor the entire edifice of their comfortable lives rested on. Often, when Alex returned from the Condé Nast office at night, Tatiana would greet her husband with a question:

"Did you make Si happy today?"

By 1968, Alex's investment in the Newhouses had paid off. At his urging, Sam and Si recruited Diana Vreeland, then the country's most innovative fashion editor, to leave *Harper's Bazaar* and become the editor in chief of *Vogue*, ushering in a renaissance at the magazine. And in a corporate coup de grace, he vanquished Patcévitch, his friend-turned-rival, after an incident that exemplified the now-entwined fates of Alex and Si. The drama unfolded during a weeklong gathering of the international jet set in Portugal hosted by a Bolivian tin tycoon, the kind of costume-ball extravaganza that was de rigueur for the social elite of the time. Sam and Mitzi attended nearly every gala and meal that week, save one: a cocktail party at their hotel thrown by Patcévitch, who had neglected to include them. Informed of the slight by her hairdresser, Mitzi was furious. Back in New York, Sam quietly asked Alex if he thought Pat was still worth keeping around. Sensing his opportunity, Alex did not say yes.

Soon after, Patcévitch received word from the Newhouses that his duties as president of Condé Nast were no longer required. He was later asked to vacate the elaborate town house on East Seventieth Street where he had lived for years. The building, Sam reminded him, was owned by Condé Nast, and another executive at the company now required the property.

A few weeks later, Si moved in.

ON AUGUST 31, 1979, from his seat in the first pew, Si watched as a thousand A-list mourners filed into Temple Emanu-El, the Fifth Avenue headquarters of Manhattan's Our Crowd Jewry, to pay respects to his father and namesake, dead at eighty-four. Among those murmuring condolences were Senator Jacob Javits, Governor Hugh Carey, and Vice President Walter Mondale; President Jimmy Carter sent a message of sympathy. A few weeks earlier, Sam Newhouse had experienced a massive and disabling stroke, the latest in a series of medical episodes that had begun in 1977 and robbed him of his energy and mental acuity. From the time of their births, Sam had intended for Si and Donald to inherit his empire. (At one point, concerned that a calamity could threaten the future of the business, he prohibited his two sons from flying together on the same airplane.) But it had taken a catastrophic health crisis for the patriarch to finally relax his grip.

For all his micromanaging, Sam had allowed Si to become the chairman of Condé Nast at the start of 1975, a move that formalized his son's leadership of the Newhouse magazines and, in the view of the family's close associates, was a tacit and overdue acknowledgment that the prodigal son had finally grown into his professional adulthood. By then, Si was in his late forties, and he had matured in his personal life, too. In 1973, he remarried, to a woman with the kind of society bona fides appropriate for the WASPy world of Condé Nast: Victoria Carrington Benedict de Ramel, an Episcopalian, half-English, half-American graduate of Brearley and Bryn Mawr and the ex-wife of a French count. Victoria personified the kind of cosmopolitan and intellectually serious image that Si had long desired for himself and the magazines he controlled. The couple shared a passion for classic movies, modern art, and the opera, embarking on regular pilgrimages to the Salzburg Festival in Austria. Victoria was fluent in French, proficient in several languages, and would later become a noted architectural historian. The days of Bachelor Si gallivanting to nightclubs with Roy Cohn were finished.

And yet, despite his bigger title, Si still never made a major decision at Condé Nast without running it by his father first—a filial reflex that, despite his occasional lamentations about it to friends, Si never really questioned or tried to change. As long as Sam was alive, Si could not shake the identity that had been imprinted on him from birth: the shy child, too timid to second-guess his father's decisions. When Sam was eighty years old, in 1976, Si and Donald strongly advised him against using $305 million of the family's fortune to acquire a Midwestern newspaper chain. Sam overruled his kids' objections and went ahead with the purchase anyway.

Now, as he sat in the gilded sanctum of Emanu-El, the encomia to his father emanating from the lectern, Si gazed at the dark wooden coffin, festooned with roses, that would be Sam's final resting place. He was a few months shy of his fifty-second birthday, and this was the first time that the specter of his father's disapproval, a looming presence in his life since childhood, had fully lifted. Sam Newhouse had never fully respected the magazines that Si had chosen as his life's work; in his mind, Condé Nast was a minnow in the Newhouse sea, an unserious realm best left to his unserious son. No longer. Si had ambitions of his own, which over the next decade would vastly expand the Newhouse empire. On the day of Sam's funeral, Advance Publications was valued at roughly $2 billion. By 1988, it would be worth $7 billion, a 250 percent increase. It would control the esteemed *New Yorker*, a revived smash-hit version of *Vanity Fair*, and the gastronomic bible *Gourmet*. Its dowdier titles would be revamped to appeal to an ascendant and free-spending aspirational class. Sam had been too set in his ways to detect the coming trend, but American culture was shifting Si-ward. The idealism of the 1960s was yielding to the materialism of the 1980s, a new preoccupation with the navel-gazing, ego-stroking life. Si, who at Condé Nast had surrounded himself with the masters of the zeitgeist, was prepared, and he had already put something into motion that marked the true start of Condé's inexorable eighties rise, a magazine whose prescient title managed to dovetail with both the spirit of the era and Si's own newfound sense of liberation: *Self*.

4

Si Finds His *Self*

At the start of 1979, the Condé Nast Publications had not launched a new magazine since the debut of *Glamour* four decades earlier. In the years since, a new crop of mass-market publications had revolutionized the magazine world, while Condé's titles effectively stagnated. *Esquire*, *Playboy*, and *Rolling Stone* found success by channeling the counterculture forces—sex, drugs, politics, and rock 'n' roll—that were rapidly reshaping society. In their pages, writers like Tom Wolfe, Gay Talese, and Hunter S. Thompson forged the New Journalism, a blend of reportage and novelistic writing that transformed American nonfiction. George Lois's covers for *Esquire*, some of which are now in the permanent collection of the Museum of Modern Art, tackled urgent issues like civil rights, the Vietnam War, and the feminist movement. An *Esquire* feature on a US Army infantry brigade was represented on the cover by a single white-on-black headline, "Oh My God—We Hit a Little Girl," prompting objections from sitting senators.

Condé had fallen behind, including with its core market of female readers. Hearst's *Cosmopolitan*, chief rival to Condé's *Glamour* and *Mademoiselle*, was revitalized in 1965 after it hired the editor Helen Gurley Brown, author of the best-selling *Sex and the Single Girl*. Brown discarded *Cosmo*'s previous emphasis on married suburbanites and turned the magazine into an enthusiastic champion of post-Friedan feminism, titillating readers with fellatio tips and a mantra of women's independence. Back at Condé, some editors at *Vogue* still wanted to airbrush out models' belly buttons when they were accidentally exposed during a fashion shoot.

"In the late 1970s, there were three tiers of magazines," recalled Graydon Carter, who was starting his career in New York around that time. "At the top is Time, Inc. Then Hearst, because they had *Bazaar*. And then there's Condé Nast. It was third-tier. It was a debutante's finishing school."

Phyllis Starr Wilson was the managing editor of *Glamour* in 1976 when she had an idea to improve Condé's appeal to the modern woman. Under the placeholder titles *Self* or *Woman*, Wilson proposed a magazine devoted to women's health and fitness, seizing on an emerging trend. Her fellow New Orleans native Richard Simmons had opened his first fitness studio in Beverly Hills three years earlier; *The Complete Book of Running*, a how-to manual for the nascent pastime of jogging, was about to become a bestseller. It was the dawn of private gyms and Jazzercise; Jane Fonda's workout tapes and Olivia Newton-John's "Physical" were around the corner. Si himself was a fitness addict who regularly worked out in the afternoons and ran laps in Central Park. He had also seen surveys that showed Condé Nast readers responded well to the occasional article about fitness that cropped up in other magazines. He gave Wilson the green light.

Starting *Self* was Si's first major decision since becoming Condé Nast's chairman in 1975, and its success set the template by which he would vastly expand his empire in the 1980s. Bucking his father's abstemious ways, Si approved what was then an unheard-of marketing budget for the launch of a new magazine: $20 million, the equivalent of roughly $80 million today. Television ads circulated in major markets ("*Self*: The First Word in Self-Improvement") and the logo was plastered on billboards, buses, and aerial banners flown over well-to-do resorts. *Self* was aimed at a growing demographic of professional women with ample disposable income, its upbeat, just-between-us-girls tone anticipating Carrie Bradshaw by nearly twenty years: "Your boss wants you to work late. Your tennis partner wants you to meet him at the club. The man in your life wants—oh well, lots of things. Have you ever gotten the feeling you have so many people to please, roles to play and things to do, you don't know who you are anymore?"

Ironically, the editor in charge of dispensing fitness tips to readers was no paragon of perfect health; Phyllis Wilson's preferred form of exercise was belly dancing. "The last thing she'd have ever done was go for a walk," one Condé editor recalled. But just as Condé Montrose Nast had exploited class anxieties in the Gilded Age, *Self* had identified a new kind of aspiration in the culture. Subscribers to *Self*—80 percent of whom worked, according to a 1981 survey, compared to half of all women—viewed financial success and social success as synonymous: to be elite in Reagan's America was to be self-sufficient, healthy, sporty, and rich. "When I got married years ago, I bought *Good Housekeeping* and *Ladies' Home Journal* to learn how to keep house," one *Self* reader said at the time. "Now, I'm trying to forget how to."

Unlike rival magazines that balked at frank discussions of money, *Self* unabashedly embraced women's pursuit of wealth and material happiness. The debut issue included a feature titled "You Too Can Fly over the Middle-Income Bracket Without Being Shot Down by Typical Female Guilt and Fear." The magazine soon rebranded itself as "The Handbook of a New Generation," with an ad campaign featuring a fashionable young woman juggling her makeup kit as she tried to leave the house in time for work.

"I Believe in My *Self*," she said, happily.

Self's brand of cheerful acquisitiveness immediately faced the kind of blowback that would be regularly lobbed at Condé Nast magazines in the 1980s: that it was a glossy vessel for a narcissism overtaking society. "Magazines used to teach social virtues. Now they preach self-fulfillment," clucked one critic. "*Self* is just the latest example of the inward turning of Americans." Perhaps, but there was no question it had struck a chord. *Self* became one of the most successful magazine launches in decades. Circulation nearly doubled in the first six months, from 300,000 to 500,000 readers; two years later, readership had soared toward 1 million. Americans were drifting from the lefty activism that had animated titles like *Esquire*, which by 1979 had fallen far from its 1960s peak. The new era was about excess and indulgence, and accidentally or not, *Self* had provided Si with a winning proof of concept. As the home of *Vogue*, Condé Nast had the right bona fides to be the arbiter of the new decade, to show the next generation of Americans how to live an elite life. What if it applied that formula beyond fashion: to health, food, lifestyle, travel, celebrity? How much bigger could it get?

Inspired, Si went on a spree. He bought *Gentlemen's Quarterly*, a sleepy men's fashion supplement previously owned by *Esquire*, and then *Gourmet*, a journal of high-end gastronomy. (Si was so eager to expand that he barely looked at *Gourmet*'s balance sheet and later wondered if he had overpaid.) Condé Nast had never published a magazine devoted to men's lifestyles or the world of cooking and food; now it had both. Random House, the book publisher that was considered the class of the Manhattan literary world, was subsumed into the Newhouse stable in 1980. Si was borrowing his father's methods, investing in money-losing properties and gambling that their untapped potential could yield a profit. But he had narrowed his focus to the upwardly mobile demographic. At Si's instructions, *House & Garden* was repositioned from a housewife's how-to manual to a chichi guide to embracing the new eighties lifestyle. Si had become alarmed at the burgeoning success of *Architectural Digest*, a California-based magazine that had supercharged the old *House & Garden* formula by filling its pages with the homes of celebrities. He replaced the veteran *House & Garden* editor Mary Jane Pool—a Condé Nast legend who had joined *Vogue*'s art department in 1946 and was still known to wear a sable cape to the office—and then intentionally sacrificed its longtime middle-class audience for a nouveau crowd. *House & Garden* was shifted to more upscale newsstands and removed from the magazine racks in supermarket checkout aisles; the price of an annual subscription tripled. The result was a steep drop-off in nationwide distribution, but an increase in the upscale readership that Si, and his growing list of luxury advertisers, desired.

Rivals scrambled to catch up with Condé's growing influence among the free-spending leisure class. In one risible example, *Esquire* experimented with printing different versions of its October 1983 issue for readers of different household incomes. Subscribers in more affluent zip codes received a cover featuring a WASPy business executive, smiling beside a headline about the world's best skiing destinations. Less well-to-do readers were mailed a version with a rumpled man chewing on a piece of hay.

Not all of Si's ideas at that time came to fruition: a Condé Nast magazine about contemporary romance, called *Love*, never got out of the planning stages. But in recalibrating his empire for the new eighties elite, Si saw an opening in the market to execute a longtime fantasy of the aesthetes and nostalgists who roamed the Condé Nast hallways, a gambit that had never been attempted by his father.

Maybe the time was right to bring back *Vanity Fair*.

VANITY FAIR MAY HAVE BEEN a glittering jewel of Condé Nast's Jazz Age glory days, but its demise during the Great Depression had mummified the brand as a relic of a bygone age. The title was borrowed from John Bunyan's *The Pilgrim's Progress* of 1678, which imagined "Vanity Fair" as a sinful bazaar ruled by Beelzebub that caters to all of humanity's earthly delights. The phrase also invoked the status-conscious plot of William Thackeray's famed 1848 novel, the story of a brilliant, vicious woman scheming her way into high society.

In the case of the magazine, the role of Beelzebub was cheerfully played by the editor Frank Crowninshield, whose first issue appeared in March 1914. A clubman and schmoozer who helped co-found the Museum of Modern Art, he made innumerable contributions to American culture; Emily Post once credited him with suggesting the idea for her book on etiquette. Under his editorship, *Vanity Fair* published Noël Coward and the humorist Robert Benchley, E. E. Cummings and Colette. Photographs came courtesy of Steichen, Horst, and Man Ray, and there were full-color reproductions of works by avant-garde painters like Matisse, Picasso, and Chagall, making the magazine among America's earliest mass-market venues for the European modernism then sweeping the world of art and letters.

Decades before *Spy* magazine and *Gawker*, *Vanity Fair* inaugurated a feature, "We Nominate for Oblivion," that skewered the potentates of the day. The magazine also offered instructional entry points for the less well-to-do. One advertisement in 1929 featured a Cubist canvas by Picasso and the eye-catching caption, "Somebody paid $3,500 for this—WHY? . . . What do you say when your pretty dinner partner asks you? Could you even tell if this were wrong side up? You've got to know. Not just gulp soup! One way to find out . . . READ VANITY FAIR." With its features on athletes, intellectuals, artists, politicians, aristocrats, and libertines like Josephine Baker, *Vanity Fair* invited readers to join a fabulous party—not unlike the ones thrown by Nast in his Park Avenue penthouse—and provided a guided, gimlet-eyed tour of the proceedings.

In the early 1980s, though, the average well-to-do American had never heard of *Vanity Fair*. Frank Crowninshield's name and legacy were mostly forgotten. But his editorial credo—his promise to capture "the progress and promise of American life"—could have been borrowed from a speech by Ronald Reagan. Once again, America had entered an age of runaway wealth creation abetted by government deregulation, with the railroad barons of Crowinshield's day substituted by arbitrageurs and junk-bond specialists. The word *yuppie* was entering the lexicon; Alex P. Keaton made his first appearance on network television in the fall of 1982. The minting of a new financial overclass meant a renewed market for cultural sherpas who could tell parvenus which artists to collect and which writers to read, what theater was worth seeing and which celebrities were worth ogling. And the long fade-out of the sixties had yielded a baby boom generation that was busy casting aside its ideals in favor of the pleasures of the material world, as embodied by the four-figure Shiatsu massagers on sale at their local Sharper Image. As Condé Nast's advertising campaign aptly put it, *Vanity Fair* was "a magazine whose time has come . . . again."

It was a fiasco almost from the start.

THE ANNOUNCEMENT, in the summer of 1981, that Condé Nast was set to resurrect the iconic *Vanity Fair* caused a stir in Manhattan's media and literary circles. In those pre-digital days, the launch of a

Richard Locke was sitting at his cramped desk in the castle-like headquarters of *The New York Times* in the spring of 1981 when his phone rang. Alex Liberman, a man he knew only by reputation, wanted to have lunch and discuss an idea. Locke found this strange: What did a fashion publisher want with a literary critic? For a moment, he hesitated.

"That's very interesting," Locke told Alex, "but at the moment I'm sort of overbooked."

The Silver Fox was undeterred. "No, Richard," Alex replied, "I'd *really* like to speak with you."

Tweedy and cerebral, Locke, not yet forty years old, was an odd choice for the rakish *Vanity Fair*. A literary critic with an impeccable Northeastern pedigree, Locke grew up in Manhattan, boarded at Lawrenceville, and studied at Harvard, Cambridge, and Columbia, taking classes with Lionel Trilling and Susan Sontag. He had worked as an editor at Simon & Schuster before joining *The New York Times Book Review*—two upstanding organs of mid-century, upper-middle-class respectability. Locke had come recommended by two influential figures in the Condé Nast orbit. One was Robert Gottlieb, the Knopf editor in chief who edited Robert Caro and Joseph Heller and had recently entered Si's employ after the Newhouses purchased Knopf's owner, Random House. The other was the novelist Francine du Plessix Gray, Alex's stepdaughter. Because he had been passed over by the *Times* to be the next top editor of the *Book Review*, Locke was susceptible to Alex's entreaties at lunch, and the two agreed to meet again at Alex's minimalist office. Locke prepared for the meeting by rooting around the *Vanity Fair* archives, and he pitched Alex on a publication that would encompass a mélange of cultural forces, both high and pop. "It wasn't just the literary magazine, it wasn't just a visual magazine, it wasn't just reviews, it wasn't just articles, it wasn't just art, it wasn't just gossip," Locke mused. "It was all of these different kinds of things brought together, in what we hoped would be a slowly evolving unity of sensibility, and ultimately some degree of celebration."

Bingo. "That's exactly the kind of thing we're interested in," Alex said.

new national magazine devoted to arts and culture was a significa[nt] event. Rumors spread about the amount of money the free-spendin[g] Newhouses were willing to commit to the project: as much as $3,00[0] ($10,000 today) for pieces of 750 words. For writers, photographers, and stylists, it was an opportunity to attract a mass audience to their work; for editors and critics, it was a chance to shift the zeitgeist. "When I was a kid, I felt I'd missed the boat—all the great magazines were gone," recalled the photographer Jonathan Becker, who was driving a cab to make ends meet until he got the call to join the new magazine. At one point, Becker had been forced to skip town for the West Coast because his tab at Elaine's, the Upper East Side literary hangout, was called in by the proprietress. "The idea that *Vanity Fair* was coming back was just a salvation," Becker said. "It was a source of excitement for everybody in the arts." Si, a longtime devotee of *The New Yorker*, was thrilled to be launching a legitimate rival that could compete in the realm of arts and culture. And it didn't hurt that owning a shiny property like *Vanity Fair*, with its Roaring Twenties lineage, could raise his own standing among New York's elite.

Alex Liberman had his own incentives. Frustrated by the lack of recognition for his art and sculpture, Alex had grown self-conscious that he would forever be known for his oversight of *Vogue*, an institution for which he cared deeply, but had come to conclude was, at heart, a trivial enterprise. A throwaway remark by Diana Vreeland, uttered while the two were sparring over some detail in an upcoming issue of *Vogue*, haunted him: "This is only entertainment." For Alex, *Vanity Fair* represented a chance for redemption, highbrow proof that his talents stretched beyond the commercial world of fashion and retail. For all the hours of calibrating skirt lengths and hemlines, Alex could not accept that a women's magazine would end up as the sum total of his life.

In this chip-on-the-shoulder spirit, Si and Alex decided to select an editor in chief whose literary bona fides were unimpeachable, whose intellectual aura would silence any critics who doubted that Condé Nast, home to frivolous and feminine titles like *Glamour*, *Brides*, and *Mademoiselle*, was capable of creating a so-called "smart magazine."

Locke was hired and set up a skunkworks on the fourth floor of 350 Madison Avenue, the Manhattan office tower that since 1973 had served as Condé Nast's headquarters; he spent nearly a year compiling a 172-page prototype issue. To this day, the cover is a knockout: an exuberant headshot of the dancer Mikhail Baryshnikov (a Liberman friend), photographed by Richard Avedon, surrounded by bright swaths of color and the *Vanity Fair* logo bannered across the top at a jaunty angle. This first stab at a modern *Vanity Fair* captured the high/low wit of the original: puckish illustrations by Edward Koren and Maurice Sendak, a feature on the newly born Prince William, an "Impossible Interview" between Bo Derek and Ayatollah Khomeini. (The latter was a revival of an old *VF* feature that imagined impertinent conversations between odd celebrity pairings like, say, Joseph Stalin and John Rockefeller.) Visually, the prototype was a feast: a black-and-white Irving Penn photograph of Luciano Pavarotti at full bellow, followed by Mick Jagger, topless and sporting a bushy Hemingway-style beard. (Annie Leibovitz had bumped into the freshly hirsute rock star in Central Park and insisted that he pose then and there.) A fine-arts portfolio included an erotic Matisse sketch and a photograph of the artist posing with a nude model. Jonathan Becker's portrait of the French film director Louis Malle, brooding and darkly handsome, added to the sense of European glamour.*

Mixed among the celebrities were signs of the magazine's literary ambitions. Locke had recruited writers more typically read in *The New York Review of Books*, the low-circulation intellectual journal that was among his chief inspirations. Robert Hughes, the erudite art critic, and Helen Vendler, a Harvard professor, came aboard, along with the novelist Elizabeth Hardwick. Publicly, Locke sounded the notes that his Condé Nast bosses wanted to hear—"We live in a world in which one can go from hearing Mick Jagger to the Metropolitan Opera's

---

* The art director for the prototype, Bea Feitler, designed *Ms.* and *Rolling Stone*, and it was her idea to bring on Leibovitz. Feitler died from cancer at forty-four, shortly before the prototype returned from the printers.

Stravinsky production to the Mudd Club," he told one journalist—but by the time the actual first issue appeared, the magazine had veered more "Rite of Spring" than Rolling Stones. *Vanity Fair*'s March 1983 debut did not feature a glitzy celebrity on the cover. Instead, readers were greeted with an illustration of the Greek god Pan playing a tune on his pipe.

It was not the sort of thing that moved magazines at the supermarket checkout line.

Inside the issue, Locke had replaced the zippy designs of the prototype with chunky blocks of text. There was a symposium on the music of Wagner and a piece by the art critic Clement Greenberg, whose famous essay "Avant-Garde and Kitsch" had been published by the *Partisan Review* forty-four years prior. The centerpiece was the unabridged text of a new Gabriel García Márquez novella, *Chronicle of a Death Foretold*, which stretched on for 102 pages. Locke deserves credit for publishing new work by a Nobel laureate, but there was a reason why *The New York Review of Books* didn't attract Condé-style advertisements from European automakers or high-end fashion brands. "The idea of publishing a memoir by the late Elizabeth Bishop—that was hot stuff for us," recalled one of Locke's deputies, Elizabeth Pochoda. "We were behind the eight ball of the cultural shift and the celebrity culture. It was at the moment when it was beginning to take over, and we couldn't have looked more fossilized." Flipping through the issue in London, Tina Brown, then the editor of *Tatler*, was appalled: "*This* is what they'd done with such largesse? This flatulent, pretentious, chaotic catalogue of dreary litterateurs in impenetrable typefaces?"

Compounding the trouble was the blowout publicity campaign that Si had mounted for his new bauble. Condé Nast had done the 1983 equivalent of going viral: the debut of *Vanity Fair* was touted on billboards and in television ads, fueled by a marketing budget of roughly $30 million in today's dollars. In a bizarre stunt, the ads featured a Leibovitz photograph of a bare-chested John Irving, the author of *The World According to Garp*, clad in a red wrestling singlet. The hype did its job: one Manhattan newsstand sold out three hundred copies in four hours, and 100,000 copies were sold nationally in three days.

Unfortunately for Si, the people who bought the magazine didn't like it. *The New Republic* wrote that "the twelve pages of ads for Ralph Lauren's clothes stand out as by far the most appealing, likable, and even interesting thing in the whole 294 pages." *Esquire*'s design maestro, George Lois, pronounced it "incredibly bad."

Si offered a feeble public defense—"We never believed we were producing a perfect magazine when we relaunched *Vanity Fair*"—but inside 350 Madison, panic set in. "This is a disaster," Si said over and over again in meetings. Feeling attacked, Locke retreated into his office, looking to some visitors like an anguished schoolboy. Alex, shocked by the vicious criticism—and ever cognizant of his place in Si's kingdom—grew increasingly anxious that he might take the blame. "It is Richard's magazine," he insisted to *The New York Times*. (In fact, one designer later said Alex had overseen the art direction and that the snoozy cover of Pan was his idea.)

At one point, Locke persuaded Truman Capote to write a gossip column; who wouldn't want to read world-class rumormongering from Capote, the sybarite who relished needling the rich? It all seemed in line with the spirit of the classic *Vanity Fair*. But when Capote's draft arrived, Locke was aghast. The celebrities Capote dished about were outdated—and in some cases, dead. Capote included a lengthy description of Greta Garbo's apartment, an anecdote about meeting Noël Coward in Portofino (Coward had died a decade earlier), and a bizarre attack on Meryl Streep's nose ("it reminds you of an anteater"). The *VF* editors rejected the column, which prompted Capote to sell the piece to *Esquire* and publicly cast a hex on Locke, grumbling, "I hope nobody ever attributes *Vanity Fair* to anybody but Thackeray."

Capote was close to getting his wish. By the time the bad reviews rolled in, Locke's second issue had already closed, meaning he would have no opportunity to respond to the feedback. And the highlight of his next issue was a twenty-five-thousand-word excerpt from V. S. Naipaul's new memoir. Alex urged Locke to loosen up—"You need to *schmooze*," he cooed at one point—but two months later, Locke was out. "From the beginning, there was a conflict between the magazine that I believe I was asked to create, a magazine of writing and ideas, or a magazine of jazzy layout and bits and pieces," Locke told reporters. "And jazzy layout won."

SI AND ALEX DECIDED TO TRY AGAIN. Locke's successor would be Leo Lerman, whose legend at Condé Nast rivaled that of the magazine whose fate now lay in his hands. At sixty-eight, Lerman had been a fixture of Manhattan's entertainment and arts world since the early 1940s. His intimates included Anaïs Nin, W. H. Auden, Maria Callas, and Marlene Dietrich, all of whom attended the martini-fueled salons he threw with his partner, the artist Gray Foy. This fabulous life was entirely self-invented. Lerman was born into a Jewish immigrant family who lived in Manhattan on East 107th Street, in the neighborhood that would later be called Spanish Harlem; his father was a housepainter. In his early teens, Lerman came across issues of the original *Vanity Fair* and was entranced by its depiction of café society; he spent the rest of his life seeking to replicate the delights in its pages. As an editor at *Mademoiselle* and *Vogue*, Lerman had published work by Rebecca West, Iris Murdoch, and his old friend Truman Capote, whom he met at a party when Capote hopped onto Lerman's back in a stairwell and demanded a piggyback ride.

Lerman was the kind of eccentric who might be shunned at a buttoned-up publisher like Hearst, but was celebrated in the stagy realm of Condé Nast. He strolled the halls in a Borsalino hat and wielded an elaborately decorated cane; a watch fob and bushy beard completed the image of an Edwardian dandy. He wrote only in purple ink—an ophthalmologist once warned his eyesight would fail him, and it was the one color he would be able to see—and he often dismissed colleagues from his office with a playful "Begone!"

To Alex and Si, Lerman's old-world charm was the perfect antidote to Locke's stuffiness, and his exacting taste in art, books, classical music, and dance seemed well suited to a cultural compendium like *Vanity Fair*. But Lerman quickly fell into the same highbrow trap as Locke. For his covers, Lerman assigned Irving Penn to shoot severe black-and-white portraits of intellectuals like Susan Sontag, Philip Roth, and

Italo Calvino, celebrities in only a very narrow sense of the word. *People* magazine featured movie and TV stars; Lerman's January 1984 issue of *VF* teased "a candid interview with screen queen Hanna Schygulla," a German actress best known for her appearances in Rainer Werner Fassbinder's films. (The issue sold terribly—surprise!) At one point, Lerman put Francine du Plessix Gray, Alex Liberman's stepdaughter, on the cover. Francine was a respected novelist, and perhaps Lerman wished to earn Alex's goodwill, but the notion that any readers beyond a rarefied slice of literary Manhattan would recognize Francine on their newsstand was laughable. Advertisers began to bail; each issue of *Vanity Fair* was thinner than the last. Lerman, whose health was deteriorating, began whittling away afternoons in his office, reminiscing about his favorite mid-century ballerinas and apologetically telling his staff, "I'm in a very *purple* mood today."

The commercial failure of these early *Vanity Fair*s was not just a result of its editors' foibles. Alex and Si had tasked Locke and Lerman with assembling a sophisticated journal of culture that appealed to affluent readers. But what Alex and Si considered high culture—products of literary and artistic seriousness, consumed by a discerning upper class—turned out to be hopelessly out of date. Elite American taste was changing. Si's parents had flocked to the opera, and Lerman had embraced the ballet to prove he wasn't just a painter's kid from Harlem. But the new American rich felt less restricted in their cultural pursuits. The New Hollywood cinema of the 1970s meant that self-styled intellectuals dissected *The Godfather* and *The Deer Hunter* with as much vigor as any novel by Joyce or Woolf. Steven Bochco's *Hill Street Blues* debuted on NBC in 1981, an early sign of television's artistic growth; MTV arrived later that year. Old hierarchies were breaking down. The strict separation of high and low art, espoused by critics like Greenberg (featured in Locke's debut issue), had been usurped in the intervening decades by Sontag's embrace of camp—the intellectual happily slumming in the lowbrow—and the rise of postmodernists like Jeff Koons, whose readymade "sculptures" of Hoover vacuum cleaners debuted at the New Museum in 1980. Si, whose own cultural tastes ran to the great Russian novels and classical music, had wanted to replicate *The New*

Yorker's role as a cultural authority in respectable upper-middle-class life. Instead, he constructed a magazine whose instincts were caught in the past.

By the end of 1983, *Vanity Fair* was still showing few signs of success. While his brother, Donald, generated big revenues at the Newhouse newspapers, Si's big bet had turned Condé Nast into an object of mockery among the elites whose approval he still craved. The posthumous disapproval of Sam, who surely would never have okayed such a lavish experiment as *Vanity Fair*, also loomed large. Si could have fired Lerman and folded his new magazine then and there, retreating to the relative comfort of a life as the man who published *Vogue*. Instead, he went for one final roll of the dice. He would turn over *Vanity Fair* to an editor four decades younger than Lerman, an upstart with little reverence for mid-century high culture, an impudent outsider who promised a fresher, zestier take on the new American establishment.

Her name was Tina Brown.

5

British Invader

In the spring of 1977, a one-act play by a young English writer named Tina Brown debuted at a fringe theater in the Shepherd's Bush neighborhood of London. Tina, a twenty-three-year-old Oxford graduate then sporting a mop of blond hair and oversized granny glasses, was a journalist with a growing reputation for coolly observed accounts of aristocrats behaving badly and humorous first-person pieces in which she, say, danced in a G-string at a strip club in Hackensack, New Jersey. ("The construction workers turned their backs and began to play pool," she reported of the audience response.) Her theatrical endeavor, *Happy Yellow*, focused on a protagonist not unlike the playwright herself. Jackie Page is a "bright, sassy London career girl" trying to break into the glamorous world of Manhattan magazines. She boasts about A-list contacts and fantasizes about a high-powered editor who will splash her work on the cover of a glossy monthly, displacing an essay by Gore Vidal. As a wide-eyed Brit in Gotham, Jackie encounters a variety of American oddities—masturbation workshops, dog motels, death therapists—that would not be out of place in a future issue of *Vanity Fair*. Driven and a bit deluded, Jackie insists to her skeptical roommates that her journalistic talent will stand out. "Watch out New York," she announces at one point. "Here I come!"

At the end of *Happy Yellow*, Jackie's dreams fizzle out. Her real-life counterpart fared better. Tina came to New York in 1983, already a hot property in the magazine world. After stints as a feature writer at *The Sunday Telegraph* and *The Times of London*, Tina, at twenty-five, had been named the editor of *Tatler*, a moribund London social gazette, which she proceeded to revitalize with a string of impudent and deeply reported scoops. Tina penetrated Princess Margaret's tropical citadel of Mustique (which she deemed a Club Med for royalty), persuaded the erotic film actress and Prince Andrew paramour Koo Stark to grant an interview, and penned an anonymous field guide to London's eligible bachelors (sample entry: "a rising young barrister with a keen interest in ladies' briefs but an even keener interest in the road to Number Ten"). *Tatler*'s investigations into Princess-to-be Diana earned Tina a guest anchor spot on NBC's *Today* show.

The coverage electrified the British chattering classes and aroused the attention of Si Newhouse, who heard about the gleeful ruckus Tina was raising during his trips to check in on *British Vogue*. Si liked *Tatler* so much that he bought it; the magazine joined the Condé Nast stable in 1982, where it remains to this day. Tina quit the editorship the following year, but Si was reluctant to let her wander off—he sensed her skills might be useful in solving the ongoing catastrophe of his *Vanity Fair*. Tina had visited New York before, exploring the city on a three-month trip after Oxford during which she sublet a rundown apartment from a death therapist, later dramatized in *Happy Yellow*. In April 1983, she arrived in more upscale fashion, taxiing in from Kennedy Airport to a room at the Royalton Hotel, not far from Condé headquarters at 350 Madison. Alex Liberman had requested her presence and the two had plans to lunch at the Four Seasons. Jackie Page's fantasy was on the verge of coming true.

"HOW DO I PIN YOU DOWN? What do you want? We need you on *Vanity Fair*!"

So Alex began his efforts to persuade Tina Brown, over a lunch of crab cocktail and sparkling water, to help him fix one of the most dire threats he had faced in his long Condé Nast career. As he introduced his guest to the status markers of the Four Seasons Grill Room—which booth belonged to Philip Johnson and which to Si; why the upstairs section was Siberia, to be avoided at all costs—Alex affected the studied, urbane ease he had honed into an art form. "I've never taken my jacket off in 50 years of Condé Nast," he once explained. "It signifies effort." He refused to wear shirts with a patch pocket sewn onto the breast, believing it would lower his status in the eyes of others. For any junior editor with the temerity to challenge his directives, Alex's flawless manners and immaculate dress sent the message that only one man fully understood the elusive mystique of Condé Nast, and it was best not to interfere.

But on this Tuesday, answers were eluding Alex. It had been only a few weeks since the disastrous debut of Richard Locke's *Vanity Fair*, the magazine Alex had bet his reputation on, and for all his years of close collaboration with the Newhouses, he knew the family had little patience for a public humiliation. His own advancing age was also on his mind: at seventy, Alex, whose cultural radar was his currency, could not afford for Si to think he had lost his feel for the zeitgeist. The bright young woman before him presented an intriguing solution. Tina's approach to covering English elites was irreverent and titillating; she had homed in on the humor and hypocrisy in Thatcher-era Britain, an apt antecedent to the Reaganism now sweeping America. Crucially, her magazine turned a profit, too: *Tatler*'s circulation grew ten times on her watch and began making money after years in the red.

Tina also offered some of the literary gravitas that Si wanted for *Vanity Fair*, which after all was supposed to compete with the vaunted *New Yorker*. At Oxford, Tina read English and dated Martin Amis; her circle included A-list scribes like Auberon Waugh (son of Evelyn) and Christopher Hitchens. Her affair with Harry Evans, the married *Sunday Times of London* editor who was twenty-five years her senior, had been a Fleet Street scandal. But by now the two had settled into a happy marriage, and Harry, among the most respected journalists of his generation, was looking for work after being ousted from his high-paying job at *The Times* by a brash new owner named Rupert Murdoch. Could there be a place at Condé for him, too? In a neat coincidence,

Tina and Harry's 1981 wedding had been held at Grey Gardens, the East Hampton estate of Sally Quinn and Ben Bradlee, the *Washington Post* editor whose great-uncle was Frank Crowninshield, of the original *Vanity Fair*. Alex may have wondered if this was fate.

Across the table, Tina's heart sped up as she listened to Alex's pitch. It had been a dream of hers to run a major American magazine, to break out from the parochialism of her native Britain, but she could not tell if Alex intended to simply hand her the reins or place her under Locke's supervision. The sorry state of *Vanity Fair* required drastic change; without full creative control, she thought the assignment would be hopeless. Her mood darkened after Leo Lerman, under the guise of friendship, let drop that Si and Alex had suggested that *he* replace Locke as the editor in chief—a sotto voce confidence that doubled as a brushback pitch. Nonplussed, she told Alex she could do a two-month consultancy, and then let's see where it goes. "It wasn't so much the job itself that scared me, as New York," Tina wrote in her diary. "I could be eaten alive in a place where I don't know anybody or know where the alliances are."

A wary courtship followed. Lerman had succeeded Locke by the time Tina's stint began in May, and he quickly rejected most of her ideas out of hand. Feeling sidelined at the *Vanity Fair* offices, Tina instead focused on meeting New York's movers and shakers while she was in town. At a Chelsea dinner party, she was seated beside Dominick Dunne, Joan Didion's brother-in-law, a former film producer then trying to make it as a novelist. Dunne was a gossip and raconteur who had drifted in and out of American high society, with the kind of insider/outsider perspective that Tina often found made for the best journalists. He was from a well-off Irish Catholic family in WASP Connecticut—"minor-league Kennedys," as he once put it—but his natty look of thick, round glasses and French-collared Turnbull & Asser shirts belied the rough edges of his life. Nick and his wife had once been celebrated for their lavish Los Angeles parties; Truman Capote, who attended a black-and-white ball thrown by the Dunnes for their tenth wedding anniversary, later stole the idea for his famous Plaza Hotel soiree, though he neglected to invite them. But Nick struggled when his marriage collapsed. He became addicted to alcohol and cocaine and fell into near-bankruptcy, reduced to selling his dog, a West Highland terrier, for $300. He was just piecing his life back together when his daughter, the twenty-two-year-old actress Dominique Dunne, was strangled by an ex-boyfriend. When Tina heard that Nick was planning to attend the murder trial, her editor's brain stirred: the combination of a grisly crime, Dunne's starry family, and his eye for society foibles felt potent. She urged him to keep a diary.

Back at 350 Madison, Tina's frustrations were coming to a head. Infuriated by Lerman's obstinance, she marched into Si's fourteenth-floor office on June 25 and informed him that she would be departing *Vanity Fair* next week, when her consultancy ended. Si hated this sort of direct confrontation; such unpleasantness was why he surrounded himself with heavies like Roy Cohn who could handle conflict.

"But the timing . . . ," Si ventured. "Leo has just become editor. He needs time."

"The magazine can no longer afford that time," Tina retorted. "The only thing I can do for you when you are ready is be the editor."

The meeting ended with no resolution. Si felt paralyzed. Lerman had been kind to him when he started at *Vogue*, one of the Condé potentates willing to mentor the callow heir in the customs of the elite. But he also desperately needed *Vanity Fair* to succeed, for Condé Nast's reputation and his own. It was by far Si's biggest gambit since Sam died, and the publishing world was wondering if the prodigal son could prove his skeptical father wrong. While Si hesitated, Tina flew back to Europe. She was about to turn thirty and figured she could easily find a job in England. But as she lay awake in her house in Pimlico, her thoughts kept wandering back to her glamorous sojourn in Manhattan, which she realized had surpassed London as the cultural and financial nucleus of the 1980s. She began taking sleeping pills for stress. When *Women's Wear Daily* phoned her in London to ask about the state of *Vanity Fair*, Tina did not hold back. "If you have the wrong editor, then there is the wrong aura," she told the paper, aware that Si and Alex would read her words. "The magazine was too dedicated to culture with a capital K, and art with a capital A. That just isn't controversial enough. It makes people yawn."

The call came in December, while Tina was lounging poolside in Barbados: her presence was requested at Si Newhouse's Upper East Side town house. Once she made it past the security guard—Victoria had insisted on hiring one after a burglary attempt—she found Si and Alex huddled together in an upstairs library. Si broke the ice by ribbing her about the *Women's Wear* comments, but after a few minutes of suspense, the offer was made: Tina Brown would become editor of *Vanity Fair* in the new year. The job had proved too taxing for Lerman, who weeks earlier had been hospitalized for a kidney stone; the public would be told he wished to return to editing and writing. Wary of gossip, the group arranged for Si and Tina to leave the house separately to avoid arousing suspicions among passersby.

Now the Cinderella routine began: Tina had to be given the trappings of a Condé Nast editor in chief. A corporate car, gym membership, and office designer were procured, along with an East Side apartment. In a sign of generosity, and perhaps desperation, Si acquiesced to a two-year contract, making Tina among the first Condé editors to secure such a lengthy commitment. Lerman was dismayed, although it was not the first or last time that Alex would ruthlessly cut loose a close friend. (A decade prior, Lerman had raged at Alex in his diary, calling him "evil—a dreadful being, a wretched murderous Russian of the blackest blood.") But Alex rationalized it all to himself by focusing on his devotion to the institution, and what he deemed his own indispensable role. The posterity of Condé Nast, he had come to believe, rested on his shoulders.

Tina's appointment was made public on January 4, 1984. The terse memo from Si described his new editor as "remarkably young." Tina had no illusions that her arrival would be met with intense skepticism from the chattering classes, most of whom assumed Si's exhumed version of *Vanity Fair* was headed back to the grave. Her editorship was the main topic of conversation at a chichi Manhattan party that week thrown by Arianna Stassinopoulos (soon-to-be Huffington), herself an Oxbridge near-contemporary of Tina's, where the discussion focused on how long she could last in the job. It looked more and more like a delusional fantasy that Condé Nast, province of women's magazines, had ever hoped to play in the first-tier literary sandbox. All Tina could do was plead her case. "I want to share my perception of what is funny, fascinating, true and beautiful," she told *Newsweek*. "And I don't want to be an editor in brief."

IT TOOK ABOUT EIGHTEEN MONTHS for Tina to fully find her footing at *Vanity Fair*, but when she was done remaking the magazine, it had ascended from an industry embarrassment to a must-read in Manhattan, Beverly Hills, and Washington, DC. Tina turned the magazine into an emblem of 1980s America, its cheerful excess and unapologetic worship of celebrity and wealth. Along the way, she innovated practices that are now so ubiquitous in the world of upscale journalism that it can be hard to imagine they hadn't always existed.

Her first issue, April 1984, opened with a Helmut Newton cover portrait of Daryl Hannah, the actress who, weeks earlier, had been launched to stardom playing a mermaid in *Splash*. Hannah posed blindfolded with an Oscar in each hand, beside the headline "Blonde Ambition." The image evoked Hollywood glamour, the scales of justice, and a frisson of kink—not an unrepresentative blend of the new *Vanity Fair*'s preoccupations. Dominick Dunne's murder trial diary, commissioned by Tina, had been a big hit in the March issue; for April, Tina asked Dunne to write on the enduring appeal of movie-star blondes, illustrated with sexy photographs of Hannah, Michelle Pfeiffer, and Kim Basinger. If the blondes titillated readers, the next page flattered their intellect: a new short story by E. L. Doctorow, followed by an excerpt from David Mamet's upcoming Broadway play *Glengarry Glen Ross*. A pair of nostalgic features about the heydays of Keith Richards and Diana Vreeland rounded out the issue, advertised on the cover with a puckish, *Tatler*-style tease: "Vreeland Remembers—Keith Richards Doesn't." All this, plus a feature on literary sex scenes, and cameos by Sting, Malcolm Forbes, Barbara Walters, and Prince Michael of Greece.

These days, TikTok and Instagram serve up a similar cultural stew: a model in a bikini, followed by an exegesis on the Israel–Palestine conflict, followed by Kim Kardashian promoting a Skims collection. In 1984, this blend was virtually unheard of. Magazines, the prevailing pulp-and-ink vessels of culture, were highly regimented: *The New Republic* for politics, *People* for gossip, *Playboy* for breasts. That a single publication might contain this mix of high and low, crude and refined, was a novelty. "No one, the makers of the magazines or the people who read them, really understood this concept of high/low," recalls Stephen Schiff, one of Tina's core team of writers. "You bought a magazine because everything in it had the same sensibility. If it was *Seventeen*, it was about women and clothes. If it was *The Atlantic*, it was about head-scratching issues. *Vanity Fair* was a magazine about both at the same time, and everything in between. And that became, very quickly, an exciting way to go."

Tina did land on one consistent theme for her magazine: money. In her short time in America, she had discovered a Manhattan awash in wealth, its upper class transfixed by the opulent lifestyles of corporate raiders like Michael Milken and Ivan Boesky, who made the delinquent toffs of *Tatler* seem quaint. The sheer fact of wealth, or becoming wealthy, was now synonymous with social status. Gone were the Mrs. Astor-esque aspersions that had previously been cast upon the nouveau: witness the social success of Saul Steinberg, the outer-borough billionaire who scandalized the Wall Street old guard before moving into John D. Rockefeller Jr.'s former apartment on Park Avenue and becoming a coveted 1980s party host. When Tina went to lunch at Le Cirque for the first time, she sized up the crowd like an anthropologist: "all the ladies who lunch in red capes and big, gleaming earrings eating pink fish." Back at the office, she ordered up a portrait of its dining room for the next issue, a field guide to the new American rich. Her social circle soon included moguls like Barry Diller, Ahmet Ertegun, and Mort Zuckerman.

For all her precocity, this was fresh territory for Tina. She was born on November 21, 1953, into an upper-middle-class family, comfortable but not posh. Her father, George Brown, was a producer of British B-movies, including early adaptations of Agatha Christie, whose career fell on hard times. Her mother, Bettina, had worked as an assistant to Laurence Olivier. Tina grew up in Little Marlow, a village northwest of London, and while she was sent to fancy boarding schools, she had a tendency to get kicked out of them. Her outsider status came in handy when she found herself inside the citadels of the ruling class: her first scoop came after she attended an off-the-record lunch at London's satirical magazine *Private Eye* and then wrote it all up in an Oxford student magazine. One friend described her, fondly, as "a police reporter for the media and political upper class."

Wealth, in one sense, had always been the underlying focus of Condé Nast, whose publications, since the Gilded Age, had offered a glimpse into the lives and habits of the well-born. What Tina recognized—ahead of Si and Alex, and certainly her predecessors Locke and Lerman—was that in the 1980s, the market for the Condé approach had vastly expanded. Just days after Si announced her appointment as editor, *Time* ran an article called "Here Come the Yuppies!" "Who are all those upwardly mobile folk with designer water, running shoes, pickled parquet floors and $450,000 condos in semi-slum buildings?" the magazine asked. The answer might as well have been the prospective readership of *Vanity Fair*. In the first three years of Tina's editorship, the number of American households that earned $50,000 or more (roughly $145,000 in today's dollars) nearly doubled in size. Popular resentment toward the rich, too, had begun to fade. *Lifestyles of the Rich and Famous* started airing the same week that Tina's first issue of *Vanity Fair* hit newsstands, tantalizing viewers with yachts, mansions, and tanned men in ascots. "It's almost as though they were tuning in to take notes on how they would take their money and spend it," observed the host, Robin Leach.

The naked aspiration of the yuppies was echoed by changes in the establishment upper crust. Whereas the old-line wealthy had once adhered to a kind of WASP *omertà*, in which the topic of money was considered, along with politics and religion, unfit for polite conversation, the rich of the 1980s felt liberated to flaunt it. "It was the first time in my life," recalled the writer Fran Lebowitz, "that people who had money talked about money all the time."

All of which boded very well for the financial future of Condé Nast. Si had bet big on magazines aimed at an upscale readership. The luxury advertisers hawking BMWs, Dubonnet, and Perrier water needed a place to reach their yuppie quarry. By amping up the eighties excess—Imelda Marcos! Scandals in the Hamptons!—Tina had delivered it:

by spring 1986, she claimed that half of *Vanity Fair* readers had a net worth of $1 million or more. A singularity of sorts occurred when, shortly into her tenure, Tina assigned a cover story on *Dynasty*, the prime-time soap about a plutocratic oil clan that debuted eight days before Reagan's inauguration and became a massive hit. Tina was desperate for its star, Joan Collins, to pose for the magazine. She made a pleading phone call—"Please, please, *please* do the cover!"—and invoked Joan's long-ago collaboration with her father in England. "You were my father's friend," Joan recalled Tina saying. "Please do it as a favor to me." There was a last-minute crisis when a former costar of Joan's accidentally shot himself on a soap opera set; the original headline, "But Darling, You Know I Am Bulletproof," had to be scrapped. Instead, the Herb Ritts portrait of Joan ran with an instant-classic headline: "She Rhymes with Rich."

IN 1985, TINA FLEW TO LONDON to report an exposé on the troubled marriage of Diana and Charles. Tossing aside the propriety usually afforded to British royals by the American press, Tina gathered all the vicious rumors about the Waleses that had been floated in the Fleet Street tabloids and repackaged them into a glossy feature for American readers, headlined "The Mouse That Roared." The story caused a scandal on both sides of the Atlantic, in no small part for Tina's conclusion that Charles was "pussy-whipped from here to eternity." In a television interview broadcast in Britain, Diana and Charles were confronted with the reporting of this upstart American magazine; the prince went out of his way to dismiss Tina's assertion that he had relied on the assistance of a Ouija board to contact his beloved late great-uncle Lord Mountbatten. "I don't even know what they *are*," Charles complained. Tina's gossipy, intrusive report was a far cry from the decorous manner in which Condé Nast publications like *Vogue* and *House & Garden* wrote about European royalty. The issue also sold extremely well, catching the attention of Tina's rival editors in the United States. The story was a starting gun of sorts for the genre of leering coverage of royal sex lives that would become ubiquitous in the international press.

About a year prior, Tina had taken a similarly brash approach to another subject that was usually handled ever-so-gently at Condé Nast: national politics. *Vogue* featured First Ladies, and Frank Crowninshield had once included Adolf Hitler on his raffish "We Nominate for Oblivion" list, but the company was reluctant to repel readers seeking an escape to the softer side of life. In 1984, Tina jettisoned this tradition and asked Gail Sheehy to cover the presidential campaign for *Vanity Fair*. Sheehy was a veteran journalist known for her immersive reporting on sex workers, drug abuse, and other gritty topics for *New York* magazine; she had also written the bestseller *Passages*, an ur-seventies examination of Americans' emotional lives. At the time, campaign journalism was dominated by the "Boys on the Bus," reporters for newspapers like *The New York Times* and *The Washington Post* who wrote up the day's proceedings and shied away from candidates' personal lives. Tina wanted a more psychological approach that considered politicians as warts-and-all human beings, something closer in timbre to the rollicking London tabloids she grew up on.

Sheehy's first subject was Gary Hart, the movie-star-handsome senator from Colorado. A rising star in the Democratic Party, Hart had unexpectedly surged in the early primaries against Walter Mondale. Sheehy discovered that Hart had maintained a years-long friendship with Marilyn Youngbird, an Indigenous woman who Hart referred to as "my spiritual adviser." Youngbird had arranged for Native American medicine people to pray for Hart's political success, including a ceremony devoted to his electoral efforts in Iowa and New Hampshire. When Sheehy asked Hart about Youngbird, the candidate promptly produced a note from Marilyn that he kept in his jacket pocket. "Go to nature," she had written. "Hug a tree. Come and say prayers with me. Nobody needs to know. It's between you and the Great Spirit."

Hart had a bit of a hippy-dippy reputation, but this was one woo-woo too many. Sheehy's article caused a sensation. When it appeared, Hart had narrowly lost the nomination, but he was jockeying for the vice-presidential slot on Mondale's ticket. The Marilyn Youngbird details deeply troubled Mondale's aides. A furious Hart had disputed Sheehy's reporting, calling it "terribly inaccurate," but the damage was done; Geraldine Ferraro was picked instead. Decades later, the episode still stings. "The story you mention was wrong then and it is still wrong," Hart wrote to me in 2023 when I inquired about his perspective on the piece. "I see no important purpose being served by responding yet again to a 30- or more-year-old inaccurate and harmful story."

The unmasking, in 1987, of Hart's relationship with an actress and former beauty contestant named Donna Rice is now viewed as a turning point in political journalism, supposedly the moment when reporters cast aside old protocols and began disclosing the more hidden aspects of a politician's personal life. (The alleged affair forced the married Hart to drop out of the 1988 presidential race, though he and Rice denied that their friendship was sexual in nature.) Sheehy's *Vanity Fair* story presaged that moment by several years. It was a portent of where American politics was headed: toward the feeding frenzy of the Monica Lewinsky scandal and the emphasis on gossip, vice, and personal foibles. Sheehy's approach was intrusive and a bit vulgar, but it not only broke news—it *was* news. Tina had taken the first step toward a glossy celebrity magazine becoming a required read (if a furtive one) in the halls of Congress and a bestseller on Washington newsstands.

But it was a very different political feature that would prove to the world—and, perhaps more importantly, to Si—that *Vanity Fair* had arrived.

ONE LATE-WINTER DAY IN 1985, Tina Brown walked into the Map Room of the White House accompanied by the Scottish photographer Harry Benson, whose visual legacy already included the Beatles' pillow fight at the Hotel George V in Paris and the first horrifying images of Senator Robert F. Kennedy on the floor of the Ambassador Hotel, bleeding to death after being shot by an assassin. *Vanity Fair* had negotiated a few minutes' access to Ronald and Nancy Reagan for a formal First Couple portrait.

Despite establishing herself on the Park Avenue and Beverly Hills circuit—collecting fancy friends like the Hollywood agent Swifty Lazar and the Republican socialite Pat Buckley—Tina had not yet secured her future at Condé Nast. Her punchy stories and lively covers (a nude, come-hither Jerry Hall greeted readers in March 1985) had people talking, but advertisers were wary, still feeling burned from the dismal failure of the overhyped Richard Locke era. *Vanity Fair*'s ad revenue fell to $4 million in 1984, down from $6.3 million a year before. Si had also just bought *The New Yorker*, his holy grail; Tina wondered if that meant he no longer needed *Vanity Fair* for intellectual bona fides. Would Si combine the magazines and exile Tina back to England?

Tina shoved those thoughts aside as the Reagans swept into the room, Ronnie in a tuxedo and his wife in a sequined gown. The shoot had been shoehorned in before a state dinner for the president of Argentina, and Tina worried there wouldn't be enough time to make the pictures pop. But Benson had planned ahead. In those pre-9/11 days, before the White House became a fortress, the photographer had managed to smuggle in a boom box, which at that moment began emitting the opening notes of Frank Sinatra's "Nancy (With the Laughing Face)."

The First Lady was charmed. "I love this song, honey," she told the president. "Let's dance."

According to Tina and Benson's accounts, Reagan briefly resisted—"We can't keep the president of Argentina waiting, Nancy"—before his wife exclaimed, "Let him wait!" and fell into her husband's arms. If it sounded like dialogue from a Fred Astaire film, the tableau of the foxtrotting black-tie couple was straight out of Old Hollywood. Tina did not dare exhale lest she break the spell. Finally, Benson urged the president to "give your wife a kiss!" Ronnie complied. The resulting photograph—the Reagans' eyes squeezed shut, their lips abutting—was unlike any previous White House portrait. Americans had seen their presidents and First Ladies in fusty wedding photos, and the Kennedys had been particularly adept at the illusion of inviting the public into their (carefully edited) family life. But here was a live glimpse of real romance, the movie-star president and his starlet bride: an instant icon of the 1980s entwinement of celebrity, glamour, and power.

Tina knew she was sitting on dynamite. To her chagrin, she discovered that while getting the pictures was one thing, getting them published was another. Her hurdle was the squeamishness of Si. For all its eagerness to play in the journalism big leagues, Condé Nast was still an institution in thrall to social protocol. Si had heard through his circle that Nancy Reagan was worried about the photos and insisted that Tina overnight copies to the White House press office—a mortifying concession for an editor accustomed to the pirate-ship independence of Fleet Street. Tina hopped the shuttle to Washington and delivered the dummy layouts herself, sweet-talking Nancy's press secretary and offering to run the "kiss" picture inside, with heels-up Nancy on the cover.

The images appeared in late May, alongside the headline "The Reagan Stomp: They Could Have Danced All Night." Si need not have worried: the accompanying article, by the Reagan sycophant William F. Buckley Jr., was a gushing tribute about how the couple had "Fred-and-Gingered-up the social life of America." Rather than let the issue passively seep into the zeitgeist, Tina booked herself onto the network morning shows to ensure that all of Middle America knew about her coup. This was the sort of thing that editors simply did not do—and while it was in the service of selling magazines, popping up on the *Today* show conveniently raised Tina's profile, too.

As Tina predicted, the Reagan issue was a sellout—and just in the nick of time. Privately, Si had decided that he had spent enough of his family's money trying to keep *Vanity Fair* afloat. He had splashed out $168 million on *The New Yorker*; maybe the tens of millions of dollars in losses on his other literary title weren't worth it. Tina was flying to San Francisco for a book fair when the early rumors emerged. Desperate, she called a colleague in New York and prevailed on him to intercept Si the next day at 6 a.m., his customary arrival time at the Condé offices. Tell Si that *Vanity Fair* had found its footing, she instructed—the buzz around the Reagan photos was immense—and he'd be a fool to pull the plug. The pitch worked: Si agreed to give Tina two more years, which she interpreted as Condé-speak for six months.

TOPPING THE STOMP WAS NO SMALL TASK, but Tina had already set another major feature in motion. A few months before Si's wobble on *Vanity Fair*, she had assigned Dominick Dunne a story in his sweet spot of sex, violence, and society: a profile of Claus von Bülow, the infamous man-about-town who had been convicted of trying to murder his wife, Sunny, with injections of insulin. That verdict had been overturned, and von Bülow was now awaiting a new trial while living with a girlfriend in Sunny's gilded Fifth Avenue apartment, while his wife lay comatose in a hospital. Tina asked Helmut Newton to fly in from Monte Carlo and accompany Dunne on the assignment. After a warm welcome, Newton, in a naughty mood, encouraged von Bülow to try on a different outfit, cooing, "Oh Claus, you would look so good in leather . . ." To Dunne and Newton's shock, von Bülow emerged in a kinky black leather jacket and gamely posed for the camera. (Von Bülow would later be acquitted.) Stephen Schiff remembered Newton's reaction when he brought the contact sheet back to 350 Madison: "*Can you believe this?!*"

Here in one story was the Tina formula: celebrity, titillation, money, and, like bitters added to a cocktail, an invigorating dash of bad taste. "You have to occasionally do things that other people say, 'My God, you know, why did they do that?'" she told *60 Minutes* when the CBS show profiled *Vanity Fair*, itself an indication of just how big her magazine had become. "If you don't, you're not alive. You're boring." Once again, Tina took an unusually active role in ensuring von Bülow would make a splash, leaking word of the leather pictures to gossip queen Liz Smith. The ensuing shock—that the aspirational *VF* was choosing to glamorize a man accused of attempted murder—convinced her to knock Matt Dillon off the cover and run von Bülow in a tuxedo instead.

It may not have been obvious at the time, but Tina's sensibility was now permanently reshaping what was deemed acceptable cultural fare for the intellectual class. The von Bülow feature was basically an upscale gossip column, dressed up in Dunne's patrician prose and Newton's arch, high-gloss aesthetic. Tina was offering elites the leeway to embrace vulgarity. "With *Vanity Fair*, you don't have to pretend that intellectual pursuits are incompatible with interest in fashion, taste, and, yes, even scandal," she wrote in a note to readers.

Tina recognized that America's Reaganite turn was fueling a new kind of cultural collapse. Status in England was conferred at birth, so posh Brits had no qualms about enjoying Monty Python alongside Shakespeare. But in America, which had no hereditary aristocracy, distinctions of taste were distinctions of class. The explosion in wealth in the 1980s destroyed those old rules. Status in America had gone postmodern. It was now less about rigid hierarchies than indulging in a cultural potpourri, whatever was trendy, popular, and *new*: a "hierarchy of hotness," to borrow a phrase from the writer John Seabrook, himself a Tina recruit. "I remember going to lunch with Tina one day and she said, 'Michael, you know the articles just have to be hot, hot, hot,'" recalled Michael Shnayerson, another *Vanity Fair* writer. "I remember her standing in a corner saying, 'Hot hot hot.'" Thanks to Tina, Condé Nast was now reflecting, and advancing, this cultural shift. "Image replaced reality," *VF* later declared in an assessment of the 1980s. "Life-style replaced life. Hype hijacked art." Even Tina was taken aback at the squares who were enchanted by her high/low mix. When Robert MacNeil, the straitlaced coanchor of *The MacNeil-Lehrer Report* on PBS, told her he had enjoyed a recent *Vanity Fair* piece on Madonna, Tina was shocked.

"Why are you reading this?" she asked.

Because, MacNeil replied, "It was right next to the Arafat story. I read that and then my eye wandered to Madonna."

Rival editors grumbled that Tina was playing to the lowest common denominator, indulging the public's baser instincts. Sometimes, the complaint came from inside the house. Si's daughter, Pamela Mensch, once lamented to her father about the changes at Condé. "For me, *Vanity Fair* was like a soft-porn magazine," she told me. "It became pretty sleazy. There was a deterioration in the values somewhere there." Si heard her out, but took no action; he was pleased with the fat advertising pages, which tripled between 1985 and 1988. "If it was making a profit," Mensch observed, "that elicited his admiration."

It was also deeply satisfying to Si that his competitors—once so dismissive of the Newhouse name—were now scrambling to keep up. Tina was poaching star writers from places like *The New York Times Magazine* and mocking her rivals in the press. "There are good things in it," she told a reporter about the *Times Magazine*. "Every fourth issue or so there's something I want to read." It wasn't just the buzz luring writers into Tina's orbit. Thanks to Si's largesse, she paid extremely well. By 1989, *Vanity Fair* writers were earning two dollars a word, double the going rate; annual contracts for some contributors topped $100,000, or $250,000 in today's dollars. *Esquire* and *New York* had to raise their rates to compete. The result was another of Tina's legacies to the culture: bringing magazine journalists, for decades an underpaid species, into the financial security of the upper-middle class. "I could send a daughter to private school and college," Shnayerson recalled. *Vanity Fair* contributors lunched at Michael's and Mortimer's, with Condé footing the bill. Tina sent flower arrangements to their homes and handed out Broadway tickets; her holiday gifts included cashmere shawls and Sony Discmans. Tina firmly believed that if writers inhabited the shimmering world they covered, access and authenticity would follow.

THE MATTER OF CELEBRITY—cultivating it, championing it, fawning over it—was the other key ingredient of Tina's *Vanity Fair*. She doused her issues in eye-popping Annie Leibovitz portraits of a sunglassed, bathrobed Jack Nicholson, flicking golf balls off the bluff of his Mulholland Drive manse; Diane Sawyer in a shoulder-baring Calvin Klein dress ("Sawyer as You Never Saw Her"); Michael Jackson midmoonwalk; an ecstatic Whoopi Goldberg submerged in a Cleopatra-like bath of milk. On its covers, *Vanity Fair* showcased the ample décolletage of Annette Bening, Madonna, Ivana Trump, Jessica Lange, Madonna (again), Kathleen Turner, Sigourney Weaver, Cybill Shepherd, Madonna (one more time), Elizabeth Taylor, and, finally, Roseanne Barr, pictured in a fox stole and blond wig and pinning her then husband, Tom Arnold, to the floor. (Headline: "Roseanne on Top—But Who's the Boss?")

This was hardly the confrontational, bite-the-hand journalism that Tina had practiced in her salad days at *Tatler*. Month after month, *Vanity Fair* elevated its subjects to the level of secular deities. The profiles that ran alongside Leibovitz's glamour shots inevitably served as tributes to the celebrity's grace under the pressures of fame, with much made about box office grosses and luminous skin. Madonna, as described in the December 1986 issue, was "a startling beauty of almost eighteenth-century purity." Nicholson, in April 1992, was "at fifty-four, the hippest guy in Hollywood . . . still ready to tear it up."

The hagiography extended to corporate executives, those pink-faced suits who had once shied away from the glitz that Tina, and the new eighties cult of capitalism, now afforded them. Steve Ross, co-chairman of the conglomerate Time Warner, posed for Annie Leibovitz in a *Lethal Weapon 2* windbreaker next to a blurb admiring his stratospheric salary; a few pages later, David Geffen lounged tanned and topless, like a Greek god, in the aqua-blue paradise of his Malibu mansion. Michael Ovitz, the CAA honcho, turned up in the same issue as Ross and Geffen, looking very master-of-the-universe for Leibovitz's camera while standing on the roof of his company's I. M. Pei building in Beverly Hills. "In Hollywood he's the dealer—the others are players," read the caption.

Ovitz happened to be one of Tina's key facilitators for gaining access to stars—seven CAA clients graced *Vanity Fair* covers in 1989—but their coziness also led to one of the more embarrassing episodes of Tina's tenure. *Spy*, the magazine started by Kurt Andersen and Graydon Carter to acidly satirize the media world, obtained a letter that Tina sent to Ovitz in 1988 asking that he participate in a *Vanity Fair* profile. It was a symphony of sycophancy.

"As I see it, the world has a very limited and unsophisticated grasp of what an 'agent' does, particularly when that agent is you," Tina cooed. "It seems to me that a better term for your role in the life of Hollywood would be a *catalyst*: activating creativity by a gifted sense of talent, material, timing and taste, plus, of course, extraordinary business acumen in putting it all together." She praised CAA's "efficiency and esprit de corps," Ovitz's "aura of leadership," and compared him to Irving Thalberg, the boy wonder of Hollywood's golden era. And while Tina apologetically explained that she could not write the profile herself, citing parenting duties for her three-year-old son, she promised that "I would be watching over it and shaping it every step of the way." (Ovitz declined the request.)

The letter's exposure only intensified the blowback from media critics who impugned Tina for what they deemed an insufficiently critical posture toward the powerful. Examples were legion: a 1988 panegyric on Ralph Lauren, "the archetypal American outdoorsman" (and a major advertiser); an unctuous 1987 cover story on Calvin Klein (ditto). Among the other advertisers enjoying kid-gloves treatment were Ronald Lauder (heir to Estée Lauder), Donna Karan, Karl Lagerfeld, Valentino, and Gianni Versace. Inside 350 Madison, *Vanity Fair* staffers sometimes glimpsed Tina's more transactional side. Stephen Schiff, a tweedy cinephile and Pulitzer finalist, was initially hired as a film critic. One day, Tina called him into her office.

"Eddie Murphy just refused to be on our cover," she said. "It seems to be about something you said." (Schiff had recently published a tough review of a Murphy flick.)

"I don't actually need film criticism," Tina continued. "I need Eddie Murphy on the cover. I love what you do—would you please do something else?" Schiff wrote features from then on.

In public, Tina shrugged off the complaints. "Actors shouldn't be subjected to the same scrutiny as a politician or a crime boss or somebody who is impacting public life," she said in 1992. Plus, she reasoned, *Vanity Fair* used the frothy lure of cleavage and gossip to entice readers for more nourishing fare, like Gail Sheehy's profile of Mikhail Gorbachev and Marie Brenner's investigation into Donald Trump's past. (Trump was so angry about that one that he poured a glass of wine down the back of Brenner's gown at a black-tie event at Tavern on the Green.) The formula was also a success: *Vanity Fair*'s ad revenue increased 60 percent each year between 1984 and 1988. Meanwhile, the entire glossy magazine industry was bending Tina-ward. In 1981, *Esquire* did not feature a single movie star on its covers; a decade later, the celebrity count had gone up to nine out of twelve issues.

TINA HAD ALWAYS BEEN a world-class self-promoter, honing her skills as a girl when she stayed up late at her film producer father's cocktail parties, where she'd be seen chatting away on the knee of the most prominent actor in attendance. As *Vanity Fair* grew, Tina was featured in Page Six and other big gossip columns as reliably as the celebrities she chronicled. "Tina almost created the whole idea of being hot at the same time she created the idea that Tina is hot," one *Vanity Fair* editor remarked.

In the eighty-odd years that the Condé Nast Publications had existed, an editor in chief had never achieved this level of infamy. Diana Vreeland may have come closest, given her outlandish declarations and frequent mixing with Andy Warhol and the Studio 54 set. But Grace Mirabella? Edna Woolman Chase? These names meant everything to fashion insiders and society mavens, but they were hardly the stuff of American dinner table discussion or prime-time news specials. Tina's notoriety, and the obvious influence she now wielded over the Manhattan and Hollywood publicity-industrial complex, meant that what went on inside 350 Madison was increasingly the subject of outside scrutiny and fascination. Tina had fulfilled the prophecy of Jackie Page, her *Happy Yellow* alter ego from 1977, who observed, "One's job isn't just a meal ticket. It's an extension of one's whole personality."

The editor-as-celebrity model had attracted a flood of advertising money and the kind of cultural cachet that Si loved. After years in the doldrums, Condé Nast was at the peak of the magazine industry. Si was besotted by his brilliant British hire; when archrival Hearst tried to poach her to run *Harper's Bazaar*, he raised her salary to $600,000 a year (plus a $1 million bonus) and forgave the $300,000 loan he had extended so she and Harry could move into a sumptuous apartment on East Fifty-seventh Street. But now the search was on for the next Tina. Si wanted to replicate her editorial magic at his other publications, to bring the *Vanity Fair* zhuzh to the rest of his empire. And Alex Liberman had introduced him to another ambitious and preternaturally talented editor who shared Tina's Fleet Street instincts, British taste, and penchant for getting into trouble in school.

Anna Wintour had arrived.

6

Enter Anna

The Temple of Dendur in the Metropolitan Museum of Art in Manhattan is dedicated to the Egyptian goddess Isis. One spring morning in 2014, the high priests of a different era gathered by the temple's sandstone columns to hail another female deity: Anna Wintour. Ralph Lauren and Calvin Klein, Donatella Versace and Diane von Furstenberg, Donna Karan and Oscar de la Renta, Raf Simons and Alexander Wang: the core of the global fashion industry had convened to witness the dedication of the Anna Wintour Costume Center, a space housing the museum's fashion exhibitions and sartorial conservation efforts. Si Newhouse beamed from the sidelines as the ceremony's host, Michelle Obama, approached the microphone.

"Two first ladies in one room at the same time," quipped another guest, Marc Jacobs.

Obama, who at that point had appeared twice on the cover of *Vogue*—she would sit for one more portrait before leaving the White House in 2016—told the crowd she had shown up for Anna: "I am here because I have such respect and admiration for this woman who I am proud to call my friend." Anna herself made no remarks, but some in the audience were surprised when, as a thunderous ovation echoed in the hall, she visibly teared up. Some of these world-famous designers owed their careers to Anna; others had angrily clashed with her. All, on some level, feared her. This display of genuine emotion from the famously flinty editor, who rarely exposed her eyes in public, did not fit the script. Anna Wintour the individual had long ago been usurped in the public imagination by Anna Wintour the institution: a cartoon of dark sunglasses and severe bob, the ice queen known by millions as the devil in *The Devil Wears Prada*. Now, quite literally, she had become a name on a museum wall.

But Anna was once an outsider to this elite world, another ambitious young editor trying to make a name for herself, desperate to gain a foothold—desperate to find a way in. This was the anxious woman riding the elevator to Alex Liberman's office at 350 Madison for a fateful meeting in 1983, three decades before she would be feted at the Met. Over and over, Anna had suffered false starts, including a stint at a doomed erotica magazine. She had just begun to find a foothold in her adopted city of New York, but a job at Condé Nast remained her lodestar. It was the place she had set her sights on since her years as a teenager in London. Even then, she knew, with a certainty that intimidated her peers, that American *Vogue* was the place she was meant to be—where her full powers could bloom. Anna Wintour's entire life had been leading to this moment.

THE WOMAN WHO WOULD PRESIDE OVER a global kingdom of taste was born into an upper-middle-class London family on November 3, 1949. Her American mother was the daughter of a Harvard Law School professor; her British father, Charles Wintour, a scion of a military family. The Wintours met at Cambridge University, introduced by a mutual friend, the future Pulitzer Prize–winning historian Arthur M. Schlesinger Jr. In 1951, Anna's older brother Gerald, then ten years old, was struck by a car and killed. According to Fleet Street lore, Charles, an aspiring journalist, was in a meeting with his boss, the *Evening Standard* proprietor Lord Beaverbrook, when a butler interrupted with the awful news; the legend goes that Charles quietly absorbed the shock and then calmly concluded his business, impressing Beaverbrook with his sangfroid. Charles went on to a long career as editor of the *Evening Standard*, one of London's biggest papers. His underlings called him "Chilly Charlie."

The tragedy of Gerald's death cast a pall over the family and strained the Wintours' marriage. Perhaps the dour mood at home forced Anna to grow up fast, or her father's elite role in London media circles imparted a certain precocity. Either way, she developed an early self-assuredness. Around age fifteen, Anna convinced her parents to grant her a private flat in the basement of their Kensington home, which she decorated with chic furnishings from the emerging designer Terence Conran. She tracked down a hairdresser whose work she'd seen in *British Vogue* and requested a then-fashionable bob. Like Tina Brown, Anna had a rebellious streak, and like Tina, she ran into trouble at school for a variety of indiscretions (one involved a too-short miniskirt) and dated older, ambitious men. She also loved magazines—as a child, she devoured copies of *Seventeen* sent by her grandmother in Boston—and the fashion scene, to the extent that her intellectually minded parents teased their daughter about her obsession with clothes. Anna dropped out of high school and decided to skip college altogether, finding an entry-level position at the London fashion magazine *Harpers & Queen*. Wintours were expected to attend Oxbridge or Harvard; Anna would be the family's sole dropout, her siblings all attending prestigious universities. "I was the one disaster," Anna said years later, half-kidding, describing the specter of her parents' disapproval as "a nightmare." Still, Chilly Charlie was onboard with her plans: it was his connections at *Harpers* that helped secure Anna the job.

But while Tina was an almost instant success, winning acclaim for her plays and assuming the editorship of *Tatler* at twenty-five, Anna's rise was haphazard, even stuttering. Four years passed at *Harpers & Queen* with little recognition.[*] In 1974, *Harpers* passed over Anna for a top role in favor of Min Hogg, the future editor of *World of Interiors*, despite Charles calling the top editor on his daughter's behalf. Frustrated, Anna hung around unhappily for a few months and then quit. Tired of London, where she was mainly known as Chilly Charlie's

---

[*] Although Anna did, during this period, secure her first-ever mention in American *Vogue*, appearing in a small photograph tucked into a report on a party thrown by a London socialite, which ran in the September 1, 1971, issue.

wayward daughter, Anna and her boyfriend, the American writer Jon Bradshaw, decamped to New York in the spring of 1975. There, she took a junior gig at *Harper's Bazaar*, from which she was unceremoniously booted after nine months. "I was told I would never understand the American market," she later recalled. It was so embarrassing for Anna that she sometimes claimed she had worked there longer.

Unwilling to concede defeat, she accepted a job as fashion editor of *Viva*, an erotic magazine owned by Bob Guccione and pitched as a kind of gender-flipped version of Guccione's more famous title, *Penthouse*. The publications shared an office, where Anna walked past contact sheets of buxom women spreading their legs. The London tabloids brayed that Charles Wintour's offspring had been reduced to working at a porno mag. In fact, *Viva*, which had once printed male nudes, was being repositioned as arty and feminist, publishing Joyce Carol Oates alongside articles about self-empowerment and achieving better orgasms. Anna hired edgy photographers like Helmut Newton and Arthur Elgort, and Guccione paid for fashion shoots in Japan and Guadeloupe. The nature of her employer was vaguely embarrassing for Anna—for a long time, she barely acknowledged the two years she worked there—but she sobbed when it closed in November 1978. It seemed like her American dream was finished.

Dejected, Anna returned to Europe to gallivant through London and Paris with a new boyfriend, a French record producer named Michel Esteban. It was a quiescent period in her career, but it yielded one of her earliest contributions to New York City culture. Anna had shared an Upper East Side apartment with a young Briton named Brian McNally; when Esteban needed to hire a manager for a clothing store he owned in Paris, Anna recommended her ex-roommate's brother. Keith McNally had worked his way up from shucking oysters to overseeing the dining room of the hip downtown restaurant One Fifth, where Anna enjoyed the eggs benedict. At Anna's invitation, Keith and his then girlfriend Lynn Wagenknecht traveled to Paris and ate their way through the city on Wintour's dime. At the end of the week, Keith decided he'd rather run a brasserie than work in retail. Back in New York, Keith, Lynn, and Brian opened The Odeon, which imported their favorite Parisian touches to a deserted block of Tribeca. The Odeon became a touchstone of the 1980s art-and-cocaine scene and defined a new genre of restaurant that spread around the country. Today, Anna remains a regular at Keith McNally's Balthazar, where she and her family are greeted upon arrival with complimentary glasses of Champagne.

Back then, however, Anna still needed to make her mark. She tried her luck again in Manhattan, this time at a new women's magazine called *Savvy*. Then a friend from London, the nightlife habitué Anthony Haden-Guest, recommended her to *New York* magazine, which was looking to hire a fashion editor. It was the spring of 1981, and Edward Kosner, the editor in chief, was eager to attract the nascent yuppie market and the lucrative advertising that catered to it. Anna got the job. On her first day, she showed up with her own clothes rack; the next morning, bemused colleagues watched as she hauled in a white Parsons desk and a chic custom chair made of bungee cords. An assistant was tasked with a daily Windexing of the Parsons desk, so Anna could be greeted by a pristine workspace in the mornings.

Then thirty-one, Anna was infused with ambition, and already yearning to understand the power structures of Manhattan. "She just wanted to know all about New York. She was trying to figure it out," said Fran Lebowitz, the writer and social observer whose advice Anna sought out that year. "She called me and she said, 'I'm the fashion editor of *New York* magazine.' I said, 'What does that mean? Isn't that like being the football editor of *Women's Wear Daily*?'" Anna began treating Lebowitz to lunches at Le Veau d'Or, a fancy brasserie on the Upper East Side, and peppering her with questions: who to know, where to go, how the city worked. "What kind of London is New York?" Lebowitz recalled Anna asking. Lebowitz told Anna the truth: "It's not any kind of London at all."

Anna was already gaining clout with major designers; once, when Ralph Lauren chewed her out at a lunch for not featuring enough of his clothes in the magazine, Lauren apologized an hour later by sending roses to her desk. And her editorial instincts were impeccable. Shortly after starting at *New York*, she introduced readers to three up-and-coming designers: Rei Kawakubo of Comme des Garçons,

Yohji Yamamoto, and a twenty-two-year-old obscurity identified in the magazine as "Micheal Kors" [*sic*]. She cast Andie MacDowell, a model who was not yet a famous actress, in a shoot that was staged on the ledge of a Manhattan skyscraper. (MacDowell, petrified she would plunge thirty stories to the sidewalk, had an anxiety attack, but Anna calmed her down.) One lively fashion spread included backdrops from of-the-moment artists like David Salle and Julian Schnabel. Not by coincidence, that one caught Alex Liberman's eye. Anna knew all about Alex's use of contemporary art in the pages of *Vogue*; in fact, she had been subtly signaling to Alex for a while, working with photographers that Alex approved of and striking up a casual friendship with Polly Mellen, a legendary *Vogue* editor. Mellen said she helped arrange for Anna to meet with *Vogue*'s editor in chief, Grace Mirabella, a summit that has since entered fashion lore. The story goes that Mirabella asked Anna what job she desired at *Vogue*, and Anna, in an atypical moment of impertinence and candor, replied, "Yours."

The meeting ended shortly afterward.

ALEX WAS UNAWARE OF THIS previous encounter with Mirabella when he finally asked Anna to visit him at his office in 350 Madison one day in 1983. Their initial conversation lasted only three or four minutes.

"What do you want to do with your life?" Alex asked.

"I want to edit a magazine," Anna replied.

Alex laughed and said he had no magazine available at the moment. Anna, who in later years would intimidate applicants with her cold demeanor in job interviews, was distraught; she walked out of the building convinced she had struck out. But Alex was impressed by her intensity, drive, and bon ton. Moreover, he believed that Anna Wintour might present a solution to a big problem: *Vogue* was getting stale.

From its earliest years in the Condé Nast empire, *Vogue*'s success relied on a fine balance: the magazine had to be elusive and accessible, sumptuous yet practical—evincing, in Mary McCarthy's words, "a democratic snobbery, a snobbery for everyone." Too highfalutin, and *Vogue* risked alienating the masses who could push its circulation above the one-million mark; too welcoming, and its illusion went *poof*.

The current editor, Grace Mirabella, owed her job to a moment when this calibration had gone awry.

Her predecessor, Diana Vreeland, had ruled *Vogue* for eight years behind a black lacquer desk in a scarlet-painted office, dispensing grand pronouncements like "un-shined shoes are the end of civilization" and demanding that her secretaries serve her daily scoop of ice cream with a precise, semi-melted consistency. Vreeland's sensuous, polychromic vision of waifs in caftans, go-go boots, and opulent furs was a great match for the sixties "youthquake" (a term she coined); she also deployed the phrase "the beautiful people" in photo essays of lithe aristocrats in repose, a glamorizing of the idle rich that would later find its apogee in Tina Brown's *Vanity Fair*.* But Vreeland's fashionably eccentric *Vogue* fell out of step as women marched into the workforce and embraced Gloria Steinem and *Ms.*-style feminism. By 1971, readership and revenue had plummeted, and Vreeland was forced out, the first of what would become many spectacular firings clumsily orchestrated by Alex and Si. Vreeland never forgave Alex for what she deemed a hideous betrayal: furious that he did not deliver the news in person, she declared, "I have known White Russians; I have known Red Russians. I have never before known a Yellow Russian." Stricken, Alex tried to smooth things over by sending one of his artworks to Vreeland's apartment as a gesture of goodwill. When a friend came to commiserate, Vreeland pointed at the painting and sniffed, "Famous last gifts."

In came Mirabella, a daughter of Italian immigrants in Newark who had worked at the magazine since 1951. Sensible and organized where Vreeland was brash and quixotic, Mirabella announced that her new version of *Vogue* would broaden its appeal. "We're going to lose that let-'em-eat-cake attitude that says that if a woman isn't Wallis

---

* "Youth Quake," Vreeland's headline for a 1965 fashion spread, is now broadly applied to radical movements led by young people, even earning Oxford Dictionaries' Word of the Year prize in 2017. Vreeland is also credited with popularizing the term *pizzazz*. "The Beautiful People" was dreamed up by a *Vogue* writer named Rebecca Warfield, a relative of Wallis Simpson's who was often referred to around the office, rather unkindly, as "Your Majesty."

Simpson, and can't afford to dress like her, then she has no place reading our magazine," she announced to a shell-shocked staff, who were dismayed by, among other matters, Mirabella's more disciplined work schedules, which put the kibosh on summer Fridays. Mirabella took over Vreeland's office and repainted the scarlet walls her favorite hue: beige. Andy Warhol, hearing of the new regime, sniffed that Si Newhouse wanted *Vogue* "to go middle-class." Alex was unperturbed. He was a realist: for all of *Vogue*'s artistry and mystique, the magazine could not retain its role as an arbiter without acknowledging that the tenor of American life was changing. Mirabella swapped out Vreeland's exotic Euros (Veruschka, Twiggy) with all-American models (Lisa Taylor, Rene Russo) who conveyed an Everywoman appeal. Idle aristos in Pucci were replaced by fresh-faced women in pantsuits, pussy-bow blouses, sportswear, and other items suited to the workplace and a professional lifestyle. Over the next decade, circulation tripled.

But by 1983, Alex was no longer so sure that Mirabella was the right woman for her job.

It was nothing personal. He liked Mirabella, even spent weekends with her and her husband, but it was clear she had dwindling currency with the designers who were defining the look of the new decade. Once again, the culture was shifting decisively: Americans were leaning into celebrity and glitz—so were the luxury advertisers that were the lifeblood of Condé Nast—and the old sartorial codes were breaking down. Yuppie women wanted playful, sexy clothes, and Mirabella was doing her best to resist the trend. "There was a lot of cashmere, a lot of Halston, a lot of minimal, and a lot of beige," recalled the *Vogue* editor William Norwich. Alex, doubtful of Mirabella's instincts, had effectively taken control of the fashion operation of *Vogue*; the joke around the office was that Mirabella was now merely "Alex's secretary." Now in his seventies, Alex relished his oversight of *Vogue*, but with Si intent on expanding his portfolio to include *Vanity Fair*, *GQ*, *Self*, and *House & Garden*, he found the workload increasingly unsustainable. "I'm overloaded," he confessed, "by Grace's dependence."

Now here was Anna. Her shoots were fresh, edgy, even kinky at times, with a feel for the avant-garde styles then sweeping New York.

Mirabella commuted to 350 Madison from the Upper East Side; Anna lived in a town house in Greenwich Village, ensconced in the downtown arts scene. She had a reputation in the industry as a brutally hard worker. And it didn't hurt that she was a fellow European.

After another meeting at Alex's Connecticut country house—Anna made sure to stop at a motel along the way to change into a very short skirt—Alex offered to create a new title for Wintour: "creative director." At first, Anna was wary: she had total freedom at *New York*, and she was unsure about accepting a vaguely defined job at an unfamiliar and rigid place like *Vogue*. Alex assured her that she could oversee her own fashion spreads; in fact, although Mirabella would remain editor in chief, Anna could report directly to him. Anna started in the fall of 1983. Alex—out of fear of confrontation, ruthless corporate savvy, or both—neglected to run any of these plans by Mirabella, who came to believe Anna had been foisted on her. On Anna's first day, Alex instructed Mirabella to personally tour the new hire around the *Vogue* office and introduce her to the staff. Those present recall a deeply awkward tableau: Mirabella in her signature beige, putting on a polite face, and Anna at her side in a black leather dress. Anna's outfit carried an unambiguous message, according to one witness: "I'm a killer."

Alex arranged for Anna to receive a byline for her fashion pages, a privilege that was unusual at *Vogue*. Mirabella became convinced that Anna was undermining her authority. And Anna, for her part, was not shy about her ultimate ambition, or her frustrations at having to defer to somebody else. "I really, in retrospect, was really frustrated," she told Alex's biographers. "I didn't have any real power or real job *per se*. I was going nuts." Working late one evening, she wondered aloud why she had to put up with it.

"It's maddening," Anna confided to a colleague, "to know you're good and to not be able to do your work."

IN THE SUMMER OF 1985, Anna finally got her own magazine—just not the one she wanted. The editor of *British Vogue*, Beatrix Miller, was retiring after twenty-one years, and Si asked Anna to fill the slot. *Brogue*, as it was known inside the company, had a rich history dating to 1916, but Anna was hesitant to move to London. She was pregnant with her first child, and her husband, Dr. David Shaffer, a South Africa–born psychiatrist who was an expert in adolescent suicide, was not able to leave his Manhattan practice. The job would also put an ocean between her and Alex, her Condé champion. Even after she accepted, Anna fretted about being forgotten; she faxed dummy layouts to New York for Alex's feedback and frequently called him for advice. Her unease extended to the atmosphere at Vogue House, Condé's London headquarters, where Anna's American-style work ethic was a bitter pill for the more leisurely staff. Grace Coddington, then a *British Vogue* fashion editor, was taken aback when Anna called a Knightsbridge restaurant to demand she return to the office from a long lunch. Lucy Sisman, a Condé art director, recalled walking into a stairwell and coming across a huddle of young *British Vogue* assistants, sobbing.

"What is this?" Sisman asked. "What happened?"

"It's Anna," one of the girls moaned. "She's making us come in before 9!"

Anna's intensity and commercial taste fit the Thatcher moment, but the Fleet Street papers had a field day, bestowing cruel nicknames—"Nuclear Wintour," "Wintour of Our Discontent"—that Anna loathed. In London, Anna gave birth to her second child, and she and David Shaffer soon grew tired of the hurdles of a transatlantic marriage; by 1987, rumors surfaced that Anna might jump to *Harper's Bazaar* or *Elle*. Si was alarmed enough to fly to London, where, over breakfast, he told Anna that he had found a place for her back at 350 Madison—just not at *Vogue*. Instead, later that year, Anna would return to New York to become the editor of a storied, if less prestigious Condé magazine, the interiors bible *House & Garden*.

Si was too squeamish to fire Grace Mirabella outright, given her decades of service to Condé Nast and Si's own aversion to confrontation. But he did not want to lose Anna Wintour. In fact, he was dazzled by her. Having relished the publicity and cachet that Tina Brown was bringing to *Vanity Fair*, Si had come to believe that all of his editors needed to embrace the eighties' penchant for celebrity. Tina's lust for publicity, her appearances in TV interviews and gossip columns, had boosted the cachet of the growing Condé empire. Advertisers were impressed, readers were excited. But Grace Mirabella was a homebody. She considered work trips to Paris "the worst possible chore," complained about Andy Warhol's "god-awful" Factory, and griped about the "ridiculously flaky" crowds at Yves Saint-Laurent's "torturous" dinners. Once, Si chartered a jet to fly Condé executives to Egypt for an extravagant benefit sponsored by Revlon, an important advertiser. Pierre Balmain staged a fashion show and Frank Sinatra crooned "My Way" in front of the pyramids. Mirabella made every effort to avoid the trip, only agreeing to join because her husband persuaded her.

Si was also conscious of Alex's advancing age. The Silver Fox showed few outward signs of fatigue, but Si relied on him for nearly all editorial matters at the company. Si worried that if Alex were to fall ill, or worse, Mirabella would struggle to successfully run *Vogue*. In a moment that Mirabella later came to rue, she was asked by Pamela van Zandt, Condé's powerful head of human resources, if she felt prepared to edit *Vogue* in Alex's absence. Wanting to appear loyal to Alex, Mirabella said she would never dream of it.

It was the wrong answer.

SHORTLY AFTER FIVE O'CLOCK on Tuesday, June 28, 1988, the phone rang inside Mirabella's Upper East Side town house. Her husband picked up, and a friend told him to turn on the TV. Liz Smith, the gossip columnist, had announced on a local newscast that Si Newhouse was making a change. Grace Mirabella was out at *Vogue*, and Anna Wintour, after less than a year at *House & Garden*, was in.

At her desk in 350 Madison, Mirabella assumed this was a mistake. Rumors were constant in the gossipy hallways of Condé Nast, and it was not the first time that whispers had reached her about an imminent ouster. Mirabella found Alex Liberman condescending and controlling; he had a possessiveness about *Vogue*, whose contents he still signed off on each month. She could not deny Alex's inherent sense of style, but Mirabella believed she had a better grasp than he did on the priorities of her readers. And she suspected that Si would not be pleased about Liz Smith speculating on the news.

A few floors above, in his own office, Alex's mind was racing. This was a fiasco.

Like most sensitive Condé matters, it was all supposed to be very discreet. In a series of lunches that spring, Alex and Si had agreed that Mirabella needed to go. *Vogue* had higher ad revenues than its competitors, but it was losing ground to *Elle*, a Parisian import that started an American edition in 1985. *Elle*'s fresh-faced models, often jumping, smiling, and frolicking in nature, made *Vogue* look formal and stodgy by comparison; by 1987, *Elle* was outselling *Harper's Bazaar*. Yet Mirabella had hardly taken any steps to keep *Vogue* current. In fact, she was put off by 1980s culture, calling herself "sickened" and "disgusted" by society's obsession with money and sex; fashion, she complained, now "had to scream wealth! class! clout!" Mirabella was especially dismayed by the popularity of the designer Christian Lacroix, blaming his influence for ushering in "a profoundly anti-woman moment." And she was unimpressed by the fact that these same values had catapulted *Vanity Fair*, and Condé Nast itself, into a new tier of influence and success.

Mirabella's own ideas, meanwhile, had failed to find much traction inside the company. When she pitched an issue devoted to women over fifty, Alex nixed the idea, saying that "nobody wants it pointed out to them that they're older than anyone else." She and Alex even disagreed over the quality of the French food at La Grenouille, one of his favorite restaurants. Mirabella believed Le Cirque was more desirable—and in the world of Condé Nast, this may have been the most serious offense of all. "All of Alex's opinions, no matter how trivial the topic, appeared to have been handed down to him by the highest authority," Mirabella would write in her memoir. "I was exhausted with trying to feed Alex's ego." Such clashes were never a good strategy at 350 Madison. By spring 1988, the question of replacing Mirabella was a matter of when, not if.

When the decision was made, Alex was aware the news could leak out. But perhaps recalling his anguished dismissal of Vreeland, he requested a pause until after the summer so he could enjoy his vacation in peace. Now Liz Smith had screwed everything up. Alex had recently assured reporters that no changes at *Vogue* were planned, but when Mirabella got ahold of him that Tuesday, he had no choice but to admit it was true. When Alex confirmed the name of her successor, Mirabella recoiled.

"Anna? *Wintour*?" Mirabella said, according to Alex's recollection. "My *god*."

At age thirty-eight, Anna had achieved her life's goal. She just didn't think it would happen in such miserable circumstances. "After it was on that damn TV program, Si went ahead without even telling me," she later recalled. "I got in that morning, and he told me that I had a new job." Her tenure at *House & Garden* had lasted less than a year. "The whole thing was so awful, and so unpleasant, and so unlike the way you think of this company as doing things."

Anna had no doubt she was the right person to run *Vogue*. "Grace wasn't strong enough," she later told Alex's biographers. "She wasn't, frankly, very bright. I mean, she had no culture." (Anna seems to have been referring to Mirabella's handling of *Vogue*'s arts and feature articles; she also called Mirabella "very good on fashion, very good on all the beauty stuff.") But Anna also believed that the fallout of Si and Alex's blundering had fallen squarely on her. The press already perceived Anna as a pitiless usurper. Now the viciousness of the Manhattan tabloids left her stunned. Liz Smith speculated in her *New York Daily News* column that Anna was picked because she was having an affair with Si Newhouse. It was a sexist accusation dismissed by both parties—Si, trying to defuse the tension, replied, "I am very much in love with my wife and my wife's dog"—but Liz Smith's column appeared on Anna's first day on the job, forcing her to deny the humiliating report at her inaugural staff meeting. David Shaffer was upset by the rumor, and it put a strain on Anna's marriage.

"You will never know how awful it was, because so many people believed that story," she said later. "Just really, everywhere you went, it was just awful. It was just beyond anything that I had ever experienced before." Si simply encouraged Anna to keep her head held high and go about her business. "He just kept telling me it wasn't so bad, and it was," Anna recalled. "It was as bad as it could get." Anna came to feel that Si was privately amused by the gossip: "He was embarrassed and liked it at the same time."

Mirabella's firing made headlines around the world, muddying Condé Nast's elegant reputation. The fashion industry was stunned that Si could discard her so abruptly after thirty-seven years at the magazine, and seventeen as its top editor. Mirabella put a fine point on it when she told *The New York Times* that her firing was "very unstylish, for such a stylish place." Even Tina Brown was rattled by Si's caprice, writing in her diary that the episode "makes one feel like the disposable help." But painful as it was, Anna's ascendance set the stage for massive changes at Condé Nast—changes that would go on to reshape the fashion world and to this day affect the choices we make at the mall, or in our bedrooms when we open the closet and decide what to wear. Anna Wintour's *Vogue* would mirror and intensify the yuppie appetite for designer clothing and European luxury brands, elevate the idea of street-style fashion, and presage the industry of stylists and celebrity brand ambassadors that have come to dominate lifestyle media. And the seeds of that legacy can be found on the cover of her very first issue, a declaration of the new that underscored Condé Nast's power to bend the culture to its will.

THE MODEL IS MICHAELA BERCU, a nineteen-year-old Israeli, who sports a winning smile and flowing hair. She is wearing a $10,000 Christian Lacroix beaded jacket and fifty-dollar department store Guess jeans. Bercu's eyes are half-shut and her stomach is peeking out, maybe accidentally; years later, Anna recalled that before the shoot, the model had taken a vacation and "gained a little weight." Today, the cover might blend in with countless other fashion glossies on a newsstand. In November 1988, Anna claimed that Condé Nast's printers were so taken aback that they called up the *Vogue* offices and asked if the wrong image had been sent by mistake.

To understand why this photograph was so shocking, it's worth considering the dozens of Grace Mirabella covers that came before it.

Every issue of *Vogue*, from the early 1980s onward, featured an almost identical close-up shot of a model's head and shoulders, her left cheek usually angled toward the reader. Sometimes she wore a hat; sometimes she wore a wig. But the covers were virtually interchangeable. Headlines consisted, in their entirety, of arbitrary, monosyllabic words like "SURE," "FAST," and the inscrutable "YOU." Celebrities almost never appeared. It was a freeze-dried kind of fashion, static and composed, with none of the kinetic energy then coursing through 1980s prêt-à-porter.

Bercu, by contrast, was photographed in the street, an It Girl strolling the sidewalks of the Right Bank. Her high/low outfit blended couture and kitsch—like Tina's *Vanity Fair*, Anna was breaking down old barriers of taste. "I wanted the covers to show gorgeous real girls looking the way they looked out on the street, rather than the plastic kind of retouched look that had been the *Vogue* face for such a long time," she later said.

Vogue, grande dame that it was, had never before put denim on its cover, even as designer jeans became a staple of Reagan-era cool. Stephen Drucker, a *Vogue* editor at the time, recalled the image as symbolizing the move from Babe Paley and Nan Kempner, the older Park Avenue matrons who were once icons of style, to the new culture of celebrities, supermodels, and obsession with youth. (Notably, Anna chose to feature Christian Lacroix, the designer singled out by her predecessor, Mirabella, as "anti-woman.") Anna underlined the shift with a cheeky, Tina-like cover line: "Haute but Not Haughty." In the 1980s, high fashion could be a joyful, informal expression of fun and freedom, accessible to anyone—or at least anyone with status aspirations and a high-limit American Express card.

Even the choice of Peter Lindbergh to photograph Bercu was a sign that Anna was willing to buck the fashion establishment. Richard Avedon, whose relationship with *Vogue* dated to 1965, had shot virtually every one of Mirabella's covers; in fact, Avedon had already provided an image for the November issue, which Anna asked him to reshoot twice. Anna never told Avedon that she had decided to go with a different photographer; Avedon discovered the snub only after the issue was printed and delivered to his studio. Furious, he severed his *Vogue* contract then and there.

Anna shrugged it all off, and six months later came her next statement of intent. In May 1989, Madonna made the cover of *Vogue*. These days, it's hard to imagine there was a time when a celebrity *wasn't* on the cover of *Vogue*: in 2022 alone, the magazine spotlighted Rihanna, Dua Lipa, Jennifer Lawrence, Jennifer Lopez, Kim Kardashian, and Serena Williams. Back then, Anna's move caused a sensation. The singer, who had recently released her provocative video for "Like a Prayer," was seen posing in a chaste swimsuit with her back to the reader, revealing none of the cleavage that Tina had highlighted to sell copies of *Vanity Fair*. But the sight of Madonna in such hallowed magazine real estate was enough of a lowbrow intrusion that *The New York Times* ran a skeptical article about the new, supposedly "hipper" *Vogue*, and the spurned Richard Avedon called it the depressing endpoint of a long degradation of *Vogue*'s standards. Anna was unbothered. "You want to be on the cutting edge. If you're not, you lose the buzz," she told *The Times*, borrowing a term often associated with Tina Brown. In fact, Tina had encouraged Anna to feature Madonna, promising her the cover would juice sales. As usual, Tina was not wrong.

This may have been the *Vanity Fair*–ization of *Vogue*, but it meant that Alex's plan had worked: Anna was keeping the magazine relevant for a new era. Like the best Condé Nast editors before her, she was determined to follow the zeitgeist. The new 1980s elite liked Madonna *and* Monet—and the mainstreaming of fashion was accelerating, whether the traditionalists wanted it or not. By the early 1990s, fashion had started to cross over from an insular, specialty-interest subculture to the klieg-light stage of mass popular culture. Supermodels like Naomi Campbell and Linda Evangelista were staples of the gossip pages; high-flying designers like Gianni Versace, Giorgio Armani, and Karl Lagerfeld became household names. Runway shows, once the exclusive domain of department store buyers and a clannish coterie of international editors, were becoming a part of the everyday media churn of tabloid papers and cable TV.

After the success of the Madonna issue, more celebrities began appearing on the cover of *Vogue*: Kim Basinger and Michelle Pfeiffer in 1991, Winona Ryder and Sharon Stone in 1993, and Julia Roberts in 1994. Movie stars had always been style icons, but now the lines between Hollywood and *Vogue*'s high-fashion milieu blurred. Designers realized that dressing a celebrity for a red carpet premiere could be a PR coup, and agents in Beverly Hills wanted their clients to benefit from the growing fashion-industrial complex. When today's publicists blast out press releases ticking off the names of the gowns, shoes, earrings, and fragrances that an actress wore to a film festival, their litanies can be traced to some of Anna's earliest decisions at *Vogue*.

In 1995, the music channel VH1 created an annual televised fashion awards show that featured models and designers alongside more mainstream celebrities. In 1996, millions tuned in for appearances by Gwyneth Paltrow, Elton John, David Bowie, and other megastars. (A taped sketch that year introduced a fictional male model, Derek Zoolander, played by Ben Stiller, and his signature look, "Blue Steel.") *The New York Times* called the VH1 Fashion Awards "the most important mass-marketing vehicle for fashion since the invention of the runway show," and Tom Ford, then the head designer at Gucci, said that "from a press standpoint, in a lot of ways, it was the most important event we did last year." Condé Nast had its fingerprints on this endeavor, too: VH1 hired Gabé Doppelt, a former girl Friday to both Tina (at *Tatler*) and Anna (at *British Vogue*), and briefly the editor in chief of Condé's *Mademoiselle*, to help oversee the awards. By 1999, *Vogue* signed on as an official co-sponsor of the show, which was rechristened as the VH1/ *Vogue* Fashion Awards. Anna made clear that it was time for the experts at Condé to take charge.

By the late 1990s, the power of a *Vogue* cover in the broader culture— to propel a career, to promote a summer blockbuster, to generate buzz around a prestige film—had become undeniable. The magazine's cover stars included Cameron Diaz, Claire Danes, Elizabeth Hurley, Sandra Bullock, Renée Zellweger, and the Spice Girls. The Miramax producer Harvey Weinstein carefully cultivated a relationship with Anna, in part to try to place the stars of his films in *Vogue*; Weinstein regularly invited Anna to movie screenings, where he assigned junior employees to monitor her reactions in the theater. Anna's pragmatism may have drained some of the magazine's old artistry, but she had seen off the ever-looming peril of *Vogue* falling out of touch. For all of Vreeland's influence in society circles, and Mirabella's agile adaptations to second-wave feminism, Anna had managed to expand *Vogue*'s influence well beyond the boundaries of mere fashion.

Now she set her sights on an even more rarefied realm: politics.

ANNA HAD BEEN EDGING INTO Hillary Rodham Clinton's circle since the start of 1993, when she sent a letter to the new First Lady volunteering her services as a stylist. The explanation, a *Vogue* spokesman said at the time, was that Clinton had been overwhelmed with requests from designers, and Anna "simply offered to sift through all of the fashion for her." By year's end, Anna had persuaded Clinton to pose for her magazine, dispatching Annie Leibovitz to the White House to capture the First Lady in a feline, jet-black Donna Karan turtleneck dress, her face tilted toward the reader with a hint of a smile. The photographs spurred debate in Washington about the complex balance of femininity and get-it-done grit that a First Lady like Clinton, a Yale-educated lawyer intent on breaking the passive tradition of her role, might want to convey. In an editor's note, Anna made clear that the magazine was firmly on Clinton's side, gushing about her refusal to be typecast "in pearls or in the pillbox hat." The buzz generated by the Leibovitz portraits affirmed *Vogue*'s power in the cultural conversation over womanhood, and cemented a growing bond between the First Lady of fashion and the First Lady of the United States.

Vogue had a decades-long history as a willing partner in crafting the public image of presidential wives. Lou Henry Hoover, wife of Herbert, posed for Edward Steichen in the magazine in May 1929, setting off a string of First Lady portraits that remained unbroken until Melania Trump. Jacqueline Kennedy, née Bouvier, had a particular affinity for *Vogue*, declaring in her early twenties, "I would like to be a top editor in

Condé Nast." Bouvier entered the magazine's Prix de Paris contest in 1951 in hopes of obtaining a year-long apprenticeship, half in Manhattan and half in Paris; she won, posed in white gloves for the March 1951 issue, and then turned down the prize under pressure from her mother. (According to one of Jackie's biographers, Janet Bouvier believed the *Vogue* prize "was like accepting a scholarship, and that was something that poor people did.") On November 22, 1963, Diana Vreeland was at lunch on the ground floor of the Condé Nast building when an editor rushed in to tell her that John Kennedy had been shot. "My god," Vreeland responded, after a pause. "Lady Bird in the White House! We can't use *her* in the magazine." (Vreeland later acceded to custom, publishing a portrait of Lady Bird Johnson—"a dark-haired, pretty woman with a twenty-inch waist"—at the White House by Horst P. Horst; the accompanying article noted her $2.98 wedding ring from Sears, Roebuck.)

Vogue's influence in elite circles meant the magazine sometimes played a larger role in advancing political agendas. In 1979, shortly after Jimmy Carter normalized diplomatic relations with China, Grace Mirabella turned to Nancy Kissinger, who was part of her social circle, for help staging *Vogue*'s first-ever fashion shoot there. Kissinger's husband Henry worked with Mirabella to secure the proper State Department clearances; the ensuing spread, photographed by Arthur Elgort, featured Nancy Kissinger modeling clothes in Beijing, Shanghai, and Hangzhou. China, recently opened to Western tourists, benefited from the prestige of appearing as a hot destination in America's top fashion magazine—and Henry Kissinger, who himself turned up in one of the *Vogue* photographs, got a puff piece to counter his controversial public image. It was the kind of soft-power diplomacy that only the corporate machinery of Condé Nast could engineer.*

Until 1998, however, *Vogue* had never featured an American First Lady on its cover. Previous editors were hesitant to yield the spot to

---

* Some political features in *Vogue* aged better than others. In August 1936, the magazine published a photo of Haus Wachenfeld, near Berchtesgaden—Adolf Hitler's holiday retreat. "The chalet has a suburban neatness," *Vogue* noted, describing one room as "a cozy podge of clocks, dwarfs, and swastika cushions."

a political figure, wary of alienating some readers and tanking newsstand sales. Or perhaps *Vogue*'s meticulous attention to social codes had precluded such a move; politics, after all, was up there with death and taxes on the list of proscribed subjects at gala dinner tables. Anna, though, had continued her steady courtship of the Clintons: in 1997, she commissioned a first-person essay from Hillary about her trip to Africa with her daughter, Chelsea, complete with a lavish Annie Leibovitz spread that ran across fifteen pages. In an editor's letter, Anna fawned with the best of them: "Although I don't know any more about Whitewater than the next person"—a studiously breezy dismissal of the Clintons' then scandal du jour—"what I do know is that Mrs. Clinton is not only very, very smart, but she also cares deeply about things we should all care deeply about."

One year later, *Vogue* was planning a feature about one of Hillary's pet projects, an effort to preserve national historic landmarks, when the Monica Lewinsky scandal broke. Whereas Anna's more polite predecessors might have dropped the idea at that point, Chilly Charlie's daughter, who had inherited her father's news instincts, leaned in. Anna told Hillary's aides that not only did *Vogue* still want a story, it wanted a full-on profile. Shortly before Thanksgiving—weeks before the president was impeached—the December issue of *Vogue* landed with a resplendent First Lady on the cover. Clinton, in a custom burgundy Oscar de la Renta gown, radiates confidence, even mirth; smiling, her eyes meet the reader head-on, a silent declaration of self amid the storm. "To have one's photo emblazoned on a *Vogue* cover offers a kind of validation that has nothing to do with policy or politics," wrote the fashion editor Robin Givhan. "It is a portrait loaded with subtext: a scorned woman victorious, proof that looking spectacular can be a satisfying form of revenge."

Here was the Condé alchemy at work: that immaculate Annie Leibovitz aesthetic, honed at *Vanity Fair*, originally used to augment a celebrity's image and now deployed as a partisan tool to rehabilitate a scandal-tarred president's spouse. The portrait, with its formal air and French Empire–style furnishings, carried a trace of the Europhilia that for decades had elevated Condé Nast magazines above the more humdrum visuals of other American rivals—indeed, Anna had told Leibovitz, before the photographer went to the White House, to "pretend you're photographing British royalty."

The cover was a massive hit, selling nearly 700,000 copies on newsstands, not far off from that year's marquee September issue, which featured Renée Zellweger. It even coincided with a rise in Hillary's approval ratings. But what really mattered—to Anna, Si, and the rest of the Condé firmament—was its cultural impact. So many articles about the cover appeared in newspapers around the world that *Vogue*'s publicity team needed a binder to compile them all. As Anna promoted the cover on CNN and the network morning shows, she managed the ultimate Condé trick of transmuting the perceived triumph of her subject matter into a victory for Condé Nast itself. "People have seen it as a vindication for her, that being on the cover of *Vogue* is beyond power and politics," Anna told *The New York Times*. "It proves in a way that she is a woman of stature and an icon to American women." The obvious implication, which Anna deftly left unsaid, was that only *Vogue* had the power to make such a resounding statement to the world.

As it turned out, Clinton said it for her. A few weeks after the issue appeared, the First Lady was at a New Year's Eve party when somebody asked about her legacy.

"Oh, I don't need a legacy," Clinton replied, playfully. "I was on the cover of *Vogue*."

7

A Man's World

By the late 1970s, Si was looking for a vehicle to attract readers who weren't traditionally drawn to Condé Nast's fashion-focused offerings: men. At the time, the men's magazine market was led by *Esquire*, the granddaddy of the genre that was founded in the 1930s and featured a testosterone-friendly mix of babes, ball games, and brown liquor, in addition to fiction and political pieces. *Playboy* had dispensed with the pretense of bikini pictures in favor of full frontal nudes, but it also published erudite conversations with novelists, philosophers, and politicians—including the 1976 interview with Jimmy Carter in which the presidential nominee nearly derailed his candidacy by admitting that he had "committed adultery in my heart." Sensing opportunity in the men's space, Si cast about for an acquisition that might fit neatly into the Condé portfolio. He found it in *Esquire*'s lesser-known, artsier corporate cousin, a fashion magazine saddled with an old-fashioned name: *Gentlemen's Quarterly*.

The *Quarterly* descended from *Apparel Arts*, a *garmento* trade publication, founded in 1931, that featured lavish illustrations of masculine finery like hosiery, ascots, and pajamas. In 1957, its owner, Esquire Inc., created a four-times-a-year consumer supplement called "Gentlemen's Quarterly," which by the next year had subsumed the *Apparel Arts* title and was spun out as a separate publication, dubbed "The Fashion Magazine for Men." *GQ*, as it came to be known, sported little of *Esquire*'s literary irreverence or hetero attitude; instead, there were blandly handsome male models and fussy style guides on when to wear an argyle sock. In 1962, President John F. Kennedy was incensed to discover that a stock photo of himself, smiling in the Oval Office in an Ivy League suit, had been used for the March cover of a magazine that his brother Robert mocked as a "fag rag."

"I never posed for any picture," JFK complained to his aides. "Any president who would pose for *Gentlemen's Quarterly* would be out of his mind."

In fact, it had long been an open secret that *GQ* was geared toward, and read mostly by, gay men. In the 1970s, under the editorship of Jack Haber, the magazine featured a full-color cast of Adonises in Speedos, men frolicking on the beach as the surf splashed their taut, suntanned flesh. This homoerotic aesthetic—which recalled the beefcake "muscle" portraiture passed among gay men like samizdat in an earlier, more closeted age—was exemplified by the magazine's key photographer, Bruce Weber, whose highly suggestive spreads of playful, libidinous young men electrified readers like Tom Ford, who subscribed as a teenager in Santa Fe.

It's possible that Si Newhouse, leafing through *GQ*'s pages, detected a kinship between the gleaming, Riefenstahl-ian bodies of its male models and the gleaming consumer goods that were regularly advertised in Condé's stable of magazines. Both represented a subtle kind of pornography that quickened the reader's pulse. The magazine's circulation was small, roughly 350,000 readers, and its owners at Esquire barely blinked when Si approached them about a possible purchase. Once again, a Newhouse saw value in a distressed asset where others did not. At the start of 1979, shortly before his father's death, Si wrote a check for $9.2 million, and *GQ* was his.

Except now he had a problem. In the early 1980s, there was still intense stigma toward gay men, and *GQ*'s reputation limited its mass appeal. "It wasn't like today, where it's okay for men to care about their style and their grooming and their clothes," one longtime editor recalled. "You were considered a little funny if you cared that much about it." Condé Nast quickly discovered that big advertisers were leery. Foreign automakers like BMW bought ads—in Europe, it wasn't unusual for men to take an avid interest in fashion—but Detroit, with its manly Ford and Dodge marques, initially said no. When a Condé adman named Jack Kliger pitched *GQ* to a buyer at Philip Morris, the tobacco man leaned back in his chair.

"You want the Marlboro cowboy in your magazine, right?"

Kliger nodded.

"Let me explain something to you," the man said. "Your cowboys are not *our* cowboys."

Si and Alex, distracted by their troubled revival of *Vanity Fair*, puzzled over how to turn around *GQ*, but little at the magazine changed until 1983, when Fairchild, a rival magazine publisher, unveiled plans for a new men's glossy called *M*. Alarmed by the competition, Alex approached Si with the idea of hiring Bob Colacello, until recently the editor of Andy Warhol's *Interview* magazine. It is fun to imagine what Colacello, an effete Republican, would have done with *GQ*, but Si was looking to hetero-ize the place, and so he cast his gaze elsewhere. He needed an editor with straight-guy bona fides, who liked cigars and baseball as much as cuff links and cashmere socks—ideally someone with foppish taste in clothes and a healthy appreciation of the female form.

Someone who used to run *Penthouse*.

LIKE CONDÉ MONTROSE NAST, Arthur Cooper was born in New York City but grew up in the hinterlands, in a fatherless household led by a strong-willed woman. Bearded and barrel-chested, Art spent his childhood in Berwick, Pennsylvania, a flyspeck factory town where he was regularly beaten up for being the only Jewish kid at school. His father died when he was young, and Art was raised by his mother. (As an adult, he mailed her cash in an envelope every week.) Art adored the classic Hollywood movies of the 1930s and 1940s, studying their lavish interiors and lush costumes. Most of all, he admired their depiction of WASP splendor, an idealized vision of the upper classes whose ranks he longed to join. "We grew up in the middle of the country, but we were close enough to big cities that we were exposed to it," said Eliot Kaplan, a friend and fellow Pennsylvanian who went on to work with Art at *GQ*. "We knew we wanted to get out."

In his youth, Art realized that clothing could be a potent semaphore of status. He began wearing double-breasted blazers—first Italian ready-to-wear, later bespoke Savile Row—and donned seersucker suits and a straw boater in summertime. His other passion was journalism. After Penn State and a stint at a Harrisburg newspaper, he made his way to Manhattan, where he wrote about culture for *Time* and *Newsweek*. From 1976 to early 1978, he was the editor in chief of *Penthouse*, the edgier, more explicit rival to *Playboy*. Afterward, he edited *Family Weekly*, a sleepy Sunday newspaper supplement that competed, feebly, with the much more widely circulated *Parade*. For a kid from coal-mining country, this was success, of a sort, but Art longed for more. On sunny days, he often walked a few blocks from his office to a pocket park by Sutton Place, where he would regard the Queensboro Bridge (Gatsby's gateway to the "wild promise" of Manhattan) and muse about his dream magazine, which he called "*Renaissance*." It would be a gentleman's guide to cultivated living: the best of fashion, food, sports, and sex, braided with the literary flair of the 1960s *Esquire* that Art revered. *Renaissance* ran the gamut of Art's own interests: basketball and horse racing and Broadway musicals and John O'Hara's short stories and Jane Austen's novels. At its heart was the yearning of a middle-class kid to belong.

At *Family Weekly*, Art tried to infuse his underpaid staff with the *Renaissance* spirit. The supplement "consisted mostly of 300-word stories wrapped around ads for porcelain dogs and tweezers," recalled Kaplan, who worked there, "yet Art somehow made us feel like we were storming Normandy in the spring of '44." The budget was tiny; when Art encouraged a junior editor to call Nora Ephron and commission an article, Ephron almost laughed in her face. Still, Art's ability to persuade big-name writers like David Halberstam and James Michener to write for him caught the eye of the Newhouses, who owned *Parade*. Si met with Art and liked him; it helped that Art's wife, Amy Levin, was the editor of Condé Nast's *Mademoiselle*. In the summer of 1983, the same year that Si brought on Tina Brown and Anna Wintour, Art Cooper was hired to replace Jack Haber at *GQ*.

To attract more readers and more ads, Art needed straight men to care about fashion and accessories and grooming and exercise. But the term *metrosexual* was still a decade away, menswear was a niche interest, and basketball players weren't yet endorsing designer suits. Back then, to appear on the cover of *GQ* was to take a risk. When Art approached William Hurt, a hot actor about to star in *The Big Chill*, about posing for the cover of his first issue in charge, Hurt's publicist balked. So, Art focused on something that straight men definitely cared about: girls. Bikini models and Hollywood starlets began appearing alongside the guides to boar-hair shaving brushes and mother-of-pearl cuff links. "What I wanted to do in repositioning the magazine was make it very clear, very quickly, that this was a heterosexual magazine," Art later recalled. He hired macho writers like Joe Queenan to write about pedicures and shampoos. David Remnick, then a twentysomething *Washington Post* reporter, was assigned stories on Russian beauty pageants and a fitness boot camp.

GQ features were witty and well reported, but also, somehow, recognizably *male*. When Remnick profiled "the smartest woman on the planet," advice columnist Marilyn vos Savant, he compared her to an "ecdysiast"—a million-dollar word for a striptease dancer—"lazing across a tiger-skin rug, eating a Popsicle and reading [Georges] Bernanos." Art, a minor-league pitching recruit in his youth, persuaded athletes like Joe Montana, Dan Marino, and Isiah Thomas to appear, a rare incursion of the sporting world into Condé's lofty realm. When Art presented Alex with a dummy cover featuring the baseball star Cal Ripken Jr., Alex was dumbfounded. "Who is this person?" he demanded. Art insisted, and the cover went on to be a hit.

Each issue was designed to make straight guys comfortable with a magazine that ultimately urged them to embrace their feminine side. Sports stars posed in Armani suits and celebrities dished on their preferred colognes, while Weber's handsome cavorting men disappeared. *GQ* covers used to feature chiseled headshots of male models, faces that would not have been out of place in a Saks catalog or a shelf of bodice-ripper paperbacks. Art brought in handsome-but-off-kilter types like David Letterman, Donald Sutherland, and Michael Caine, offering a more accessible entry point for the average male reader. This *GQ* was something new: a fussy, fashion-forward lifestyle guide that hetero dudes could live with.

So, what kind of lifestyle was *GQ* selling? If *Playboy* evinced a hoary masculinity, *GQ* showcased a kind of elevated WASP splendor, a blend of *The Official Preppy Handbook* and proto–Patrick Bateman materialism that mirrored the mores of the Eastern establishment. It was aspirational, authoritative, and useful for arrivistes—the same formula that Condé Montrose Nast used at *Vogue* and *Vanity Fair* in a previous gilded age. And the eighties were the right moment for it. Fitness fads and the Wall Street boom meant that yuppie guys were looking for new ways to flaunt their lifestyles, from overpriced Filofax organizers to overpriced exercise bikes. With its careful balance of clothes and cars, aftershave and supermodels, the magazine gave men outside of urban and gay circles permission to express a sense of style. "For men, it had some fantasy," said Jack Kliger, "but it was a fantasy about what they wore and what they drove, not who they slept with."

In 1988, the magazine touted a survey, "The American Male Opinion Index," that painted a national portrait of male vanity and insecurity: two-thirds of the respondents, it claimed, spent thirty minutes or more each day on grooming. *GQ* was normalizing the notion that men, like women, cared about their appearance. "It helped make it okay," recalled one former executive, "for men to actually put moisturizer on their hands."

At the same time, the nation's managerial class was no longer exclusively male. "Now with women in the workforce, men have to look good, too, to compete," a *GQ* executive told a reporter. How to be a man in the 1980s was becoming an increasingly fraught question, and *GQ* was convincing readers that it had the answers. By 1985, its circulation had grown past 700,000; by decade's end, its formula had spawned an entire newsstand's worth of copycats. "Men, it seems, read," *The New York Times* observed in 1990, reporting on a recent crop of sensitive-yet-manly publications. "Even more revelatory, men shop, cook, go to movies, play with their kids and—Are you ready?—have feelings. So, why shouldn't they have their very own magazines to lead them through the labyrinth of life?"

Around the time that Art started at the magazine, *GQ*'s brash young publisher, Steven Florio, presented a thesis statement of sorts. (In magazine parlance, a title's publisher is in charge of business operations like ad sales and marketing, while the editor in chief oversees all editorial matters.) *GQ*'s ideal reader, Florio said, is "the first one in his family to graduate from college, who wants to drive a BMW and dress well. It's new-money. It's ethnic. It's young Black men, young ballplayers, young Hispanics, young Italians, all of whom have come into a new lifestyle and need some direction." This was the inclusive kind of exclusivity that Condé Nast thrived on. And Art's idea of good living came from the heart of the American establishment. A summer fashion spread highlighted the dressing habits of Gerald Murphy, the wealthy expat who moved to the French Riviera in the 1920s and popularized espadrilles and Breton stripes. One article focused on the personal style of an unlikely role model: the head of the English department at Phillips Academy—Andover, the high-prep enclave. "The Natty Professor," as he was dubbed by *GQ*, boasted of his eclectic wardrobe, which included three-piece Burberry suits, cowboy boots, and women's leather jackets, because they "are often crafted with more finesse and style." A regular feature called "Expensive Habits" promoted luxuries like a Charvet shirt—"For $300 apiece, you deserve perfection." The leading men's magazine of the 1960s, *Esquire*, had skewered the American elite; in the 1980s, *GQ* became the market leader by embracing it.

One day in the late 1980s—there is some confusion about the year—Art and Jack Kliger trekked to a meeting with Alex and Si. Inside Alex's stark white office, Alex observed that chic women were often described as looking like a page out of *Vogue*; *GQ*, he proposed, needed a similarly pithy way to convey the essence of what the magazine stood for. Art proffered an idea: "Personal Style for Men." *GQ*, he argued, showed classy men how to behave in the world: the smartest watches to wear, the best Globe-Trotter suitcase to lug. It should be required reading for men seeking the kind of cultivated life that *Vogue* presented to women.

Alex turned his gaze to a mocked-up photograph of a man in fine leather shoes and linen pants. Quietly, he took a pen and scrawled a phrase above the picture:

"Very *GQ*."

After a silence, Art spoke up. "That's it," he said, as the others nodded.

To this day, being "*GQ*" remains a byword for being a well-dressed, stylish man. The magazine "turned those initials into an adjective," the menswear designer Alan Flusser would say years later. "Art raised the consciousness of what it meant for a man to be fashionable."

EVERY YEAR FROM 1986 TO 1996, *GQ* beat *Esquire* in advertising pages. William Hurt's long-ago rejection had turned into a running joke for Art, who boasted to friends that Hurt would now "crawl across the desert" to be on the cover. Brandon Tartikoff, the TV executive, was so excited about his cover that he accosted an editor on a flight to find out if his issue had outsold Ted Danson's. *GQ* was also minting literary talent. Art asked a Brit named Peter Mayle to write about traveling in France, an article that led to his best-selling *A Year in Provence*. Michael Kelly, who went on to edit *The Atlantic*, reported from Baghdad. When Art bought the rights to a short work of fiction called "Thirty Dildoes," which had been rejected by *Harper's*, he called up the author's agent, Binky Urban.

"I'll buy this on one condition," Art said. "I want to change the name."

"What do you want to change it to?" Urban asked.

"'Sixty Dildoes.'"

Condé opened a string of international editions, hoping to make the phrase *GQ* into a global byword for *suave*. European men, whose own easy enthusiasm for men's fashion had influenced Art, were now importing back *GQ*'s version of their own *sprezzatura*, a neat transatlantic feedback loop of stylish masculinity. In 1996, the magazine created its annual Men of the Year Awards—an essentially meaningless prize that doubled as a hugely successful marketing campaign. The awards were handed out at a $2 million ceremony at Radio City Music Hall that was later broadcast on VH1.

Si liked his editors to live the upper-class lifestyle they peddled. He didn't have to tell Art Cooper twice. Art wore candy-striped Turnbull & Asser shirts and stocked his sixth-floor office with rare fountain pens and ashtrays from European hotels. He borrowed $1 million from Condé Nast to buy a country house on Candlewood Lake in Connecticut, where he hosted lavish staff retreats at Si's expense. Years earlier, toiling away at *Family Weekly*, Art had daydreamed about a grand apartment by the East River; now he was living in a co-op on Sutton Place South. His pride and joy, however, was a different kind of status marker, the sort of thing that *really mattered* in 1980s Manhattan: a dedicated corner booth in the Grill Room of the Four Seasons, arguably America's most famous power-lunch spot. Art was a wine snob and gourmand who clinched a permanent spot for himself at the restaurant after publishing a flattering profile of its maître-d', Julian Niccolini. (Headline: "Julian of the Spirits.") Most weekdays, Art turned up at the Grill Room shortly after noon, ordering a martini and an extremely expensive bottle of Sassicaia wine, a progenitor of the Super Tuscan reds that *GQ* helped popularize. The bill could stretch past $500, but per long-standing policy, Art never saw a check; lunch for Condé Nast editors was charged to the company's tab.

As the 1990s dawned, the workplace culture at *GQ* stayed locked in time, more akin to the *Mad Men* world of the fifties and sixties. Art would squire models like Heidi Klum to the Four Seasons restaurant and then brag about it to his readers, highlighting Klum's tight T-shirt and low-cut jeans and concluding, "It's very nice to be the editor in chief of *GQ*." After a post-lunch sambuca, Art might work a few hours before inviting favored staff members to drinks in his *GQ* office around 5 p.m. Writers of a certain vintage recall Art sipping Stoli on the rocks out of an old Penn State tumbler, holding court over the strains of Sinatra. By the late nineties, his alcohol consumption sometimes got out of hand. "You never wanted to have an afternoon meeting with Art," recalled one former colleague, noting that the editor became progressively grumpier and drunker as the day went on. At the retreats at his summer house, Art liked to pit writers against each other on the tennis court, once awarding the winner a free Hugo Boss suit; by the time the cheese course arrived at dinner, Art could be blindingly drunk and hurling insults.

Chauvinism was rampant. At the magazine's Christmas party in 1997, Art paid models to parade around in scanty, red-leather Santa's helper outfits with fishnet stockings. Adrienne Miller, who started as an editorial assistant in 1994, encountered routine misogyny during her time there: a coworker admiring a photograph and exclaiming, "That's the best set of tits I've seen all year"; a male colleague calling her into his office to ask, "What's your favorite part of sex?" In a particularly unpleasant incident, which Miller later disclosed in her memoir, she and another young female assistant were taken to lunch by a *GQ* journalist and "a notorious restaurant maître d'." Miller confirmed to me that the man was Julian Niccolini. She recalled that Niccolini repeatedly shoved his tongue into the women's mouths as they shared a cab back to the office; their colleague in the front passenger seat never turned around. (Niccolini told me that he had no recollection of Miller or this incident, adding, "Everybody can come up with their own ideas.") In 2016, Niccolini pled guilty to misdemeanor assault after a female patron charged him with sexual abuse, telling investigators that he tried to kiss her, ripped her bra, and tried to pull down her stockings; he was forced to resign from the Four Seasons two years later.

Miller, who attended state school in Ohio and knew virtually nobody in media circles when she arrived in New York, now credits *GQ* with ushering her into the city's literary milieu. She went on to be *Esquire*'s literary editor for nearly a decade, publishing work by George Saunders and David Foster Wallace and winning the National Magazine Award for fiction. Her three years at *GQ*, Miller recalled, were both challenging and illuminating, opening her professional horizons and revealing the rigid limits that women faced in the media world.

"It was such an unbelievably complicated, ambivalent experience," she said, "because I knew how lucky I was."

FOR ART'S FAVORED FEW, a job at *GQ* could be life-changing in different ways.

Alan Richman was an army vet who had manned a machine gun in Vietnam before turning to sports writing in his native Philadelphia. He was eking out a meager journalist's living, occasionally contributing wine columns to *Esquire*, when Art Cooper called one day and asked if he wanted to write about food for *GQ*. "I never had any intention of being a food writer," he told me when we met for lunch at a diner near his home in Westchester. "It never crossed my mind." Food writing in those days was relegated to restaurant reviews and dedicated magazines like *Gourmet*. Thanks to *GQ*, Richman soon found himself living like a king. Art dispatched him to Monte Carlo for a five-night stay at the Hôtel de Paris. His assignment: eat an elaborate meal at Alain Ducasse's three-Michelin-star hotel restaurant. Ten times in a row. "Too Much Is Never Enough," Richman's essay about the experience, was a classic Condé confection of exotic opulence and European society—good taste on several levels. "I couldn't believe things like this happened in the real world," Richman said. "I didn't think this world of lavishness still existed." In 2008, Richman flew business class to Tokyo for a fourteen-day stay at the Park Hyatt (of *Lost in Translation* fame) for a feature on eating non-Japanese cuisine in Japan. When he handed in a $14,000 expense account, an editor asked him, "Is that all?"

But the real indulgences came during trips to Milan and Florence for the Italian menswear shows, which Art arranged for Richman to attend, all-expenses-paid. When I asked why the company would spend thousands of dollars to fly a food writer to a fashion event, Richman smiled. "My job," he explained, "was to order wine." Art wanted Richman to coordinate pairings for the dinners that he threw for important Italian advertisers. With no internet at his disposal, Richman racked up long-distance phone bills with sommeliers to locate the pricey Barbarescos and Barolos that Art preferred. "If Art didn't like it—god forbid," Richman said, shaking his head years later. In the competitive, status-conscious world of Condé Nast, choosing the wrong varietal could be a serious offense. Richman recalled Art once asking Robert Draper, a new *GQ* writer, to pick the pairing. When Art took a sip and grimaced, Richman snuck a peek at Draper and thought, "He's *done*." Two decades later, Draper stands by his choice: he maintains that the wine he recommended that night came from the sought-after Italian vintner Josko Gravner, now considered a pioneer of orange wines. "That moment at the Milan fashion shows was a pretty minor event for me," Draper told me, "and it's been a source of bemusement that I keep running into people that Alan has told one form or another of this tall tale."

After the decadence of the 1980s and 1990s, *GQ* ran into trouble in the new millennium. British imports like *Maxim* and *Stuff* were hawking a crasser, dumbed-down version of *GQ*'s aspirational approach, and readers were lapping it up. These so-called lad mags were all dessert and no vegetables: acres of areolas with none of the literary talent or long-form journalism that Art admired. They were also cheaper to produce and popular with the young men that advertisers coveted. Art begrudgingly tried to adapt. In 2001, a *GQ* cooking page featured a buxom model with her face cropped out, holding a tray of chicken tenders beneath her chest. "Breasts for Guests," read the headline for an accompanying recipe. Some editors cringed when *GQ* ran a cover photograph of a topless Tyra Banks, hair partially covering her breasts; the headline read, "Tyra, Please Pull Your Hair Back!"

At one point, Art got roped into a public feud with Greg Gutfeld, the libertarian editor of *Stuff*, who had published a cartoon mocking Art as overweight and bald. Art fired back a letter calling him boorish and ignorant, which Gutfeld gleefully leaked to the *Daily News*. "We were making fun of the *GQ* guy who thinks an eight-thousand-word piece on his dying dog was the greatest thing ever," Gutfeld told me years later, with pride. *Maxim* and *Stuff*, he said, "were magazines made for guys who don't read magazines." It was a harbinger of a coarser turn in the culture. Gutfeld eventually migrated to television, where he became a late-night host on Fox

News. Today, he is a pro-Trump TV star who commands a nightly prime-time audience of millions.

WITH *MAXIM*'S CIRCULATION prancing past *GQ*'s, Si Newhouse decided that a change was needed. Si asked Art to step down in early 2003, eventually replacing him with a deputy, Jim Nelson. Like other felled Condé potentates, Art was devastated. "He was so lost and brokenhearted afterward," recalled Kate White, a former colleague who went on to edit *Cosmopolitan*. "It was so much a part of his identity." Si, as he did with the editors he liked, tried to soften the blow: Condé gave Art airline tickets for an around-the-world trip—and rumor had it that Si agreed to keep footing his bills at the Four Seasons.

It was there, on June 5, 2003, shortly after his retirement party, that Art sat down for lunch in his usual corner banquette with David Zinczenko, the editor of *Men's Health*. As he ordered a Dover sole, Art rubbed his neck and complained that he was sore after a morning workout; he had recently taken up a faddish exercise routine, "Power of 10," that emphasized weightlifting over cardio. Art excused himself from the table and laid down on a leather couch by the bar overlooking East Fifty-second Street. When Alex von Bidder, the restaurant's co-owner, asked if anything was amiss, Art waved him off: "I'm fine. I overdid it a bit. Would you please call my wife?" Zinczenko told the staff to call an ambulance. Art had suffered a stroke, and fell into a coma; four days later, he died, almost twenty years to the day he started at *GQ*. He was sixty-five.

Tragedy aside, there was a kind of romance in Art dying where he did. His protégée Kate White considered it an apt twist of fate: "It's as if it was scripted by Art." He had spent his life longing to be at the epicenter of the establishment. When he arrived, he bent it to his will, reshaping the habits and priorities of a generation of men who, like him, yearned to be, or at least look, elite. *GQ* set the course for a new kind of masculinity, the metrosexuality, dandyism, and male self-care that have since saturated the culture. To be "very *GQ*" is still to emulate Art's imagination of the good life: WASPy, Europhilic, denoted by a crisp tuxedo and perhaps a pair of velvet slippers. These days, it's vanishingly rare that a single editor, or single publication, could ever replicate such an effect. "*GQ* is an aspirational book," Art once said, of the magazine he curated. "You feel like you crashed a very civilized cocktail party, and everyone's too civilized to throw you out."

8

The Ballad of Donald and Si

In May 1984, the cover of *GQ* featured a Richard Avedon portrait of a handsome thirty-eight-year-old in a suit, with bushy eyebrows and a mercurial, closed-lip smile. "SUCCESS," read the headline. "How Sweet It Is." The man in the photograph was Donald Trump.

The author of the accompanying article, a magazine writer named Graydon Carter, zeroed in on Trump's outer-borough tells ("cuff links: huge mollusks of gold and stone the size of half-dollars") and outsize vanity, like the Lucite-framed copy of a *New York Times* profile that he kept on the windowsill in his office. "Did you ever pass Trump Tower at night and see the way it glows?" Trump asks Graydon as they glide down Fifth Avenue in his stretch limo with "DJT" vanity plates. (Trump brags about the TV, radio, and wet bar he's installed in the back seat.) This is the bombastic, barking, dissembling, self-mythologizing Trump that millions of Americans would soon come to know, captured by Graydon like a lepidopterist impaling a monarch. "I'm a first-class sort of person," Trump says in closing. "I only go first class."

Among the many readers who relished the article was Si Newhouse. And not just the writing: Si, who pored over circulation numbers, discovered that the Trump cover had sold much better on newsstands than comparable issues of *GQ*, an early example of the Trump Bump. As a celebrity, Trump was irresistible, and his unapologetic embrace of 1980s excess resonated with the younger yuppie readers, particularly men, who were flocking to *GQ* and other Condé publications. Si had acquired Random House, the prestige book publisher, in 1980, and the success of the Trump article prompted an idea. At a Random House sales conference in the Bahamas a few months later, Si instructed his team that securing a Trump book was a priority. "This Trump fellow was more than a comer," Si told the group. "He had arrived." Si soon took matters into his own hands: he rang up Trump himself. The whole thing, the book's editor, Peter Osnos, recalled years later, "was very definitely, and almost uniquely, Si Newhouse's idea."

Trump agreed to take a meeting. Si asked Osnos and Howard Kaminsky, the Random House CEO, to join him at the pitch in the developer's twenty-sixth-floor office at Trump Tower overlooking Central Park, a self-styled shrine to The Donald festooned with his press clippings and magazine covers. To help Trump envision the book's possibilities, the men brought along a prop: a hefty Russian novel dummied up with a dust jacket featuring a photograph of Trump looking triumphant in the Trump Tower atrium, with his surname emblazoned in oversize gold typeface.

Trump's only suggestion: "Please make my name much bigger."

The Art of the Deal was in motion.

Si authorized a $500,000 advance, later split between Trump and his ghostwriter, a magazine journalist named Tony Schwartz. The book, released in November 1987, went on to be a smash hit that earned Random House millions and spent forty-eight weeks on the *New York Times* best-seller list. It was also a prime example of Si's unseen hand in shaping American culture. The book catapulted Trump into bookstores and airport cafés across the country, morphing a provincial New York personality into a national pop culture product for the first time. He was interviewed by the *Today* show, Barbara Walters, David Letterman, Phil Donahue, *People* magazine, and a dozen local TV stations. Tina Brown ran an excerpt in *Vanity Fair*. Si, who rarely spoke publicly, accompanied Trump to a Memorial Day booksellers' convention in Washington, where he declared he had made two great decisions in his publishing career: buying Random House, and convincing Trump to write a book. At Trump's request, Si even ordered his warehouses to reopen over Christmas week so that a thousand copies could be flown to Aspen during Donald's ski vacation.

Trump, the avatar of the arriviste eighties, whose obsession with wealth paralleled the driving impulse of Condé's magazines, seemed both a byproduct of, and fuel for, Si's personal ideal of American glamour. Like Si, Trump was an outer-borough scion who outperformed his old man, transcended déclassé roots, and remade himself as a Manhattan king. At the black-tie book party, held under the waterfall in the Trump Tower atrium, Trump greeted well-wishers with Si standing by his side.

THAT SI WAS THE INSTIGATOR of Trump's first major media venture is a legacy that the Newhouse family isn't eager to discuss. Si's daughter, Pamela, cringed when I raised the subject with her. "I just don't know whether Trump would have gotten that show"—*The Apprentice*—"but for the success of that book," she said, ruefully. "So, my father, in a way, put Donald Trump on the map. It is a source of deep regret to everybody, to think that. But how would he have ever known?"

Perhaps Si had sensed the national fascination with Trump and made a shrewd business decision. But the reality was that he and Trump had a powerful friend in common: Roy Cohn, the pugnacious lawyer who had been Si's confidant since Horace Mann. And the ties between Cohn and the Newhouses extended well beyond a childhood friendship.

After the Army-McCarthy hearings in 1954 left his career in disarray, Cohn started his comeback by securing a general counsel position with Henry Garfinkle, one of the country's most powerful newsstand magnates and a close family friend of the Newhouses. In 1959, after Sam Newhouse purchased Condé Nast, Cohn and Garfinkle helped ensure that *Vogue, Glamour, Mademoiselle*, and other Condé titles were placed in prime positions at tens of thousands of newsstands across the country, enticing a new group of readers. The magazine arm of the Newhouse empire succeeded in no small part thanks to Si's old pal. Cohn went on to represent the Newhouse family across a variety of legal matters, from union disputes at the family's local papers to individual divorces. A master at manipulating older, powerful men, Cohn cultivated his friendship with Sam Newhouse, even claiming that Sam bailed him out when he had money troubles. "He reached into his drawer and got out his checkbook and he wrote me a check for half a million dollars," Cohn said. "He told me not to worry about repaying him."

As young men, Si and Cohn vacationed together in Havana, Acapulco, and Palm Beach. After Si's divorce, Cohn's friends claimed that Sam, concerned his son could become involved with a socially unsuitable woman, paid Cohn a retainer to keep an eye on Si's dating life; Cohn supposedly once steered Si away from a potential marriage match that Sam deemed ill-considered. When Cohn was thrice tried—and thrice acquitted—in federal court on charges ranging from fraud to blackmail to perjury, Si sat vigil in a Manhattan courthouse for every day of the trials. Just as Alex Liberman had introduced Si to the world of high culture, Roy Cohn was his mentor in the dark arts, explaining how to navigate the corridors of political and corporate power.

And there is little doubt that Cohn and Si discussed *The Art of the Deal*. Cohn, who was Trump's lawyer and Pygmalion, was almost certainly the conduit by which Trump and Si first met; both men attended Cohn's raucous birthday parties at Studio 54. Cohn saw the potential boost that a best-selling book could provide for Trump, and the opportunities that Si's empire offered for mythmaking. (Random House later offered Cohn a hefty sum for his memoir; "I didn't see how we could not do it, given how close he was to Newhouse," recalled Robert L. Bernstein, the president of the publishing company at the time.) Si, self-conscious about his reputation in the insular publishing world—and aware of the Random House old guard's skepticism about their *nouveau* owner—was eager to show he could deliver a hit.

"There's no question the Trump thing was Roy's idea to Si," recalled Peter Osnos. "Si says, 'Roy Cohn says he's an amazing guy, the magazine sold like hot cakes. We gotta go see him.'" To use a corporate term that the litterateurs of Condé might have sneered at: it was synergy.

THE SUCCESS OF *THE ART OF THE DEAL* permanently yoked Trump and Si, and by extension the editors of Condé Nast, together. In the years that followed, Trump turned up regularly in the pages of Condé magazines. The flashy developer was only the latest in a long line of parvenus who sought Condé's status-bestowing power, but few others had the kind of leverage that his friend Cohn held over Si—and the entire Condé universe knew it.

Tina Brown once received a call from Si, who relayed that Trump was upset about an upcoming item in *Vanity Fair* revealing that knobs had been falling off the doors inside Trump Tower. Si expressed concern that Trump might cease advertising in his magazines. The story was killed. Only as Trump's businesses began to unravel did Tina publish a probing piece by the investigative journalist Marie Brenner, which plumbed Trump's mendaciousness and his collapsing marriage to Ivana. Among other revelations, Brenner reported that Trump kept a volume of Hitler's speeches in his bedroom. ("*If* I had these speeches, and I am not saying that I do, I would never read them," Trump told Brenner.) The article also included a prescient quote from a Trump lawyer: "Donald is a believer in the big-lie theory. If you say something again and again, people will believe you."

Graydon Carter, who unwittingly set the groundwork for *The Art of the Deal* with his original *GQ* profile, had gone on to fillet Trump in *Spy* magazine as a "short-fingered vulgarian," solidifying Donald's image as a poster child of stomach-churning eighties excess. But after Si hired Graydon in 1992 to take over *Vanity Fair*, the editor displayed a newfound graciousness toward his former foil. In 1993, Graydon took Trump as his guest to *Vanity Fair*'s table at the White House Correspondents' Association Dinner. "We buried the hatchet over lunch months ago," Graydon breezily told *The New York Observer* at the time. "Donald and I have a healthy, ironic relationship." Trump returned the hosannas, with an edge: "I've called him one of the most upwardly mobile people I know," he said of Graydon, "and I mean that." Later that year, Trump invited Graydon to his blowout wedding at the Plaza to Marla Maples.

It is an irony worthy of *Spy* that in March 1994, the same month the satirical magazine announced it would shut down, Donald Trump appeared, with his new bride and baby, on the cover of Graydon's *Vanity*

Fair. "I sort of admire him after all this time," Graydon told a reporter, "in the way that former enemies can have a grudging admiration for each other."

At *Vogue*, emblem of elegance, Anna Wintour had also made room for The Donald, for the same reason that enticed Si in the first place: Trump moved product. In May 1990, Wintour was looking to reprise the enormous success of her Madonna cover from a year earlier. Ivana Trump came to mind. She and Donald were in the midst of a not-so-conscious uncoupling that had turned into a national soap opera. Anna had her doubts, asking a colleague if an Ivana cover would be "too tacky." But she cast those misgivings aside, tasking André Leon Talley and the photographer Patrick Demarchelier with turning Mrs. Trump into a vision worthy of *Vogue*. "The Real Ivana" was a rah-rah feature that congratulated its subject on "coming out of her nightmare." The cover sold 750,000 copies, a massive hit; it meant so much to Ivana that she hoarded hundreds of copies of the issue, which were later discovered in her town house after her death.

Anna had no illusions about the calculation she had made. "Ivana was thrilled with the cover and the article. As she should be," Anna said at the time. "It sort of gave her a whole new lease on life." Then she laughed. "Gave *Vogue* a boost, too."

For his part, Alex Liberman was appalled. "I should turn in my grave, if that's the correct expression," he confided to his biographers, referring to the feature as "Anna's idea." Alex, the old lion, still believed in his bones that *Vogue* carried something of a sacred mission, to expose its readers to the superlatively attractive in life and culture. "It had to be the best," he said. "Well, I can't say that Mrs. Trump is the best."

That Anna could override Alex's hesitation spoke to the changing dynamic inside 350 Madison as the 1990s dawned. Then in his late seventies, Alex retained the editorial director title and, crucially, the ear of Si. (His vanity was also intact: asked by a colleague which actor might play him in a movie, the aging Alex replied, "Tom Cruise.") But he was deferring to the younger generation more than he used to. At the urging of a young *Vogue* editor, James Truman, Alex had begun occasionally exchanging his suit-and-knit-tie uniform for Yohji Yamamoto jeans and sneakers. Visitors to his Connecticut weekend home recalled him listening to Milli Vanilli and Madonna as he painted; another Condé bright young thing, Linda Wells, brought him CDs by the hip-hop artists MC Hammer and Bobby Brown. In a sense, Alex's effort to keep up with pop culture was a testament to his aesthetic antennae: in the highly volatile world of glossy magazines, where editors and publications could be equally disposable, he grasped that the only formula for long-term success was change.

ANNA MAY HAVE HAD THE IVANA BUMP in mind when she decided to feature Trump's third wife, Melania Knauss, on her cover in February 2005. (Marla Maples never made a *Vogue* cover, but the magazine did showcase her in an obsequious 1996 feature about the spa at Mar-a-Lago.) In 2004, Trump had proposed to Melania at the 2004 Met Gala—theme: "Dangerous Liaisons"—piggybacking on the *Vogue* publicity machine surrounding the event. He then tapped a former *Vogue* publicist to represent Melania in her discussions with Anna about a potential cover story. Once again, Talley was tasked with the class-up work, posing Melania in a John Galliano gown; the accompanying article, "How to Marry a Billionaire," included fawning quotes from designers like Manolo Blahnik, who cooed, "She is a true beauty. She has it." An editor's note from Anna insisted that Donald had a "good-natured, kindhearted side." Readers were being indoctrinated in the idea that the Trumps represented the pinnacle of wealth, success, and glamour—that they *deserved* the discerning imprimatur of *Vogue*.

Anna and André attended Donald's wedding to Melania at Mar-a-Lago—as did Bill and Hillary Clinton. At one point, Anna offered Trump's daughter Ivanka a plummy position at *Vogue*, traditionally reserved for the children of the high-born. Ivanka politely declined, telling Anna that she wanted to focus on real estate. But Donald's reaction was telling. He repeatedly asked his daughter to reconsider, to the degree that Ivanka found herself taken aback. "It was a bit disconcerting to me why he was pressuring me to take the job at *Vogue*," she said. "I was a little bit upset about it."

In March 2011, Trump began publicly espousing racist "birther" conspiracy theories about President Barack Obama. He and Melania attended that year's Met Gala in May; they were invited back for the 2012 fete, too. Trump appeared, for the final time, at *Vanity Fair*'s Oscar party in February 2011. By then, however, his old feud with Graydon Carter was on the verge of being revived. The next month, *Vanity Fair*'s website published an item mocking his White House aspirations, under the headline, "Donald Trump Still Really into the Donald-Trump-is-Running-for-President Story." Trump fired off a furious reply, written in gold Sharpie, that invoked their old eighties rivalry, even needling Graydon about the collapse of *Spy*. "Graydon—I know far more about you than you know about me," Trump wrote. "You never got the 'Trump thing.'" Graydon gleefully published the letter on *Vanity Fair*'s website. He then requested that his web team mock up "a proclamation call for Trump to prove his hair is real."

"Trump must present a notarized certificate from his barber and/or dermatologist that it's real to soothe concerned citizens of the 'hairers' or whatever we want to call the movement," a *VF* editor wrote to colleagues, relaying Graydon's instructions under the subject line "Urgent project."

A couple days later, Graydon commissioned a blog post making fun of Trump's stone-faced look at that year's White House Correspondents' Dinner. The article carried a *Spy*-style headline—"Every C-SPAN Shot of Donald Trump Looking Angry About Seth Meyers's Donald Trump Jokes"—and asked "whether *The Washington Post* brought a life-size marble bust of Trump to the dinner instead of *The Apprentice* impresario himself."

Trump in turn began regularly mocking Graydon and *Vanity Fair* on his Twitter account, even invoking his *Art of the Deal* publisher: "If the great Si Newhouse were still running @CondeNastCorp, he would fire Graydon Carter immediately—circulation tanking." (In 2013, when the tweet was sent, Si was eighty-five and had stepped away from day-to-day management.) Graydon dutifully framed each tweet and hung it outside his office, quipping, "This is the only wall Trump's built." In late 2013, after *Vanity Fair* published an article about fraud charges levied against Trump University, Trump lashed out at "dopey Graydon Carter" and a restaurant that he owned, the Waverly Inn, tweeting that it served the "worst food in city." The quote has appeared at the top of the Waverly menu since.

As ever, this was a mutually rewarding pas de deux. Graydon buttressed his political bona fides and silenced critics who had accused him of going soft since his *Spy* days. Donald had *Vanity Fair*, a big, juicy symbol of the elite liberal media, as a convenient piñata. In a sense, the men were Bizarro World versions of each other: status-conscious, thrice-married masters of the Manhattan universe with singular hairdos. Both found fame in the 1980s; both owed their success, at least in part, to Si Newhouse. Again and again, Condé Nast had brought them together. It had one more extraordinary summit in store.

SHORTLY AFTER HE SECURED THE PRESIDENCY in November 2016, Donald Trump made the rounds of the Manhattan media institutions he revered. He jousted with editors and reporters at *The New York Times*, where I witnessed his glee at commanding the undivided attention of the newspaper of record. He taped an interview with Lesley Stahl for *60 Minutes*. And then, two weeks before his inauguration, he visited the Condé Nast headquarters at 1 World Trade Center to sit with the most famous magazine editors in the world.

The meeting was Anna Wintour's idea.

Even as Trump traded blows with one star Condé editor, he had kept up relations with another. In December 2012, at the height of his Graydon-bashing era, Trump extended some rare praise when rumors emerged that Anna was under consideration for an ambassadorship to Britain or France. "I am happy to hear that Pres. Obama is considering giving Anna Wintour @voguemagazine an ambassadorship," Trump tweeted. "She is a winner & really smart!"

In 2016, however, Anna took the unprecedented step of issuing *Vogue*'s first-ever political endorsement: of Hillary Clinton. The decision made sense given the women's long-standing ties: Anna had helped dress Hillary since her days as First Lady, hosted fundraisers for her, and frequently served as a financial and social connector. Anna had taken Huma Abedin, Hillary's longtime aide, under her wing after the implosion of her husband, Anthony Weiner, in a sexting scandal; Abedin spent long stretches at Anna's country estate in Long Island. (When Abedin wrote a memoir, Anna proposed the title *Truth Hurts*, but the publisher opted for the more cryptic *Both/And*. Anna later recycled "Truth Hurts" as the cover line when *Vogue* ran an excerpt.) Rumors again flew that Anna was eyeing an ambassadorship, maybe to the United Kingdom, in a prospective Hillary Clinton administration. When Anna gathered her stunned staff to acknowledge Trump's victory, her voice quavered and she cried.

But it was unlike Anna, ever meticulous in her social chess moves, to leave herself so exposed to an adverse outcome. (Presumably, she genuinely saw no possibility that Trump might win.) Access to the White House mattered for *Vogue*, which had always considered the First Lady important to cover. Compounding Anna's problems, she had been overheard by a British tabloid musing that Trump had only sought the presidency for personal financial gain. She quickly apologized, and days later, made a covert visit to Trump Tower to pay her respects face-to-face, slipping in through the building's residential entrance to avoid detection by the photographers staking out the main lobby.

Trump figured Anna wanted to grovel for an ambassadorship. Instead, she invited him to 1 World Trade to clear the air. Notably, Trump agreed without insisting that the editors come to him; the only other media institution Trump deigned to visit while president-elect was *The New York Times*. "It just shows that it was a priority for him," Hope Hicks, Trump's 2016 campaign press secretary, told me, of his mindset at the time. "*Vogue* is *Vogue* and *The New York Times* is *The New York Times*. We can tweet that they're failing, all of that stuff, but it still has a certain prestige to it, and he recognized that."

When Anna met with Graydon in her office to break the news of the upcoming summit, it did not go over well.

"There's a meeting I would like you to come to . . ." Anna began.

"Okay, sure."

"... with Donald Trump."

Graydon's face dropped. "You've got to be kidding me."

Besides his objection to Trump, Graydon was also dismayed that Anna had agreed for the meeting to be off the record, which he believed made the conversation journalistically useless. (When Trump visited *The New York Times*, the newspaper insisted that the discussion be on the record, to the extent that I was invited to attend as the media reporter and report the proceedings on Twitter in real time.) Anna pressed her case, and Graydon eventually relented.

Early on January 6, 2017, as an icy wind vexed Manhattan, Anna greeted the president-elect and his entourage—which included Hicks and Kellyanne Conway—in the 1 World Trade Center lobby. It all seemed like an amusing anachronism. Condé Nast was struggling to persuade readers and advertisers of the relevance of print magazines in a digital age. Yet here was the president-elect, ascending in a high-speed elevator to the forty-second floor, where he entered an executive conference room with floor-to-ceiling glass windows overlooking the Hudson River and the Jersey City skyline. From his Trump Tower condo that morning, Donald had proudly informed the public via Twitter that Anna had personally invited him. In a subtle nod to the Roy Cohn years, he added a shout-out to Si's nephew, by then a top family executive: "Steven Newhouse, a friend." Ringing the conference table were the company's editors in chief, including his old nemesis-turned-friend-turned-nemesis Graydon, and David Remnick, whose post–Election Day essay for *The New Yorker*'s website had been titled "An American Tragedy." These were the gatekeepers whose respect Trump, for the moment at least, still desired.

The discussion covered Putin, feminism, climate change, hate crimes, race, and abortion. Things were mostly cordial. Spotting Graydon, Trump joked, "I can't even believe we're sitting near each other in a room like this." (On this isolated point, Graydon agreed.) An uncomfortable moment came when one editor said Trump's campaign was the reason that swastikas were spray-painted on her children's playground; Trump angrily rejected this notion, invoking his daughter Ivanka, who had converted to Judaism before her marriage to Jared Kushner.

For the most part, though, Trump appeared to be on his best behavior. This was Condé Nast, after all. "He left feeling like, 'I didn't come out of that any worse than when I went in,'" Hicks said.

In hindsight, the meeting was something of a final stand between Trump and the company that had done so much to boost his profile. In October 2017, after his chaotic first nine months as president, Anna appeared on the late-night show of James Corden and declared that President Trump would not be invited back to the Met Gala. An attempt by *Vogue* to photograph Melania Trump for the magazine earlier that year had fallen through when the First Lady declined, apparently because Anna would not guarantee her the cover. "They're biased, and they have likes and dislikes," Melania said later of the magazine that seventeen years earlier had paid for her bridal shopping spree in Paris. "It's so obvious, and I think American people and everyone sees it." *Vanity Fair*'s website resurfaced the magazine's most famous Trump-bashing features and published tough reporting on his messy personal life and finances. The #Resist readership rewarded VF.com with record traffic. After Trump responded on Twitter by rebuking "the really poor numbers of @VanityFair," the magazine plastered the insult on its next cover, verbatim.

In his scathing tweet, Trump also included a prediction about the career of the man who had penned the *GQ* profile that, three decades earlier, and unbeknownst to all involved at the time, had set in motion the journey that would take Donald Trump, improbably, all the way to the apex of American life: "Graydon Carter, no talent, will be out!"

Twenty-four hours later, Condé Nast announced that subscriptions to *Vanity Fair* had soared.

9

Philistine at the Gate

By the late sixties, Samuel I. Newhouse Sr. was already a very rich man, enjoying the hefty profits of his mid-market newspaper empire. His purchase of Condé Nast in 1959 had added a dollop of glamour to his public profile, but his peers considered those women's magazines an anomaly in the Newhouse portfolio, which mostly consisted of workaday papers based in locales such as Staten Island, New Jersey, and Syracuse. Sam, born in a Lower East Side tenement to Jewish immigrants, owned a co-op on Park Avenue, but he could not buy his way into the upper social echelons of the establishment.

But, just maybe, he could buy *The New Yorker*.

Like many other totems of the American elite, *The New Yorker* had Gatsbyesque origins. It was the creation of Harold Ross, a high-school dropout who grew up poor in Utah, and Raoul Fleischmann, the Jewish heir to a yeast fortune. Two men from outside the WASP establishment turned their Jazz Age journal into a beacon of sophistication, edited for those who aspired to belong to, or at least converse with, the intellectual gentry. The magazine's mockery of upper-class mores—the social anxiety of William Hamilton's cartoon WASPs; Charles Barsotti's dogs who dryly reenacted the therapy sessions and business lunches of well-to-do professionals—only fueled its appeal to affluent mid-century readers. It was an effective editorial strategy, and a profitable one, too; at one point in the magazine's glory years in the 1950s and 1960s, the sales department had to turn away advertisers. Under the genteel command of William Shawn, Ross's legendary successor as editor in chief, *The New Yorker* published the pantheon: Updike, Cheever, Baldwin, Kael, McPhee, Salinger, a procession of twentieth-century stars. Eager to emphasize exclusivity, the Fleischmann family refused to solicit new subscribers, although discounts were quietly offered to undergraduates at the better universities. For a good chunk of the twentieth century, the magazine's painterly covers became a synecdoche of cosmopolitanism in American living rooms, an efficient way to declare one's allegiance to higher cultural planes.

In the late 1960s, Sam Newhouse arranged a meeting with Peter Fleischmann, Raoul's son and the magazine's heir apparent. The men met at the Newhouse residence, where Sam walked the scion to his study and began his pitch. Sam was a seasoned cajoler and dealmaker, but Fleischmann ended things quickly. He was not impressed by Sam's newspapers. And as far as that frivolous magazine division, Condé Nast, was concerned . . . well, the less said about that, the better. *This* was the guy who thought he could run *The New Yorker*?

"It didn't last long enough for me to finish my drink," Fleischmann later recalled.

This rebuff was a great disappointment of Sam's career, and it did not go unnoticed by his son. Si Newhouse had watched his father build a multimillion-dollar media empire whose reach extended around the country and into Europe. Sam had namesake buildings at universities and donated enough money to Lincoln Center to ensure one of its theaters would be named after his wife. Si now owned Random House and was the superintendent of *Vogue*. And yet he knew exactly how the Newhouses continued to be perceived: arrivistes grasping for status.

In 1984, the younger Newhouse finally saw his chance.

The plot kicked off in the Upper East Side auction room of Sotheby's, a prime gathering spot for the Eastern elite. As bids flew for a Hockney painting, Si was deep in conversation with Donald Marron, a PaineWebber banker he knew from the board of the Museum of Modern Art, another signifier of membership in Manhattan high society. PaineWebber controlled a key tranche of stock in The New Yorker

Magazine Inc., the publicly traded parent company of the magazine, and Marron confirmed to Si that the rumors were true: the shares might be in play.* By then, *The New Yorker*'s financial health had unraveled, and Fleischmann fils had proved to be an unsteady steward. Circulation had barely budged in the 1980s, and although the magazine still eked out a profit, its ad revenue had fallen nearly 40 percent in two years. Fleischmann had rejected shrewd proposals like investing in the American edition of *Elle*, in part because William Shawn objected, turned off by the idea of sharing a corporate owner with a fashion magazine. Instead, Shawn was enthusiastic about an all-French edition of *The New Yorker*, edited by himself. When *Elle* became a smash hit, *The New Yorker* saw none of the rewards.

Si embarked on a series of financial maneuvers to secure a sale, although once he expressed interest, it felt inevitable to many on Wall Street that the magazine would ultimately be his. Si had access to an enormous family fortune, and he was willing to overpay for what he wanted: a few years later, he would shell out $17 million for a Jasper Johns painting called *False Start*, an auction record for a work of a living artist. (The dealer Leo Castelli estimated that Si paid at least $8 million above the going price; Si later sold it at a loss.) Now Si was aggressively bidding for a different kind of masterpiece. He offered a significant premium over the share price, completing the acquisition in March 1985. Fleischmann had resisted Si's father, but with his investors eager for a payout, he didn't have the luxury of saying no to the son.

Even after Fleischmann accepted the deal, trading his family heirloom to a rival scion, he privately dismissed Si as a parvenu hell-bent on social acceptance. As Fleischmann's wife, Jeanne, would later bitterly recall: "He wanted to buy it for his mother and put it on the coffee table. His father had wanted to buy it for the same reason. It was a classy thing to have." In fact, at that time, Si might have been the only

---

* In a neat bit of Condé backscratching, *House & Garden* published a lavish spread of Marron's Manhattan apartment about four years after this encounter at Sotheby's. Marron's wife, Catie, said that she had casually mentioned to Si that she loved decorating. He invited her to "come work at *House & Garden*," where she became a contributing editor; she went on to work for *Vogue*.

living Newhouse who thought buying *The New Yorker* was a good idea. According to Si's daughter, Pamela Mensch, Donald Newhouse objected to the deal, as did the other Newhouse relatives who oversaw acquisitions at Advance Publications. The family had already sunk tens of millions of dollars into another Si plaything, *Vanity Fair*, which was gaining in cultural currency but not yet turning a profit. The Newhouse newspapers, overseen by Donald, enjoyed fat margins, and Donald had led speculative investments into a promising technology called cable television that was starting to catch on. Now Si wanted to spend more of his inheritance on yet another magazine whose financial prospects looked iffy at best, at a price—$168 million, or roughly $475 million in today's dollars—that many analysts agreed was overinflated. "The decision to buy *The New Yorker* was not a corporate one; it was personal, and lonely," Mensch recalled. "I doubt my father had ever before made a decision unsupported by his kinsmen." But Si dug in, arguing that *The New Yorker* was a cultural institution of national importance, and the rest of the family ultimately deferred to his wishes.

The acquisition announcement, in March 1985, set off a hysteria. *The New York Times* carried two front-page stories about the news. One staff writer deemed the purchase "a deliberate affront to every artist, writer and editorial staff member"; another compared herself to Blacks in the antebellum South. "I do feel a little bit like a slave went on the block," the writer Emily Hahn told the paper. Things only got crazier. Over the next two years, Si would confront a full-scale staff rebellion, make national news by firing Shawn, and find himself accused of coarsening American letters. With these philistine Newhouses intent on desecrating an icon, it was widely concluded that the best days of *The New Yorker* were behind it.

THE ANTI-NEWHOUSE VIEWPOINT, encouraged by the soon-to-be-exiled Shawn and his disciples, ignored several inconvenient facts.

In truth, *The New Yorker* had grown out of step with affluent 1980s audiences, who were losing interest in the magazine's sentimental visions of a fading upper crust lifestyle. There were interminable articles devoted to topics like the future of wheat. E. J. Kahn Jr.'s five-part series on staple food plants opened with a thirty-one-page essay on corn. The new American elite craved glitz and consumption, not agricultural dissertations or the bons mots of high-WASP writers such as George W. S. Trow. A magazine defined by its feel for the establishment had failed to keep up with the establishment. And the business staff had little interest in change. Shortly after Si's takeover, the ad sales department balked at a suggestion to solicit subscriptions by mail in order to boost circulation—a ubiquitous magazine industry tactic which *The New Yorker* had avoided for the past fourteen years. "We don't want anyone who isn't interested in us first," one *New Yorker* marketing director scoffed. In a vow of editorial independence, published in the magazine shortly before Si's acquisition was finalized, Shawn wrote that "we have never published anything in order to sell magazines, to cause a sensation, to be controversial, to be popular or fashionable, to be 'successful.'" If he had, perhaps *The New Yorker* would not have withered financially and lost the support of its backers.

Rattled by the sale and the reputation of his new owner, Shawn seemed to misapprehend the degree to which Si Newhouse held him and his magazine in awe. Si had worshiped *The New Yorker* since boyhood, telling his children that a subscription was a prerequisite for living a cultivated life. Shawn's sway over his writers, and his ability to attract the finest literary talent, struck Si as a kind of magic, and by some accounts, he genuinely wanted Shawn to serve out the rest of his career in the Newhouses' employ. "I've never seen Si so excited about anything," Roy Cohn said after the *New Yorker* purchase. "It's like the crown jewel." Hoping to allay Shawn's fears, Si guaranteed him editorial independence and created a firewall between *The New Yorker* and Condé Nast, installing the magazine in a separate arm of the Advance empire so as not to "taint" its writers with the perceived shallowness of *Vogue* and its glossy ilk. In his first meeting with the staff, Si tried to cut the tension with an attempt at humor. "You mean you don't want Jerry Hall on the cover of *The New Yorker*?" he asked, referring to the current issue of Tina's *Vanity Fair*, which featured the Texan model and Mick Jagger paramour wrapped in a bedsheet and not much else.

The line didn't land quite as Si had hoped; a mocked-up *VF* cover was soon circulating in the *New Yorker* office, featuring Eustace Tilley's head pasted atop Hall's seminude torso.

The dynamic deteriorated from there. "Si has got himself some of America's glories," Leo Lerman noted in his diaries, "but also a nest of seething neurotics, making fantastical demands." Shawn, in particular, was sensitive to any hint of meddling, having been accustomed to a level of hands-off ownership that would be unimaginable now (and was barely imaginable in 1985). According to Calvin Trillin, Peter Fleischmann "was so careful about not interfering with the magazine that Peter never complimented Shawn on a piece in *The New Yorker*—because that would imply there were pieces that he didn't like." Staffers were also appalled when *Newsweek* published a story that mentioned Si's friendship with Cohn, whose values represented everything their liberal, literary set despised. Jonathan Alter, who wrote the *Newsweek* article, recalled the horrified reaction: "The *New Yorker* people were calling me up and screaming: '*What do you mean, Roy Cohn?!*'" The genteel *New Yorker* staff was revolting against its arriviste owner. In her private notes from the time, Lillian Ross, the veteran staff writer and Shawn's longtime mistress, described Si as "very much the ravenous Jew now in the country club. Looking around hungrily." (Ross and Shawn were themselves Jewish, and not known to be anti-Semitic, but they were quick to condemn evidence of social climbing, a trait they considered vulgar.)

The backlash intensified when a new publisher, Steven T. Florio, entered the picture. Florio was the star salesman who had reinvigorated *GQ*: an earthy, cigar-smoking thirty-six-year-old Italian American from Jamaica, Queens, whose swagger, mustache, and loudly striped suits made him look like he'd burst from a Dick Tracy comic strip. Florio came to Condé Nast in 1979, imported from *Esquire*, where he was advertising director. Hugely charming and unabashedly crude, Florio was a boiler-room type who got results by carousing with clients and browbeating his staff. At *GQ*, he boosted ad revenues and helped shed its "gay" reputation to broaden its appeal to mainstream readers. Si loved the fact that Florio made him money. But he was also drawn to

Florio's wiseguy image, so redolent of the studio-era gangster movies that Si adored and regularly rewatched in the screening room at his Upper East Side town house. Florio, the outer-borough peacock, stood out from the refined staff of *The New Yorker* "like he was an alien," Ken Auletta recalled. In her private notes, Lillian Ross compared his appearance to a thug "who takes the prisoner to [the] back room and applies lighted cigarettes to bottoms of the feet." In May 1985, weeks after his purchase, Si named Florio the next president of *The New Yorker*. Understatement was all well and good when it came to the articles, Si figured—but maybe the sluggish sales force could use a kick in the caboose.

Florio charged in like a rhino. He cleared out the old-guard circulation and sales staff, most of whom considered the idea of aggressively marketing their magazine to be a gauche undertaking at best; their reputation in the advertising world was summed up as "We'll tell you whether you can be in *The New Yorker* or not." Florio's pride in these firings didn't engender much appreciation in the office. "I just blew it out of here with a fire hose," he bragged of his dismissal of the sales team. Under his guidance, *The New Yorker* created a direct-mail campaign to entice new subscribers—the first time it had actively solicited new readers since 1971. Florio introduced tear-out cards for advertisers like L.L.Bean, allowed a gatefold cover featuring a Ford Taurus, and ran lengthy advertorials that mimicked editorial content, business-side intrusions that would have been unthinkable under the Fleischmanns. A market survey was mailed to subscribers, asking readers their reactions to statements like "I am envious of friends who are more affluent" and "I like to think I'm a bit of a swinger." The editorial staff was so insulated from commercial imperatives that some writers were horrified when Florio had the temerity to run ads that filled up half a page, rather than the small squares that ran next to articles, almost in deference to the pristine text alongside. (Full-page ads remained out of the question.) But the real pearl-clutch moment came when Florio accepted an advertisement for Obsession, the Calvin Klein fragrance, featuring a mass of lithe nude bodies shot by the photographer, and one-time *GQ* favorite, Bruce Weber. Sexy ads were virtually ubiquitous in the mid-1980s glossy magazine trade. But they were considered heresy at the prudish *New Yorker*, where Shawn once insisted that a writer change the word *pissoir* to "a circular curbside construction."

Soon, Florio hit on his next horrifying initiative: TV ads. Shawn disdained television, even devoting a hundred pages of a 1980 issue to George W. S. Trow's remonstrance against the medium, "Within the Context of No Context." But Florio, with Si's approval, believed *The New Yorker* needed to reach younger readers—not just because advertisers preferred them (although they certainly did), but also to prevent the magazine from sleepwalking into obsolescence. The result was a series of commercials dramatizing *New Yorker* articles that aired in prime time during popular shows like *Miami Vice*. One spot featured a scene straight out of a soft-core erotic thriller: a voyeur sitting in his car on a luridly lit street, gazing at a beauty strolling by in a body-hugging pink dress. In voiceover, we hear, "I sat in the dark, and imagined flirting with a pretty Latin girl in a short, tight, shiny dress, her skin perfect and brown." The sequence ends with the revelation that the sultry sequence was adapted from "Driver," a short story by Frederick Barthelme in a recent issue of *The New Yorker*.

Cue the slogan: "Yes, *The New Yorker*."

The ad represented everything the staff had feared about the "Condé" influence. Privately, Shawn was incensed, while the smooth-talking Florio euphemistically told the *Times* that the editor was merely "energized by the more aggressive selling of his words." But what was so wrong with aggressive selling, anyway? The magazine's subscriber base was loyal but aging; as Florio put it, "The *New Yorker* reader is a 64-year-old member of a bird-watching club." What good was all that exquisite prose if few people under the age of fifty were reading it? Si had kept his word and refrained from weighing in on Shawn's editorial decisions. But that meant many of the same sloggy pieces still appeared week after week; one year after the Newhouse purchase, the magazine ran a three-part series on identifying the World War II–era remains of GIs in New Guinea. *The New Yorker* once set the cultural agenda for upper-middle-class elites. Now it dawned on Si that Shawn, who had recently turned seventy-nine, had failed to grasp that the tastes of that elite had changed. Fifteen years earlier, Condé Nast shivved Diana Vreeland to save *Vogue*. It was time again to sharpen the knife.

OVER HIS DECADES LEADING CONDÉ NAST, Si Newhouse fired many powerful people. None of these ousters caused a firestorm like that of William Shawn.

The precise chronology remains in dispute, but many accounts agree that Si urged Shawn for months to identify a suitable successor, and Shawn's ideas failed to please. Jonathan Schell, a Shawn protégé (and school chum of his eldest son, the actor Wallace), was not well liked among the staff; Charles McGrath, a bookish, soft-spoken type, was respected, but lacked the kind of charisma that Si preferred. Meanwhile, Si had grown close to Robert Gottlieb, the rock-star editor in chief of Knopf. Gottlieb had discovered Joseph Heller's *Catch-22*, along with countless other literary bestsellers, and he had been working under the Newhouse umbrella since 1980, when Advance Publications acquired Knopf's parent company, Random House. Si and Gottlieb had a lot in common. Both were secular Jews who grew up in New York; they liked to watch old movies together and wore the same sort of conspicuously slouchy clothes. Gottlieb even encouraged Si to dress comfortably in the Condé offices, urging his billionaire friend, "You don't need to impress anyone." Si liked the idea of Gottlieb running *The New Yorker*, but he was hesitant to guillotine Shawn too soon. Then, one day in January 1987, according to Gottlieb's account, Shawn went to lunch with Si and, out of a sense of good-soldier obligation, asked a bold question: "Mr. Newhouse, would you welcome my leaving sooner rather than later?"

Startled, and rather delighted that Shawn had offered his own head on a platter, Si nodded yes.

"Then I will," Mr. Shawn resolved.

Thrilled, Si marched straight to Gottlieb's office to share the news: He was to replace Shawn at once. Gottlieb, however, suspected that a consequential miscommunication had occurred. The well-meaning Shawn had failed to realize the consequence of his words, thinking he was merely proposing to Si a gradual timeline for a departure, not tendering an immediate resignation. Si, ever allergic to small talk and dillydallying, was convinced Shawn had yielded the position, which was now his to reassign. "The ultra-forceful Newhouse and the passive-aggressive Shawn were constitutionally incapable of understanding each other," Gottlieb would write years later.

This interpretation may explain why Si was convinced he had done nothing untoward, and why Shawn and his allies came to believe he had been unceremoniously ousted. Regardless, Shawn was stunned when Si walked into his office and handed him a pre-written press release announcing his "retirement." It was as if a bomb went off at 25 West Forty-third Street. Lillian Ross, who had urged her colleagues to greet Si with chants of "Shame, shame," after he first bought the magazine, organized a protest letter urging Gottlieb to reject the job; it was signed by 154 writers, artists, and editors, including the reclusive J. D. Salinger. The letter, after a dutiful review by the magazine's fact-checkers, was hand-delivered to Gottlieb—who then received a phone call informing him he had been given an incorrect copy. Could he hold off on an answer until the "correct" version could be obtained? "This did not speak well for the efficiency of the gang on 43rd Street," Gottlieb noted dryly in his memoir.

Gottlieb politely declined the staff's request that he turn down the editorship, and on February 13, 1987, Shawn left the *New Yorker* office for the final time. As it often did at Condé Nast, an unpleasant exit came wrapped in the balm of generous severance. Si extended to Shawn whatever amount of money he needed to live comfortably in retirement and provide for his daughter, Mary, who had autism and had been institutionalized since she was young. Si also offered Shawn an office at 350 Madison, but Shawn declined, citing his dislike of the building's elevators. Instead, Shawn accepted a workspace from an unlikely source: Lorne Michaels, the *Saturday Night Live* impresario, whom Lillian Ross and Shawn had befriended when she researched an article about him for *The New Yorker*. For several years, the wizened, genteel Shawn toiled away at his editing projects inside Michaels's personal corner office at his company, Broadway Video.

It was there, in exile, that Shawn and Ross, who quit after his ouster, wrote a feature-length screenplay about a philistine fashion publisher who purchases a famous literary magazine called *Info* and proceeds to wreck it. "The rag-pickers have got to us," moans one of the *Info* writers upon hearing about the sale, a nod to Sam Newhouse's old nickname. The script is a vivid snapshot of Condé Nast's reputation in the late 1980s. Si's stand-in is Ron Farley, son of Dottie (a dig at Mitzi) and owner of the magazines *Style*, *Onslaught*, *Attitude*, *Man's Way*, *Lawn & Home*, *Urbs & Suburbs*, and *Me*, whose cover features "a smiling model with inch-long, tombstone teeth" in "a low-cut bosom-revealing gown." ("The worse *Info* is, the better it is for business," Ron declares.) Gottlieb is rendered as Sheldon Laibrook, a nebbish with a habit of "fraudulent 'intellectual' double-talk." When the Lillian Ross character, Wendy Marigold, pitches a serious feature about wealthy horse owners, Sheldon leeringly requests the *Vanity Fair* version: "Tell me how they spend their *nights* in Kentucky. The high life. The revels. The kinkiness. The partying."

"Their *nights*?" Wendy asks, horrified.

"Nights. The sex. The bi-sex. Liven it up. That's what people want to know."

The screenplay includes a blowout party at the Metropolitan Museum's Temple of Dendur, seemingly a parody of Tina's *Vanity Fair* soirees, complete with a Tama Janowitz type (Bam Horowitz) who snorts coke, carries a red balloon around, and asks, "Who's got the most power? The Pope or Donald Trump?" Ross and Shawn, who detested the Condé-ization of the book world, include a literary agent who declares, "Don't think books. Think deals!" and an anxious intellectual who wonders, "Is Magic Realism on its way out?" Wendy/Lillian denounces Ron/Si—"I despise the slop you pour out over the world!"—and Andrew Mann, the Shawn-like editor of *Info*, compares his magazine to a moral crusade: "There are cynics who accuse us of thinking that we are working as though we think we are saving Western civilization. For all I know, maybe we are."

The screenplay ends with Mann restored to his rightful editorship and, oddly, Wendy married to Sheldon Laibrook, although not before she has carried on a covert affair with an Arab sheikh who reminisces about his childhood enjoyment of the "talking camels" in *Info* cartoons. The script was never produced. The 1980s celebrity-industrial complex, wrought in no small part by the Condé Nast blend of art and commerce ("Don't think books. Think deals!"), had little use for a lamentation on a literary paradise lost.

BACK IN REAL LIFE, Robert Gottlieb was neither the change agent that Lillian Ross had feared nor that Si Newhouse had hoped.

Gottlieb's eye for literary talent was unsurpassed; Le Carré, Cheever, Morrison, and Robert Caro were among his writers, and he would later edit Katharine Graham's Pulitzer-winning memoir. But his bookish personality and kitschy interests—he was among the world's leading connoisseurs of plastic handbags, even publishing a book about his collection, which he kept on shelves above his bed—didn't quite mesh with the energies required of a weekly periodical. "He wasn't interested in journalism. He wasn't interested in getting the story," Calvin Trillin told me many years later. "America was not one of Gottlieb's interests, except in a sort of a camp way. I remember my first conversation with him. He thought a good American story would be about a toilet museum that one of the bathroom companies had." Gottlieb's eccentricities could be charming—he kept a toaster in his office that, on an hourly basis, popped out slices of plastic bread—but his self-satisfied demeanor did not help matters. Tina Brown claimed that Gottlieb, at a dinner party, told her blithely that, as an Englishwoman, she "could never understand *The New Yorker*."

To be fair to Gottlieb, Shawn was a near-impossible act to follow. Tina, watching the drama unfold from her offices at *Vanity Fair*, was appalled at the intransigence of the old-guard *New Yorker* staff, especially when one complained to her that Gottlieb was now assigning stories, rather than allowing writers to germinate ideas on their own. It was the endless freedom afforded by Shawn, Tina believed, that had led *The New Yorker* into the dreary indulgences that repelled modern readers and had stripped the magazine of any urgency or cultural vim.

From Si's perspective, however, there was one key area where Gottlieb's skills fell hopelessly short: his congenital aversion to the spotlight. Si, so introverted and awkward in private settings, liked to live vicariously through the exploits of his butterfly editors. Tina and Anna Wintour, with their whirling social calendars, offered Si the perfect entrée to the elite circles he adored. All the publicity also drummed up business for Condé and kept the luxury advertisers keen. Gottlieb was the inverse: soon after his appointment at *The New Yorker*, he attended a ballet performance and became deeply uncomfortable when he realized dozens of people were staring at him. "It confirmed my long-standing belief that being a public figure is hell," he later wrote.

Gottlieb, who once bragged that he had never visited a magazine office before Newhouse offered him the *New Yorker* gig, also retained a snobbishness toward Condé Nast, insisting that he had nothing to do with that glossier, tawdrier arm of Si's empire. So critical was this distinction to Gottlieb that, more than thirty-five years after he was named editor, he declined to speak about the subject. "I never worked for Condé Nast," he wrote in a message a year before his death in 2023. "When I was at *The New Yorker* it was completely separate. My (very happy) relationship was with Si Newhouse directly. I just don't have a single thing to say about CN."

That relationship notwithstanding, Si had come to believe that Gottlieb's approach was no longer working. The subscription rate barely moved; financial losses were still adding up. Si had withstood all those slings and arrows from the literary set because he believed the Condé buzz machine could coexist with *The New Yorker*'s gravitas. But Gottlieb was, at his core, a preservationist. He enlisted Ingrid Sischy, the hip editor of *Artforum*, to remake the front-of-the-book culture listings, "Goings On About Town," but his indifference toward infusing topicality and celebrity into the magazine left it out of sync with the broader culture. "*The New Yorker* is no longer a kind of secular religion, as it once was," Hendrik Hertzberg, a one-time lion of the magazine, wrote in a sour 1989 assessment of Gottlieb's early tenure, echoing a widely held view that *The New Yorker* had become an ossified curio of fading WASPdom—"merely a magazine," in Hertzberg's subtle dagger. For

Si Newhouse, these words would have carried an extra sting. He had achieved a lifelong dream—his father's dream—to control an American literary treasure. But the reputation lingered of the chiffonier, that insult that had originated with the magazine's own A. J. Liebling. Despite his trust in Gottlieb, Si had gotten no closer to reviving *The New Yorker*'s reputation—or his own.

10

Eustace Tina

At the start of the 1990s, Robert Gottlieb may have been stumbling at *The New Yorker*, but Tina Brown was riding high. Her *Vanity Fair* was the red-hot center of the Condé Nast universe, each of its glamour-soaked issues a monthly distillation of the culture. Si had spent the prior decade in acquisition mode. He added *Gourmet* to the Condé stable in 1983; debuted *Condé Nast Traveler*, an upscale Baedeker edited by Tina's husband, Harold Evans, in 1987; and purchased the downtown cult fashion magazine *Details* in 1988. But it was a blowout party thrown by Tina that captured the raw cultural power of Condé Nast writ large.

Vanity Fair's fifth anniversary bash in 1988 took place at the Diamond Horseshoe club in the basement of the Paramount Hotel near Times Square, a defunct 1940s-era supper club revived for the night by Tina with the help of Studio 54 impresarios Steve Rubell and Ian Schrager and the go-to event designer of the era, Robert Isabell. Amid an Old Hollywood backdrop of white limos and cigarette girls in Carmen Miranda turbans, celebrities from every sphere waltzed in past the flashbulbs of the paparazzi, like an issue of the magazine come to life: Liza Minnelli, Norman Mailer, Halston, Swifty Lazar, Jacqueline Bisset, Jackie Collins, Kurt Vonnegut, Tom Wolfe, Gloria Vanderbilt, Donald Trump, Ron Perelman, Julian Schnabel, Bianca Jagger, Bill Blass, Barbara Walters, Henry Kissinger, and Reinaldo Herrera, who took charge of a midnight-hour conga line. Like a basketball coach, Tina laid out a man-to-man defense: each of her writers and editors was assigned to look after particular VIPs, with highly specific instructions on flattering their ego or ensuring they did not duck out early. The excess was palpable: gold-painted palm trees flown in from Miami; sixteen female saxophonists dressed head to toe in Calvin Klein. This was the apotheosis of the Condé edict that editors become something more than rearrangers of pretty words and pretty pictures: for Si, the ideal editor in chief was a curator of the culture. Si himself presided and, sloughing off his usual shyness, delivered a speech—"*Vanity Fair* fever is sweeping the country!"—reveling in the elite stratosphere that Tina had created for him.

The event itself "was a strategic decision to revive the sense of cultural elitism that was part of the premise of *Vanity Fair*," an executive later recalled. Si was bankrolling his own version of Condé Montrose Nast's lavish soirees on Park Avenue: extravaganzas of the good and the great that doubled as highly effective tools to dazzle advertisers and advance the commercial prospects of the publisher's brand. The party laid bare how the Condé Nast of the 1980s had perfected the art of harnessing glamour as a corporate tool, to be manufactured, marketed, and ruthlessly exploited for its own corporate interests. The fact that Tina commissioned the former proprietors of Studio 54 to design the event—and assigned her celebrity wrangler Jane Sarkin, who started her career as Andy Warhol's receptionist at *Interview*, to oversee the guest list—neatly tied this pinnacle of 1980s New York excess to its 1970s antecedent. Schrager and Rubell themselves would go on to popularize the concept of boutique hotels, transposing the tax-evading, coke-bingeing antics of their youth into the legitimate realm of high-priced lodgings, whose swishy bars and dim lighting epitomized the louche decadence of the 1990s and pre-crash 2000s. Condé Nast repaid the favor: when the duo opened the Royalton Hotel on East Forty-fourth Street, Tina and other star editors made it their regular canteen, fueling a happy cycle of hype that benefited all parties.

Vanity Fair's influence was bending the culture in more profound ways, as well. In the spring of 1989, Tina was invited by Anna Wintour to attend a tribute to her psychiatrist husband, David Shaffer, recognizing his contributions to research on youth suicide. Tina was moved when William Styron, the hugely successful author of *Sophie's Choice*, stood up from his seat and spoke about his struggle with clinical depression and suicidal ideation. At the time, depression was not widely understood as an illness, and the act of suicide carried a similar stigma. Tina made a beeline to Styron and asked if he might consider writing about his experience for *Vanity Fair*, an essay that she imagined "would be news and literature combined."

Styron had first revealed his thoughts on the subject a few months prior in a *New York Times* op-ed, but a national magazine represented a much broader platform. When his article ran in *VF* in December 1989 under the headline "Darkness Visible," a phrase that Tina borrowed from *Paradise Lost*, it caused a sensation. Letters poured in from Americans who had struggled to explain similar demons to family members and friends. Clipped, photocopied, and passed around by hand, the essay offered a way for sufferers to articulate what Styron called "the diabolical discomfort of being imprisoned in a fiercely overheated room." Tina had offered Styron whatever length he needed, and his essay ran at fifteen thousand words. The following year, Styron expanded the article into a short book, a bestseller that prompted a wave of similar memoirs depicting struggles with depression; Elizabeth Wurtzel's *Prozac Nation* was published in 1994. It was a signal moment in the mainstreaming of mental health. "Out of a great deal of luck and timing," Styron recalled, "I was able to be the voice for a lot of people"—a role that Tina and *Vanity Fair* had instigated.

This was not the first time that Tina had reoriented the conversation around public health. In 1987, she commissioned a story on the lethal toll of AIDS on New York's creative community. Mainstream publications had been slow to acknowledge why so many young and middle-aged artists, writers, and actors were dying, in part because many of the victims and their families, frightened by the still-potent stigma around homosexuality, had sought to hide their diagnoses until the end. (*Vanity Fair* itself had done plenty to glamorize Ronald Reagan, who did not deliver a speech about the AIDS epidemic until late in his presidency, by which point nearly twenty-one thousand Americans had died.) Tina decided to publish a gallery of fifty black-and-white photographs, annotated with each victim's name, profession, and the age they died. "AIDS: In Memoriam" was modeled after a celebrated issue of *Life* magazine in 1969, "One Week's Toll," that included photographs of 242 American soldiers who had died during a recent week in Vietnam. Readers were confronted with the sheer scale of the carnage; Tina's AIDS gallery had a similarly powerful effect. "It was bringing AIDS out of the closet," said Michael Shnayerson, who wrote the accompanying article. "There was still no recognition of its impact, or the toll it was taking on people in the arts."

The feature included the fashion designer Perry Ellis and the decorator Angelo Donghia, whose *New York Times* obituaries did not mention AIDS as the underlying cause of their deaths. Shnayerson had been tasked with convincing relatives and friends to allow their deceased loved one's photograph to appear—for some, a terrifying prospect. He spent hours with the celebrity hairdresser Maury Hopson, who recounted the final days of his lover, Way Bandy, a makeup artist to the stars who died at age forty-five. Recalling the interview to me thirty-six years later, Shnayerson began to cry. Hopson's account was so heartrending that Shnayerson devoted the final portion of his article to it, printing many of his words verbatim. "I wanted to let him speak," he told me. "There was nothing more powerful than what he was saying. And Tina ran it just like that."

But arguably Tina's biggest splash as editor of the magazine came in the summer of 1991, with the publication of a nude photograph of the actress Demi Moore, pregnant, one hand casually draped across her breasts, the other supporting the sphere of her swollen belly. When the image appeared on the cover of the August 1991 issue of *Vanity Fair*, it caused a national scandal.

Demi, who was fresh off her blockbuster turn in *Ghost*, was already comfortable with Annie Leibovitz, who had shot her wedding to Bruce Willis in 1987. For the couple's personal use, Leibovitz also photographed Demi unclothed while she was pregnant with their first child, Rumer. Now Demi was pregnant again, with Scout, and Tina wanted to feature her on the cover. An initial shoot was called off because Demi had dyed her hair blonde for a movie called *The Butcher's Wife*, and the *VF* crew preferred her in her usual guise as a brunette. Later, at the reshoot, Demi posed in a flowing green gown by Isaac Mizrahi. There were no plans for her to pose nude, but Leibovitz asked Demi if, as a gift, she would like a companion set of disrobed photos to go with the earlier ones. The images were not intended to be seen by the public. When Tina saw the contact sheets back in New York, she was mesmerized. Would Demi let them use it? Leibovitz got on the phone and, to Tina's shock, convinced the actress to say yes. Alex Liberman tried to talk Tina out of it, telling her, "I don't think so; I think it's rather too vulgar." Tina had a great deal of trust in Alex's instincts, but in this case, she overruled him. (Later, Alex would happily claim the Demi photo as one of his great moments at Condé Nast.) When Tina ran it past Si, he looked pensive for a moment and then acquiesced: "Why not?"

Leibovitz's portrait was unadorned and unashamed, a riposte to an emerging 1990s pop culture awash in sex, but uncomfortable with its potential consequences. Several major supermarket chains balked at carrying the issue on their newsstands. So Ron Galotti, Tina's macho publisher at *Vanity Fair*, dreamed up the idea of shrink-wrapping the magazine in white plastic that cropped Demi's body below the head. It looked like a peekaboo issue of *Penthouse*, which only fueled the runaway sales. Within days, it had sold out across the country. One magazine store in Ottawa, Canada, received a thousand calls from customers asking if its shipment had arrived. "I guess they want to be first on their block to own it," an employee mused. Phyllis Schlafly denounced it as "sickening, cheap sensationalism." At least fifty-nine American newspapers ran stories about it. The cover turned up on network television shows for eight days in a row, and ABC News named Leibovitz its "person of the week."

The New York Times ran an assessment by its art critic, Roberta Smith, who called Demi "the ultimate yuppie madonna"—and observed that Leibovitz's career arc from counterculture icon *Rolling Stone* to the materialist glitz of *Vanity Fair* reflected the embrace of popular culture "by the American corporate structure." Indeed, Leibovitz had in recent years created a series of advertisements for American Express, perhaps the ultimate status symbol of American yuppie splendor. (In a neat corporate ouroboros, Leibovitz's Amex ads sometimes appeared alongside her editorial work in Condé magazines.) The Condé Nast alchemy had struck again, merging a cultural cause—in this case, female empowerment—with pecuniary reward, a feat that the firebrand intellectual Camille Paglia found both revealing and delightful.

"Isn't it ironic that capitalism, not feminism, brought this one about?" Paglia quipped at the time. "There is no benevolence here. There's sheer manipulation and salesmanship. And, again, I'm for it!"

Crassly motivated or not, the uproar sparked by Demi's naked body busted old taboos. A glossy magazine had managed to open the door for a more frank cultural conversation about pregnancy. Every subsequent *People* and *Us Weekly* headline celebrating an actress's baby bump owes it a debt. Demi later wrote that she found the accompanying article, by Nancy Collins, demeaning, given its focus on her diva-like demands for private jets and on-set psychics. (The piece also included a quote from the director Joel Schumacher comparing Demi to "a young Arabian racehorse.") But for Tina, the fallout of the cover image was a kind of culmination, perhaps even a vindication, of the philosophy of celebrity and provocation that she had infused into American media, and the brickbats she had endured because of it. In a triumphant staff memo—"Demi Does a Million"—Tina congratulated her *Vanity Fair* team on the stupendous newsstand sales, up 77.6 percent from the year prior. The number of issues sold by then: 1,087,000.

"Any ideas for next August?" Tina asked, puckishly.

THINGS WERE GOING A LITTLE MORE QUIETLY at *The New Yorker*.
Gottlieb had made improvements on the margins, but the consensus was that his magazine was still mostly a snooze. "A piece on a collection of plastic guitar picks?" E. J. Kahn Jr., a contributor since 1937, remarked after happening on a Gottlieb-approved "Talk of the

Town" item about the subject. "I don't know. Then you read it, and you find out that it wasn't even the world's best collection of plastic guitar picks. It was the *second* best collection. Mr. Shawn would never have approved of that." One columnist observed that Gottlieb's magazine "doesn't do celebrities, it doesn't do sound bites. Like Custer's troops at the Little Big Horn, it stands proudly, and perhaps vaingloriously and foolishly, trying to fight off the utterly relative and transitory 'values' of our age, which circle it howling like Red Indians." Famously, it didn't end well for Custer.

In public, Si studiously backed the soft-spoken Gottlieb, praising his preservationist instincts and dismissing the critics who, Si believed, wanted the magazine to "run pictures and run color and run stories on Harry Helmsley," the scandal-tarred real estate magnate. Privately, though, he was worried. Si was something of a gambler: in his twenties, a friend recalled, he learned Yiddish phrases so he could play games of chance with the Seventh Avenue *garmentos* he'd met through *Vogue*. Now Si had invested much of the Newhouse legacy in the wager that he could prove himself a capable steward of a literary treasure. Steve Florio had channeled his inner Barnum to improve the magazine's advertising and marketing effort, but by the start of 1992, *The New Yorker* was still in the red. Worse yet, it had little cut-through in the national conversation. Si didn't really mind losing the money: between the local newspapers, with their fat margins, and his brother Donald's shrewd investments in the bustling cable industry, the family business was doing gangbusters. But the losses from its magazines were only worth it if the editors achieved the right level of renown, if the articles received notice on the morning shows and in gossip pages—if the glossies functioned as a highly tangible reminder of Si Newhouse's ringmaster role in the culture. And plastic guitar picks weren't going to cut it.*

Si raised the subject with Tina in January 1992, in his usual sidelong manner. "How much do you read *The New Yorker*?" he asked, somewhat

---

* *Glamour* did make money, and lots of it. The magazine's focus on beauty and makeup made it more accessible than *Vogue* and more broadly appealing to the middle and working classes. For decades, *Glamour*'s success helped offset the excesses elsewhere at Condé Nast.

to her bewilderment, during a meeting in his spare executive office at 350 Madison. Tina was well acquainted with Si's sphinxlike utterances. Not quite knowing where he was going, she hedged: "Not much lately." The seconds ticked by. Finally, Si asked how she might go about editing it. For Tina, the timing was apt and inapt at once. Her son, Georgie, who had been born two months premature, had learning disabilities and would later be diagnosed with Asperger's; Isabel, her daughter, was not yet two. The notion of spending less time with her young offspring immediately struck her as painful. But professionally, Tina was also feeling antsy. Over the years, she had been tempted by opportunities elsewhere: Condé's great rival Hearst hoped to put her in charge of *Harper's Bazaar*, and Barry Diller had mused about putting her in charge of a Hollywood movie studio.

She'd turned them both down. Condé Nast was the closest that the late twentieth century had come to reassembling the great Old Hollywood culture factories of the 1930s. Overseen by a Jewish outsider, employing the finest artisans and visual technicians of its day, the company generated a voluminous output of entertainment products celebrating the wit and manner of upper-class splendor that were then transmitted to the hinterlands, where the masses could marvel at and consecrate the most beautiful women and men of the day. In 1992, Condé Nast was MGM and RKO rolled into one. And Tina, for all her discomfort with Si's defenestrations of Grace Mirabella and William Shawn—her awareness that her mercurial Medici could withdraw his patronage, with little warning, at any time—still appreciated the freedoms and benefits that only the Newhouses could provide. Condé Nast, for all its growth in the 1980s, was still run like a mom-and-pop—or, rather, a bro-and-bro, with siblings Si and Donald in charge of every aspect of its privately held operations and accountable to no one besides themselves. This was why, when Si wanted to stop Tina from leaving for *Bazaar*, he offered to pay in perpetuity the long-term medical expenses of her aging parents in Europe; why he threw in a five-digit annual clothing allowance. Plus, as the Demi Moore cover proved, Americans were talking about *Vanity Fair*, not a lesser title at Hearst.

Still, Tina was stirring for a new challenge, something more intellectually stimulating than the world of Hollywood that she and *Vanity Fair* increasingly inhabited. Seated beside Richard Gere at a gala dinner, Tina had struggled to muster the energy for small talk, finally asking the actor, "What are you working on?"

"My spiritual life," Gere replied.

Gottlieb, meanwhile, had an inkling that his close friend Si was not entirely happy with his tenure. But he liked his version of *The New Yorker*: the Jane and Michael Stern exegeses on chilies, John McPhee's novella-length meditations on geology. Years later, in his memoir, Gottlieb bragged about publishing "a piece that had a radical influence on the way bats were perceived and treated in America." (He meant nocturnal mammals, not Louisville Sluggers.) Confirming the qualms of people like Calvin Trillin, who questioned Gottlieb's lack of interest in topical journalism, he continued to edit the full-length books of favored authors like Robert Caro while putting out a weekly magazine.

One weekend in Palm Beach, in early 1992, Si and Gottlieb took a walk along the sand. Si made clear that he needed to make a change; according to Gottlieb, Newhouse said the magazine was everything he had hoped for, "but he didn't like the demographics." Privately, Gottlieb wondered if Si was under pressure from his more cost-conscious brother, Donald, who had never been keen on the *New Yorker* purchase in the first place. But blithe as ever, the editor took it in stride. "I'm good at putting out the magazine the way it is," Gottlieb declared later that year. "I didn't want, nor was I really equipped, to rethink the magazine to the extent that Si came to want."

Newhouse could be ruthless in cutting down his editors, but when it came time to formally dismiss Gottlieb, he felt racked with guilt. In 1971, after he fired Diana Vreeland, a vivid nightmare jolted him awake; in 1992, Si suffered through a sleepless night before he sat down with Gottlieb one day in June for their usual lunchtime sandwiches. (Gottlieb was not a Four Seasons guy, which in Condé world was part of the problem.) After delivering the news, Si immediately offered a consolation prize—and here was where the singularity of the Newhouse empire came into play. For his five years of service at the magazine, the company would pay Gottlieb roughly $350,000 a year for the rest of his life. Gottlieb died thirty-one years later, in 2023, at age ninety-two. By a conservative estimate, Advance Publications paid him about $10 million over three decades to *not* work at its magazines. No wonder that Gottlieb, after being fired from the most prestigious job in literary journalism, denied any rancor. Asked by a reporter how he was feeling, he invoked the title of a campy country song about a lovestruck newlywed: "I'm the happiest girl in the whole U.S.A."

Gottlieb would later claim that at the time of his firing, Si had not yet made up his mind about a replacement. Was this true? Tina Brown said that Si's official job offer arrived in the middle of June 1992; startled, she asked if she could take the summer to consider. The next day, Si showed up in her office and asked, "Did you make up your mind yet?" Gottlieb, meanwhile, had flown to Japan with Ingrid Sischy to judge a literary translation contest. Si planned to reveal everything upon Gottlieb's return in July. This, in hindsight, was laughably optimistic, given the speed at which gossip traveled inside Condé Nast. When the news started to leak, during the last weekend in June, Si moved up his big announcement. A sleep-deprived Gottlieb found himself fielding reporters' phone calls from his hotel room in Tokyo. Tina's accession was seismic enough to merit the front page of *The New York Times*, although it was widely assumed that the woman who turned the flailing *Vanity Fair* into a global phenomenon had always been at the top of Si's wish list of candidates he wanted to take charge of the jewel in his magazine crown.

But as Graydon Carter tells it, he had *The New Yorker* before Tina did.

BEYOND THE FACT THAT HIS BYLINE was hard to forget, E. Graydon Carter would have come to Si Newhouse's attention by 1984 at the latest, when he wrote the Donald Trump profile for *GQ* that generated the idea for *The Art of the Deal*. In 1986, he and a former *Time* colleague, Kurt Andersen, founded a new monthly called *Spy*. Plucky and scathing in its satire, *Spy* combined investigative reporting, inventively droll prose, and visual pizzazz to lay bare the foibles and excesses of status-crazed 1980s Manhattan. Among the magazine's pranks was to mail checks of smaller and smaller quantities to wealthy celebrities and wait to see who was avaricious enough to cash them; Trump redeemed a check for thirteen cents.

Two years into *Spy*'s run, Si approached Graydon and Kurt about acquiring a 25 percent stake in the magazine. This was somewhat surprising, since Condé Nast—and, in particular, Tina Brown and *Vanity Fair*—was among *Spy*'s favorite targets. Si himself would be cited in its pages for "his famous aversions to leisure and interaction with other human beings"; he also fell for the check prank, cashing one worth sixty-four cents. Perhaps Si wanted to use his money to neutralize a threat. Or, as a magazine enthusiast, he may have simply been impressed by the quality of the product. (Likely a bit of both.) In any case, the deal was never consummated, though the possibility prompted a spirited discussion in the *Spy* offices about what Si might choose for his first cover. The consensus: "Those Nasty Men at the IRS," a joke about Si and Donald's epic, years-long tax dispute over their father's estate, which they eventually won.

Graydon had also developed a powerful friend inside Condé Nast: Anna Wintour. In later years, long after both editors ascended to imperial status, the Anna–Graydon alliance would sour, and in 2016 it was Anna, by then Condé's artistic director, who informed Graydon of the budget reductions that partially prompted him to quit. But in the 1980s, the two admired one another, a Canadian Anglophile and a Brit bonding over their emerging success in Manhattan media. "We were friends," Graydon recalled to me. "We'd have dinner and things like that. She was really cozy and conspiratorial. I had great affection for Anna."

Graydon wrote for *House & Garden* prior to Anna's takeover of the design magazine in 1987. Impressed by his work, she brought Graydon along with her to *Vogue* the following year, awarding him a contract to write features. The notion that the chief *Spy* man, who had made his reputation scorching the ruling class, would accept a side hustle at *Vogue* raised some eyebrows. Graydon acknowledged that while there was a conflict of interest, he would not modify *Spy*'s approach toward covering Condé Nast. Besides, he told a reporter, he needed the gig "to stave off poverty, make a car loan, and pay for my kids' school."

In truth, it was a shrewd move by both. Graydon, who may have suspected that *Spy*'s flame would burn brightly but quickly, burnished his journalistic reputation and laid some groundwork for a future career move. Anna, meanwhile, could brag to Si that she had successfully coaxed the city's most scathing satirist into the Condé tent. ("I figured it was a protection racket situation," Graydon told me, "but I was fine with it.") *Spy* tended to give friends a pass from the usual acid bath treatment, and indeed, Anna, despite her notoriety and sway in late 1980s New York City, was conspicuously absent from the magazine's pages. Si also got off relatively easily: In a 1987 *Spy* feature about New York's vertically challenged power players—"Little Men: How the Runts Have Taken Over"—the diminutive Newhouse was mentioned only in passing, whereas Lawrence Tisch was labeled a "dwarf billionaire" and Henry Kissinger a "socialite–war criminal." At one point, Susan Morrison, *Spy*'s executive editor (and a former *Vanity Fair* staffer), pitched Graydon on a regular gossip column about goings-on at Condé Nast. It would be called "The Women," a nod to the Clare Boothe Luce play from 1936 about the lives of pampered Manhattan socialites. Graydon nixed the idea, although he did not prevaricate about the reason: he didn't want to offend Si, whose paychecks from *Vogue* helped cover his children's tuition. (Actually, Si may not have minded: years later, over dinner at the Connaught in London, Si told Graydon that he'd always wanted *Spy* to run a Condé gossip column, "so I would have known what was going on.")

By 1992, Anna would have been aware that Si was seriously considering a change at *The New Yorker*. It is likely that she recommended Graydon, if not for *The New Yorker* per se, then as a potential editor in chief. At Condé, Si acted as an emperor: his whims alone determined the fate of even the most powerful editors. (The brutal backstory of Anna's own accession was proof enough of that.) Elevating Graydon would gain Anna another ally at the top ranks of the company—one who owed his career at Condé to her. The move would also prevent Si from appointing a new, unknown rival who might threaten Anna's status in the Newhouses' court. No slouch himself, Graydon had also taken steps to attract Si's attention. In 1991, *Spy* was sold off to outside investors, and Graydon left to assume the editorship of *The New York*

Observer, a weekly that chronicled the city's power elite. Although the paper was mainly read in pockets of the Upper East Side, Graydon sent copies to friends at the Condé Nast offices in London and Paris. When Si toured his European outposts, he kept spotting the pink-hued *Observer* on his editors' desks. As Graydon put it later, "He thinks this is a fucking international hit!"

The call finally came. Si wanted to meet.

"I've got two things, and I wonder if you would be interested," Si said, after he and Graydon sat down inside his apartment overlooking the East River. "*The New Yorker* or *Vanity Fair*."

For once, Graydon was speechless. Two thoughts flashed through his head. The first was how far the boy from Ottawa had come. Here he was, on the cusp of taking over the magazine he had worshiped for much of his life, that had fired his youthful desire to attain the heights of urban sophistication. The second was: "Jesus Christ. *Vanity Fair*?" Thanks to all the nasty things *Spy* had written, half the staff probably wanted him dead. And now he was supposed to be the editor? How the hell was that going to work?

"You know, to be honest," Graydon began, "we've made fun of *Vanity Fair* for the last five years . . ."

Si cut him off. "Okay. *The New Yorker*."

Graydon staggered out of Si's apartment barely believing what had happened. He'd been sworn to secrecy, but Si said the announcement would come soon. "One hundred percent," Graydon told me, when I pressed him on whether Si had explicitly offered him the job. "We had a salary—everything." Graydon told only his wife, children, his agent, and his best friend. In the evenings, he sketched out his plans for the magazine, using a code name: "The Pencil." Then, shortly before he was expecting the news to become public, his phone rang. He picked up and immediately recognized the voice of Anna Wintour.

"It's the other one," she said.

Graydon froze. "I don't know what you mean."

"It's the other one," Anna said again. "Act surprised." *Click.*

About an hour later, the phone rang again. "It's not going to be *The New Yorker*," Si Newhouse told Graydon. "It's going to be *Vanity Fair*."

Recounting the story to me thirty-one years later in his Greenwich Village apartment, Graydon showed no sign of bitterness. "I have no idea what happened," he said. "My guess is, Tina probably thought, you know, 'If anybody's going to have *The New Yorker*, it's going to be me.'"

He added, "I don't blame her."

AFTER MY CONVERSATION WITH GRAYDON, I contacted Tina Brown. I told her I was hoping to get to the bottom of what I called an "enduring mystery," the precise sequence of events that led to her selection as editor in chief of *The New Yorker*.

"It's one of the enduring mysteries to me, too," Tina replied, "and sadly so entrenched in Graydon's head, it has led to decades of unfounded bitterness towards me."

Tina cited her 2017 book, *The Vanity Fair Diaries*, which dates her first discussion with Si about *The New Yorker* to a lunch at the Four Seasons on July 12, 1988, when he asked her opinion of the magazine's performance. She wrote that Si brought up *The New Yorker* again three months later, but, Hamlet-like, did not seem sure if he wanted to offer it to her or not. Tina said she encouraged Si to keep Gottlieb in place for the time being, in part because of her ambivalence about the strain on her family of running a weekly magazine. More explicit discussions followed in January 1992.

"Si first talked to me about editing *TNY* as early as 1988, and far from grabbing it out of Graydon's clutches, I was ambivalent about it all the way through to 1992, when he conclusively and directly offered it to me," Tina told me. "I was very attracted to it creatively, but with two small children, one of them with special needs, I was concerned it would add impossible strains to family life. I also felt that Gottlieb should be given more time, or it would be impossible to step into the roiling *TNY* office still furious about the firing of Shawn.

"By 1992, I was beginning to feel ready to make the change and was being courted by several other media companies, but I still felt I couldn't do the *TNY* job unless I could persuade my mother to move to the US and help with the kids. She did and I accepted. Never at any time throughout all this did Graydon's name come up to me as a possible alternate candidate."

Tina described herself as "bedeviled by Graydon's angry recollection."

"Clearly, Graydon wouldn't make up his version," she said, "so I am perfectly willing to believe that Si was also talking to him in the early nineties. I know he did talk to Ed Kosner* about *TNY* at some point in the late eighties, but went off the idea.

"By the way," Tina added, "Si never asked me whether I thought Graydon would be a good editor of *Vanity Fair*! Again, you might think my opinion, as essentially its founder editor, would have been useful. Most people thought that if I left, I would be succeeded by Adam Moss,† and I was surprised by the Graydon pick as he had no experience with glossies, but he turned out wonderfully well. So all I can think of is this is how it went down: Si talked to Graydon about the job—perhaps as a backup, given my own hesitancy for so long—and then simply went off the idea. Why, I don't know. Perhaps Alex was against it.

"It was classic Si MO," Tina added. "BUT IT HAD NOTHING TO DO WITH ME!"

Si, for his part, publicly addressed the rumor in 2000, telling a journalist that he was not attempting to leverage Graydon's interest to entice Tina to take on the role. "I talked about both jobs being open," Si said of his conversations with Graydon. "At the time, it was not clear that Tina felt she could handle *The New Yorker*, that she was ready to deal with a weekly, so there was some uncertainty. However, my feeling at the time was that Tina would accept *The New Yorker*, as she did, and I was thinking of Graydon more in terms of *Vanity Fair*."

However it happened, it was Tina's magazine now.

---

* Edward Kosner, who edited *New York* magazine from 1980 to 1993, and hired Anna Wintour as its fashion editor.

† Adam Moss, the founding editor of the innovative weekly Manhattan magazine *7 Days*, who went on to edit *The New York Times Magazine* (1998–2003) and *New York* (2004–2019). In 1992, Moss was a consultant at *The New York Times*, where he was instrumental in creating the newspaper's Styles section. Tina included Moss, along with Graydon Carter, in a photo spread of top magazine editors in the December 1989 issue of *Vanity Fair*.

11

Lapses of Taste

Tina's tenure at *The New Yorker* is still recounted by her detractors as a series of blasphemies wrought upon the institution. When rumors first swirled that she might replace Gottlieb, John McPhee referred to the dangling prospect of a Brown editorship as "the joke of Damocles." Now, on the last day of June 1992, the *New Yorker* staff had been hastily gathered into a conference room where Si Newhouse, dressed surprisingly formally in a light green suit, welcomed them by announcing, "The rumors are true." He extolled Tina's talents and deployed the word *evolution*, to the disquiet of the old-guard writers watching him. Si offered only vague answers about what he wanted for the magazine, besides that it would remain a weekly. Then he was gone.

Tina, who had burst into tears that morning when she announced her departure to the *Vanity Fair* team, arrived later in the afternoon to meet with department heads. Outwardly, she was noncommittal about her plans—keep the cartoons, maybe add a black-and-white photograph or two—but her mind was whirring. In Tina's view, *The New Yorker* was an elegant, elderly patient on life support, easier to praise than to read. Shawn and Gottlieb had effectively taken a literary jewel and embalmed it, preserving its vaunted traditions but leaving it stuck in an outmoded mid-century WASPiness. Tina found inspiration in Harold Ross's original Jazz Age incarnation of the magazine, copies of which she had picked up at The Strand, particularly its irreverence and thumb-in-the-eye takes on the nouveau riche. She also believed its writing staff had become sclerotic with what she later called "an underbelly of mediocre talent—people who thought that they were good because they were there, as opposed to being there because they were good." It would not have been lost on Tina that some of the most exciting literary chroniclers of 1980s New York were coming from outside the magazine; it was only after Jay McInerney was fired from his job as a *New Yorker* fact-checker that he published his breakthrough novel, *Bright Lights, Big City*.

"It was ten years into dying, maybe more," Tina later claimed, of the magazine she inherited. "If I hadn't come in at that moment.... It really was on its last legs, is the truth."

Her changes happened quickly. Hendrik Hertzberg, the former staff writer who had artfully filleted Gottlieb's tenure, returned as her executive editor. Tina named James Wolcott, one of her *Vanity Fair* stars, as *The New Yorker*'s television critic. She revived "Shouts & Murmurs," a forgotten humor feature from Harold Ross's era, and decided to make it the back page of every issue. Maurie Perl, her public relations guru at *VF*, arrived, too, with plans to modernize the magazine's publicity and marketing efforts. For the first time, summaries appeared below headlines, and author's names were transferred from the end of an article—where they had been tossed in, almost as an afterthought, and denoted with a retiring em dash—to the start, billboarded in the magazine's signature Rea Irvin typeface. At the time, these innovations were widely received as something of a scandal; *The New Yorker*, after all, was a publication so immune to broadening its appeal with readers that it had barely bothered to include a table of contents until the 1970s. Back then, when the editor Daniel Menaker, a fact-checker at the time, mused to a colleague that some subscribers might appreciate a legible table of contents—you know, to help guide them through the articles—his coworker scoffed.

"It's none of the reader's business what's in the magazine," she said.

Tina had asked Si to take the summer to finalize her plans before formally taking charge, and she and Harry escaped to a dude ranch in Wyoming for a recharge before her October debut. It was there that she decided on her first cover, one of six possibilities that she had commissioned from *New Yorker* illustrators to make a conspicuous statement about the magazine's new management. Laying out the options on her duvet, Tina alighted on an Edward Sorel sketch of a bare-chested, leather-clad punk reclining in the back of a Central Park hansom cab, the top-hatted driver looking startled. Over the last two decades, Tina had been the Oxford prodigy shaking up London society and the precocious twentysomething who conquered America. Now she was thirty-eight years old, with two young children, a seven-figure salary, and full entrée to the elite circles of Manhattan, Washington, and Hollywood. But to her old-world doubters, she was still the barbarian trying to breach the gates.

She went with Sorel.

It's hard to imagine, in today's fractionalized media environment, just how much attention a single print magazine could attract in that pre-digital era. So scrutinized were Tina's first issues that even typos—Dan Aykroyd as "Ackroyd"—received coverage in the press. (Tina pointed out that publications like *Newsweek* never faced that level of criticism, and her ally Hertzberg dove into *The New Yorker*'s archives to see if its reputation for scrupulousness was itself factually wanting; he reported finding more than three hundred instances of past errors.) The talk show host Dennis Miller asked if Tina would photograph John Updike in the nude. There were sexist barbs, like one *New Yorker* veteran who called her "a great girl wearing the wrong dress." The editorial page of *The New York Times* would later rebuke her for sullying the magazine with "a tarty breathlessness."

Sometimes, the criticism was paired with a denigration of Si's own supposedly unsuitable background, another echo of the opprobrium that the Newhouses had faced since Sam's first days in the publishing business. "A great American magazine falls into the clutches of a Staten Island newspaper mogul who goes out and hires a British editor who seems to know this country mainly from television and movies," lamented Garrison Keillor, the snobbish public radio personality who worked at *The New Yorker* under Gottlieb and quit the day that Tina's appointment was announced.

Inside the building, the skepticism and hostility persisted. At one point, the magazine's cartoonists believed there was a conspiracy afoot to banish them in favor of Annie Leibovitz portraits. Tina's emphasis on "buzz," a word that William Shawn despised, was anathema to the magazine's old guard, who viewed themselves as the last defenders of high-minded cultural values they feared were draining from American life. Many *New Yorker* veterans prized a tone of leisurely understatement; their articles were meant to maintain a studied distance from anything that smacked of commercial intrusion. William Shawn once balked when he learned that an actor and director—Mel Brooks, according to several accounts—had asked for his *New Yorker* profile to run around the same week as the opening of his new film, *High Anxiety*. Shawn made sure that wouldn't happen, reasoning that readers would find it distasteful, even vulgar, for a *New Yorker* article to be construed as a form of publicity. (The profile was eventually published ten months after the movie's release, under the headline "Frolics and Detours of a Short Hebrew Man.")

The magazine had a long tradition of publishing journalism that made an enormous impact, including milestones like John Hersey's "Hiroshima," the devastating account of six survivors of a nuclear attack that occupied an entire issue in August 1946; Rachel Carson's "Silent Spring" of 1962, which begat the modern environmentalist movement; and Hannah Arendt's serialized examination of the Adolf Eichmann trial, in which she coined the concept of "banality of evil." These were articles that, like the rest of Shawn's magazine, were intended to be timeless, or at least, out of time—as accessible to the reader who bought an issue on the newsstand as the one who unearthed it in an attic years later. That its back issues tended to stack up on nightstands and country house bedrooms was a feature, not a bug. Counterintuitively, the magazine was a news periodical that allowed its readers to escape the static of everyday life, to immerse themselves in whatever rabbit-hole world a writer had spent months—or even years—spelunking and then meticulously conjured in sparkling prose.

Tina believed that the magazine needed more of a newsroom's cadence to break out in the increasingly crowded media world of the

1990s, a world that her *Vanity Fair* had helped forge. "The important thing is that all by itself the magazine makes news and people are talking about it," she said. She recruited writers who had experience scoring scoops. David Remnick, hired in 1992, brought the energy of a former *Washington Post* Moscow correspondent; Jane Mayer, a *Wall Street Journal* veteran, came aboard, along with the famed investigative journalist Seymour Hersh. Ken Auletta, approached in 1992 to write about the media industry, said he would take the job if Tina agreed to pay for him to travel for four months, interviewing CEOs and moguls around the country, before he had to write a single article. Tina said yes—and added a clause to Auletta's contract guaranteeing him first-class airfare. She also brought modern methods to *The New Yorker*'s vaunted fact-checking department. The team had long relied on phone calls to subject experts and a collection of reference guides; Tina arranged for access to the electronic research database LexisNexis and doubled the size of the team, from eight checkers to sixteen. Whereas writers were once allowed to report and tinker on articles for months, even years, on end, Tina began aggressively assigning breaking news stories—and demanding they be submitted in less than a week.

She was particularly puzzled by the magazine's tolerance (and ongoing paychecks) for the longtime staffers who failed to produce any writing of note. The most egregious example was Joseph Mitchell, a legendary chronicler of New York City life who walked into the office every weekday morning, shut his door, and then departed around 5 p.m. Since 1964, he had not published a word in the magazine. "Joe Mitchell would suddenly float into my office wearing a trilby hat, like the ghost of Christmas past or something," Tina recalled. "I would think, 'Wait a minute. I thought that you were dead.'" Tina did try to coax some material out of Mitchell, urging him to write about a fire at Manhattan's Fulton Fish Market and to contribute a short remembrance of William Shawn for a tribute after the former editor's death in December 1992. Mitchell, who died in 1996 and suffered from depression much of his adult life, always declined.

Tina modeled the kind of editorial cadence she expected, routinely editing multiple drafts of stories into the wee hours. Writers became accustomed to her 3 a.m. faxes, with thousands of words marked up in pen and comments scrawled in the margins. She also continued her practice from *Vanity Fair* of axing or shelving finished stories at the last minute if something timelier emerged, prompting some staffers to call her "the Terminator." "Tina wanted something in the magazine every week that was right on the news, something you couldn't get elsewhere," said Jeffrey Toobin, another of her early hires. "That saved the magazine. I don't know if it would still be in business without that."

Not all of her efforts were successful. When Tina wanted to re-energize "Talk of the Town," famed for its sophisticated take on Manhattan life, she hired Alexander Chancellor, the Old Etonian former editor of London's *Spectator*, to oversee the section. Chancellor, it turned out, knew very little about life in New York. On his walk to work one morning, a few weeks into the job, he stopped by Rockefeller Center to see the installation of its famous Christmas tree. Chancellor told bemused colleagues how fascinated he was by the ritual and that he planned to write an article about it. A more experienced editor, Charles McGrath, gently discouraged him—the tree, a tradition since the thirties, was not exactly news—and the piece was killed; Chancellor left the magazine a year after that.

But Tina had otherwise taken the lumbering ocean liner of the magazine's editorial system and begun molding it into a speedboat, equipped to handle breaking news. And in the summer of 1994, a story broke that put *The New Yorker*, for the first time in years, at the forefront of the American news cycle.

JEFFREY TOOBIN WAS AN ASSISTANT United States attorney in Brooklyn who had freelanced for *The New Republic* when a friend, David Remnick, recommended him to Tina. He wrote "Talk of the Town" pieces and, in the summer of 1994, a longer feature about television tabloid shows like *Hard Copy* paying cash for interviews, a practice that damaged the credibility of key witnesses and had derailed several criminal investigations. One such witness was a woman who said she had seen O. J. Simpson driving erratically in Brentwood on the night that his ex-wife, Nicole, and her friend Ron Goldman were murdered. Tina encouraged Toobin to drop everything and fly to Los Angeles to see what he could dig up. "There's no story in New York," Tina told him. "Just go."

Before he left, Toobin called Alan Dershowitz, who had taught him criminal law at Harvard and was now a member of O.J.'s defense team. Dershowitz suggested that he look into a LAPD cop named Mark Fuhrman. At the LA County courthouse, Toobin was directed to a subterranean warehouse of crumbling dockets, where he found Fuhrman's lawsuit seeking a disability pension because, the cop claimed, he had been psychologically harmed by his years of interacting with Black people. (Fuhrman lost the case.) Toobin photocopied the file and made his way to the Century City office of O.J.'s attorney Robert Shapiro, where he bluffed his way inside. Shapiro had just posed for a picture by Richard Avedon, who Tina hired in 1992 as the first-ever staff photographer for *The New Yorker*; after the O.J. murder first broke, Tina had assigned Avedon to shoot portraits of both the prosecution and the Simpson defense team. Flattered by the attention, Shapiro agreed to speak with Toobin, and the reporter promptly shared what he had discovered.

Shapiro looked back at him. If you think that's bad, he said, wait until you hear about the planted glove.

This was a significant scoop. Toobin had received a preview of the stunning defense strategy that O.J.'s lawyers were planning to unleash: that a racist cop had taken outrageous steps to frame the football star for the crime.* Toobin typed up the story that afternoon from an office overlooking the La Brea Tar Pits. It ran, days later, in the next week's *New Yorker* under the headline "An Incendiary Defense." The article made waves even before the physical issue hit newsstands that Monday. Because Maurie Perl had instituted a system of previewing newsy articles to other media outlets, wire services picked up the story on Sunday night. Toobin's reporting was the lead story on many Sunday evening newscasts, and he was quickly

---

* *Newsweek* reported on the defense strategy the same week as Toobin's article, although its story included fewer details.

booked onto *Charlie Rose* and *Larry King Live*. Tina hired a service that flew a banner advertising the scoop above nearby beaches, in case any summering *New Yorker* readers had left the issue behind at their Manhattan apartments. Perl estimated that the coverage of the article, in just the first two days after publication, reached roughly 170 million people.

Any media organization in the 2020s would kill for that kind of attention, and that kind of earthshaking scoop. In 1994, *The New Yorker* came under intense attack. Toobin was accused of carrying water for O. J.'s defense team by injecting their highly speculative glove theory into the mainstream. "I want to welcome *The New Yorker* to the field of tabloid journalism," quipped Mike Walker, a gossip columnist for the *National Enquirer*. "If we had printed what Jeffrey Toobin printed in *The New Yorker*, there would be so much gnashing of teeth and wailing throughout the land." Walker was speaking on an episode of ABC's *Nightline* devoted to the media frenzy surrounding the case; when the ethics of Toobin's reporting came up, Fred Barnes, a senior editor at *The New Republic*, called it "bad journalism." Toobin defended himself by pointing to the care with which he had written his piece: twice, he had described the defense theory as "monstrous," and the article closes with a warning of the ominous implications that it carried for the tinderbox of race relations in post–Rodney King Los Angeles. The final sentence, a quote from Dershowitz, is a clear signal to readers of those dangers: "Once I decide to take a case, I have only one agenda: I want to win. I will try, by every fair and legal means, to get my client off—without regard to the consequences."

"Because I wrote about O. J., I was a symbol of the stuff people didn't write about," Toobin recalled when we met at a diner on the Upper West Side to talk about the article. "O. J. was the classic high/low story. It was about fundamentally what Black people think about the criminal justice system, which is a very serious subject. But it was also Kato Kaelin, the Dancing Itos, were Marcia Clark and Chris Darden fucking? All that silly stuff. It was illustrative of a lot of things." One *New Yorker* stalwart, the heterodox cultural critic George W. S. Trow, was not convinced. He was so incensed by the magazine's coverage of the Simpson case that he resigned, writing a fiery letter to Tina that accused her of "kiss[ing] the ass of celebrity culture." Tina riposted that she was distraught, "but since you never actually write anything, I should say I am notionally distraught."

Tina had once described *Vanity Fair* as "the great high/low show," juxtaposing "Demi Moore's pregnant belly" with "Martha Graham's dance aesthetic." But it was arguably her *New Yorker* that achieved the distinction of a true postmodern magazine. It is striking to realize the degree to which her tenure, so controversial in its day, laid the template for our modern notion of upper-middlebrow journalism. Malcolm Gladwell, hired by Tina in 1996, began his witty explorations into pop psychology that became national phenomena and made his name an adjective, "Gladwellian." Susan Orlean interviewed Mark Wahlberg about his Calvin Klein underwear ads. Tina asked Gay Talese to tackle Lorena Bobbitt. In 1993, Tina assigned James Wolcott an article on Rush Limbaugh, the trash-talking conservative radio star who was quietly on his way to becoming one of the foremost forces in American culture. Her hires included now-stalwarts of the magazine like Hilton Als, Anthony Lane, and Dorothy Wickenden. Tina's ethos was a mix of hard-nosed reporting, literary flourish, true-crime titillation, and highbrow pop culture criticism, served up in dishy, easy-to-digest fashion. Back at *Vanity Fair*, Tina once admonished one of her top editors there, and later at *The New Yorker*, David Kuhn, to rewrite the "boring" headline and display type he had drafted for an article by the legendary choreographer Agnes de Mille.

"Don't you get it?" Tina asked, impatiently. "Our job is to make the sexy serious and the serious sexy."

This was, of course, a great way to sell magazines. But in the context of *The New Yorker* in particular, Tina's approach was giving elite Americans permission to think seriously about subjects that the old version of the magazine had rarely deemed worthy of deep consideration: tabloid scandals, hit sitcoms, right-wing demagogues, porn stars. She wasn't so much dumbing down *The New Yorker* as expanding the universe to which it applied its smarts. When Tina dispatched the feminist writer Susan Faludi to cover the plight of male actors in California's adult film industry, the resulting article appalled some readers; the headline was "The Money Shot," and it was almost certainly the first time that *The New Yorker* printed the word *cum*. But Faludi's piece is a triumph of literary journalism, empathetic to its subjects and almost scholarly in its interrogation of modern masculinity. (Sample sentence: "A porn shoot is an intricately delineated ecology.") The tone was wry at times, but Faludi took seriously an American demimonde that most mainstream publications treated with condescension or point-and-laugh immaturity. What appeared week to week in *The New Yorker*, house organ of the tasteful monied classes, was reshaping the kind of cultural fare that readers felt comfortable consuming. Would the vogue for true-crime podcasts among the public radio set have happened without Tina paving the way? Or the elite embrace of HBO dramas like *The Sopranos*, which would become the subject of university symposia? When magazines became eligible for Pulitzers, in the 2010s, *The New Yorker* received one of its first prizes for, of all things, television criticism.

After two years of Tina at the helm, the magazine's circulation was up by 30 percent, from roughly 630,000 to 817,000. But her internal critics viewed those statistics as merely another sign that Tina's pursuit of buzz had lowered institutional standards. The resentment simmered until three years into her tenure, when it burst spectacularly into public view. The culprit was one of the most popular celebrities in America: Roseanne.

TINA MAY NOT HAVE ANTICIPATED the backlash that ensued when she decided to feature Roseanne Barr in *The New Yorker*, but it wasn't the first time she'd encountered the shit-stirring power of the comedienne's blue-collar charms. The December 1990 cover of *Vanity Fair* was an arresting Annie Leibovitz photograph of Roseanne in a *Dynasty*-style fur stole, straddling the prone body of her then husband, Tom Arnold. It horrified high-society readers, one of whom confided to Dominick Dunne that the magazine had "gone too far this time." In early 1995, Tina asked her theater critic John Lahr to write a profile of Roseanne, which ran for nineteen pages under a headline touting "her real importance in America's comedic tradition: the essence of her art and how she used it to make rage about sex and class funny." Lahr accurately captured Roseanne's gleefully déclassé persona. Throughout the article, the actress liberally deployed the word *fuck*—a word once verboten in the magazine's pages—and at one point is quoted instructing her critics to "suck my dick." This kind of thing was, to put it mildly, a departure from the usual *New Yorker* tone.

Tina loved the article, and she decided to double down. Shortly after Lahr's profile appeared, she flew to Los Angeles and spent three hours with Roseanne at her Brentwood mansion. There, she pitched an idea: *The New Yorker* was planning a special double issue that would interrogate the state of American womanhood. How would Roseanne feel about guest-editing it? Plans were drawn up for Tina and a pair of her top deputies to spend three days at Roseanne's house for a brainstorming session with the comedian and her friends, a group that eventually included the actress Carrie Fisher. (Tina thought it would be fun to ask Roseanne about the "cost per minute" of her marriage to Tom Arnold, "and what you get for your money.") Word of the summit promptly leaked, prompting Ian "Sandy" Frazier, a staff writer since 1974, to quit. "If the magazine were to fail, I would rather that it fail as itself, and not as some weird hybrid entertainment publication," Frazier told the Associated Press. Tina shot back that Frazier was unfamiliar with the magazine that employed him: "If you ask Sandy about the last six issues, he won't be able to tell you what's in them."

The outcry outside the magazine was even more intense. Maureen Dowd published a *Times* column headlined "Eustace Silly," in which she observed that both Tina and Roseanne were "slaves of the buzz." Tina defended her decision: "It will be great to bring that iconoclastic, fresh voice into the corridors of *The New Yorker*, to stop the kind of earnest, passé, cliché-ridden approach to women's issues that starts to rise like a mushroom cloud over a meeting." Several months after the "Eustace Silly" column, *The New Yorker* published an unflattering assessment of Dowd's writing by James Wolcott under the headline, "Hear Me Purr."

(Tina had long been attentive to the *Times* columnist's critiques; back at *Vanity Fair*, she once referred to her in an internal memo as "The Dowd." Still, at one point, Tina tried to hire her to serve as *The New Yorker*'s Los Angeles correspondent; Dowd declined.)

The "Special Women's Issue" was published in February 1996, featuring a feminine "Eustacia Tilley" in a low-cut dress on the cover, and a clarification that while Roseanne had acted as a consultant, the actress had not, in fact, edited any of the actual printed words. And what exactly was in this issue that caused so much agitation and fuss? The table of contents is a Murderers' Row of writing talent: Katha Pollitt on the demonization of poor women, Francine du Plessix Gray on aging, poems by Mary Karr and Joyce Carol Oates, and an affecting, almost painfully tender reflection by Wendy Wasserstein on her relationship with her oldest sister. Tina suborned Wolcott into contributing a wry account of the backlash against Barr—"Semicolons our forefathers had died for were being sacrificed in a bonfire of cheap celebrity"—that identified the Roseanne Resistance as "a sort of rhetorical class warfare carried on under the guise of Good Taste. It's the last refuge of a snob." And, indeed, the last refuge of an earlier generation of *New Yorker* readers and writers, who still clung to a retrograde version of the magazine that no longer clicked in the culture of the 1990s.

One last *scandale* arose from the issue's publication. Tina had commissioned an essay by the cultural critic Daphne Merkin about her fetish for spanking and sadomasochism. The article, "Unlikely Obsession," is a gripping personal account, in which Merkin plumbs the origins of her kink and its role in her romantic life, entwined with an erudite review of the literary and psychoanalytic history of bondage, including discursions into Jean-Jacques Rousseau's predilection for spanking and the Luis Buñuel film *Belle de Jour*. Such an essay, published in the 2020s, would barely register in the sea of sexual confessionals that at this point have become near-mandatory for mainstream outlets like *The New York Times Magazine*. In 1996, Merkin's article shocked the literary world. The week the issue hit newsstands, a mother at Merkin's daughter's school accosted her to ask if she was crazy. She received a call from a friend who had just returned from a dinner party where her article was the topic of fierce debate; guests were wondering what Daphne looked like, her turn-ons and turn-offs. "I froze internally," Merkin recalls. "I kept thinking, '*I wrote this while my parents were alive?!*'"

The tut-tutting stretched across the country: *The Seattle Times* ran an editorial deriding the article as "warmed-over prurience." Merkin received dozens of letters from readers, some horrified, others delighted to see their private thoughts expressed so unabashedly in public. At one point, a friend spotted a personal ad in a Midwestern newspaper: "SWM seeking Daphne Merkin type for mutual involvement and pleasure." Her byline had morphed into a symbol, a reminder of the immense reach of weekly magazines before the revolution of the internet.

Looking back, Merkin's essay broke a taboo that paved the way for Jane Pratt's *xoJane*, online sites like Thought Catalog, and the soul-baring and sexually candid first-person pieces of *The Cut*. It sent a signal, to a status-conscious audience, that it was okay for women to write about their erotic life in the pages of an upstanding magazine. David Remnick, Tina's successor, would later say, semiseriously, that he was proud of having been the first editor to get the term *blow job* into the magazine.* "People were proprietary about *The New Yorker*, and saw it still as the 'clinking glasses in the Connecticut suburbs' way, as a bastion of WASP rectitude," Merkin told me, of that earlier age. "The feeling was, 'Our *New Yorker* doesn't touch this.'" The fact that Tina had encouraged her, Merkin said, spoke to the magazine's newfound vigor and relevance. She considered it a feminist statement, too.

"No one called Mailer confessional, and what else was he?" Merkin said. "No one questioned Updike when he wrote about pink vulvas."

ONE OF TINA'S ENDEAVORS to boost readership would have a long-lasting effect on the broader media industry. Together with her

---

* "Blow job"—*New Yorker* style mandates a space—appeared in an article by Tad Friend, "Remake Man," in 2003. Remnick's quip is technically correct, but the plural form first arrived in the magazine under Tina, in a Mary Gaitskill short story about a sexual encounter, "Turgor," in 1995.

publicity maven Maurie Perl, Tina created what became known as "The Hot List." In 1992, there was no "Politico Playbook," and it would be another decade before ABC News created "The Note," widely viewed as a progenitor of morning email tip sheets. Setting the national news agenda had to be accomplished on a person-to-person basis, assignment editor to assignment editor. At enormous expense, rumored to be about $1 million annually, Perl arranged for copies of each week's *New Yorker* to be couriered directly to the homes or offices of influential journalists, politicians, morning TV bookers, chief executives, and opinion leaders. These were the influencers before influencers: the behind-the-scenes gatekeepers of the mass media platforms that were, at the time, the only means of communicating widely with movers and shakers. The hand-deliveries happened on Sundays, after the magazine had been printed, but before it hit newsstands on Monday morning. Every network news anchor received a copy; so did every living president. Al Gore and Bill Clinton were on the list, along with Peter Jennings and Dan Rather. Stacks of copies were dropped off in the cloakrooms of the Senate, the House of Representatives, and the Supreme Court, along with the newsrooms of *The New York Times* and *The Washington Post*. The list itself was a closely guarded secret. Because it was updated frequently by Tina and Maurie, it represented a real-time inventory of who was up and who was down. To be included on Tina's distribution list—with its high concentration of Manhattan, Beverly Hills, Georgetown, and Mayfair postcodes—quickly became a status symbol of its own.

Before Tina introduced this practice, Condé Nast's publicity team relied on a small circle of media and lifestyle reporters, some at barely noticed trade papers like *Ad Age*, to drum up attention. But Tina wanted her stories read immediately by media's big hitters, who could then amplify *The New Yorker*'s reporting through their own news outlets. It was no longer enough for someone to stumble on an article while waiting at the doctor's office. "The way Tina looked at the magazine, it needed to be talked about," Calvin Trillin recalled.

Perl, who cut her teeth in PR at ABC News working with Barbara Walters, knew Sundays were an agenda-setting day in the American news industry: over coffee and pancakes, journalists watched political talk shows like *Meet the Press*, perused the fat Sunday newspapers, and tuned in for *60 Minutes* in the evening. "By the time *The New Yorker* got into people's mailboxes on Monday or Tuesday, you'd be behind the curve," she recalled. Perl also liked to put her thumb on the scale; when Tina published an enormous Janet Malcolm essay on Sylvia Plath, Perl's team called reporters with the "suggestion" that the piece be compared with a previous lengthy *New Yorker* classic, Hersey on Hiroshima. These methods were widely adopted. Today, nearly every leading publication and TV network issues press releases that loudly tout scoops, major investigations, and groundbreaking essays.

The New Yorker began receiving so much press attention under Tina that other Condé Nast editors, including Art Cooper at *GQ*, requested Perl's services, or phoned her for a personal tutorial on how to inject their content into the cultural bloodstream. "The questions journalists once asked themselves on the eve of publication were: Is this smart enough? New enough? Important enough?" observed *The New York Times*, in a mid-1990s report on Tina's influence. "Now they are just as likely to ask: Will there be a buzz?"

Did Tina go too far in her pursuit of buzz? Her track record was not entirely clean. Ethics issues cropped up early in her tenure. An unsigned "Talk of the Town" piece about the criminal trial of a former East German strongman, Erich Honecker, was revealed to be written by Honecker's lawyer's spouse. ("Questions were not asked that should have been asked," Tina conceded.) Michael Ovitz, Tina's muse from *Vanity Fair*, was mentioned ten times in a special issue on movies. A Richard Avedon fashion spread that depicted the model Nadja Auermann in carnal ecstasy with a skeleton ran for twenty-six pages and seemed hopelessly out of place; the shoot cost so much money that a mortified *New Yorker* editor later shredded the expense sheet out of embarrassment. Tina was fixated on topicality, sometimes to a fault; when John Seabrook approached her with a draft of an article titled "The Man Who Invented the Intermittent Windshield Wiper"—which, among other topics, digressed into Thomas Jefferson and the history of American patent law—she was unimpressed: "Too much then, not enough now." A joke went around that Tina had left a disapproving note on a draft of an article: "Galley five and no celebrities yet." Even her fans allowed that Tina sometimes privileged flash above substance. Anthony Lane recalled pitching her a story on *The Invention of Love*, Tom Stoppard's play about the English poet A. E. Housman. Tina paused to consider the idea.

"Is Housman hot?" she asked.*

For her part, Tina described her methodology as a kind of furtive delivery system for status-conscious readers. She believed that modern audiences, distracted by cable television, talk radio, and other droning forms of lesser media, needed an extra pull to engage with the more thought-provoking articles she put out. "My goal, far from being to dump the long, serious, *traditional* pieces of *The New Yorker*, had been to find new ways to market them so that they will be read by a new and younger audience—and therefore preserved," she said in 1994. "The newsier piece acts as the tugboat or the seduction point for the reader to pick up the magazine and become engaged. They then find themselves in a friendly mood towards the more challenging and quieter pieces." She also didn't mind a touch of the vulgar. "Tina always said a lapse in taste was an absolutely essential ingredient to her philosophy," recalled Ruth Ansel, one of her art directors at *Vanity Fair*. "If something wasn't exactly beautiful or refined, she would want it because it had power and it had impact. Things that are too tasteful are too safe."

In this, Tina was ahead of the curve. Some of her supposed offenses from that era now look downright quaint. "Tina decided there should be a fashion issue, and Richard Avedon would become the lead photographer," said Stephen Schiff. "And that was just a huge controversy. It was like, 'How dare you? This is *The New Yorker*!' Can you imagine that *that* was a controversy?"

From his executive suite inside 350 Madison, Si Newhouse happily

---

* In 1986, Tina sent a sharp memo to the senior *Vanity Fair* staff after a writer who had seen an early preview of David Lynch's *Blue Velvet* failed to warn her that the film would strike a cultural nerve. "I personally detested that movie," Tina wrote, "but when I caught up with it last week, I could see why everyone is talking about it, and that is a good enough reason to be featured in *Vanity Fair*."

watched all of this unfold. Technically, Si had adhered to his original agreement to wall off *The New Yorker*'s operations from the rest of Condé Nast. In practice, there was little separation. Tina still reported directly to Si, and when *The New Yorker*'s publisher, Steve Florio, left to become Condé Nast's chief executive, Florio's brother Tom stepped in to take his place. Under Tina, *The New Yorker* was fulfilling the Condé mandate of telling Americans which subjects were worth thinking about. In fact, it was telling more Americans than ever before. The magazine's circulation had stood around 500,000 subscribers when Shawn was replaced in 1987; it rose above 600,000 under Gottlieb. In 1996, circulation was at nearly 870,000.

It all came at a price: *The New Yorker* was now losing tens of millions of dollars annually. Tina's innovations were not cheap. She paid hefty fees to her writers and ran up production costs by tearing up issues at the last minute. Si did not relish accumulating debts; the bloody trail of decapitated editors in his wake offered proof of that. But it was obvious that Tina's work at the magazine was satisfying him on a different, perhaps deeper level. Si had shown little interest in the newspaper side of his father's empire—the "hard news" side, where matters of import, at least by Sam's standards, were reported and discussed. His brother, Donald, had taken up oversight of all that. The fact that *The New Yorker* was now a player in the world of current affairs meant that Si had finally achieved the kind of legitimacy of which his father, perhaps, would have approved. Maybe Sam never thought he had it in him.

In the Condé Nast offices—amid arguably the planet's most heavily groomed and well-coiffed workforce—Si was often seen wearing a wrinkled *New Yorker* baseball cap, above a faded *New Yorker* sweatshirt. At his summer home in Bellport, Long Island, Si kept a Boston Whaler at a local dock that he sometimes liked to aggressively steer around the harbor.

A friend recalled the boat's name as *Eustace Tilley*.

12

Life as a Party

One day in 2006, Graydon Carter touched down in Venice to attend a global retreat at the Hotel Cipriani for high-ranking editors and executives at Condé Nast. The launch of *Portfolio*, Condé's new high-end business magazine, was a few months away, and a handful of copies of a dummy issue had been printed and distributed on a strictly confidential basis.

Jon Kelly, a twentysomething then working as one of Graydon's assistants, had flown in on a redeye from New York, and he was in his hotel room when the telephone rang. Graydon was on the other end. The editor couldn't find his copy of the *Portfolio* prototype. He must have misplaced it on a boat ride in town.

"Look," Kelly recalled Graydon telling him, "you've got six hours to find this thing. Otherwise, we're screwed."

Kelly was jet-lagged, newly arrived in a foreign city, and he needed to locate a single issue of a magazine that was sitting in the back of one of hundreds of boats that spent the day crisscrossing 150 canals. He figured he had one option: bribery. Hanging up, Kelly opened the safe in his hotel room and removed an envelope that contained 10,000 euros in bills—his usual allotment of petty cash for an overseas trip. Given the uncertainties of international travel, it was standard practice at Condé for assistants to carry a significant amount of money, the better to ease the burdens of important editors in chief.

Kelly slipped a 1,000-euro tip to the head gondolier at the Cipriani, who agreed to ferry him to what seemed like Venice's equivalent of a maritime parking lot. Another hefty tip convinced the on-duty clerk to rummage for the missing issue. The Condé gods were smiling that day: the *Portfolio* turned up, and a grateful Kelly shelled out another 1,000 euros as a finder's fee. The issue was returned to Graydon with time to spare.

In his quarter century as editor in chief of *Vanity Fair*, Graydon Carter surfed the crest of Condé Nast decadence. He established himself as an impresario of Hollywood, Washington, and Manhattan, famous for his double-breasted suits, flowing white hair, and seven-figure salary. This identity, and the highly agreeable lifestyle that accrued to it, was almost entirely a product of his own invention. Like his forebears at Condé Nast, Graydon was a conjurer: he dreamed of a fantasy Manhattan life, willed it into being, and made himself the star of the show.

Edward Graydon Carter was born on July 14, 1949, to a middle-class family in Toronto. His father had been a Royal Canadian Air Force pilot in World War II, who, after a short stint as a shopkeeper, returned to the service to fly Lancasters and Sabres. When Graydon was a toddler, the Carters sailed to Europe, where his father trained pilots in Germany; the family spent time in England and France, returning to Ottawa the year he turned seven. Graydon, who shared a bedroom with his younger brother, was the kind of child who was impatient to become an adult. He admired the well-dressed neighbors who sipped cocktails at his parents' weekly bridge games and studied the wry sophisticates of screwball comedies like *My Man Godfrey* and *Twentieth Century*. At eight years old, he watched *Sweet Smell of Success*, the Burt Lancaster film set in the world of Manhattan gossip columnists. Graydon was intoxicated by its vision of ice-cold martinis, private telephones at the 21 Club, and rain-soaked New York streets glowing in neon light. "I could hardly wait," he recalled, "until I could smoke cigarettes and have cocktails and get dressed up and play bridge."

Academics were an afterthought; he preferred learning from magazines like *Esquire*, *Life*, and *Time*. After Graydon graduated from high school, an aunt referred him to the Canadian National Railway, where he worked as a telegraph lineman in rural Saskatchewan. He rode in a boxcar with ex-convicts; at the time, his hair was grown out hippie-style, and a foreman forced him to shave his head. Graydon, who traveled with a knapsack of books by Kerouac, calls this one of the great periods of his life, and it's clear, looking back, that he was experimenting with new identities. At one point, he informed his railroad compatriots that he was a Jew. (He isn't.) "I thought, if you're going to be an intellectual in New York, you gotta be Jewish," Graydon explained years later. "It was so much more exotic than what I really was."

Self-invention became the project of Graydon's youth. He spent a few years working at a government accounting department, then helped draft speeches for the office of Pierre Trudeau, then the prime minister of Canada. He pitched himself to publications as a political cartoonist and wrote a spec script for the sitcom *All in the Family*, in which the Bunkers inherit $1,500 from a dead aunt. Along the way, he took classes at the University of Ottawa and Carleton University, but never earned a degree. Instead, Graydon, then known to friends as "Gray," found his footing at *The Canadian Review*, a tiny magazine about literature and politics. He joined as the art director in 1974 and eventually became editor, growing circulation to a respectable fifty thousand readers. At the *Review*, Graydon added an *E.* to the front of his byline and set up a spacious office with a fireplace and a long leather couch. A colleague later remembered him wearing white pants to the office, so regularly that they wondered if he owned a single pair that he cleaned and pressed at night. "Carter had an understanding I've always admired," said Jonathan Webb, an editor at the *Review*, "that you can create a reality by creating the trappings of it first."

His stewardship of the *Review* reflected an entrepreneurial streak that Graydon had long nurtured. In a prescient 1975 essay, written when he was twenty-six, Graydon reflected that he had "always fluctuated on the edge of a career in journalism, or one in business. There are possibilities of course that 'the twain might meet,' but for the most part, one would have to combine the most outrageous set of talents to nimbly walk the tightrope that divides the two fields." He added, "The thought of spending my nights lounging around the Rideau Club,* with favourite cronies, sipping Port and smoking cigars, while organizing and putting through profitable mergers and takeovers, really brought out the Dow Jones in me."

In 1977, however, the *Review* went kaput, with tens of thousands of dollars in debt.† Undeterred, Graydon drove a beat-up BMW to Manhattan a year later, where he talked himself into a job at *Time* magazine. An outsider among Ivy Leaguers, Graydon wore his ambition literally on his sleeves, going to work in neatly tailored suits. (He once showed up to a party wearing spats, although, years later, he claimed he had done so as a joke.) Restless to move up in the world, Graydon left for a senior editor role at a start-up magazine called *TV-Cable Week*, only for it to fold weeks later. He ended up at *Life*, where he spent lunch breaks with his friend Kurt Andersen mapping out *Spy*, which they hoped would blend the insouciance of *The New Yorker* in the 1920s, *Esquire* in the 1960s, and *Rolling Stone* in the 1970s. Named for the gossipy magazine that James Stewart's character works for in *The Philadelphia Story*, *Spy* would cast an irreverent eye on Gotham, skewering the city's potentates in politics, publishing, and finance. "New York bristles with power and hubbub, glamour and squalor, extravagant effort and astonishing rewards," Graydon wrote in his business plan. "It is a spectacle, packed to overflowing with rascals and entertainers and madmen and geniuses." Among the inspirations was Graydon's old childhood favorite, *Sweet Smell of Success*, in which all of Manhattan's elites live in fear of a powerful newspaper columnist; *Spy* winked at the movie by attributing some articles to J. J. Hunsecker, Burt Lancaster's role in the film. It wasn't long until Graydon became a fixture of the New York social whirl, a well-dressed imp with a poison pen.

By the early 1990s, Condé Nast was a charter member of the media establishment that *Spy* loved to needle. But Si Newhouse could not help but appreciate Graydon's gumption. He loved the same old Hollywood

---

* An elite private social club in Ottawa, founded in 1865 and popular with high-ranking government ministers.

† Graydon told *Maclean's* in 1987 that he eventually paid off his creditors.

films as Graydon, whose WASP affectations hit a Condé-friendly note of gently ironic grandeur. Plus, Graydon was funny: *Spy* once knocked Canadians for being so polite that they said "thank you" to their bank machines. So Si was receptive, in 1991, when Graydon called and asked to meet.

On a cold morning, around 6 a.m., Graydon arrived in Si's spare, all-white office, ready to pitch him an idea for a newspaper. The meeting went fine, until Graydon stood up to leave and the tail of his whipcord Chesterfield coat caught his drinking glass, which was filled with iced café au lait. Graydon watched, in a kind of slow-motion existential horror, as coffee and ice cubes arced through the air and splashed, Pollock-like, onto Si's pristine carpet.

Fuck, fuck, fuck.

"Everything I could ever humanly want to do in life, he owns," Graydon remembered thinking. Near tears, he looked at Si helplessly.

"I'm so sorry."

"That's okay." Si shrugged. "I do it all the time."

The newspaper idea never took off. But a year later, Si would tap Graydon as the next editor of *Vanity Fair*. The kid from Ottawa had clawed his way to the inner circle. It was the start of one of the most miserable years of his life.

CONDÉ NAST'S ANNOUNCEMENT, in June 1992, that Graydon Carter would succeed Tina Brown at *Vanity Fair* did not go over well in Hollywood. At a James Taylor concert, Warren Beatty told a journalist that people were uneasy and that *VF* was ceding its Los Angeles territory, "now that Tina's gone." Beatty's response was typical of the showbiz royalty who were worried about the fate of their favorite magazine, whose soft-focus cover stories were seen as a reliable driver of box office sales. Under Tina, *Vanity Fair* had come to play an important symbiotic role in the Hollywood celebrity-industrial complex. Now Si had put a fox in charge of the henhouse.

Graydon wasn't particularly thrilled about the situation, either. After leaving *Spy* in 1991, following its sale to outside investors, he had spent a year remaking *The New York Observer*. (His first issue foreshadowed some future preoccupations, like an article about "Two Brothers from Queens"—Harvey and Bob Weinstein—who "resemble car salesmen in both appearance and manner.") Then came Si's bait-and-switch with *The New Yorker*. Now Graydon had to prove himself capable of succeeding arguably the most famous magazine editor of the era. He quickly recruited the acid-tongued British essayist Christopher Hitchens and the crack investigative financial reporter Bryan Burrough, a coauthor of *Barbarians at the Gate*. But Graydon knew it was *Vanity Fair*'s access to Hollywood that kept the magazine in the zeitgeist, reeling in readers and ads. The skepticism of stars like Beatty represented a serious threat.

Graydon had also come to believe that Tina's loyalists were plotting against him. A *VF* mailing list of celebrities, media machers, and other VIPs who received advance copies, maintained by Tina's PR guru Maurie Perl, disappeared during the transition. The advance issues stopped going out, and the VIPs got the impression that the new editor had gone out of his way to snub them. Tina was also a conspicuous no-show at Si's big welcome party for Graydon, and her allies who remained at *VF* sniped to the gossip pages about the stumbles of the new boss. The whole thing still rankled Graydon thirty years later. "I always thought she left them behind," he said of Tina and her acolytes, "just so they would be able to tell her how fucking catastrophic I was." Graydon's early issues included a memorable cover of the singer k. d. lang being shaved in a barber's chair by Cindy Crawford, a witty Herb Ritts image that captured the trend of lesbian chic. But it was obvious to the outside world that *VF* was struggling. Advertising sagged, and *The New York Times* declared the magazine "out of the spotlight." Critics called it *Vanishing Flair*. Four months into his tenure, Graydon admitted to an interviewer that he sometimes felt "a little bit like the new bride in *Rebecca*."

Everything changed when he decided to throw a party.

Since 1964, Irving "Swifty" Lazar had hosted Hollywood's premier see-and-be-seen soiree, an annual Academy Awards watch party that by the early 1990s was held at Wolfgang Puck's Spago. Swifty was a legendary talent agent who had represented icons like Humphrey

Bogart and Lauren Bacall. He masterminded his party like a Lilliputian Stalin, enforcing a seating chart that separated A-listers from B-listers, and chastising guests who attempted to stand up and use the restroom during the ceremony. Entry was coveted and sternly policed; in 1983, on assignment for *Time*, Graydon himself donned a tuxedo and tried to sweet-talk his way past the door. The valet refused to even park his car.

When Swifty died in 1993, Graydon seized his chance. What if *Vanity Fair* sponsored a shindig of its own? Graydon imagined the party as a marketing coup for the magazine and a way to repair strained relationships on the West Coast. Instead of being the scary guy from *Spy*, he would reintroduce himself to a wary film industry as a welcoming, free-spending host. And he was certain that Si Newhouse would approve. Like Graydon, Si was intoxicated by the romance of the movies, telling friends that "if I'd had my choice of what to do with my life," he would have been a magazine editor—or a film director. (Si's remark, recounted by Robert Gottlieb, helps explain why he conceived of Condé Nast as an old-fashioned movie studio—and hints at the pressure he felt from his father to set aside artistic longings in order to become the custodian of the family business.)

For the venue, Graydon zeroed in on Morton's, the West Hollywood power restaurant popular with studio moguls and both of the powerful Michaels—Ovitz and Eisner—who loomed over the business at that time. But when he called the restaurant's owner, he discovered he was too late: a producer named Steve Tisch had already booked the venue for an Oscar party of his own. Tisch, the scion of an East Coast corporate dynasty, had once been described by Graydon's *Spy* as a "primogeniture loser." Perhaps Tisch hadn't read that issue, because when Graydon called and suggested he serve as cohost, the producer agreed.

In a sense, Tisch acted as Graydon's Trojan horse, a Hollywood player with real credibility—he had co-produced the Tom Cruise megahit *Risky Business*—whose presence sent the message that *VF*'s new editor was now willing to play nice in the celebrity sandbox. It was just one salvo in a charm offensive launched by Graydon shortly after he took over the magazine. One of his early gestures was to invite the powerful gossip columnist Liz Smith to lunch, where, by her account, "he extended to me these abject apologies for the way he had treated me at *Spy*." The old Graydon had derided Smith as "an egregious bum-kisser to the famous and the wealthy" and "the best argument for licensing journalists." Condé-ized Graydon invited her to pose in *Vanity Fair*, where she appeared, in Converse sneakers and an Anna Sui dress, in a splashy Steven Meisel photo spread on grunge.

Graydon also wanted to enlist Jane Sarkin, Tina's longtime celebrity wrangler, who was well known for her formidable Rolodex of agents and publicists. At *Spy*, Graydon had alienated Sarkin in spectacular fashion when he obtained and printed Tina's sycophantic and embarrassing letter to Michael Ovitz. Sarkin, who was on her honeymoon in Bermuda when the issue appeared, had to leave the beach to take calls from a furious Tina, an incident she later described to me as "the worst moment of my career." When he took over *VF*, Graydon believed it was imperative that he keep Sarkin from departing, and he quickly fell on his sword. "Oh my god," he told her, when they met face-to-face. "I'm the worst person in the world." Sarkin stayed.

To repair his relationship with Barry Diller, the entertainment tycoon that *Spy* often referred to as "gap-toothed," Graydon called on a friend of his: Diller's wife, Diane von Furstenberg. "If it hadn't been for my wife, I probably wouldn't be speaking to him twenty-five years later," Diller told me. Within a year of Graydon's arrival at *VF*, Diller agreed to lend his star power to a party that the magazine was throwing in Washington before the 1993 White House Correspondents' Dinner. There, the mogul said to a reporter the magic words:

"Graydon's been rehabilitated."

The inaugural *Vanity Fair* Oscar party, held in March 1994, would be the capstone of this latest reinvention of E. Graydon Carter. Sarkin persuaded Tom Cruise and Nicole Kidman to show up. Then came Liam Neeson and Natasha Richardson, Candice Bergen and Anjelica Huston, Nancy Reagan and Gore Vidal. Prince mingled with Lee Iacocca and James Carville as Annie Leibovitz snapped photos. Graydon stood at the entryway and personally greeted everybody who walked in. There were some snubs—Jack Nicholson and Demi Moore were no-shows—and none of the night's big award winners made an appearance. But one important guest was pleased: Si Newhouse, who shared door-greeting duties with Graydon and was thrilled to see the Hollywood he had worshiped since childhood brought to glamorous life.

It was immediately clear that the *VF* party had pull: one producer showed up despite the fact that the magazine had accused him, in its current issue, of illegally importing rare antique coins. Doubling down, Graydon devised a special "Hollywood Issue" that he timed for the following year's Academy Awards. It included a gigantic photography portfolio of stars, studio bosses, directors, and screenwriters, shot by Leibovitz and Herb Ritts, and a foldout cover featuring ten of the world's most in-demand actresses, including Kidman, Uma Thurman, and Julianne Moore, posing in slinky lingerie. One newcomer on the cover was Gwyneth Paltrow, whose breakout role in *Seven* was months away; she was still obscure enough that *VF*'s publisher had to explain to the ad sales staff how to properly pronounce her name. Paltrow, who was photographed in a gown, was the only actress on the shoot who did not strip down to her underwear. "I can't," she told the *VF* team. "My parents will kill me."

The Hollywood Issue was a huge seller, but it also drew accusations of racism, for featuring too few Black directors and actors, and sexism, for the way it had depicted one of Hollywood's most powerful women. Sherry Lansing, then the chairwoman of Paramount Pictures, had agreed to appear, but when the shoot fell through, Graydon decided to use a years-old picture, shot by Leibovitz for an American Express campaign, in which Lansing posed poolside in a revealing swimsuit. Lansing never received a heads-up, and the photo ran, pinup-like, under the headline "Working Girl." Lansing, the first woman to lead a Hollywood studio, was furious. "I started to scream when I saw it," Lansing told the *Los Angeles Times*. "It diminishes the accomplishments of all women, not just in our business, and it shows a great insensitivity to the changing role of women in the world today and how we feel about ourselves." And yet, when that year's Oscar party kicked off at Morton's, there was Lansing, smiling and posing with the editor in chief. The two had made up over lunch a few days before.

Like his Condé forebears, Graydon had learned to weaponize exclusivity. "It's not just about those you invite," he liked to say about his party. "It's about those you don't invite." In the mid-1990s, there were no social media platforms for celebrities to advertise their decadent lifestyles and A-list friend circles. With dozens of news crews from around the world covering the red carpet, an appearance at the *VF* Oscar party became a coveted symbol: a modern version of Mrs. Astor's old Four Hundred. The saturation of star power in the room—what the writer Frank DiGiacomo called a "panorama of encyclopedic celebrity"—confused even the pros: when the talk-show host Regis Philbin saw Cate Blanchett at the party, he exclaimed that "Gwyneth" looked great. (His wife, Joy, had to correct him.) Will Smith and Sandra Bullock queued at the entrance like any other bridge-and-tunnel partygoers. Even Warren Beatty became a regular at Graydon's table.

Entrée was tantamount to a cosmic signal that one's achievements—or notoriety—had resonated in the culture. "Everyone's trying to get on the front page here," said Matt Drudge, who attended in 1998, two months after he broke the Monica Lewinsky story on his website. Lewinsky herself was invited to the 1999 edition, where guests remarked upon her physical similarities with another attendee, Shoshanna Lonstein, Jerry Seinfeld's much-younger former girlfriend. When Lonstein clumsily delivered a tray of coffee to Graydon's table, Fran Lebowitz was audibly unimpressed.

"I'm sorry," she told Lonstein, "we asked for Monica."

Lonstein left in a huff. "You mean to tell me," Lebowitz said, "Jerry Seinfeld's ex-girlfriend doesn't have a sense of humor?"

Civilians and celebrities alike went to elaborate lengths to gain access. One year, a woman snuck in posing as a service worker, hid in a restroom stall for hours, and then wiggled into a formal dress, only to be discovered by security guards who hauled her away. One *VF* editor was offered $30,000 for a pair of invitations. Bronson van Wyck, an aspiring party planner, took advantage of *VF*'s policy of allowing in all of the night's award winners. In 1998, van Wyck rented an old Oscar from a pawnshop, affixed a custom plate with his name and "Best Sound Editing" (not a real category at the time), and showed up in a white stretch limousine. The bouncers waved him in, and he returned the statuette the next day.

Jane Sarkin, holder of the official guest list, was once approached by a woman in a formal gown who demanded entry.

"I *need* to come in," the woman explained to Jane. "I'm Jane Sarkin."

When Ernest Lehman, the screenwriter of *Sweet Smell of Success*, attended one year, it was a neat bookend to Graydon's youthful fantasies. *Vanity Fair*'s editor had manifested this night out of raw ambition and a hustler's nerve, the same combination that had driven another outsider, Condé Montrose Nast, to gather the leading lights of entertainment and society in his Park Avenue penthouse seventy years earlier. By the time the Oscar-shaped topiaries were dismantled from the Morton's driveway, and the 3 a.m. stragglers stumbled into the predawn California chill, a new status marker had been carved in the cultural bedrock. Condé Nast was once again the proprietor of the most famous celebrity party in the world.

BACK AT CONDÉ HQ, Si was pleased by all the buzz—and the happy symbiosis between the party and the prestige of his magazine. Graydon's Hollywood Issue became a perennial bestseller and a magnet for advertisers, with agents and publicists demanding spots for their clients. "People needed that cover to get their price up for a movie, to compete with other people in the movie, to explain why they couldn't be on a panel because the other actor on the panel wasn't in the same league," Sarkin recalled. "It was so powerful." Si took advantage, asking Graydon to arrange breakfasts with his favorite movie stars during Oscar week; one *VF* veteran recalled seeing Si, Graydon, Cruise, and Kidman dining together at the Hotel Bel-Air.

For all these reasons, Si was happy to approve the party's ever-expanding costs. At one point, Condé Nast paid for residents who lived next to Morton's to vacate their homes and stay at a hotel in the days leading up to the party—making it easier for *Vanity Fair* to erect its security tents and giant Oscar figurines. Graydon, always an aesthete, now had the budget to indulge his more fanciful whims. Invitations were sent on watermarked Benneton Graveur stationery, printed in Paris. Cigarette girls in dresses designed by Mick Jagger's girlfriend L'Wren Scott paraded around the room. The famed chef Thomas Keller of Per Se provided hors d'oeuvres (caviar macarons, truffle lasagna). In 2012, *VF* arranged for an apple farm to fit a custom-built vise around hundreds of budding Red Delicious fruits, applying pressure that interrupted the natural flow of the crimson pigment. The vise, molded in the form of two Art Deco letters, compressed the apple as it grew, leaving the mature product imprinted with a distinctive monogram: "V.F." Packed into straw-padded boxes, the apples were then flown to California to be used as centerpieces on the Oscar party tablescapes, in between the ironically served In-N-Out cheeseburgers. The coordination involved in creating this disposable party favor, for the fleeting delight of millionaires, was just one of a thousand details that *Vanity Fair* devoted to each year's extravaganza.

Riddled with anxiety when he started at *VF*, Graydon now grew more comfortable with the trappings of his rank. By the mid-1990s, he had moved his family from a West End Avenue rental into a spread at the Dakota, which he decorated with model sailboats, an eighteenth-century French cherrywood dining table, and a bust of Napoleon. (Later, he moved to a West Village town house. Condé Nast provided loans to help secure both residences.) Always dapper, he amassed a collection of bespoke Anderson & Sheppard suits, and increasingly relied on his Condé-provided Russian chauffeur, Sergei. His tricorn swoop of silver hair became a calling card of its own; Graydon's email signature includes an Al Hirschfeld sketch of himself, complete with a "NINA" hidden in his coiffure.

Vanity Fair's floor at Condé Nast gradually became a physical expression of his exacting taste. Graydon's blond-wood office resembled a set from mid-century Manhattan workplace movies like *The Best of Everything*; he didn't have a pneumatic tube, but a glass panel in the wall could be discreetly slid open for his assistant to pass him notes. A constant hum of jazz—Stan Getz, Duke Ellington—wafted from a Bang & Olufsen speaker and a Camel Light was usually on Graydon's lips or in a vintage ashtray, even after New York City enacted its indoor smoking ban in 2003. Rubber-soled shoes were banned (Graydon disliked the squeak); Dunkin' Donuts cups were verboten (too gauche);

Britishisms were always preferred ("dinner jacket," never "tux"). His assistants had to keep a clutch of pencils in a cup on his desk sharpened to the precise point where they generated a satisfying scrawl, but did not disintegrate upon impact. Printouts had to be prepared with binder clips, not paper clips. *Never* paper clips.

A signal task for Graydon's assistant was to fetch the editor's briefcase from the town car he took to work. After a driver sent notice that Graydon was on his way, the assistant jogged to the elevator, descended to the sidewalk, and grabbed the bag from the back seat while Graydon swept into the lobby hands-free. When the workday ended, the process repeated in reverse. "Will you do the honors?" Graydon asked, and the briefcase would be toted down to the car. In an episode of the sitcom *30 Rock*, Alec Baldwin's character, Jack Donaghy, employs the services of an "office replication service" to construct an identical mahogany workspace for himself while traveling. In real life, Graydon achieved the next best thing. If he was staying a few days at, say, the Hôtel du Cap-Eden-Roc in Antibes or the Four Seasons in Milan, an assistant sometimes flew out ahead of time to prepare his hotel suite. The same meticulous tablescape of pencil cups, stationery, and ashtray that greeted him each day at his Condé desk would be awaiting him on arrival.

His assistants learned that one grave error was to allow Graydon to answer his phone and hear someone else's assistant on the other end. According to a former employee, Graydon once picked up expecting to speak with the superagent Ari Emanuel.

"Hi, Ari."

An assistant's voice chirped back: "Please hold for Ari."

"I will not hold for Ari," Graydon replied. "He called me." *Click.*

Some ego, perhaps, was to be expected. Graydon was enjoying his spoils. "The basic atmosphere of *Vanity Fair* is kinda like *Spy*, only with money," he told a journalist after a few years on the job. Whereas Graydon was once eager to win the respect of celebrities, he now had a way of striking fear into their hearts. One year, when the Carter family rented a summer cottage in East Hampton, Graydon was dropping off his kids at the Jitney when he bumped into the *Sex and the City* actress Kim Cattrall, who was boarding the same city-bound bus. When Graydon got back to his office on Monday, he received an urgent message from Cattrall's publicist: "Kim wanted to let you know that the reason she was on the Jitney was because her Bentley was in the garage."

"That was the saddest thing I've ever heard in my life," he recalled.*

As cutting as Graydon might be, he could also be generous and loyal, particularly with many of the younger editors and writers in his employ. Turnover in the top ranks at *Vanity Fair* was rare, and to this day Graydon still works closely with members of his old team from *Spy*. He sent Champagne to friends on birthdays and gave holiday gifts like linen pocket squares. When the political writer Todd Purdum, whom Graydon had recruited from *The New York Times*, wrote a controversial article for *VF* about Bill Clinton's post-presidential carousing, there was fierce blowback from Clinton's allies. Purdum and his family took a trip to Paris to get away from it all; Graydon called and told him to put a few hotel nights and dinners on Condé Nast.

There was a caper-like quality to life at *VF*. One year at the National Magazine Awards, Graydon was so put off by the rubber-chicken catering that he called his office and requested takeout for his entire table. Two assistants arrived in the Waldorf-Astoria ballroom with bags of gourmet sandwiches, which they proceeded to hand out to the magazine's staff—"Who wants tuna?"—as less-flush competitors picked at their limp salads. But Graydon also sometimes surprised his minions by revealing a neurotic side, particularly when Si's phone extension appeared on his office line. "There's a 1 percent chance I'll be fired," Graydon would say before trudging off to see the boss. If Si had a specific request, it took precedence: once, when Si expressed curiosity about the Paris Hilton sex tape, a phalanx of *Vanity Fair* assistants was mobilized to find him a copy.

Amid this fussiness and frivolity, Graydon also ran a magazine that made news. In 1996, an investigative piece by Marie Brenner on Jeffrey Wigand, a former research executive who'd blown the whistle on Big Tobacco, inspired the Al Pacino film *The Insider*; Graydon published

---

* A spokeswoman for Cattrall told me that the actress was unaware of any call made to Graydon on her behalf, and that she has never owned a Bentley.

the article even when major cigarette brands pulled their ads. In 1998, *VF* published a glamorous photo shoot featuring Monica Lewinsky, shot by Herb Ritts on the beaches of Malibu. Lewinsky had bumped into Maureen Orth, the wife of news anchor Tim Russert, at a party in Washington and gushed about *Vanity Fair*; Orth, who wrote for the magazine, arranged an introduction with the editors. The pictures, which evoked 1950s-style pinups—Lewinsky wore blue jeans and a gingham shirt in one; in another she danced with a sunlit American flag—were dissected on all three network newscasts and *Larry King Live*. Maureen Dowd mocked the shoot as "sickening," but she also acknowledged that "getting your own photo shoot in *Vanity Fair* has become the premier achievement in our celebrity-mad culture."

The Ritts shoot is notable in light of the 2010s re-evaluation of Lewinsky as the victim of a global pile-on, when a new generation asked why the young intern had been subjected to so much cruelty. In one sense, *Vanity Fair* had gotten there first: in December 1998, the month of Clinton's impeachment, the magazine included Lewinsky in its year-end Hall of Fame, recognizing her as a victim of a media that "project[ed] every dark wish, sociological cliché, and erotic fear onto her" and left her "deprived of her voice." "This is a melancholy story," *VF* concluded, "covered in shame." In 2014, when Lewinsky wrote her first extensive public commentary on the scandal, she did so in the pages of *Vanity Fair*. The essay, "Shame and Survival," came about after Graydon referred Lewinsky to a British public-relations adviser who had worked with Kate Middleton and David Cameron. The redemption narrative they crafted kicked off a campaign that turned Lewinsky into a sought-after speaker on cyberbullying and public shaming, and the heroine of a sympathetic Ryan Murphy TV docudrama. More than two decades into his tenure, Graydon was still shaping the zeitgeist.

LEONARD DOWNIE JR., the executive editor of *The Washington Post*, was onstage at a management retreat in Maryland on May 31, 2005, when the cell phone in his pocket started to ring . . . and ring, and ring.

The buzzing was so persistent that Downie, trying to concentrate on his remarks, shut it off. Finally, he spotted the chairman of *The Post*, Donald Graham, whose family owned the newspaper, beckoning him from behind a door. Downie walked over.

"You better call Woodward," Graham said.

That morning, *Vanity Fair* had published an explosive scoop: it unmasked Deep Throat, the famously anonymous source whose confidential tips fueled Bob Woodward and Carl Bernstein's reporting that brought down Richard Nixon. Deep Throat's secret identity was among the most enduring mysteries in American journalism, and, up until that day, was known only within a vanishingly small circle of *Post* journalists. Yet here was W. Mark Felt, formerly the number two official at the FBI under Nixon, revealing his critical role in political history—not in the sober newsprint of *The Post*, but in the pages of a magazine whose cover featured Nicole Kidman promoting the film *Bewitched*.

Woodward and Bernstein, who had promised to shield Felt's identity until his death, were caught by surprise: Graydon never contacted them ahead of publication, to minimize the risk that they would publish first. John D. O'Connor, a lawyer representing Felt's family, had first pitched the story to *People* magazine and the book publisher HarperCollins, requesting payment in exchange for the information; both turned him down. *Vanity Fair* reached a different accommodation: the magazine paid O'Connor roughly $10,000 to write the article, and the Felt family retained the potentially lucrative film and book adaptation rights. It was the biggest journalistic coup of Graydon's tenure—ABC broke away from a live presidential press conference to report the news—and it underscored *VF*'s ongoing relevance in Washington. The magazine's annual party after the White House Correspondents' Dinner, which originated as a reception in Christopher Hitchens's apartment, had become the apex of the capital's social calendar, an infusion of glamour into a district of drab. The event even caught some blame for fueling Washington's fixation with celebrity: in 2012, during the Obama years, George Clooney, Reese Witherspoon, and Woody Harrelson all attended. If Tina's "Reagan Stomp" cover hinted at a coming fusion of Washington and Hollywood, Graydon's annual soiree embodied it.

Back in New York, Graydon pursued other projects that blurred the line between his role as a chronicler of the culture and an active participant. He bought and revived a pair of classic restaurants, the Waverly Inn and Monkey Bar, that became living manifestations of his magazine's "who's in, who's out" vibe, with seating charts curated by Graydon's assistants on a daily basis. Condé Nast had no formal ties to these ventures, but the clamor for reservations (and the paparazzi regularly parked outside) added to the company's mystique. With Barry Diller, Graydon coproduced a documentary on the producer Robert Evans, *The Kid Stays in the Picture*, that premiered at Cannes; later, he produced a Broadway show about the agent Sue Mengers with Bette Midler. Graydon's social circle increasingly consisted of the wealthy moguls and Hollywood grandees whose doings he had once skewered in *Spy* and now often celebrated in *Vanity Fair*. At one point, he accepted a $100,000 payment from the producer Brian Grazer after he recommended a book about a math genius; the ensuing movie, *A Beautiful Mind*, had won the 2002 Oscar for Best Picture. That year, Grazer and the film's director, Ron Howard, were included on *Vanity Fair*'s New Establishment list.

All this extracurricular activity raised grumbles inside Condé Nast that Graydon was distracted from his day job. Some readers noticed a staleness creeping into the magazine's pages. In 2011, a reporter for *The New Republic* calculated that one out of every three issues of *Vanity Fair* since 2003 included at least one article either focused on a member of the Kennedy family, written by a Kennedy, or mentioning a Kennedy on seven or more occasions. Graydon proffered a defense—"They are the totemic figures of the last great years of the American Century"—but the survey fueled an impression that his magazine, ostensibly a champion of the vanguard, was overly fixated on the past.

Still, the allure of the Oscar party endured. For each new generation of Hollywood stars—many of whom had grown up absorbing the party's mythology, and dreaming of one day attending themselves—Graydon's invitation still counted as an official confirmation that, in the eyes of the town and the culture at large, one had arrived.

"I try not to be too aware of powers-that-be giving you approval," said the actress Greta Gerwig, who first attended in 2013. "But I would like to think that somewhere, in the internal workings of *Vanity Fair*, they said: '*Yes*, Greta Gerwig. You can now be part of this.'"

13

Age of Empire

The pink ribbon is a globally recognized symbol of breast cancer awareness. Its ubiquity is in large part due to Condé Nast.

In 1992, Alexandra Penney, then the editor in chief of *Self*, was compiling a feature on breakthroughs in breast cancer research for her October issue. The cause was important to her—she had friends who had battled the disease, and some who had died from it, and it had also claimed the life of *Self*'s founding editor, Phyllis Starr Wilson, in 1988. The red ribbon symbolizing AIDS had recently entered the mainstream, and a woman in California, Charlotte Haley, had gained notice for mailing out peach-colored "breast cancer awareness ribbons" from her dining room to bring attention to the paltry funding dedicated to the disease. Penney called Haley and offered to join forces on a national ribbon campaign—to which Haley said no. Condé Nast, she explained, was too commercial. Undeterred, Penney conferred with Condé's lawyers, who advised that a change in color would allow the idea to go forward. "I was sitting there thinking—what's very female?" Penney recalled. "Pink. It got into my head."

Penney called Si Newhouse and pitched him on the idea of binding an actual pink ribbon into every copy of the October issue. Si told her to forget it—think of the cost! So, Penney contacted Evelyn Lauder, the cosmetics magnate and a major Condé advertiser, who had herself survived breast cancer and become active in the cause of finding a cure. A year earlier, the women had collaborated on an issue of *Self* that included a "cancer-cure report," with articles on mammograms and new treatment methods. Lauder told Penney that she would distribute 1.5 million pink ribbons at her cosmetic counters around the country, with a card describing how to perform a breast self-exam. The October 1992 cover of *Self* touted a "Hot Celebrity Workout" and "10 Ways to Find Real Love"—and the image of a pink satin ribbon, "pinned" to the cover with a trompe-l'oeil safety pin, with a message: "Support Breast Cancer Awareness Month." Readers were invited to send a self-addressed envelope to the Condé offices and receive a pink ribbon back. "Wear this ribbon," Penney wrote in her editor's letter, "and make a difference."

The collaboration between *Self* and Lauder spawned a cascade of activism that has raised hundreds of millions of dollars for research in the thirty-three years since. Every October, pink is ubiquitous, from police departments touting pink handcuffs, to pink-painted fire trucks at local parades—even a pink spotlight aimed at the White House. Charlotte Haley's refusal to cooperate with Penney also presaged future criticisms of so-called "pinkwashing"—the idea that corporations exploit the feel-good branding of the ribbon to project an image of good citizenship, while doing little to remove carcinogens from their products or fund research to prevent or alleviate the effects of the disease. That the pink ribbon emerged from the image-obsessed corridors of Condé Nast adds another layer of irony—and yet, the movement may never have become as successful without Condé's power, access, and reach.

"At the time, we all knew somebody who had died; the statistics were terrifying," Penney recalled. "And nobody was talking about breast cancer." Looking back thirty years later, she felt only pride. "All I ever thought about was that the ribbon was everywhere," she said. "Look at what one idea could do."

The ribbon was a testament to the extraordinary impact that Condé Nast was having on the culture in the 1990s. Ten years after he brought aboard Tina, Anna, and Art Cooper at *GQ*, Si had seen the clout of his empire expand well beyond expectations. International editions of *Vogue*, *Vanity Fair*, and *GQ* were on newsstands in Europe, Asia, and

South America. Condé had muddled through an advertising dip in the 1990 recession and come out the other end, launching a new title, *Allure*, as the economy began to recover. *Allure* was arguably the first beauty magazine to take a journalistic approach to the then-burgeoning world of cosmetics. At seventy-eight, Alex, then in the twilight of his career, became deeply involved in its development, calling its editor, a former *New York Times* journalist named Linda Wells, at odd hours to impart sporadic nuggets of inspiration. Wells might answer her phone only to hear Alex say two words—"Dash! Vitality!"—and then a dial tone. Alex would call back a moment later, shout, "Style! Verve!" and hang up again.

Overseeing *Allure*'s avant-garde design was Polly Mellen, the exacting *Vogue* editor who issued pronouncements like "I'm feeling the color *toast!*" and had been responsible for, among other indelible images, the famous Avedon photograph of Nastassja Kinski erotically entangled with a snake. The British editor Grace Coddington had recently arrived at Anna Wintour's *Vogue*, and by Mellen's recollection, did not wish to work alongside her. So Si called Mellen to his office and suggested she join *Allure* as creative director.

"I don't want to go there, Si," Mellen replied.

"Well, what would you like, Polly?"

"I'd like my own magazine."

"Let's do this as an interim thing," Si replied, diplomatically. Mellen stayed for eight years.

The debut issue, in March 1991, was a signature Condé high/low blend of luscious visuals and literary writing—elevated craftsmanship applied to the most superficial of subjects. Wells commissioned an essay by Betty Friedan, who wrote about why feminists "don't have to go to war against love or lipstick." *Allure* was engineered to reassure readers that caring about the way they looked was consistent with leading an enlightened life. "Beauty is news," Wells wrote in her introductory note. "It is frivolous and serious, a mirror of society and a bit of frippery." What better slogan for Condé Nast itself?

Allure secured its true legacy in 1996, when Wells dreamed up the Best of Beauty awards, a mix of service journalism and clever marketing.

The cosmetics industry was booming—Sephora would open its first New York City boutique in 1998—and Wells felt shoppers needed a guide to the enormous number of products flooding the market. Initially, Si hated the idea. "This is going to be career suicide," he told Wells when she pitched him on the awards. *Allure* relied on cosmetic companies to advertise; what would L'Oréal think if the magazine told readers to buy a Lauder lipstick instead?

When the first batch of awards were published, in October 1996, *Allure* did no marketing or promotion, and some Condé executives privately hoped the feature would vanish into the ether. (Even Wells, in a letter to readers, acknowledged the awards could prove "a bold, even foolhardy move.") Fearing a backlash, Wells sent hand-delivered copies of the issue to the presidents of Chanel and Estée Lauder, accompanied by sprays of flowers. She needn't have worried: the companies began calling to report that readers were tearing out pages from the *Allure* awards to use as a reference guide when they shopped in a store. To Wells's shock, the cosmetic brands now wanted to reproduce the *Allure* seal of approval on the labels of their own products, and were willing to pay Condé Nast for the privilege. The perceived authority of Best of Beauty would soon create significant revenue for *Allure*—yet another successful monetization of Condé's aura of exclusivity. "The seal did more for the magazine than everything else," Wells told me. "I think the seal was responsible for keeping the magazine alive for so long." Indeed, Condé Nast shut down *Allure*'s print magazine in 2022. The Best of Beauty awards, considered the Oscars of the cosmetics world, live on.

AT *VOGUE*, ANNA WINTOUR was also wielding her power to shape the industry her magazine covered.

The reach of Condé Nast allowed Anna to single-handedly determine the fates of many designers—and therefore whose clothes would be coveted by the new class of American strivers. *Vogue* had always maintained close relations with the luxury world; in the 1960s, Diana Vreeland wooed Seventh Avenue *garmentos* and even provided them with sketches of her preferred designs. Ruth Ansel, a *Vogue* art director, recalled an anecdote about Vreeland glancing out a window at women on a Manhattan sidewalk and pointing out their footwear. "You see those women in those go-go boots?" Vreeland said. "I made them!"

Anna went further: she not only placed her preferred designers in *Vogue*, she also recommended their services to the executives who were forging today's modern fashion conglomerates. Anna put John Galliano in touch with the mogul Bernard Arnault, who hired Galliano to design for Givenchy and Dior. Marc Jacobs, another early Anna favorite, was later selected by Arnault to run Louis Vuitton. "She was the discoverer," Arnault said of Anna's influence. (Jacobs was never shy about being in Anna's debt. After one runway show, he raced to Anna's seat and dropped to his knees, beseeching her, "How did I do?") After Michael Kors, discovered by Anna back in her *New York* magazine days, ran into financial problems in the mid-1990s, Anna talked him up to her industry contacts and later helped midwife a $100 million sale of his company. When Anna organized *Vogue*'s hundredth-birthday party at the New York Public Library, in 1992, Karl Lagerfeld made a twenty-four-hour trip from Paris to attend. "I just came for Anna Wintour," he said. "For a one-night stand."

For the cover of *Vogue*'s centennial issue, Anna winkingly restaged a classic Irving Penn photograph with a bevy of supermodels—but instead of couture, the women were clad in mass-market jeans and dress shirts from the Gap. This was the new high/low *Vogue*, the fashion corollary to Tina's postmodern *Vanity Fair*: the imprimatur of Condé Nast updated for a more informal era of elite living.* Debutante balls and other vestiges of Mrs. Astor's New York had yielded to Wall Streeters in Japanese suits ordering bottle service at Tribeca nightclubs. Inside 350 Madison, even Alex Liberman had taken to wearing Comme des Garçons. And Anna was about to project these social shifts onto an even bigger national stage.

---

* Anna's editorial approach did have its critics. Grace Mirabella, in a 2000 interview, said her successor's *Vogue* suffered from "a rather severe, monied sensibility at the expense of real-world grace and beauty."

The Costume Institute gala, held annually by the Metropolitan Museum of Art, was for years the kind of fusty, high-WASP ritual of philanthropy and cheek-kissing that seemed to only exist in the pages of an Edith Wharton novel. Its roots date to 1948, when the museum threw a midnight ball in the Rainbow Room and charged guests fifty dollars a head. *Vogue*'s editor at the time, Edna Woolman Chase, was on the first organizing committee, and the magazine's ties to the event deepened after Diana Vreeland became a special consultant to the institute following her Condé defenestration. Vreeland jazzed up the soiree, but the scene remained a redoubt of aging fixtures of New York society, basically as parochial as an Upper East Side tradition could get.

When Pat Buckley (wife of William F.) stepped aside in 1995, after seventeen years in charge, Anna was asked to help reimagine the event for a new era. The idea stemmed from a pair of Anna's best-connected friends: Oscar and Annette de la Renta, the fashion designer and his socialite wife, who were donors to the Costume Institute and well acquainted with the *Vogue* editor's skills. (For years, Anna has vacationed at a villa designed by de la Renta in the Dominican Republic.) Anna was an important figure in the fashion world, but conveniently not a designer whose presence might pose a conflict of interest as the museum decided whose clothes to feature in each year's exhibit. Anna's instinct was to re-create, in the decorous and imposing halls of the Met's Fifth Avenue home, the imaginative fashion fantasies that played out in the lavish pages of her magazine. She persuaded Chanel and Versace—loyal *Vogue* advertisers, whose clothes Anna frequently wore—to contribute $500,000 to sponsor the event; Robert Isabell, the party planner who had devised several of Tina's *Vanity Fair* fetes, confected a gigantic Christmas tree of roses.

Anna flexed her editor-in-chief powers to haul in several gossip columns' worth of fashion stars and celebrities as guests. Karl Lagerfeld, Ralph Lauren, and Calvin Klein turned up, along with Claudia Schiffer, Richard Gere, and Henry Kravis. Kate Moss vanished into a ladies' room as her escort, Marc Jacobs, and a *Vogue* editor hollered her name outside, and Barry Diller struggled to reach his dinner table amid the sea of eight hundred well-groomed attendees. André Leon Talley, the on-again, off-again *Vogue* editor and Anna's on-again, off-again consigliere, coolly observed the proceedings and offered a reporter a prescient remark.

"This," Talley declared, "is Anna Wintour's great ascension into the social firmament."

Si Newhouse was there that night, too. His parents had attended balls like this, upper-crust events that were staples of the Park Avenue calendar. Now Si, as Anna's patron and benefactor, had become the event's de facto host. The guests still joked about Si's mumbling and his awkward mien, but it was a nervous laughter. Si was now the sovereign of this elite, his will carried in the fiefs of fashion, entertainment, and celebrity by regents like Anna Wintour. Increasingly, the American zeitgeist was produced, packaged, choreographed, and marketed by the forces of Condé Nast.

Frank DiGiacomo, who chronicled the Met Gala's transformation for *The New York Observer*, sensed "the collective coming-out for a new social order," a contemporary elite "whose position in the food chain is determined not by bloodlines but by blood, sweat, tears and a big bank account." The night before Anna's Met debut, the cable channel VH1 had staged the first live telecast of its fashion awards. The ceremony seemed to cement the marriage of fashion and mainstream popular culture that Anna had been driving forward with her celebrity-flecked *Vogue*. "The future is, after all, getting the clothes and images to the masses," one nominee told *The New York Times*. "My own personal goal is go mass. I'm not interested in being limited, insidery." Madonna, whose *Vogue* cover in 1989 had irked Grace Mirabella and repulsed Richard Avedon, received an award as Karl Lagerfeld and Gianni Versace sat in the audience and applauded. The *Times*'s fashion critic, Amy Spindler—whose role at the newspaper had only been created a year before, in recognition of the growing mainstream interest in the field—approved of the cultural amalgamation that the award show represented. "Fashion needs to be a part of a wider creative world," she wrote, "or it's only relevant to itself."

That the mainstreaming of fashion also happened to be the mainstreaming of Anna Wintour was a testament to Anna's unusual combination of editorial and entrepreneurial skills—and, for Condé Nast, a very happy alignment of incentives. As fashion got bigger, *Vogue* got fatter: more and more advertisers flocked to its pages, including the new luxury conglomerates that benefited from the growing public fascination with designers and stylists. Anna, in turn, used the Met Gala to further expand her once-provincial world. After a year off in 1996, when her rival Liz Tilberis of *Harper's Bazaar* took over hosting duties, Anna returned to the gala in 1997 with the most potent weapon in her celebrity arsenal: Madonna. The Material Girl was a neat fit to perform at that year's Costume Institute show, "Gianni Versace," a tribute to the recently murdered designer: both were agitators of Italian heritage who subverted Catholic iconography in their work. But the idea of unleashing a provocateur like Madonna in the Met's hallowed galleries proved too much for one doyenne. Jayne Wrightsman, a major collector and donor, took umbrage at this intrusion of low culture into high, and reportedly threatened to resign from the museum's board. In a sign of the times, the Met sided with its newer patron, Anna Wintour. Madonna attended that year's gala, and when a reporter asked about the dustup, the pop star shrugged.

"I don't even know who Jayne Wrightsman is," she said.

Anna next took charge of the event in 1999, the year she turned fifty, and she never again relinquished control. The 1999 edition was the fullest expression yet of how she viewed her role at *Vogue*: not merely an editor, but a grand convener of the culture. Her guests included Gwyneth Paltrow, Liam Neeson, Harvey Weinstein, Henry Kissinger, Jerry Seinfeld, and Ellen Barkin, a crew that ranged well beyond the runway. Perhaps Anna had sensed Si's satisfaction with the success of Graydon Carter's Oscar parties, and felt a need to compete. There are those around Anna who say she has an intrinsic need to outdo her own last act. Whatever the reason, Anna topped herself by arranging a performance by Sean "Puff Daddy" Combs, who sang his hit "I'll Be Missing You" alongside a live children's choir. After Combs left the stage, he was accosted by a towering white man in a tuxedo.

"Hello, Puff Daddy," the man said. "I'm David Koch." The billionaire industrialist smiled at the rapper. "You're a helluva performer."

Embedded in this moment were the seeds of what the Met Gala would become under Anna: a globally recognized spectacle and a staggering demonstration of Condé Nast's cultural sway. Even as Condé shrank and its magazines' influence ebbed—as *Vogue* itself drifted from its central role in the fashion world—the Met Gala reached new levels of opulence. In 2010, Anna installed a thirty-foot-tall hot-air balloon from South Dakota in one of the museum's interior courts. Today, the red carpet is covered live on television and *The New York Times* dedicates more than a dozen staff members to a live blog of the proceedings. As with its Condé cousin, the *VF* Oscar party, an invitation to the Met Gala is now among the most coveted tickets on earth. Minuscule details, like the order in which stars approach the carpeted staircase, are decided by Anna alone. George and Amal Clooney were granted a private bar so that they could decompress away from the crowd; a stash of European Coca-Cola was locked in an office so that Karl Lagerfeld could enjoy his favorite beverage. In total, Anna's Met Gala has raised more than $250 million for the Metropolitan Museum's Costume Institute, making the event one of the world's most successful philanthropic efforts in support of a cultural institution. As the excess increased, so have the prices; the ticket that cost fifty dollars in 1948 was $75,000 in 2024. Even Nan Kempner, the wealthy socialite, eventually became uneasy about the sheer scale of it.

"I just think it's terribly expensive, and I've been doing this party for God knows how many years," she said in 2003. "It seems to me it's gotten a little out of hand."

BY 1998, CONDÉ NAST HAD SET ITS SIGHTS on a new home for its glossy brand of luxury consumption: the former Soviet Union.

The idea of launching a *Vogue Russia* may have seemed odd, given the country's history of vilifying Western decadence. But the collapse of Communism had ushered in a nascent market economy that was birthing a new leisure class. Designer brands from Europe opened boutiques in a glitzy Moscow mall, and oligarchs' wives and girlfriends wanted the looks from Paris runways. *Vogue* executives sensed opportunity—and, amazingly, given the potential for ironic disaster, allowed a BBC camera crew to tag along. The ensuing documentary, *To Russia with Vogue*, is an eye-popping testament to the stumbles of Western businesses seeking riches in the new Russia and the grandiosity of Condé Nast, a company convinced of its civilizing powers in a harsh and unchic world.

"I feel a sense of mission that I don't feel in other places," Si's cousin Jonathan Newhouse, who led the international division, tells the camera as he tours the penthouse offices in Moscow that Condé leased for its local *Vogue* staff. "We talk about the fight between Communism and capitalism, or between totalitarianism and freedom," Newhouse continues. "But there was another battle, and that is the battle between ugliness and beauty. Without beauty, people suffer. And I think one of the reasons Communism fell was not only economic, or political—but because it was so ugly."

British Vogue staff members were flown in from London to train the Russian hires, including a domineering editor in chief with an Anna Wintour–like bob. Condé paid $2 million for billboards and television ads—one slogan was "In Russia. At Long Last."—and organized an elaborate launch party with guests like Donatella Versace and Karl Lagerfeld, to be held at a museum of Russian history on Red Square. The *Vogue Russia* team was busy ordering decorations and flowers from England when, days before the first issue's debut, the Russian economy collapsed. "They devalued the ruble?" asks a dumbfounded party planner. "*This morning?!*"

The Western luxury goods advertised in the magazine doubled in price overnight. As bread lines and bank runs break out in Moscow, the BBC crew catches *Vogue* editors debating whether to use a photo of the actress Julia Ormond for their next cover, and if the picture looks too much like something that would run in *Cosmopolitan*. Despite a "crisis discount" for advertisers, sales dry up. After the Red Square party is canceled, Jonathan Newhouse flies in to rally his troops. "Russia has a culture, a history, a greatness which few nations can equal, and a future, a great future," he says, noting his family's Russian ancestry. "One can't expect a transition from seventy years of Communism to a free-market society to be smooth." He continues, "We have kind of a sense of mission, that what we're doing really is important to the life of the people here.... We think *Vogue* matters, and in this country, *Vogue* is going to matter a lot." Newhouse was correct, to a point: *Vogue Russia* survived its initial crisis and eventually reached 800,000 readers, and Condé Nast added Cyrillic editions of *GQ, Tatler, Glamour,* and *Architectural Digest,* a full suite of lifestyle porn for Russia's new rich. But after Vladimir Putin invaded Ukraine in 2022 and enforced draconian censorship laws, Condé shut down its entire Russian operation. Even *Vogue* could not art-direct its way out of that one.

Condé's foray into Russia is understandable in light of the company's strategy for international growth: when a country with an emerging capitalist economy developed a new upper-middle-class, Condé Nast was there to swoop in with its guides to a lavish lifestyle. Luxury brands, themselves seeking a foothold in these regions, used the magazines to introduce their products to a fresh consumer base. Local readers felt affirmed that the likes of *Vogue* and *Vanity Fair*—world-famous emblems of the elite—considered their country worthy of attention and investment. In the BBC documentary, a *Russian Vogue* editor can be seen crying with joy as she flips through the pages of the inaugural issue. Condé's entry was a sign that a country had arrived.

It was all in keeping with the company's imperial moment. By the start of the 2000s, the sun never set on Si's global empire. *Vogue* had spawned editions across Europe, Asia, South America, and the South Pacific; one could do worse to trace the rise of global consumerism by dating the magazine's subsequent outposts in China (2005), India (2007), and the Persian Gulf states (2017). "The Arabs deserve their *Vogue,* and they've deserved it for a long, long time," said *Vogue Arabia*'s first editor in chief. Condé relied on a licensing model not unlike the Four Seasons hotel chain: while the properties were often locally owned, the proprietors were trained in the high standards expected of the brand, traveling to New York or London to watch more experienced *Vogue* editors in action. And unlike Si's profligate kingdom in Manhattan, the international division, run by Jonathan Newhouse from Condé's British headquarters, Vogue House, was reportedly profitable. "We covered our poor American brothers and sisters," quipped Bernd Runge, a former Condé executive who helped launch dozens of its global magazines.

There was precedent for this international reach. In the early years, Condé Montrose Nast shipped copies of American *Vogue* to London for distribution across Europe, until naval conflict broke out in the early years of World War I and nonessential imports like magazines were cut off. Nast responded by founding *British Vogue* in 1916, the first European edition of any major American fashion magazine. (*Harper's Bazaar* did not expand to Britain until 1929.) He followed with *Vogue Paris* in 1920, cementing the power of the Condé brand across three fashion capitals. Because Gilded Age Americans fetishized European design and taste, ideas about style typically traveled westward across the Atlantic; Nast's magazines helped reverse that flow, for the first time granting editors in New York a say in European trends. "*Vogue* carries to the four corners of an eagerly waiting world the secrets of the distinguished circle united through its efforts," the French poet Paul Géraldy wrote in 1923. Well before the rise of luxury conglomerates like LVMH, Condé magazines were serving as an early adhesive for the global elite.

AS HIS KINGDOM EXPANDED, Si decided he needed a palace to match.

Condé Nast had occupied its 350 Madison Avenue building for over twenty years, its entrance aptly nestled in between the flagship stores of the old-money men's clothiers Brooks Brothers and Paul Stuart. In 1996, the powerful developer Douglas Durst decided to build an office tower on a dilapidated site at the corner of Forty-second Street and Broadway, above the shuttered husk of a Nathan's Famous hot dog franchise. This was a big bet: Times Square, once the bustling heart of Manhattan, had dwindled into a seedy district populated by porn shops and third-run movie theaters, a symbol of New York's urban decay. Si smelled an opportunity. Condé Nast had the mystique that city officials hoped could revive that section of Midtown, and Durst was on the hunt for a big-name tenant to attract investment. The 350 Madison office, meanwhile, was aging and cramped, with the Newhouses forced to lease space in neighboring buildings to accommodate their growing stable. Si secured a below-market rent, naming rights for the building, and millions of dollars in state and local tax breaks. In exchange, Condé Nast would move two blocks west to Times Square.

It might as well have been New Jersey. Inside the company's status-crazed halls, editors agonized over the gaucheness of their new location and whether Condé's coveted 880 telephone prefix would move with them. (In the early 1990s, "880 Girls" was a common phrase in certain Manhattan social circles, referring to young women who worked at Condé with access to the hottest fashion and beauty products. The 880 prefix did not make it to the new building, although the 212 area code remained.) The added distance to Mangia, the high-end Italian lunch spot that delivered hundreds of dollars' worth of grilled eggplant each day to Condé staffers, was a matter of intense debate. An internal booklet about the move took pains to reassure editors that their new individual offices would contain sufficient closet space for their coats.

Si, however, viewed the new headquarters, dubbed 4 Times Square, as an opportunity to announce his company's dominance to the world. He spent an estimated $100 million on airy, light-filled interiors and state-of-the-art environmental features like solar panels and sustainable wood furniture. At 350 Madison, the windows opened to the street so editors could smoke at their desks; at 4 Times Square, they were sealed shut to minimize energy use. (One person familiar with Si's office swears that he installed a sole working window so that his pet pug could breathe fresh air.) Still, Si was aware of the grumbling. One day, over lunch, he and James Truman—Condé's editorial director and the man Si had put in charge of the relocation—hit upon an idea to make the move more palatable. They would build a cafeteria.

For a company whose backbiting culture was often compared to a high school, this was almost too on the nose. But dining had long played a crucial role in the Condé Nast mythology. Alex Liberman's insistence that Tina Brown sit in the correct tier of the Four Seasons

Grill Room (floor level, never mezzanine) had given way, by the early 1990s, to the much-studied seating hierarchy of 44, the restaurant at the Royalton Hotel that became known as "Club Condé." The restaurant, which opened in 1991, was steeped in Condé Nast: its British proprietor, Brian McNally, was longtime friends with Anna Wintour, who once put McNally's wife and daughter on the cover of *House & Garden*, with an accompanying feature written by Truman. Anna's patronage on opening day announced the arrival of an all-important new spot for the company.

Starting in 1992, the power triumvirate of Anna, Tina, and Graydon permanently occupied three of the Royalton's coveted lime-green banquettes; the fourth was left open for whichever A-lister had a reservation that day, although it was always available for Si in case he decided to come by. McNally kept a hefty folder at the hostess stand with a frequently updated directory of every Condé masthead. "Sometimes, Brian would ask, 'Whose number is this?' when a reservation would come in," recalled Gabé Doppelt, a former Condé editor. "I would look it up in the directory, and I'd say, 'Oh, a junior editor at *Glamour*,' which basically informed him that he could put them near the kitchen." VIPs, meanwhile, received service fit for a sultan. When Anna walked in for lunch, a cappuccino would be waiting at her table when she sat down. This was the result of an elaborate behind-the-scenes ballet: Because Anna sometimes arrived early or late, a designated kitchen worker began preparing cappuccinos ten minutes before her stated reservation time. If the drink sat for two minutes with no sign of Anna, it would be dumped out (or sent to another unsuspecting diner) and a new one was made. Dana Brown, who worked at the Royalton as a barback before joining *Vanity Fair*, calculated that nearly a dozen cappuccinos might be drawn and discarded in order to coordinate this perfect handoff.

To create his own hotspot inside 4 Times Square, Si had one person in mind: Frank Gehry, the world-renowned architect who at the time had never completed a project in New York City. Si and his wife, Victoria, an architectural historian, had met Gehry at a dinner party in Los Angeles in the early 1990s, where they discovered mutual passions for contemporary art and classical music. In 1995, Si and Victoria commissioned Gehry to build a new country home for them on the waterfront in Bellport, Long Island. The project fizzled, so Si, eager to find another collaboration, proposed that Gehry take on the new Condé offices instead. Gehry demurred, but when Truman suggested a cafeteria, the architect was intrigued. He knew that a project involving Condé Nast was sure to attract outsize publicity, and that Si's taste for cutting-edge design meant he could indulge his more imaginative and costly whims.

The result was the most scrutinized and celebrated corporate cafeteria in the world. Gehry's design, hashed out over several brainstorming sessions with Si, Victoria, and Truman, called for thirty-nine imitation-leather banquettes; highly amused by all the attention paid to the Royalton's seating chart, Gehry had decided that in his Condé canteen, nearly every table would be a booth. Blue titanium panels grew like stalactites from the room's perimeter walls, creating recesses that housed the lush banquettes and seemed to encourage furtive gossip. Seventy-six unique panels of sinuous Venetian glass dangled overhead, and the tabletops were made of taxi-yellow plastic laminate, perhaps a nod to the industrious city outside. Informed by Truman that Condé employed "mostly young women who were quite conscious of their appearance and their body shape," Gehry decided to affix distorted mirrors to the columns bracketing the cafeteria's exit doors, so that passersby looked smaller and thinner. "It was a very witty architectural gesture," Truman recalled. "He created something that encouraged performance, and made people look good and feel good." Idiosyncrasy, the indulgence of the rich, also had its place: garlic was banned from the cafeteria kitchens solely because Si abhorred it. Depending on who you ask, Si spent anywhere from $10 million to $30 million to enact Gehry's avant-garde vision. Truman laughed when I suggested that Si may have wanted an in-house dining room so he could save money on all those pricey lunches at the Royalton.

"There was no cost savings involved in this cafeteria, I assure you," he said.

When it opened, in 2000, Gehry's cafeteria received its own architectural review in *The New York Times*. "The company's fashion and beauty magazines offer monthly reflections on the human form as a universal intersection between nature and culture," wrote Herbert Muschamp. "Gehry has provided an ideal background for those who put out these primers in cultivation." An invitation to eat in this private sanctum of the Condé elite became a new status symbol in New York. Journalists offered inventive interpretations of the abstract design, with one describing the space as "slightly vaginal, accented by hanging chrome lamps which look like Fallopian tubes." According to Truman, Gehry's inspiration was more ecclesiastical than erotic. Early in the planning process, Gehry presented Truman and Si with a postcard of a Bellini portrait of Jesus wearing a blue robe; the architect pointed out Jesus's elbow, where the garment's sleeve concertinaed into a series of subtle folds. "Jesus was forgotten fairly quickly," Truman said, "but the beauty of the color and texture of the folds was the inspiration."

As always, Condé Nast was a trendsetter: in the years after it signed a lease at Times Square, the neighborhood became one of Manhattan's hottest commercial districts, with MTV, Reuters, and ABC News all moving in. And the endless tabloid coverage of the cafeteria's seating arrangements and celebrity sightings highlighted the ongoing public fascination with Condé Nast itself. What was it *like* to work with editors who spawned a thousand gossip items, who glided through the streets of Manhattan and Paris in the back seats of town cars, who paraded in custom Chanel suits and Manolo Blahniks in front of the paparazzi? *Vanity Fair* made celebrities of Hollywood agents and Wall Street corporate raiders; *Vogue* made A-listers of couturiers. Now, thanks to Tina, Anna, and Graydon, the stardust was falling on another once-obscure class of cultural gatekeepers: magazine editors. Life inside Condé Nast was becoming more decadent, more lavish, and more scrutinized than its Gilded Age progenitors could ever have imagined.

14

"Do It All Grandly!"

At its peak, Condé Nast was a bizarre, sui generis world that was simultaneously dysfunctional and successful. Because Si had endured his father's disappointment, he was driven to dominate his competitors in a manner that Sam would have approved. And because, as a young man, Si had experienced the wrong side of snobbery's sting, he was determined to signal his astuteness, his exquisite sensitivity to taste, an endeavor to which he applied the multibillion-dollar fortune at his disposal. "Si used money far more strategically than many people realized," recalled Katrina Heron, an editor in chief of *Wired*. "Rather, every penny went to satisfy his idea and expression of empire. He created a calculated fiefdom of which he was completely and autocratically in control."

Thus the culture of Condé Nast became an extension of Si's id. Budgets were for the unimaginative; to care about a budget was to reveal oneself as insufficiently devoted to the pursuit of excellence. This was a land of unspoken codes and byzantine social rules, proficiency in which was required in order to succeed. The proper knotting of an ascot; the angle of a tie bar; how you dressed, how you spoke, where you went, who you knew—these considerations mattered deeply. What might have been superficial in other contexts took on outsize importance at a company defined by its mastery of perception and the minutest criteria of caste. Once, Alex Liberman overheard an editor mispronounce

Françoise de la Renta—Oscar's first wife and a *Vogue* editor herself—as "fran-SWAH," not the correct "fran-SWAZZ." Alex's eyes narrowed. The editor was out of a job weeks later.

"That was the kind of thing that would kill your career," recalled one *Vogue* veteran. "It revealed you were not a truly worldly person."

Those who thrived there recall a paradise; those who flailed, a perdition. Oddly enough, the most widely known pop cultural depiction of the company, the Meryl Streep and Anne Hathaway film *The Devil Wears Prada*, is perhaps the most accurate. Not because the movie gets all of the details right (it doesn't), or because *Runway* and Miranda Priestly are exact stand-ins for *Vogue* and Anna Wintour (they aren't), but because it captures the anxiety and ambition, self-discipline and self-regard, seriousness about silly things and silliness about serious things that defined the modern Condé Nast.

JOAN KRON WAS A SOUGHT-AFTER magazine writer in the 1980s when she was contacted about the possibility of taking over the editorship of *House & Garden*. A meeting with Si went well, and she left with the sense that the job might be hers.

Then Alex Liberman asked her to lunch at La Grenouille.

"He insisted that we have asparagus," Kron said. "When the asparagus comes, it's sitting in oodles and oodles of dressing." Kron, hoping to appear fastidious, used her salad fork to pierce the stalks. "And Alex proceeds to pick up his asparagus and eat it by hand! Which I learned later was the European style." She did not get the job.

"This is what I failed at," Kron told me, laughing about it years later. "Eating asparagus."*

Lucy Sisman was a highly respected graphic designer when Liberman summoned her to his weekend estate in Connecticut to discuss a position at *Allure*, then still in the prototype stage. He greeted her

---

* Years later, Kron would be hired as a writer at *Allure*, where she became a leading authority on plastic surgery. She told me that she crossed paths with Alex at the magazine's kickoff party. "We finally got you, my dear!" he said cheerfully, omitting any mention of the asparagus incident.

in painters' overalls and invited her to take a ride around the property in his muscle car. Soon, she was hanging on for dear life. "He drove with reckless speed, like some sort of rally driver," she recalled. "I was gripping the handles." (One of Si's friends recalled a similarly terrifying experience, in which the publisher tore his small boat around the crowded harbor near his country house in Bellport, Long Island.) Alex's assessment of Sisman's ability, she said, "was as much about my endurance of my terrifying ride as it was about anything else." Sisman got hired. "I was just grateful I'd worn flat shoes."

Lots of Condé alums recall just how important it was to master the folkways of the place. "I had to learn how to speak like a Condé Nast person," said Jennifer Barnett, who grew up as a Navy brat and had no connections in Manhattan media when she moved to the city from Virginia in 1999. She was eking out a living at Hearst's mid-market magazine *Redbook* when a chance encounter on the L train led to a job at *Teen Vogue* in 2004, the year after the magazine launched. "I would have worked at any publication at Condé Nast," she recalled. "It seemed really fun and really glamorous." She paid for a manicure and a blowout before her interview; when she was hired as the magazine's managing editor, "I felt like I was Willy Wonka with the golden ticket."

Even though she was bowled over by the glamour of her new workplace, Barnett quickly learned to adopt a default insouciance. "An editor in the elevator would say, 'I'm going to have cocktails with Heidi Klum because she's launching her Birkenstock line,'" she recalled. "Everyone around nodded like, 'Yes, of course that's what you're doing.'" Language itself became a balancing act, with staffers feeling an implicit pressure to express themselves only in euphemistic, status-saving terms. Once, Alex objected when a colleague used the term *flee* to describe his family's escape from Bolshevik Russia. "No, no. I didn't flee," Alex clarified. "It was an orderly exit."

"You never say anything to anyone directly," Barnett recalled. "You couch it all in flattery, and insinuation, which I did not know how to do. It was all very polished." When a stylist botched a photo shoot, it was up to Barnett to break the news that the feature had been killed. "The way I had to do it was convey to her how much she was loved.

'*Everyone* loves you! Amy [Astley, *Teen Vogue*'s editor at the time] adores you.' Just reinforce how *fabulous* they were. And then you'd literally slip it in. I would say, 'We've gone in a different direction.' So flattering and so gentle. There was never to be a harsh word directly. If you were getting fired, you'd barely know." Indeed, one Condé Nast employee was fired on the office elevator between the twelfth and fifteenth floors. His boss was leaving on vacation and asked for help carrying luggage to the lobby. As the car descended, the following scene played out:

"Darling, I had a wonderful idea: Why don't you become a contributing editor?"

"Am I . . . fired?"

"Nothing like that, really, dear!"

The man deposited his boss into a waiting limousine. When he walked back into the building, a personnel director was waiting for him: "If you have a minute, follow me into my office." The deed was done.

Liberman once confided his own subtle method of severing ties:

This is what I find best. Do it at the end of the day, not early. Just before they're about to leave, go to their office, not yours. If you can sit next to them, on a couch, or a chair side by side, it's better than doing it over a desk. Touch them—their shoulder, their elbow—and call them by name. Say, "George, may I be completely frank?" They always say yes. Then you can put the knife in and gut them right away. "All right, George. It's not going to do. They're going to fire you tomorrow, so clean out your desk tonight. There's nothing I can do." There. You've said it. Don't try to explain; they'll go on for some time. Steel yourself and listen. Listen for as long as you possibly can as they unburden themselves. When you can't bear it a moment longer, calmly reach into your jacket and take out your agenda. Turn to a date two or two and a half weeks from that day, and make a lunch date. Do it someplace public, like the Four Seasons or Le Cirque. Say, "I don't want to lose you, George. Let's have lunch on the twenty-whatever." Never break that lunch date, ever. And remember, they think they still might get something from you, so they won't be nearly as nasty as they could be.

It was all of a piece with the conspicuous *civility* of the place, which prevailed even at moments of extreme ruthlessness. Condé's swans were serene on the surface, even as they furiously kicked their legs underneath. "There was a way to comport yourself that was very strict," recalled Linda Wells, who started her career at *Vogue* and then edited *Allure* for twenty-four years. "If you worked at *Vogue*, you had to embody the *Vogue* attitude. You might be making $10,000 a year and not be able to buy a movie ticket, but you had to be the biggest snob ever about which caviar was served, or would you have it with Champagne or sparkling wine." The implicit pressure to live stylishly was intense. "We were in heels, Manolos," recalled Plum Sykes, who joined *Vogue* in the late 1990s. "It was considered extremely unprofessional to go into the office in flat shoes. Maybe a pair of Chanel ballet flats, but a pair of brogues, absolutely not." Sykes had a reputation as a quintessential "*Vogue* girl": an Oxford grad with London society connections, rail-thin, hardworking, and a fixture of Manhattan's junior party scene. "The clothes that people wear here in the day are probably clothes that normal people would wear on their most glamorous night out of the year," Sykes said. "Who is going to wear a chiffon Dolce & Gabbana skirt like this to the office? Only me! Or only someone who works at *Vogue*."

Sometimes, conforming to Condé's expectations meant changing more than one's outfit.

Right out of college, Carolyne Volpe landed her dream job as an assistant in the beauty department at *Vanity Fair*. She was over the moon; Volpe loved magazines and she was excited to work with Sun-Hee Grinnell, the magazine's uber-chic beauty editor. A few days into the job, Grinnell approached Volpe with a request. There was already another woman named Caroline working at the magazine, and it was confusing to have two. It would be a lot easier if Volpe went by her given name, Lynden, instead.

"I really like the name 'Lynden,'" Grinnell told her, "so I'm going to call you that."

Volpe had gone by Carolyne, a nickname bestowed by her parents, since she was an infant. On a dime, Carolyne was no more. "I was absolutely terrified of her," Volpe recalled. "I would do whatever she said." All her post-college friends know her as Lynden Volpe, the name she still uses professionally. Her mother was dumbfounded—"Why would you decide that?" she asked her daughter—but looking back, Volpe sees changing her name as just a natural part of fitting into the glam world of Condé Nast. Her boss "definitely wanted things a certain way, and wanted things to appear a certain way," Volpe said. "She thought it was a chicer, more unique name, which it probably is."

"Basically," Volpe added, "anything she would have said to do, I would have said yes."

IN NAVIGATING ALL THESE TACIT EXPECTATIONS, it helped to be rich. Nepotism was a fact of life at Condé Nast—at one point, dozens of Newhouses were employed throughout the company—and coveted, if menial, entry-level jobs often went to the well-connected. Tina Brown hired Angela Janklow, daughter of her powerful literary agent Morton Janklow, at *Vanity Fair*, where one eyewitness recalled Angela installing a light-up makeup mirror at her cubicle. The extended Janklow network was a noted beneficiary of Tina's largesse: the November 1986 issue of *Vanity Fair* included an article by the writer Barbara Goldsmith, represented by Janklow; an article on the Lincoln Center Theater, where Janklow's wife, Linda, was a director; an article on Warner LeRoy, Janklow's brother-in-law; and an article by Angela. The apparent coziness was so glaring that *The New York Times* ran an item about it—only to backtrack a day later in an unusual "editors' note," informing readers that the newspaper "possessed no evidence" of any favoritism toward the Janklows at *Vanity Fair* and dismissing its own article as "unwarranted." The fact that this quasi-correction appeared at all was, ironically, an even clearer sign of Janklow's—and Tina's—influence in Manhattan media circles.

At Condé, pedigree had a professional purpose, too. Its magazines *needed* the sons and daughters of aristocrats to ensure continued access to the rarefied worlds they covered. If *Vogue* wanted to photograph the private gardens of, say, a minor Spanish royal, it helped to have the aristocrat's backgammon partners on speed dial. Hence the hiring of Prince Michael of Greece as a contributor to *Architectural Digest*, in case an editor wanted to stage a shoot at a palace on Corfu. Some well-heeled employees didn't bother to cash their payroll checks at all, prompting awkward reminder calls from the Condé accounting department. One grandee requested that her payments simply be forwarded straight to the New York City Ballet.

It also helped to be European. Kate Reardon was a well-bred nineteen-year-old in London in the late 1980s when she idly told a woman at a party that she wanted to work in magazines. The woman suggested she write to a friend: Bernard Leser, then Condé's president. Suddenly, Reardon was on a flight to New York for an interview. Reardon figured somebody was impressed by her chic London postal address, or assumed she was Leser's goddaughter. "I had absolutely no qualifications," she recalled. "I had been given two weeks' work experience at British *Elle*, but I hadn't turned up for the second week because I was bored." She was immediately hired as an assistant at *Vogue*, a coup she attributed to her posh English accent. (Telephone etiquette was an important focus at Condé Nast, where for decades new hires attended an orientation session on the proper way to answer calls and take messages.) Reardon soon found herself at a lavish *Vogue* photo shoot with Alec, Stephen, and William Baldwin, and a catered sushi lunch. "All my friends were at some excruciating B-level university in England and I was fawning around in stretch limos with Patrick Demarchelier and all the Baldwin brothers at once," recalled Reardon, who went on to become editor in chief of Condé's British magazine *Tatler*. "It was heaven."

But creating glamour wasn't always so glamorous. One exacting editor charged her assistant with the less-than-exalted task of removing the blueberries from her morning muffin; the editor preferred the *essence* of blueberries, she explained, but not the taste of the berries themselves. Vera Wang was a wealthy former debutante when she was hired as an assistant to Polly Mellen at *Vogue*. Wang showed up for her first day of work in a crisp white YSL dress. "Dearie," Mellen told her, "you're going to have to go home and change out of that dress, because you're going to be on the ground here crawling around" on the floor of the fashion closet. The Herculean trials of Anna Wintour's fleet of assistants (she usually employs two or three at a time) have passed into magazine legend: the 7:30 a.m. arrivals, the relentless flood of need-it-now tasks, from ferrying her clothes to the elite dry cleaner Madame Paulette to monitoring the tracking devices of her goldendoodles. Instructions for many of these responsibilities were maintained in a twenty-one-page booklet presented to her assistants upon hiring.

Anna's brusque management style has fueled her intimidating public image. One *Vogue* editor was in a meeting with Anna when the telephone rang; Anna answered, then grabbed a tube of lipstick and scrawled a message on a sheet of paper that she silently handed across the desk: "Please leave." But her workplace behavior did not substantially differ from those of hard-charging male chief executives in other competitive industries, who often rely on underlings to handle personal errands and evince little patience for ineptitude. The enduring caricature of Anna as a sadistic boss speaks in part to the sexist attitudes through which her career—along with the broader domain of Condé Nast—is often perceived.

FOR MIDDLE-CLASS MORTALS hoping to gain entry to Condé Nast, the application process could resemble an admissions interview at a finishing school. For many years, applicants for entry-level positions were administered a typing test—fifty words a minute, six mistakes allowed—as a minder watched over their shoulder, highlighting mistakes with a red pen. Polly Mellen was known to drop a pencil on the floor during an interview; if the assistant didn't lean down to pick it up for her, they were dismissed. In 1951, when a twenty-one-year-old Jacqueline Bouvier applied for a position at *Vogue*, one of the standard questions on the Condé Nast employment form was "Are you a Communist?" (Bouvier's answer: "No.") Condé also sought information about an applicant's hobbies, club memberships, and "amusements" (Bouvier: "riding, theatre and tennis"), a not-so-subtle way of discerning social rank that indicated a fitness for Condé's upper-class culture.

By the mid-1990s, the divining of status persisted in other ways. In 1994, applicants to become assistants at *Vogue* were presented with an impromptu oral exam: four typed pages of 178 notable people, places, institutions, literary titles, and other cultural ephemera, all of which had to be identified on the spot. It was at once a test of elite cultural literacy, and a striking declaration of the sort of shared knowledge and values that mattered at a place like *Vogue*—which, like the rest of Condé's magazines, was itself a monthly dispatch of people, places, and ideas, both high and low, that its editors believed a discerning citizen ought to know about. The ideal candidate would recognize Fassbinder as the New German Cinema director, Evan Dando as the lead singer of the Lemonheads, the Connaught as the London luxury hotel, and the opening sentence of Proust's "Swann's Way." Devised by the *Vogue* editors William Norwich and Charles Gandee, the list is an insight into the status-conscious universe that Condé wanted employees to be conversant in, even those whose main role at the company would be fetching cappuccinos for their boss. Want to be a part of Condé Nast? This was your obstacle course:

Pedro Almodóvar
American Psycho
Marian Anderson
April is the cruellest month
Richard Avedon
Azzedine Alaïa
Robert Altman
BAM
Barbarians at the Gate
St. Barts
Anne Bass
Cecil Beaton
Sandra Bernhard
Bernardo Bertolucci
Manolo Blahnik

Molly Bloom
Mary Boone
Breathless
Tina Brown
Holly Brubach
CAA
Jane Campion
John Cassavetes
Chateau Marmont
Tina Chow
Claridge's
Eldridge Cleaver
Francesco Clements
The Conformist
The Connaught
Quentin Crisp

Mrs. Dalloway
Evan Dando
Angela Davis
Day of the Locust
Norma Desmond
Leonardo DiCaprio
Barry Diller
DKNY
Dolce & Gabbana
Isadora Duncan (How did she die?)
Marguerite Duras
Marian Wright Edelman
8 1/2
Michael Eisner

Bret Easton Ellis
Esalen
Even Cowgirls Get the Blues
The Face
Jerry Falwell
Fassbinder
Fear of Flying
Henry Fielding
Karen Finley
Eric Fischl
Gennifer Flowers
For a long time I used to go to bed early
Eileen Ford
"44"
Jean Michel Frank
Stephen Frears
Freud: Bella, Lucian, Sigmund
Squeaky Fromme
Larry Gagosian
Jean Paul Gaultier
David Geffen
Frank Gehry
André Gide
Romeo Gigli
Ruth Ginsburg
Jean-Luc Godard
The Good Soldier
C. Z. Guest
Jessica Hahn
Ashley Hamilton
Eve Harrington
Jean Harris
Juliana Hatfield
Haute Couture
Hermès
Jenny Holzer
Humbert Humbert
Iman
Derek Jarman
Jim Jarmusch
Tom Jones
Neil Jordan
Jules and Jim
Louis Kahn
Rei Kawakubo
Ken Kesey
Jack Kevorkian
Anthony Kiedis
Anselm Kiefer
Jamaica Kincaid
Larry Kramer
La Dolce Vita
Christian Lacroix
Karl Lagerfeld
Le Corbusier
Annie Leibovitz
Fran Lebowitz
Courtney Love
David Lynch
The Magic Mountain
Janet Malcolm
Robert Mapplethorpe
Peter Martins
Hattie McDaniel
Jay McInerney
Steven Meisel
Susan Minot
MOCA/MoMA/La Mama
Kate Moss
Vladimir Nabokov
Liam Neeson
S. I. Newhouse
Frank O'Hara
Oribe
Our Lady of the Flowers
Out
Michael Ovitz
Palais-Royal
Bob Packwood
Paris, Texas
Irving Penn
Père Lachaise
PETA
Pink Flamingos
Place des Vosges
Sylvia Plath
Ezra Pound
Prada
Prescriptives
Wolfgang Puck
The Raleigh
Charlotte Rampling
Herb Ritts
Gena Rowlands
Dominique Sanda
Ed Schlossberg
Jean Seberg
The Seventh Seal
Donna Shalala
Cindy Sherman

Randy Shilts	Jon Stewart	Veruschka
Andrew Shue	Ben Stiller	Diana Vreeland
Siegfried & Roy	Stonewall	George Wallace
Mona Simpson	Studio 54	Wendy Wasserstein
Anna Deavere Smith	Niki Taylor	John Waters
Anna Nicole Smith	Trash, Heat, Flesh	Veronica Webb
Paul Smith	James Truman	William Wegman
South Beach	Christy Turlington	Wim Wenders
Spago	Cy Twombly	The White Album
Special K	Gus Van Sant	Wigstock
Gayfryd Steinberg	Eddie Vedder	Billy Wilder

"We did it as much for ourselves as for our colleagues and for the applicants," Norwich recalled. "I thought it was too long, and Charles thought it was too short!" The list performed its function: Norwich confirmed that he weeded out several *Vogue* applicants who had never heard of Diana Vreeland.

Being in charge of a Condé Nast publication carried its own highly specific set of expectations. When the editor in chief of *Wired*, Katrina Heron, flew to New York to meet with her new bosses, she booked a modest room at the mid-market Royalton. Steve Florio chastised her and told her to switch to a hotel more commensurate with her position. She ended up at the St. Regis on Fifth Avenue, which was several times the price. "Good," Florio said, when he heard about her new digs. "When people have breakfast with you, they *want* you to be staying at the St. Regis."

Lucy Sisman, the art director at *Allure*, was similarly scolded when she attended her first Paris fashion week as a Condé employee. The phone in her undistinguished hotel room rang, and she heard Alex's voice on the other end.

"I understand that you're not staying at the Ritz."

"That's right."

"My art directors stay at the Ritz."

"There was a kind of largeness to being an editor in chief that was an uncomfortable role for me," recalled Linda Wells, who was a reporter at *The New York Times* when Alex recruited her to edit *Allure* in 1990. "As a reporter at the *Times*, your job is to be watching what happened, to essentially be invisible. And suddenly I *had* to be visible and be a public person. I had to entertain, and go to benefits and co-chair benefits, and get press. It was so foreign to me. Like, *boom*, I had to be it. I never anticipated that part of the job." Dominique Browning, the editor who relaunched *House & Garden* in 1996, would be hauled into Steve Florio's office to be reprimanded: "You're not in Page Six enough. We need to see you wearing more designer clothing." Those who felt uneasy about embodying the Condé brand tended not to last long at the company. When John Leland, a mild-mannered *Newsweek* editor, was hired in 1994 to run the edgy Condé men's magazine *Details*, he was presented with a major perk: a leased Mercedes sedan. "I wasn't that interested, but they felt I should have a car," Leland recalled. He felt uncomfortable driving in a luxury vehicle—"it was a carjacking waiting to happen"—and eventually swapped it out for a more modest Saab convertible. Later, Leland chafed when his bosses dispatched him to hobnob with Gianni Versace at the Milan men's fashion shows, a milieu where he felt woefully out of place. Leland tried to democratize the articles in *Details*, hoping that readers in their twenties and thirties would find their own lives and challenges reflected in its pages. Democracy, it turned out, was not desirable at Condé Nast: he was ousted after ten months.

BUT IF YOU MADE IT AT CONDÉ NAST, you reaped the spoils.

The mandate to live expensively had deep roots in the company's DNA. In 1928, when Edna Woolman Chase was planning to build a country home on Long Island, Condé Montrose Nast offered her a gift of $100,000—$1.8 million in today's dollars—for its construction. Edward Steichen, the pioneering fashion photographer, received a $35,000 contract to shoot for *Vogue* and *Vanity Fair* in 1923—$625,000 in today's dollars. Alex Liberman believed deeply in this tradition. For decades, he served as the in-house philosopher of excess, defending the company's decadent spending as the necessary price of achieving artistic excellence. Alex was a proselytizer of waste—creative waste. It cost money to generate the avant-garde design, iconic photographs, and ambitiously reported journalism that distinguished Condé Nast from its competitors, to reach the heights that Alex believed were necessary for the company to be, as he put it, "one of the great civilizing forces in America." Thanks to Alex's ideas and Si's largesse, Condé culture boiled down to a simple dictate: it was always better to spend than not to spend.

Editors were encouraged to toss away photo shoots and kill expensive articles. When *Vogue* commissioned Irving Penn to photograph a broken Champagne glass, Alex insisted that the magazine smash a hundred samples from Cartier in order to procure the perfect image. "We were always given this idea that you had to aim for some sort of artistic perfection," said the photographer Sheila Metzner, another Liberman protégée. "Your references were the greatest movies, or the greatest books, or the greatest artists—and whatever you had done before, you had to do better than that." This was the mandate that allowed Diana Vreeland, in the 1960s, to spend tens of thousands of dollars insisting that Richard Avedon twice reshoot a fashion spread on the color green. Vreeland wanted the hue to resemble the baize of a billiards table, and upon reviewing Avedon's contact sheets, she was convinced the photographer hadn't gotten the color quite right. Finally, fed up, Avedon tore off a strip of felt from an actual pool table and presented it to Vreeland's office. See? he demanded. It's the right hue.

"Oh," Vreeland said, distractedly. "But I meant a billiard table in the late afternoon sunlight!"

Vreeland once flew David Bailey to India for a shoot involving white tigers that never ran. Recalling that the British photographer Norman Parkinson had glimpsed fields with white horses on a trip to Tahiti, she enlisted him to return to the island, "select the finest Arab stallion," and drape the animal in mounds of silver and gold fabric. Upon arrival, Parkinson was told that all of the white horses had been eaten by French colonizers. When a (brown) stallion was finally located, and weighed down with 150 pounds of fabric, the horse got spooked and leaped into the air, sending the fabric flying. A pony had to be used instead.

When Polly Mellen came over from *Harper's Bazaar* in 1966, her first assignment was "The Great Fur Caravan," a five-week-long, first-class tour of Japan with Avedon and the model Veruschka, accompanied by enormous trunks of winter clothing carried by a crew of local laborers.

"Money," Mellen told me fifty-six years later, "was not something that was given a thought."

The grand only got grander when Si Newhouse took full control of his father's company, and Condé's revenues and relevance began to swell. Alex, who saw no distinction between creative pursuit and financial comfort, believed that the propagators of Condé's luxurious dreamland ought to live inside the lives they conjured on the page. "I believe that money should be used to facilitate a creative life and to eliminate fatigue," he said. "I take taxis all the time; I find them restful and stimulating." Shortly after Grace Mirabella assumed the editorship of *Vogue* in the early 1970s, Alex called her to his office at 350 Madison and offered some advice on an upcoming shoot she was overseeing in Paris. "Take the Concorde," Alex instructed. "Spend a lot of money. Get yourself there in the most expensive way possible, take pictures over ten times if you need to. *Do it all grandly!*"

Perks were legion. One *Vanity Fair* editor, on assignment in London, lived in the Dorchester hotel with her husband and children for a month—with a separate room reserved for their full-time nanny. A *VF* writer flew back and forth to London for a ten-minute interview with Tony Blair. Todd Purdum estimates that he spent $100,000 on an article for Graydon about London's financial industry that never ran. Once, Annie Leibovitz ran up a $475,000 bill for a Hollywood Issue shoot that involved an elaborately constructed set that traveled from Los Angeles to New York to London. ("It was like Vietnam, the expenses," Graydon recalled.) Over lunch with Si, Graydon gingerly broached the subject.

"I do have to talk to you about something," Graydon began. "It's a good-news-bad-news situation."

"What's the bad news?" Si asked.

"I think we just shot the most expensive cover in magazine history."

"How much?"

"$475,000."

Si paused. "What's the good news?"

"It looks like a $475,000 cover."

Si was fine with it.

In fact, the notion that an editor might concern herself with a subject as gauche as money was viewed as . . . déclassé. "If you're not 10 percent over budget," *GQ*'s Art Cooper once told a colleague, "you're a wimp." During one pleasant period, Condé editors were allowed to have Federal Express pick up their luggage and ship it to their hotel ahead of them, so they could travel light. Around the same time, an assistant at the magazine happened to glance at Annie Leibovitz's expenses for a single photo shoot and realized it was more than they made in a year.

The company footed the bill for any number of eccentric costs. When the writer Ann Patchett flew to the Amazon for a story in *Gourmet*, she stumbled on a turtle for sale at an outdoor market. She called her editor, William Sertl, to see if Condé would pay for her to buy the animal and save it. Sertl approved, citing a policy "that permits writers to expense any animal that rhymes with the name of their editor." Max Vadukul, a staff photographer at Tina's *New Yorker*, was in India, staking out the Catholic mission of Mother Teresa, when his team sought shade under a nearby tree. A monkey clambered down a branch and snatched a bag containing thousands of dollars in cash out of his editor's pocket—the funds for the entire rest of their stay. Vadukul's assistant sent a fax to Condé Nast (complete with a drawing of a monkey) that explained their predicament, and the company wired over thousands more.

Photo shoots were particularly elaborate affairs. In 1988, the *Vogue* editor Stephen Drucker spent three weeks in Kenya for a safari-themed shoot with the actress Kim Basinger. Twenty-three trunks of clothing and props were shipped to the African heartland, where a large crew slept in tents equipped with electricity and working toilets. The shoot was a disaster. Basinger's couture high heels kept sinking into the mud. Polly Mellen, the fashion editor, rented a falcon and chained it to Basinger's wrist; terrified, the actress was in a near panic that the bird would peck her face. At one point, a team of assistants was tasked with surrounding Basinger with a canopy of parasols to protect her skin from the hot sun. Sheila Metzner, surveying this chaotic and confused scene, turned to Drucker and whispered, "There is such truth in this moment." (Later, the older English gentleman who was serving as *Vogue*'s safari guide sidled up to Drucker. "Is it really like this for you 365 days a year?" he asked.)

In 1989, Tina Brown paid for Leibovitz to fly forty-one thousand air miles in first class—and develop 1,500 camera rolls, at a time when film processing was hugely expensive—to create a massive end-of-the-decade *Vanity Fair* portfolio of stars like Rupert Murdoch and Michael Jackson. Later, when Leibovitz balked at a *Vanity Fair* contract renewal, Si instructed Graydon Carter to acquiesce to the photographer's request for a $250,000 salary boost, on top of the hundreds of thousands of dollars she was already paid each year.

"Don't nickel and dime her," Si said.

In a practice dating to mid-century, Condé also provided access to "petty cash," a perk in which magazine staffers could walk up to an in-house teller, working behind a bank-like glass window in 350 Madison, and request money to pay for incidental expenses, including, but certainly not limited to: lunches, dinners, breakfasts; taxi rides, dry cleaning, gym passes; movies, Broadway plays, concerts; cigarettes, six-packs, and bottles of Champagne. Recipients were expected to sign for the cash, which was kept in a physical vault inside the Condé building. The amount of money that was disbursed could be stunning. In the early nineties, Hamilton South, Tina Brown's editorial promotions director, was wrangling a major Hollywood event for *Vanity Fair* on the Sony Pictures studio lot, where he was having trouble coaxing unionized workers into performing tasks outside of their usual duties. The solution, he discovered, was to hand over envelopes of money. During a three-month period, South withdrew "many many thousands of dollars" from the petty cash window in New York, and brought it to California to use for bribes.

By the late 1980s, black cars, queued and purring outside the Condé Nast offices, had become an icon of the company and its swagger. A generation of Condé personnel enjoyed the pleasures of Big Apple Car Service, the company's hired fleet of limousines and town cars.

High-ranking editors were often granted a personal full-time driver, available at all hours of the day. (An option of smoking or nonsmoking car was provided.) Stacks of Big Apple vouchers were kept in every magazine's office, readily disbursed to assistants and interns who needed to zip a rack of skirts to a fashion shoot or collect contact sheets from a star photographer's studio. The rides, charged directly to a central Condé Nast account, occurred more or less unsupervised; any employee could hop into a Big Apple car and specify where they wanted to go, no questions asked. Some advantage-taking occurred. Eliot Kaplan, a *GQ* editor, said he took a black car to his chiropractor appointments twice a week, and the car waited for him outside until he came out. At least one editorial assistant used a car for a drug run. Another high-ranking editor routinely called a Big Apple car to pick up his Chinese takeout, charging Condé for an empty vehicle to ferry around a box of lo mein. Si got wind of that one—and he signed off. As Si explained it: Condé did not have to answer to shareholders, and it was important to keep valued employees happy.

Big Apple Car signed its contract with Condé Nast in 1988, the year Anna Wintour took over *Vogue*. By the early 2000s, the account represented 30 percent of Big Apple's annual revenue. As many as 170 Big Apple cars handled Condé rides on workdays between noon and 7 p.m., but few of the well-coiffed passengers knew much about the company behind this most indispensable of perks. Big Apple Car was owned and operated by a woman named Diana Clemente, the eldest daughter of one of New York's last Mafia kingpins. Her father, Anthony Spero, a Bonanno family consigliere, ran his enterprise from an unassuming building in Bath Beach, Brooklyn, that also housed a pet shop called And Your Little Dog Too; the car service headquarters were next door.* Big Apple became so ingrained in Condé's corporate culture that a dedicated dispatcher was stationed at the building: Louis "Red" Menchicchi, a cigar-smoking, suspender-wearing Staten Islander who wielded a beeper and a walkie-talkie to direct the endless stream

---

* Spero had two pursuits—executing the duties of La Cosa Nostra, and breeding champion pigeons—and he was sentenced to life in prison in 2002 for ordering three homicides.

of limo traffic. (At Christmastime, he dressed up as Santa Claus.) Menchicchi went fishing with Steve Florio, and when Florio's daughter got married in Florida, Menchicchi attended as a guest; Diana Clemente went, too. Even after the 2008 stock market crash, when Condé's finances were flagging, the Newhouses ensured that the black car culture would continue. When the family negotiated a move to 1 World Trade Center in the early 2010s, hours of discussions with the landlord concerned the logistics of ensuring that town cars could easily access the building without interference from the post-9/11 security apparatus at Ground Zero. When Art Cooper was pushed out of *GQ* in 2003 after a twenty-year tenure, he wryly acknowledged his favorite amenity in a farewell toast. "I shall miss seeing you," Art told his fellow editors, "but I'll probably see you more than you think. I've accepted a job as a Big Apple VIP driver."

Perhaps the most legendary perk of all were the interest-free loans offered to top editors and executives, allowing them to live in the sorts of opulent apartments and homes that regularly appeared in the pages of their magazines. Condé signed on as the mortgage guarantor, or in some cases purchased a property outright, with the editor only responsible for monthly costs. Longer-serving editors, in subsequent contract negotiations, sometimes earned a forgiveness of the loan, which effectively added ownership of a multimillion-dollar property to their compensation packages. Condé was the lender on a $1.64 million mortgage for Anna Wintour's Greenwich Village town house in 1993. Advance Publications, Condé's parent entity, lent Graydon Carter $3.8 million for his four-story Greek Revival–style town house on Bank Street in the West Village. When David Remnick and his family bought an Upper West Side duplex in 2000, listed at $3.25 million, Advance secured the loan. It wasn't only editors in chief who benefited. Grace Coddington, one of Anna's top deputies at *Vogue*, borrowed $400,000 from the company when she bought a West Village apartment; Maurie Perl, the company's head of public relations, received assistance when she bought on the Upper West Side. Condé secured mortgages for the *New Yorker* writer Adam Gopnik (Upper East Side), the *Lucky* editor Kim France (Carroll Gardens),

Art Cooper's *GQ* successor, Jim Nelson (Chelsea), the *Cargo* editor Ariel Foxman (West Village), and the *Self* editor Alexandra Penney, who moved into an apartment in River House, overlooking the East River, where she still lives decades later.

These were life-altering gifts. Looking back, it's astounding to think that writers and editors were rewarded to this extent. For a chosen few creative New Yorkers, Si Newhouse was a startlingly effective engine of social mobility. But it all had a purpose. Si wanted his company to represent the acme of luxury and excellence. Editors used their grand apartments to host parties for celebrities, socialites, important advertisers, and business tycoons. It was a critical part of the Condé mystique, the magic that made it a source of envy from rivals and a magnet for readers and advertisers alike. "We were expected to be walking billboards for the fantasy we were selling," the *Vanity Fair* editor Dana Brown observed. Si wanted Condé Nast to be the lushest, wealthiest, most exclusive party in the world.

IN A SENSE, ALL THIS LUXURY was nirvana for a magazine editor: endless funds for the most ambitious aesthetic pursuits. "The mandate from Si was, 'You are wildly creative and talented, and here's an open line of credit,'" recalled a former executive. "'Make me the most fabulous magazine that drives the zeitgeist.'" Yet the charmed life of virtually no budgets doubled as a gilded cage. Editors in chief were often kept in the dark about the financial performance of their magazines, leaving them constantly guessing as to where they stood with the boss. For all of the seemingly mindless profligacies that made up day-to-day life at Condé Nast, Si Newhouse refused to overspend a penny of the currency he considered most precious of all: control.

Sarah Slavin, a longtime Condé Nast executive, offered an example of how this system worked. In the 1970s, Slavin was working at *Vogue*, where she was expected to oversee the magazine's finances. One day, she received a call from Billy Rayner, Condé Nast's editorial business manager and one of the few people at 350 Madison who actually kept track of the spending at every magazine. Rayner was himself the sort of high-status, impeccably connected character who often found a professional home at Condé Nast. His mother was a Palm Beach society fixture and his aunt, Betty Parsons, ran a famed Manhattan gallery that exhibited paintings by Alex Liberman; during summers home from boarding school in the 1950s, Rayner lived with Betty on Long Island and befriended Jackson Pollock and Mark Rothko. His first wife was Chesbrough (Chessy) Hall, a socialite who became a famous decorator; Chessy's stepfather was Iva Patcévitch, then the president of Condé Nast, where Rayner, formerly a stockbroker, went to work. Although Rayner had a genteel, kooky reputation—he was often seen wearing his telephone headset upside down—Slavin was leery of him. She knew that *Vogue* had been spending a *lot* of money, even by its own lavish standards, and this was the call to the principal's office she had been dreading.

Inside his tastefully decorated office, Rayner gestured for Slavin to have a seat.

"Sarah," he began, in a plummy tone, "you're spending an awful lot of money on models."

"Oh dear. I'm so sorry. How much did I spend?"

Rayner laughed and sat back in his chair. "Oh," he said, dismissively, "you don't need to know that! Just spend less."

Dumbfounded, Slavin walked back to the *Vogue* offices and informed Grace Mirabella that Condé Nast had decided the magazine was overspending on models.

"How much did we spend?"

"I don't know, ma'am. He won't tell me."

Mirabella sighed and shook her head.

There was, no doubt, a gendered aspect to all of this. The majority of Condé Nast's workforce and customer base were women, but almost all of the business executives who controlled the company's purse strings were men. While Condé was a rare company in the 1970s and 1980s where women could ascend to positions of tangible influence, their power was, for the most part, limited to the editorial side of the shop. Tina's managing editor at *Vanity Fair*, Pamela Maffei McCarthy, recalled asking a Condé production manager how much it would cost to delay a print run, since she wanted to correct a mistake that a late fact-checking call had turned up. "Don't you girls worry about what things cost," the manager replied. Linda Wells encountered similar challenges at her magazine, *Allure*, in the 1990s. "We would not receive any guidance on what would be an appropriate amount to spend," she recalled. "It was infantilizing. There was an element of 'You've got the keys to the kingdom,' and there was an element of 'We're just little ladies who will be patted on the head.' In the end, it wasn't a good thing."

Mirabella, who as editor of *Vogue* was among the world's most important cultural arbiters, was left hugely frustrated by this dynamic. When Condé decided to raise the newsstand price of *Vogue*, she learned of the change from a rival publisher, not from Si or Alex. In her memoir, she recalled confronting Si and asking to be made a vice president of Condé Nast, with a direct say in the business operations of her magazine. "What do you want to do that for?" Si replied. Tina was adored by Si, yet she routinely found herself enraged when he made major business decisions without her. "Si was extremely secretive and precipitous in his decision-making," Tina told me. "He maddened editors all the time by firing their publishers and replacing them without any conversation at all with the editor, even though the editor-publisher relationship is so critical, and you would think he might have at least asked how they felt about it." Tina's eventual departure from *The New Yorker* would be prompted in part by Si's refusal to offer her a more direct financial stake, such as equity in the success of her magazine.

In 1994, Alex, who had endured a series of heart attacks and bypass surgeries, agreed to step down from the omnipotent editorial role he had occupied for more than thirty years. At eighty-one, he had spent more than half a century at Condé Nast. This was a moment that Si had long feared—he and Alex were so close that they eventually lived in the same luxury high-rise building, overlooking the United Nations—but it also presented an opportunity to signal a new direction for his magazines. Several accomplished women were clear candidates to succeed Alex. Anna had become the world's most powerful stylist and had revived

Vogue for the celebrity-soaked, youth-obsessed 1990s. Tina had proven her facility with pizzazz at *Vanity Fair* and literary journalism at *The New Yorker*. There was also Rochelle Udell, an accomplished creative director who designed Calvin Klein's Brooke Shields denim campaign and had taken up a powerful advisory role at Condé, consulting on *Self*, *Mademoiselle*, *House & Garden*, *Glamour*, and *The New Yorker*. Elevating a woman to the most influential job in American magazines, at a company whose overall readership skewed female, would have amounted to a profound statement by Si.

He picked a man instead. James Truman, thirty-five, was a puckish Brit who had worked under Anna at *Vogue*, where he donned skinny suits and dated a string of socialites. He became the editor of *Details*, Condé's edgy young men's magazine, and transformed it from a Manhattan cult favorite to a mass-market success, but that was the extent of his achievements. Pretty much all of Condé was shocked by Si's pick, given the talents of the women that Truman was competing against. It fell to Alex to blurt out the truth. "It is better for a man to be in this job, because you deal with other men," Alex told a reporter for *New York* magazine. "The business side is nearly all male, and you deal with the engravers, printers, all these things. And I think the women editors are more receptive to something from a man, and there may be female resentment, jealousy. Is that very sexist, what I am saying?"

Alex's candor buttressed an anecdote involving Ruth Whitney, the longtime editor of *Glamour*, who once presented Condé sales executives with an upcoming issue that included a story tentatively titled "The Glass Ceiling."

"What is the glass ceiling?" one of the salesmen asked obliviously.

"John," Whitney replied, "you're standing on it."

Male editors were not immune from Si's condescension, either. When Harry Evans, Tina Brown's husband and a famous journalist himself, launched the high-end leisure magazine *Condé Nast Traveler* in 1987, he was informed by his superiors that he did not need to follow a budget. Bewildered, Evans called up Louis Gropp, then the editor of *House & Garden*, to ask how he could gauge his magazine's financial progress. "Well, you might get a call if you've spent a lot of money," Gropp explained. "Somebody from the accounting department. They'll be soft-spoken, and very polite, and if you can explain things reasonably and coherently, they'll thank you, and you'll never hear about it again."

EFFORTS TO REIN IN RUNAWAY SPENDING had been sporadically tried and promptly discarded over the years. In the 1920s, Condé Montrose Nast hired an efficiency engineer at *Vanity Fair* who deposited a slip on every writer's desk in the morning noting exactly how many minutes they had been late arriving to the office. Frank Crowninshield crumpled these up and threw them in a wastebasket. In the mid-1980s, a Condé Nast executive named Linda Rice decided to give efficiency another shot. Rice had started as a production manager at *Vogue* dealing with the humdrum logistics of getting the magazine to the printers; she got along well with Alex Liberman and rose to become one of Condé's top executives. Rice was taken aback to discover that, unlike most of its competitors, Condé Nast had no internal computerized budgeting system. Virtually all spending decisions were made on the fly, with Si verbally approving any overages (and he almost never said no to his favorite editors). Alex, for his part, detested paperwork—"Typing stifles creativity," he once told a colleague—and preferred to run the business on instinct. "He'd get the idea that this is *not* the year to send sixty-five giraffes from the south of Africa or India to the Arctic," one executive recalled.

Rice took it upon herself to devise an accounting system to keep track of the costs of each photo shoot. Instead of an editor unilaterally ordering pricey retakes, they would now be expected to plan ahead, submitting a form that delineated the precise costs of travel, models, props, and photographers, and obtaining a superior's sign-off. All was going smoothly with plans to introduce the new system until Alex got ahold of the new form. Rice received a phone call asking her to come to his office. When she walked in, Alex was sitting calmly behind his white Parsons desk. He picked up a copy of the budget form, raised his hands above his head, and theatrically tore the sheet in half.

There was a reason that editors at Hearst, envious of their profligate rival, developed a nickname for Condé Nast: "Our Irrational Competitor."

15

Up Is Up

All the runaway spending finally reached a crisis point in 1998, in the form of an investigative report by the *Fortune* magazine writers Joseph Nocera and Peter Elkind. In a way that few others had done before, the journalists threatened to puncture the plush mystique that Si and his editors had carefully cultivated around their magazines. For all the tales of excess spending, zero-interest mortgages, Concorde flights, and eye-watering budgets, *Fortune* had uncovered an inconvenient fact: Condé Nast did not make much money.

The world's most glamorous magazine publisher had ended 1996 with $55 million in profit on $750 million in revenue. When Nocera and Elkind tallied up the losses at *The New Yorker*, which at the time was still housed in a separate division of Advance Publications, the profit margin across all of the Newhouse magazines nosedived to roughly 5 percent. (At the time, other magazine companies had margins that were three to four times higher.) *Fortune* reported that *Cosmopolitan*, the flagship monthly at buttoned-up rival Hearst, made about as much money in 1997 as every Condé Nast title combined.

The Newhouses' private ownership model had always shrouded the internal economics of their magazines, and Si and Donald's determination to keep their business under family control meant that public disclosure rules did not apply. But it had never been spelled out in such black-and-white terms the degree to which Condé Nast remained Si's plaything, a glamorous money pit bankrolled by the Newhouses' far more lucrative holdings in newspapers and cable television. Some Condé executives speculated that the family viewed its entire magazine division as a useful tax write-off. "The money was in the newspapers that Donald ran," recalled one former executive. "Condé Nast was the beautiful pretty girl you have on your arm—the glam, the fun, the reputation and prestige. Frankly, they didn't care whether it made money." Si had purchased *The New Yorker*, *GQ*, and *Architectural Digest*, invented *Self* and *Allure* and *Traveler*, and overseen the advent of the *Vanity Fair* Oscar party and *Vogue*'s annexation of the Met Gala. The chic little business his father had bought was now an empire. But for all the influence the magazines wielded, the Newhouse brothers' rough financial formula remained the same: Donald made the money, and Si spent it.

The *Fortune* article proved especially embarrassing for Steve Florio, the brash-talking publisher and favored corporate son of Si, who in 1994 had been named president of Condé Nast. Queens-born and Long Island–raised, the tall and bearish Florio carried himself with a salesman's braggadocio. He was central casting's idea of an eighties businessman: bushy mustache, double-breasted suits with gold buttons, a carouser with an office stocked with sailboat paraphernalia who ate nearly every lunch at the Four Seasons. Like many of his fellow Condé strivers, Florio was the author of his own myth. Over the years, he had claimed to have served in the military, played minor-league baseball, earned an MBA, studied premed, and spent a year after college "as a career counselor in some of the tougher neighborhoods in New York, convincing kids with backgrounds similar to mine to stay in school." The *Fortune* reporters discovered that none of this was true. Florio had also frequently fibbed to the press about *The New Yorker*'s financial performance, claiming that the magazine was raking in cash when it was actually bleeding out.

When *Fortune* approached Condé Nast's publicity department for comment about all this dissembling, a spokeswoman offered up a matter-of-fact explanation: "The company policy back then was to say we're not losing money."

After all, Condé's success was predicated on its expert curation of a kind of American fantasy life. Why not extend this worldview to the bottom line, too?

Inside the company, Florio's reputational issues extended beyond doubts about his truthfulness. He was a fount of dirty jokes and sexual banter, in a manner that would never fly in today's corporate world and barely flew then. One editor recalled Florio throwing a party for advertisers during New York's Fleet Week, and sending word to *Vogue* that he needed young female assistants to attend as eye candy for the clients. The same editor observed Florio, during an office evacuation shortly after the 9/11 terror attacks, hugging young women on the ad sales team as they loitered on the sidewalk.

Florio's chauvinist behavior set the tone for Condé's macho business side, which stood out against the more feminine spaces of its lifestyle magazines, many of which were led by female editors in chief. One high-ranking female editor kept a private file at her desk of Florio's more offensive comments and misdeeds; given the mercurial atmosphere at Condé, she figured it would boost her leverage in negotiating an exit package in case she ever found herself abruptly fired. Florio, for his part, made no apologies about his hyperaggressive style. "I was not short on nerve or ego, and I carried a heavy chip on my shoulder," he wrote in a proposal for a memoir that he later abandoned. "I was, after all, Steve Florio: the Godfather, the Samurai, the leader, the warrior."

Si liked warriors. He had been drawn to bruisers since childhood, when he cultivated Roy Cohn as his friend and protector. Tongue-tied as a boy, Si may have appreciated the security of a silver-tongued spokesman; he also had a fascination with gangster movies, with their romantic portrayals of the heavy. The blue-collar Florio represented the striver that Si, for all his wealth, still identified with—that grinding mentality that Sam Newhouse had embodied, too. "Si likes it when people are controversial; it adds a little excitement to his life," recalled Eddie Hayes, a longtime lawyer and fixer for Condé Nast. "Si likes tough guys."

At a company where perception trumped *everything*, it was no surprise that the sales guys crafted their public image as meticulously as any editor in chief. They lived as large as the fashionistas they serviced, wearing bespoke Italian suits and lunching at the Four Seasons. Florio, whose BMW license plate read "MAGAZINE," hosted corporate retreats at the posh Ocean Reef Club in Florida, where one year he distributed a color headshot of himself, complete with a silver frame, as a keepsake for the attendees. ("I'm going to keep it visibly displayed where I can look at it for inspiration," one publisher quipped.) He bought a boat that he sailed around Long Island Sound, where he finagled a membership to the WASPy Seawanhaka Yacht Club, not far from his palatial home in Oyster Bay.

Another tough guy was Ron Galotti, a Montecristo-smoking, Zegna-suited salesman who emerged as Florio's rival for Si's affection. Galotti was the son of a liquor store owner in Peekskill, New York, whose father died when he was nine; he barely graduated high school and went into the air force. An early marriage ended after his young son died in a car accident. Galotti got started in publishing at *Home Sewing News*, a Seventh Avenue trade rag, before joining Hearst in 1978; Si poached him in 1982 with a big salary boost. At Condé Nast, Galotti liked to brag about spending $50,000 a year on cigars. One year, he shipped his Ferrari Testarossa to Colorado so he could impress an advertiser who was opening a hotel in Telluride. (He was briefly detained by local cops who caught him doing 130 miles per hour on a back road.) Galotti dated the supermodel Janice Dickinson; after she broke up with him, he moved on to a journalist, Candace Bushnell, who kept a public diary of their relationship in a column she wrote for *The New York Observer* called "Sex and the City." She gave Galotti a nickname—Mr. Big—and recounted one of his favorite phrases: "Abso-fucking-lutely." Later, at one of the premiere parties for the HBO adaptation, Galotti instructed the actor Chris Noth on the finer points of enunciating the term.

They may never have been as famous as Tina Brown or Anna Wintour, but the fact that Condé Nast's publishing executives had public personas at all spoke to the unusual nature of life in the Newhouse kingdom. "I used to tease people and say my life is better than James Bond's," said Tom Florio, Steve's younger brother and a veteran Condé executive himself. "Because nobody was trying to kill me. But I had everything else that motherfucker had." Hearst, with its more staid corporate culture, frowned on sales heads showing up in the gossip pages; Si wanted the Condé aura to permeate all corners of his empire. He had calculated from the start that the more exclusive the company appeared, the more ads it could sell, and the more luxury brands would clamor to pay for space in its pages. Galotti, when he became publisher of *Vogue*, refused to hand out complimentary copies, reasoning it would make the magazine seem cheaper and less exclusive.

And the publishers knew that Si kept close track of their work. The *Fortune* article revealed that, while Si could be sanguine about a lack of profit, he had no patience for a decline in ads. He counted every advertisement in every issue published by a Condé Nast title, and did the same for his competitors. Any sign of a drop-off prompted a flurry of scribbled notes on his signature legal paper, which came to be known internally as "yellow snow." Si's publishers had a saying—"Up is up"—that became a mantra of the Condé sales side. It meant more pages, more advertisers, more buzz—no matter the cost. "Succeed, succeed, succeed," recalled Mitchell Fox, a longtime Condé Nast publisher and executive. "Si admired someone who communicates to the world that they are successful. He wants to see his guys be fighters. It's okay to get knocked down, put on the mat, but you better know how to get up and fight on."

Florio, an inveterate fibber, interpreted this mandate as an excuse to make the numbers look good, even if they weren't. Temperamental types like Galotti, who called himself "the dictator" in the office, used it as a reason to rebuke underlings. More than two dozen members of his staff quit or were fired over the course of two years. "Was I a motherfucker? Absolutely," Galotti told me. "But nobody pays you a million dollars a year and wants you to come back into the office rested and smiling. They want you soaking wet." Once, when he was the publisher of *GQ*, Galotti got into a shoving match at a Bergdorf Goodman party with a fashion editor who had written unfavorably about the magazine. After the incident made the gossip columns, Florio supposedly smoothed it over by telling Si, falsely, that Galotti had lashed out because the journalist "said something about Italians and Jews."

"You'd never know when something would set one of them off," said one veteran Condé executive. "It was not only allowed; it was encouraged. I think Si liked the sport of it."

Inevitably, lines were crossed. Richard Beckman was a British sales executive, hired by Steve Florio in the mid-1980s, who later became publisher of *Vogue*. His nickname was "Mad Dog." In June 1999, at a company sales meeting, Beckman reportedly insisted that two senior female *Vogue* employees, an advertising executive and a fashion director, kiss one another in front of their colleagues—and then pushed their heads together, badly injuring the ad executive's nose. She resigned and threatened a $10 million lawsuit that Condé apparently settled for between $1 million and $5 million. According to Anna Wintour's biographer, Amy Odell, Anna was "appalled by the incident," but *Vogue*'s managing editor told her that Anna "wouldn't have thrown down the gauntlet" with Si and demand that he fire one of the company's favored executives. Si made Mad Dog apologize to the staff and seek counseling, but he let him stay on at *Vogue* for another three years—before promoting him to a more powerful role as chief marketing officer of the entire company. Beckman remained at Condé Nast until 2010.

IN THE MONTHS BEFORE the *Fortune* article appeared, Tina Brown had grown restless at *The New Yorker*, and increasingly frustrated with her longtime patrons at Condé Nast. Her magazine was still surfing the zeitgeist, and Tina's provocations were still making headlines, like her dishy first-person account of a lunch with Princess Diana and Anna Wintour at the Four Seasons, which *The New Yorker* published days after the princess's death. The article aired Diana's private thoughts on the Windsors ("Charles is not a leader. He's a follower.") and was said to have irked Anna, who had expected the conversation to remain private.

But Tina's late-night editing sessions had taken a toll, and she was feeling stymied by Si, who had rejected her ideas for expanding into ventures beyond a weekly print magazine. Her ties to Hollywood meant that she grasped the commercial and cultural possibilities of adapting for film and TV. Back at *Vanity Fair*, Tina had hired Susan Mercandetti,

Ted Koppel's producer at ABC, and sat her next to Si at a Manhattan dinner in order to pitch him on a *VF* television series. "I was prepping the hell out of it," Mercandetti recalled, "really thinking through my thought process." When she arrived at her seat, "Si turned to me, before the first course was served—I didn't even have water in my glass—and he said, 'I know you're going to try to talk me into giving you a television show, but there's no way I'm doing it. It's a magazine, and it's never going to be a television show.' And he turned to his other side, and that was the end of the conversation."

Tina tried again at *The New Yorker*, arguing that Condé could take a cut of prospective box office receipts or start an in-house production company. She also advocated for in-person conferences where the hoi polloi might pay for the privilege of attending talks with the movers and shakers to whom her magazine had access. A quarter century later, these sorts of extracurriculars are rampant in the journalism world: witness *The New York Times*'s DealBook Summit, or the popular "ideas" festivals sponsored by *The Atlantic* and, yes, *The New Yorker*. But in the late 1990s, Si remained fixated on the print magazines that were at the core of his success. Tina's entrepreneurial interests, Si worried, threatened to dilute *The New Yorker*'s aura; he viewed himself as the caretaker of a cultural treasure that, axiomatically, was a physical product made of pulp and ink. Recall, too, the slings and arrows that Si suffered when he purchased the magazine, when he dared to enact innovations like full-page advertisements and color photography. As a Newhouse, Si was sensitive to accusations of crassness; Tina's ideas, forward-looking as they were, likely struck him as exposing the magazine, and his own reputation, to undue risk.

Si, however, was not the only mogul in Tina's social orbit, and Michael Eisner and Mort Zuckerman were urging her to embrace the seismic changes looming in the media world. She was also upset by a drumbeat of headlines calling attention to the financial woes of her editorship. Under Tina, *The New Yorker*'s cultural acquisition cost was staggering: all those six-figure writing contracts, hefty kill fees, and indulgent Avedon photo shoots added up. If you had to put a price on buzz, it might be $80 million, a conservative estimate of the amount that

The New Yorker reportedly lost between 1993 and 1997. (*Fortune* would later report, in 1998, that the magazine had lost $175 million since it came under the Newhouses' control.) When Steve Florio was named president of Condé Nast, in 1994, he was replaced at *The New Yorker* by his younger brother, Tom Florio, whose early friendship with Tina—she gave him a personalized Edward Sorel sketch for his fortieth birthday—soured as ad sales lagged. Tina was convinced the losses were not her fault—that she had tried to make her budgets and that Si had saddled her with a publisher whose salesmanship failed to keep pace with her own.

The Florio *frères* soon had a dramatic falling-out that entered Condé Nast lore. In January 1998, Steve publicly likened *The New Yorker*'s financial performance to a "nosebleed," and blindsided his brother by telling *The Wall Street Journal* that Tom was now "informally" reporting to him. Meanwhile, Si was moving forward, over Tina's objections, with a plan to fold *The New Yorker* into the rest of Condé Nast, breaking a promise he made when he purchased the magazine that it would remain a separate entity. Shortly before Memorial Day weekend, Tom was expelled from *The New Yorker* and reassigned to *Condé Nast Traveler*. Si had appointed a new publisher, David Carey, without bothering to consult with his editor first. When Si called Tina at home to deliver the news, he was met with a glowering silence on the other end of the line.

Like many a Condé editor in chief before her, Tina was running up against the limits of Si's largesse: he would gladly bankroll her gilded professional life, while refusing to relinquish a modicum of control. And another media honcho was in hot pursuit.

In 1997, Tina had finally gotten a green light from Si to pursue one of her pet projects: the Next Conference, a gathering co-sponsored by her friend Michael Eisner at the Walt Disney Company. Held on Disney's Florida campus, the $500,000 event featured a cavalcade of VIPs, including Vice President Al Gore, whose trip to the event on Air Force Two was reportedly reimbursed by Condé Nast. Tina accepted a private jet ride back to New York with another attendee, the Miramax mega-producer Harvey Weinstein. When Weinstein and his brother, Bob, learned that Tina's five-year contract ran out in July 1998, he pitched her on an enticing vision: a new magazine where Tina could control both the editorial *and* the business side, with an equity stake in the profits (never a possibility at Condé), and a books-and-film division to boot. Tina was exhausted by the day-to-day work of publishing a weekly; her mother, who had been fading from cancer, had died on June 30. A wunderkind about to turn forty-five, Tina found herself pondering a next act. She called Harvey five days later.

On July 8, around 9 a.m., Tina walked into Si's office and resigned. She was moving from the House of Newhouse to the House of Weinstein: leaving one culture-shaping, status-craving Jewish mogul for another.

Si was stunned by Tina's defection—and he grasped its relevance as a moment of truth for his stewardship. When he purchased *The New Yorker* in 1985, the magazine had technically been subsumed by a separate arm of his family's holding company, Advance Publications. He was now planning to move it officially under the Condé Nast umbrella, a capstone to his decades of work changing the company's image from a mere fashion publisher to one of literary respectability. This had, predictably, not gone over well among some of the magazine's stalwarts. "To graft it onto the faceless corporate entity of Condé Nast is going to be the end of the old, authentic *New Yorker* identity," one griped at the time. Now Si watched as the woman who had almost single-handedly reinvented his family business, who had fueled Condé's rise from mom-and-pop shop to glittering powerhouse, walked out of his office for the last time.

What followed was one of the great steeplechases in American journalism.

Si drew up a list of potential replacements. One was Peter W. Kaplan, the editor of *The New York Observer*. Kaplan was a keen chronicler of status and a romantic about journalism and New York City, whose witty newspaper had more cachet among the cognoscenti than its low circulation numbers would suggest. Editing *The New Yorker* was a childhood dream of his, and when he was summoned to Si's office, he suffered a bout of nerves. That morning, he cut his face shaving, and a friend had to point out, minutes before the meeting, that Kaplan had neglected to remove a speck of bathroom tissue from his cheek. At the interview, Kaplan became distracted by one of the framed *Krazy Kat* cels hanging on Si's wall; he apparently spent a large chunk of their conversation enthusing about old cartoons and animated movies. Kaplan did not get the job.

Graydon Carter says that Si approached him about replacing Tina at *The New Yorker*, and that he passed; two others familiar with their conversations said that Si and Graydon mutually agreed that moving him off *Vanity Fair*, then riding high, would be counterproductive. David Remnick, the prolific Pulitzer Prize winner on Tina's staff, was also on the short list, though Si initially had doubts, telling a colleague that Remnick might make *The New Yorker* too "Washington think tank." In fact, Si's top choice was more than two thousand miles outside of New York, lacing up his boots for a weekend of hiking in the forests of Washington state, when a call came in from a 212 area code.

"Don't go anywhere," Tina Brown told Michael Kinsley. "Si Newhouse wants to talk to you."

Kinsley, then forty-seven, was among the most admired journalists of his era, a polymath Rhodes Scholar who edited *The New Republic* and cohosted CNN's *Crossfire*. In 1995, Microsoft had tapped him to create an online publication called *Slate*. (The idea was so ahead of its time that for several years Microsoft distributed a printed version called *Slate on Paper*.) It was Friday morning in Seattle when Si reached Kinsley; by Saturday, the editor was standing in Si's apartment, admiring the Andy Warhol Marilyn on the wall. Three hours later, according to Kinsley, Si offered him the editorship of *The New Yorker*, with a $1 million salary and a $5 million signing bonus. "To the extent he had a strategy at all, it was to bowl me over with money," Kinsley recalled, "and he succeeded at that." Kinsley was elated but disoriented; things were moving very fast, and he asked for a beat to speak with his wife. Si, who wanted to announce Tina's successor by Monday, reluctantly agreed. They met again on Sunday, for a dinner with Donald Newhouse, and upon parting, Kinsley promised a final decision by morning.

Fifteen minutes later, he walked into his room at the Helmsley Hotel and found a message to call Si.

The publisher's voice crackled over the receiver. "You seem reluctant."

"It's a big decision," Kinsley replied, "but if I do it, I assure you I'll be energetic and enthusiastic."

Condé Montrose Nast, the preacher's grandson from Missouri who founded Condé Nast Publications in 1909.
(Everett / Shutterstock)

Frank Crowninshield (and friend), the dapper Jazz Age editor of *Vanity Fair*.
(George Karger / The Chronicle Collection / Getty Images)

(Zine Artz / Alamy Stock Photo; Retro AdArchives / Alamy Stock Photo; Zine Artz / Alamy Stock Photo; Heritage Image Partnership Ltd. / Alamy Stock Photo)

Samuel I. Newhouse Sr., born Solomon Neuhaus in a tenement building on the Lower East Side of Manhattan. He built a newspaper empire and purchased Condé Nast in 1959, eight years before this photo was taken. *(Jack Manning / The New York Times / Redux)*

Inset: Samuel Irving ("Si") Newhouse Jr., in his Air Force uniform in an undated photograph. (*Courtesy of Jane Marks*) *Above*: Si and his first wife, Jane Franke, in a booth at El Morocco, one of the Manhattan nightlife hotspots that they frequented together in the 1950s. (*Courtesy of Pamela Mensch*)

Mitzi Newhouse, Si's status-conscious mother, who adored couture and the arts, with Sam on vacation in Acapulco in 1968. (*William E. Sauro / The New York Times / Redux*)

Si and Jane's holiday card in the mid-1950s. Copies of *Vogue* can be seen stacked on the coffee table. (*Courtesy of Jane Marks*)

Si Newhouse, bachelor at rest, as pictured in the April 6, 1966, issue of *The New York Times*. His "houseboy" Pedro ("one of the great luxuries of the world," according to Si) is pouring his tea. (*Don Hogan Charles / The New York Times / Redux*)

Diana Vreeland, the editor in chief of *Vogue* from 1963 to 1971, seen in the magazine's offices in the Graybar Building by Grand Central Terminal, selecting designs and garments for an upcoming issue. Photographed on May 1, 1963. (*Ben Martin / Archive Photos / Getty Images*)

Alexander Liberman, for more than thirty years the editorial director and all-powerful creative force of Condé Nast, at the dedication of his sculpture, *The Way*, at a park near St. Louis in May 1980. "I believe that money should be used to facilitate a creative life and to eliminate fatigue," he once said. "I take taxis all the time; I find them restful and stimulating." (*Bettmann / Getty Images*)

Two British editors entered the Condé Nast orbit in 1983 and came to define its new era of power and cultural influence. *Left*: Anna Wintour on the steps of the Metropolitan Museum of Art in New York after a Costume Institute event in December 1989. (© *Dafydd Jones*) *Above*: Tina Brown at *Vanity Fair*'s Phoenix House benefit in Los Angeles, March 1990. (© *Dafydd Jones*) *Below*: Tina being interviewed by *60 Minutes* at the *Vanity Fair* offices, 350 Madison Avenue, in 1990. (© *Dafydd Jones*)

A few months after Tina took over *The New Yorker* in 1992, Simon Doonan included this papier-mâché version of her in a Barneys holiday window that paid tribute to the magazine. A featured quote: "Every so often you have to bite the hand that reads you."
(*Jim Lorelli / WWD / Penske Media / Getty Images*)

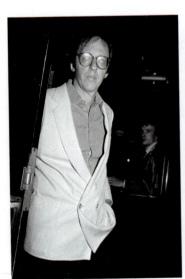

William Shawn's successor and Tina's predecessor, the cerebral Robert Gottlieb, at a party at Mortimer's in 1983.
(*Tony Palmieri / WWD / Penske Media / Getty Images*)

David Remnick, who succeeded Tina in 1998, photographed in the *New Yorker* offices in 2000.
(*Robin London / Hulton Archive / Getty Images*)

Graydon Carter introduced the *Vanity Fair* Oscar party in 1994. The soiree quickly became the hottest ticket in Hollywood and one of the most famous parties in the world. Here, Graydon looks dapper on the red carpet in 2000.
(*Ron Galella / Ron Galella Collection / Getty Images*)

Graydon boogeying with Madonna at the 1999 party at Morton's restaurant.
(© *Dafydd Jones*)

Donald Newhouse and Si Newhouse greet guests at the 1997 party.
(© *Dafydd Jones*)

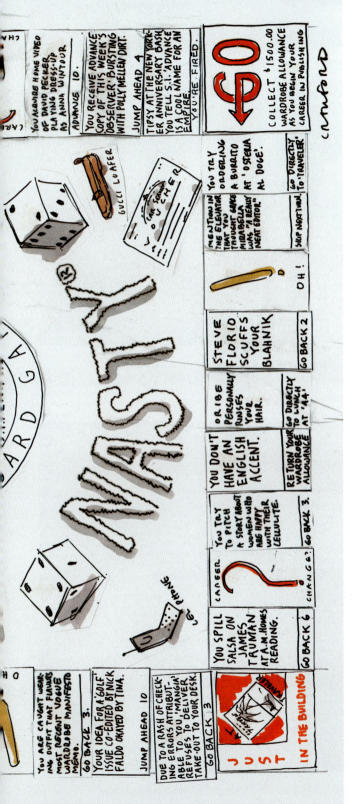

Condé Nast: The Board Game, as imagined by the *New Yorker* cartoonist Michael Crawford in 1996.

Crawford, an astute chronicler of manners, distributed copies of this homemade, madcap Monopoly-style board to friends and coworkers. The game is a wry encapsulation of the folkways and idiosyncrasies of Condé Nast at its 1990s peak. Among the illustrations are a sketch of Steve Florio's sailboat, a Big Apple Car voucher, and Si's beloved pug, Nero. The restaurant at the Royalton Hotel, "44," is cited in several squares; known as the Condé canteen, it was where top editors held court from dedicated banquettes.

Crawford died in 2016. I am grateful to his children, Farley and Miles, for tracking down this piece in his archives.
(@michaelcrawfordart, courtesy of Farley Crawford Bliss and Miles Crawford)

Donald J. Trump at the 1987 book release party at Trump Tower for *The Art of the Deal*, with his wife, Ivana, and the man who hatched the idea for the book, Si Newhouse. (*Ron Galella / Ron Galella Collection / Getty Images*)

Trump in conversation with Anna Wintour in the front row of a fashion show at the Plaza Hotel in 1995. (*David Turner / WWD / Penske Media / Getty Images*)

Annie Leibovitz, whose dramatic portraiture helped define the look of the revived *Vanity Fair*, poses in 2009 in front of her famed photograph of a nude and pregnant Demi Moore, which caused a national sensation when it ran on the cover of *VF*'s August 1991 issue. (*Sean Gallup / Getty Images*)

Twenty-four years later, Leibovitz made headlines again with her photographs of Caitlyn Jenner, which made the front page of newspapers around the country (three examples, above) and prompted a statement from the Obama White House. (*Richard Levine / Alamy Stock Photo*)

André Leon Talley, who would go on to become creative director and editor at large at *Vogue* under Anna, at the Fire Island Pines on August 9, 1976.
(Pierre Schermann / WWD / Penske Media / Getty Images)

Ron Galotti, the hard-charging publisher, and his then-girlfriend, *Sex and the City* writer Candace Bushnell, at the Bridgehampton Polo Club in August 1995. Galotti was the inspiration for Bushnell's character Mr. Big. (© *Dafydd Jones*)

Arthur Cooper, longtime editor in chief of *GQ*, and Estella Warren at a *GQ* party, April 2000.
(Patrick McMullan / Getty Images)

Steve Florio, Anna Wintour, and James Truman, who succeeded Alex Liberman as editorial director in 1994, at a mid-nineties fashion show in New York.
(Catherine McGann / Hulton Archive / Getty Images)

Graydon and Anna, 1996. (© *Dafydd Jones*)

Frank Gehry's celebrated Condé Nast cafeteria in 4 Times Square. The sinuous, blue-hued titanium folds were inspired by a Bellini painting of Jesus. (*Michael Appleton / The New York Times / Redux*)

Oprah Winfrey at a party at Balthazar celebrating her October 1998 cover of *Vogue*. The issue became a massive bestseller. (*Richard Corkery / NY Daily News Archive / Getty Images*)

Louis "Red" Menchicchi, the cigar-smoking Staten Islander who directed black car and limousine traffic outside of 4 Times Square. (*Don Hogan Charles / The New York Times / Redux*)

Members of the Condé Nast union demonstrate on a picket line outside 1 World Trade Center, January 2024.
(*Angela Weiss / AFP / Getty Images*)

A live elephant was rented at exorbitant cost to create this 2008 image for *Portfolio* magazine.
(*Phillip Toledano / Trunk Archive*)

Anna Wintour receives the Presidential Medal of Freedom from then-president Joe Biden at the White House, January 4, 2025.
(*Chris Kleponis / AFP / Getty Images*)

Following page: Anna on a New York City subway train, 1992.
(© *Dafydd Jones*)

Manhattan & Bronx via Lex Av Express

1595

"I'm starting to feel reluctant, too," Si said. "I think it would be better to call it off."

Kinsley froze. Grasping for words, he told Si, "This is going to be embarrassing for both of us." A few Newhouse-ian mumbles later, the call, and the prospective editorship, was finished.

"I was really angry," Kinsley told me. "I sulked for a while. What annoyed me, in some ways, was that he offered it to me and then withdrew it with the same 'who cares?' attitude about the consequences. That's something that only a rich man would do." At the time, Kinsley considered himself adept at handling wealthy benefactors, but Si's caprice left him confounded. "He was very nice," Kinsley said, "until the last phone call."

The episode revealed a fundamental truth. Condé Nast was Si's passion project, and he wanted the men and women he entrusted with it to share that passion. He didn't like losing money, but he didn't particularly care about making heaps of it, either. At the time, his brother, Donald's, newspaper holdings were still generating enormous profits, and the family had made shrewd investments in lucrative cable television systems. The Newhouses, in other words, were doing just fine—which meant the Condé magazines could remain Si's plaything, the asset whose dividends accrued in status, not dollars. Kinsley would have made a fine magazine, even an exceptional one. But Si's idea of a great editor was shaped by Alex Liberman, Diana Vreeland, and Tina Brown: creative iconoclasts who never doubted their fitness to dictate the culture to the world. That Kinsley hesitated at all, when the prize of *The New Yorker* was in his grasp, must have struck Si as hugely concerning. So, he turned to a different option: the bookish son of a dentist, not yet forty years old, who had little editing experience but a sparkling prose style and a bloodhound's nose for news.

Perhaps most importantly, when Si offered him the job, David Remnick did not hesitate to say yes.

REMNICK ONCE WRYLY REFERRED TO his upbringing as "Springsteenian." Both he and Bruce grew up in the New Jersey suburbs, where Remnick's father, a dentist, practiced from a home office, and his precocious son perused the magazines piled up on the waiting room table. *Esquire* and *Rolling Stone* were favorites; *The New Yorker* was not. "I didn't know how to read it, which is to say, I didn't know how to understand it," Remnick recalled. "It seemed like something from Greenwich, Connecticut, or Princeton, New Jersey, which is to say, two places I knew nothing about." New York City, just across the Hudson River from his home in Hillsdale, "was a million miles away and twenty-five minutes away, and I wanted to bridge that twenty-five minutes and million miles as quickly as possible."

Remnick edited his public high school's paper, *The Smoke Signal*, then went on to Princeton, where he studied comparative literature and wrote a thesis on Walt Whitman. As an undergraduate, he wasn't lacking for confidence. When John McPhee, a *New Yorker* staff writer since 1965, accepted Remnick into his Princeton creative writing course, McPhee asked if he'd been concerned about being rejected. "That never crossed my mind," Remnick replied. An internship at *The Washington Post*, the summer after he graduated, led inadvertently to his *New Yorker* debut. The magazine often republished examples of poor newspaper writing in a recurring feature called "Block That Metaphor!," and in 1981, the editors singled out an infelicitous phrase from an article about the Miss America pageant: "Deanna Fogarty, Miss California 1979, is acting sexy. Sexy like a Muriel cigar commercial. Lips pouty and pursed. Eyebrows arched and hips akimbo." The sentence is attributed to "David Remnick in the Washington Post," along with a sly comment: "1979 was the year of the contortionist."

"Five people tore that out and sent it to me," Remnick later recounted. "I thought, 'I've finally made *The New Yorker*, and now I can die in shame.'"

That gaffe aside, Remnick earned a staff job at the *Post*, where he demonstrated an unusually wide range, writing on crime, boxing, tennis, celebrities, and Soviet dissidents. Remnick disliked Washington—"He said there were no decent bagels," recalled Sally Quinn, who sat beside Remnick at the paper's Style section—and, in 1988, he accepted a job at the paper's Moscow bureau. There, he chronicled the fall of Communism, which became the basis of a Pulitzer Prize–winning book,

Lenin's Tomb. He was Tina's first major hire, in 1992, and became one of her most prolific and versatile writers, profiling Mike Tyson, Ralph Ellison, Luciano Pavarotti, the Russian writer Aleksandr Solzhenitsyn, and Pope John Paul II.

In the days after Tina resigned, Remnick met twice with Si, once while wearing a Leon Russell T-shirt he'd bought at a concert. Si peppered him with questions about how he might run the magazine; he spent the weekend writing a lengthy memo that he handed in on Sunday night. On Monday morning, July 13, Remnick was having his hair cut when Steve Florio called and said, breezily, "I guess if you don't fuck it up, you'll be the editor of *The New Yorker*." Remnick was soon face-to-face with Si, who said he planned to announce the promotion in a half hour.

"Do I get to make a phone call?" Remnick replied. It felt a little more like being arrested than being offered the job of a lifetime.

By 11 a.m., *The New Yorker* officially had a new editor in chief—and he had to turn out an issue by Friday. Remnick had not edited a publication since *The Smoke Signal*, and not everyone at the magazine understood the logic. "David getting picked was like Sarah Palin," one editor said, recalling the confusion. "'*Him?*'" But the bulk of the staff greeted Remnick with an ovation that morning, and Calvin Trillin, a *New Yorker* writer since 1963, declared it a smart choice. "I had steeled myself for the possibility of some Condé Nast trend-hound arriving with his black shirt buttoned up to the collar and telling us we needed to pay a little more attention to the club scene," he said. "It never occurred to me that anything this sensible would happen." Remnick's catholic taste made him an apt Tina successor: like her, he believed high and low culture were equally worthy of thoughtful scrutiny. Tina's incursions into ostensibly lowbrow subjects like Roseanne Barr had been met with censure, but now the culture was catching up. *The Sopranos* would debut on HBO six months into Remnick's tenure, kicking off an era of literary television that put the medium on par with novels and the theater. Bill Clinton was about to be impeached, merging the sober business of governance with tabloid scandal. And Jon Stewart was in talks to become host of *The Daily Show*, where a younger generation of educated, upwardly mobile elites—that is to say, the kind of people who subscribe to *The New Yorker*—would soon turn for their news. Remnick liked mixing the silly and the serious, the poetic and the profane, an egalitarian editorial ethos that fit the times. "A balance between stardust and heft," as he later put it.

Tina was busy starting *Talk* magazine with Harvey Weinstein, but Remnick retained many of her core staff writers and artists—the DNA of *The New Yorker*, in many ways, remained hers—while also hiring new critics like Peter Schjeldahl and persuading Woody Allen to start contributing again after a long drought. Si's sentimental view toward the magazine, which remained his favorite of the Condé stable, allowed Remnick some breathing room. "David's mandate, such as it is, has nothing to do with ad pages or revenue," Si said. "I think he has got to discover his own magazine for himself."

One early Remnick highlight grew out of an unsolicited pitch by an unknown writer—or, technically, the writer's mother. Remnick's wife, Esther Fein, a reporter at *The New York Times*, was approached one day in the newsroom by a colleague touting an essay written by her son. "I hate to sound like a pushy mom, but I'm telling you this with my editor's hat on, not my mother's hat on," the woman said. "It's really good, and it's really interesting, but nobody will look at it, nobody will call him back." The woman was Gladys Bourdain, a *Times* copy editor, and her son was named Anthony. His essay, "Don't Eat Before Reading This," which Remnick published in April 1999, was a merciless, hilarious, and sometimes revolting peek into life at a Manhattan brasserie. It got Anthony a book deal, which led to a pair of TV shows; soon, he was one of the most famous chefs in the world.

Tina had been burdened with shaking off the cobwebs that had accumulated from the Shawn years. Remnick inherited a newsier machine, more attuned to the rhythms of post-millennium culture and already accustomed to breaking big scoops. In 2004, the investigative journalist Seymour M. Hersh exposed the torture of Iraqi prisoners in the Abu Ghraib prison in three devastating *New Yorker* articles, reshaping the national conversation around the Iraq War. Lawrence Wright published a bombshell investigation into the Church of Scientology in 2011. Remnick created features like "20 Under 40," a list of fiction writers to watch, and, in 2000, broke decades of precedent by putting a photograph on the cover, sneaking a William Wegman portrait of a Weimaraner dog into an illustration of Eustace Tilley. These were the kinds of heresies—brazen salesmanship, gimmicky lists—that sparked revolts among the Shawn-era staff and brought Tina no end of public grief. By the early 2000s, however, they were welcomed as innovations in a changing industry. Remnick even succeeded at executing the sorts of entrepreneurial ideas that Tina had hoped to implement, only to be blocked by a reluctant Si. In May 2000, for the *New Yorker*'s seventy-fifth anniversary, the magazine threw a New Yorker Festival, three days of events where readers could travel to New York to meet their favorite writers or see live interviews with stars like Paul Simon and Jon Stewart. After years of bleeding money, *The New Yorker* broke even in 2001, and reportedly earned a profit of $2 million in 2002. "In your own quiet ways you must be very proud," Si wrote to Remnick and his publisher, David Carey, in 2004. "As I am of my association with you and your wonderful magazine."

For Remnick, the excitement has never faded. He once marveled at the fact that he could now assign stories to his former mentor at Princeton, John McPhee. "I have to tell you, it was a very strange and wonderful feeling," Remnick said, "to call up John and say, 'Well, whaddaya got?'"

16

A House Divided

Si was pleased with his magazines' sway in the realms of fashion, food, entertainment, literature, and travel. Condé Nast had a foothold in nearly every sphere and phase of human life, telling readers how to be a young adult (*Mademoiselle*), attract a spouse (*Glamour*), and marry them (*Brides*); how to cook (*Gourmet*), groom (*GQ*), primp (*Allure*), and vacation (*Condé Nast Traveler*); what clothes to wear (*Vogue*), what culture to consume (*Vanity Fair*), and what ideas to take seriously (*The New Yorker*). But there was one element of aspiration that he still wanted to conquer—how to live—and that desire led to one of his last significant acquisitions: *Architectural Digest*.

Since 1911, Condé Nast had published *House & Garden*, a magazine about decoration, furniture, and residential design. Condé Montrose Nast had spotted a market of newly affluent women who wanted guidance on how to express their status in the home, a service that he was happy to sell to them. The magazine's archives trace the evolving grammar of the American upper- and upper-middle-class lifestyle. Servants, silent and liveried, show up in early issues and gradually disappear, supplanted by the ideal of the domestic hostess, cheery master of her kitchen. With mid-century highways came features on carports and beach bungalows, novel accoutrements for a middle class newly empowered to escape the city. By the 1960s, the look is pure WASP splendor: "Take-Along Shelters," a 1964 spread on summer activities, features a green-and-white canopy perched atop a station wagon as navy-blazered spectators tailgate at a polo match. Each month, *House & Garden* exported the aesthetic standards of the Eastern establishment: cashmere sweaters were patched and threadbare, wainscoting scratched and patinaed; nothing had too much flash or glitz. In the so-called "shelter" category of magazines, *House & Garden* stood out as the arbiter of sensible domestic style.

Then, in 1970, a woman named Paige Rense walked into the offices of a second-tier publication in Los Angeles to apply for a job.

The Architectural Digest (the *The* later disappeared) got started in 1920 as a quarterly trade publication for the builders and architects fueling Southern California's real estate boom. In the haute design world, it was an afterthought, underfunded and unloved. *House & Garden* ran photos by Irving Penn and Edward Steichen, and treated interiors the way *Vogue* treated fashion, employing squadrons of stylists to curate a just-so aesthetic of burnished old-world charm; one editor in chief paid for an entire reshoot to replace a wilting amaryllis with narcissus. The *Digest* didn't print covers in color until 1964, and its writers had to beg the boss for money to travel from Los Angeles to San Francisco.

In the late 1960s, the *Digest*'s owner and publisher, Cleon "Bud" Knapp, hatched a plan to improve his magazine's reputation by appealing to a more affluent readership. Paige, a diminutive forty-one-year-old blonde in oversized eyeglasses, had little knowledge of architecture or design; her peripatetic writing career included a stint at a publication called *Water World*, for which she interviewed skin divers. If she possessed any visual sense, it came from the LA-area thrift shops where she hunted for recycled dresses. When Knapp asked Paige how she might make his magazine better, she thought to herself, "I couldn't make it any worse." At the time, Paige had her hopes set on a job at *Women's Wear Daily*, but she lost out to a journalist with experience at *Delicatessen News*, a restaurant trade paper. So she became an associate editor at *Architectural Digest* instead. The job would eventually make her a pillar of Condé Nast, a global tastemaker and perhaps the single most powerful person in the world of interior design. Her whims would influence the living spaces of millions of Americans who aspired to emulate the rich.

It was an unlikely destiny.

She was born, in 1929, in an Iowa farm town, to a woman who gave her up for adoption when she was about a year old. No one remembered the baby's name, so her adoptive parents called her Patricia. Her adoptive father, a school custodian, was abusive, and after the family moved to Los Angeles, she left home at fifteen to escape him. Like Sam Newhouse and Anna Wintour, she never finished high school. Patricia restyled herself as Paige, and worked a few low-level jobs; by her late thirties, her biggest success was publishing a short story in *Cosmopolitan*, about an ambitious single girl in New York whose roommate dated wealthy men. "Sherry believed in just two things," Paige wrote of her protagonist. "Never sleep with a man who isn't rich, and don't tell the truth when a lie will work better." Wealth intrigued Paige, as did independence. She kept a collection of autographs of strong women, like Dorothy Parker, who had managed to succeed on their own terms in a man's world.

Six months after starting at *Architectural Digest*, she seized her chance. On April 9, 1971, the magazine's editor in chief, James Bradley Little, was murdered outside a club in Los Angeles. Little was in the parking lot with his partner when a pair of men clambered into the back seat of his car, robbed them, and shot Little in the back of the head. The assailants were never caught. Paige persuaded Bud Knapp to put her in charge. She studied European shelter magazines and hired fixers in London and Paris to arrange access to the homes of celebrities like Coco Chanel. The odds were against her: Condé editors still referred to *AD* as "Architectural Disgust," a tawdry product made by tacky Angelenos. Paige was desperate for an edge.

She found it by flouting the long-established ethics of shelter media. Paige told decorators that she was willing to publish their own photographs of their designs—effectively ceding editorial control in exchange for access, and saving *AD* a considerable amount of money on original photography. She spun this tactic as a virtue—that unlike the snobs at *House & Garden*, she would merely "report" objectively on how rich people lived. The strategy worked: Angelo Donghia and

Tony Duquette, two of the era's most influential interior designers, gave Paige exclusive photos of their latest designs. *House & Garden* typically published snippets of a house—a kitchen here, a mudroom there—to maintain aesthetic standards and, its editors reasoned, to provide better practical tips to middle-class readers. Paige went for lengthy, almost voyeuristic photo spreads, allowing readers to gawk at every detail of each room. Today, we call this "real estate porn." In the 1990s, one designer dismissed it as a print version of *Lifestyles of the Rich and Famous*: "It's all, 'Look at me! Aren't I expensive?'" Another designer described Paige's taste as "very California. Need I say more?"

Paige didn't mind being mocked as vulgar when her sales were this good: between 1971 and 1989, circulation at *Architectural Digest* climbed from 50,000 to 625,000, and annual ad revenue grew from less than $1 million to an astonishing $46 million. The exclusives rolled in, with issues devoted to the lavish homes of Marlon Brando and Madonna, Truman Capote and Liza Minnelli, Woody Allen and Cher. Readers loved it. Paige negotiated the first pictures of Ronald and Nancy Reagan's redesign of their private living quarters in the White House, beating *House & Garden* for the exclusive.

Si Newhouse was also watching, with growing concern. It was increasingly evident that Condé's *House & Garden* was falling out of touch. *Architectural Digest* was flashy and acquisitive, a perfect complement to the *Dynasty* aesthetic of the 1980s. It also featured on-trend designers like Michael Graves, whose creations were defining the look of the yuppie age. Even Alex Liberman, who privately considered *AD* to be hideous, was forced to admit that the magazine "has the hideousness that will attract." Paige, it seemed, had out-Condé'd Condé. "*House & Garden* got the people who had the palazzo in the family for five hundred years," said Joan Kron, a journalist who chronicled the design magazine wars. "At *Architectural Digest*, it was new money, it was big money. Paige was like Barbara Walters: she wanted to get the stars."

In the early 1980s, Si and Alex ordered a redesign of *House & Garden* in an effort to replicate Paige's success. Out went the longtime editor Mary Jane Pool, a Diana Vreeland protégée and thirty-five-year Condé veteran; in came thicker paper stock and a new focus on ultra-high-end homes, ideally occupied by a celebrity. Paige fought back: she sent word to designers that if they shared their work with *House & Garden*, they would be banned from *AD*—for life. "It was never discussed, but I instinctively knew that I was to show my work exclusively in *Architectural Digest*, something like being under contract with a major Hollywood film studio," one interior designer recalled. Paige once paid $20,000 to a competing magazine, *Interiors*, to kill their piece on a new boutique hotel in Washington, DC, that Paige wanted to feature in *AD*. The *Digest* also borrowed a Condé high/low trick by hiring literary talent like John Updike and Arthur Miller to write about topics like bathroom design; years before Graydon Carter's *VF* Hollywood Issue, it dedicated an issue to movie star homes. The introduction of the AD100, a list of prestigious decorators, cemented Paige's arbiter status.

In the summer of 1987, Si decided *House & Garden* had not done enough to compete with *AD*'s garish fantasia. Its editor, Louis Oliver Gropp, was on vacation in Newport Beach, California, where he used a pay phone once a day to check his messages. One afternoon, he received word that Si wanted to talk. "Lou, have you been reading *Women's Wear Daily* while you've been on vacation?" Si said. "There have been a lot of stories that Anna Wintour is going to become the editor of *House & Garden*."

Gropp froze. "Is that true?" he asked.

"Yes," Si replied.

One month later, Gropp found himself presiding over a lavish design awards ceremony at the Plaza Hotel, sponsored by Condé Nast, that doubled as his own memorial service. Word was out that Anna was in, and the decorators and architects in the audience were already flocking to the chic Englishwoman who was newly in their midst. Because Si, at that point, was still reluctant to fire Grace Mirabella, he had decided on *House & Garden* to provide Anna a useful test of her ability to revamp a title. Anna renamed the magazine *HG*—an echo of *Architectural Digest*'s nickname of *AD*—and upped the celebrity quotient, running lavish spreads of homes owned by Bette Midler, David Hockney, Karl Lagerfeld, and Michael Chow. Sheila Metzner photographed the succulents in David Lynch's garden. Anna also emphasized fashion: an article about seating featured models in high heels balancing on designer chairs. Anna brought energy—even her cover lines ended in exclamation points ("Simply Chintz!")—but the old-guard design world balked at this blending of decor and fashion. "Apparently I am now working for 'House & Closet,'" quipped John Richardson. Other nicknames included "House & Garment" and "Vanity Chair." One whimsical photo spread, featuring celebrity hairdressers in a garden cutting topiaries, was met with particular disdain. Readers were so puzzled that Condé Nast set up a 1-800 phone line to field subscriber complaints and cancellations. "I was shocked to receive so much hate mail my first week," Anna recalled.

The Wintour era at *HG* lasted barely ten months. In June 1988, Si Newhouse announced Anna's departure for *Vogue*. Her replacement, Nancy Novogrod, remembered Si coming to her office to gush over the latest pages from *AD*: "Look how dramatic this is. Look at how wonderful." Novogrod lasted for five years; like Gropp before her, she learned of her ouster by telephone, while hosting a dinner with advertisers at North Carolina's High Point furniture market in April 1993. It turned out she wasn't just losing her job—Condé Nast was closing *House & Garden* entirely. Secretly, Si had been courting Paige through a mutual friend, the decorator Mario Buatta. At a meeting at the Hotel Bel-Air, Si told Paige that he would purchase *AD* on one condition: that she come with it. If he couldn't beat *AD*, he would buy it. In 1993, the Newhouses paid $175 million for *AD* and its sister publication, *Bon Appétit*, a significant premium over the magazines' annual revenues. After ninety-two years, *House & Garden* was dead.

Paige now took her place among Condé's most powerful editors. Designers showered her with gifts. "Decorators would say to me that they would take Paige to dinner, and look in Cartier's window, and she would admire a pair of earrings, and they would send it to her the next day," Kron told me. "And she didn't send it back." Paige was not shy about the quid pro quo arrangement with many of the brands she showcased. "Let's say there are two carpet manufacturers," she said at a 1997 industry luncheon. "One supports us with advertising. They don't ask for anything, they just give us their money. The other doesn't give us their money. Why would I give credit for the one that doesn't support us with their advertising? Why should I slap the other one in the face?"

Paige published spreads on Gore Vidal's home in Ravello, Estée Lauder's Palm Beach manor, and Michael Bloomberg's restoration of Gracie Mansion in New York. Just as *Vogue* gradually replaced models with celebrities, the cover of *AD* increasingly became a showcase for movie stars: an issue featuring Jennifer Aniston was one of its biggest-selling ever.

In 1995, Si announced a revival of *House & Garden*, citing a comeback in the American housing market. Paige was furious. "I killed it once," she declared. "I'll kill it again." The new *House & Garden* editor, Dominique Browning, soon discovered that sharing a corporate owner with Paige would do her no favors. When Mario Buatta bumped into Browning at a gala, the designer blanched. "I can't be seen talking to you," he whispered. "Paige is here." David Carey, the new *House & Garden* publisher, learned that Paige was telling decorators that if they cooperated with Browning, *AD* would never feature their houses again. Carey was flabbergasted: Why would Si allow one magazine to so brutally undercut the other? Carey brought the matter to Si and suggested there could be benefits to collaboration, but the boss was unmoved.

"If it's not her, it's going to be someone else," Si told Carey, dismissing his concerns about Paige. "Figure it out."

This exchange captured one of Si's key precepts: competition was always good. He liked watching his editors joust over the same celebrity exclusives and the same luxury advertisers, figuring that intramural rivalries would force every magazine to raise its game. Si didn't mind when Anna Wintour sent a memo to the *Allure* staff, with a list of photographers who, Anna maintained, were exclusive to *Vogue* and therefore could never appear in *Allure*'s pages. Graydon Carter used to tell his staff never to discuss magazine business in the company elevator, "because the competition is going up and down with you." He had fond memories of how one *Vanity Fair* publisher, Mitchell Fox, found subtle ways to undercut the in-house competitors at *Vogue*.

"He'd be on a sales call, and a woman would say, 'Well, you know, I'm putting a lot of my money in *Vogue*,'" Graydon recalled. "And Mitch says, 'Don't get me wrong. Our receptionist, she loves *Vogue*! When she gets on the subway to go home to Queens, she just reads that thing cover to cover.'"

Paige eventually made good on her vow of corporate fratricide. In December 2007, Condé closed *House & Garden* again. Browning walked into work on a Monday morning and was told to clear out her things by Friday night. Weeks later, at an Upper East Side dinner for the AD100 attended by the grandees of the design world, Paige luxuriated in her victory. The death of *House & Garden*, she crowed, was "richly deserved."

Paige retired in 2010, when she was eighty-one, but her magazine's uncritical worship of wealth and real estate extravagance lives on in the cultural fabric. The many online purveyors of lavish Instagram and TikTok house tours owe *AD* a debt for pioneering this shameless genre of voyeuristic fix, and websites like Zillow allow users to gaze into elaborate properties they will never buy. As income inequality has worsened, and home ownership itself became a more distant goal for millennials and Gen Z, the complicated appeal of real estate porn—its blend of pleasure, envy, and enchantment—has only grown.

17

Technical Difficulties

One day in the mid-1980s, Alex Liberman was standing in the *Vogue* art department as an executive tried to show him how to use a newly purchased digital layout system. After a few minutes, he lost his patience.

"*Computers!*" Alex declared, with his usual haughty flourish. "It's a phase."

Joan Juliet Buck, editor of *Vogue Paris* in the 1990s, once asked an executive at Condé Nast's French headquarters to purchase computers for the staff.

"*Non*," came the reply.

Flummoxed, Buck argued that her editors needed internet access to stay in electronic touch with designers and their colleagues in New York, London, and Milan. The executive sniffed, "They'll be playing solitaire all day long."

By 1994, the fashion team at *Allure* had made a great leap forward: a single computer was installed, for the use of the entire department. In 1995, Steve Florio was asked by Charlie Rose if he had concerns about the coming world of "electronic publishing." "I don't worry about it," Florio replied. "I mean, the fact of the matter is, what we're talking about here are ideas. And whether the record is on a 78 or a cassette or a CD-ROM, or whatever, you still want to hear the music."

"When the electronic revolution is here," Florio added, "we will have the content that the people that develop the system will want."

The internet broke Condé Nast. No major magazine publisher anticipated the profound changes that the web would bring to the ways that people consumed news and information, images and words. But in Condé's case, the dawn of the digital world carried an extra payload, perhaps the most lethal of all: it introduced the means of cultural curation to the masses. For a company founded on the precept of exclusivity, whose business model and social clout hinged on its perceived expertise in taste, this was existential. Looking back, the moments when Condé *did* innovate on the web—when it published early online recipes and the first online slideshows from fashion shows in Europe—are all the more agonizing because Si and his deputies never pursued them to their logical, profitable ends. For years, the company's web teams were starved for resources, even as editors dreamed up innovations that, if nurtured correctly, might have secured Condé's pre-eminence for a new generation. "You're going to have to go a long way on the Internet to compete with the way we produce words and images in the magazines," Thomas J. Wallace, Condé Nast's editorial director, confidently told *The New York Times*.

He uttered those words in the summer of 2008.

"The digital world wasn't the Condé Nast world," said Deborah Needleman, whose ideas for online growth at *Domino*, a beloved and short-lived Condé magazine that she oversaw in the 2000s, were met with ambivalence and neglect. "They wanted to stay on the mountaintop."

SI HAD ANTICIPATED the consumer capitalism explosion of the 1980s. But when it came to the internet, he was a skeptic. In the early 1990s, it seemed axiomatic to Si that the lushness and sheen of physical magazines was what announced Condé's authority to the world and enticed high-spending advertisers to show off luxury goods in immaculately art-directed pages. He was also a wealthy magnate in his late sixties, who from childhood had loved the ink-and-pulp romance of print. The early internet, with its janky visuals and fragile dial-up connections, hardly seemed like much of a threat.

One Newhouse, however, was intrigued.

Steven O. Newhouse was the oldest son of Si's brother, Donald, and he had grown up in the Park Avenue apartment directly underneath Sam and Mitzi. Steven attended Collegiate and Yale, the old-line elite education that had eluded his father and uncle, and as a teenager he worked classifieds at the Newhouse-owned *Newark Star-Ledger*. Like Donald, Steven had an unassuming side. Touring one of his family's newsrooms, he reported feeling self-conscious, as if he "was being shown off as a curiosity"; when he transferred to a Newhouse-owned paper in Springfield, Massachusetts, he insisted on working the night shift. In 1983, at age twenty-six, Steven took over as editor of *The Jersey Journal*, a community paper covering the North Jersey suburbs, where he would remain for a decade, toiling in a nondescript Jersey City office that was a river and a world away from his uncle's Condé Nast kingdom.

Steven appeared destined to succeed his father in overseeing the sleepy, if dependable, newspaper side of the Newhouse family dynasty. But in the early 1990s, Steven, seemingly alone among his family members, took an interest in the internet. "No one else in the business really cared or wanted to pursue new media," he recalled. "I elected myself." Steven joined a program at MIT's Media Lab examining the effects of digital technology on the news business, where he encountered an early version of a web browser. At the urging of the lab's director, Nicholas Negroponte, Steven persuaded his family to invest $3 million, reportedly in exchange for a 15 percent stake, in *Wired*, a new magazine in San Francisco about technology. *Wired* was in the process of creating *HotWired*, the first commercial online magazine, and Steven decided the local Newhouse newspapers should go online, too. In those early internet days, he had little trouble securing domain names like NJ.com, Cleveland.com, and Syracuse.com, all of which were still readily available. "If I had been really smart, I would have bought a thousand of the best URLs and made hundreds of millions of dollars," Steven said years later.

It was right around then that Rochelle Udell ran into trouble with a turkey.

Udell, a longtime editorial director at Condé Nast, was hosting Thanksgiving dinner at home in 1994 when she realized she could not fit two whole birds into her oven. Was it possible to roast a turkey on an outdoor grill? Her collection of *Gourmet* and *Bon Appétit* back issues yielded no answers, so Udell logged on to America Online, a dial-up internet service just starting to attract a following. At 6:20 a.m. on Thanksgiving Day, Udell posed her question to a chat room called "AOL Talk Turkey." Within minutes, she had more than twenty answers. Users followed up throughout the day to see how her meal was turning out.

Dashing between her kitchen and desktop computer, Udell was struck by an insight that many of her peers in publishing would take years, even decades, to fully comprehend. The internet was a wellspring of spontaneous communities, like-minded groups of people bonding across time and space over shared interests and desires—not unlike the readers of a magazine. Monthly subscribers were essentially signing up for a club, their membership (and whatever perceived status it conferred) signaled by the titles they kept on the coffee table. But instead of the one-way direction of editors declaring what to do and think—with feedback limited to the slow and highly mediated format of letters to the editor—the web allowed for instantaneous and interactive connections. It was a conversation, not a decree. And Udell, who had helped create the visual identities of *Self*, *Vogue*, and Robert Gottlieb's *New Yorker*, believed there was no company better positioned to spark a conversation than Condé Nast.

After the holiday break, Udell approached the Newhouses. Condé was sitting on an incredible archive of recipes from *Gourmet* and *Bon Appétit*; why not put them online? Time Inc. had just launched Pathfinder, a website with articles and photographs from *Time*, *People*, and *Fortune*; other magazine publishers were experimenting with packaging CD-ROMs with print issues. Udell explained how recipes could be indexed based on ingredients, letting readers quickly sift through thousands of options. A website about food and beverage, she argued, could promote Condé's lifestyle expertise. Steven endorsed her plan, and Si agreed—to a point. He told Udell that Condé would pay for the site, but it needed a unique name. Gourmet.com or BonAppetit.com, Si declared, were off-limits.

It was, in hindsight, a grievous error. Condé Nast controlled some of the most powerful brands in the world of lifestyle journalism. Yet, given the opportunity, it declined to plant those brands in the virgin soil of the web. Si, who did not use the internet, viewed the online world as untamed territory. He had built his empire on the mantra that perception was everything, and the potential of tarnishing *Gourmet*'s immaculate image by tossing it onto the web—an inchoate realm of gossip, porn, and god knows what else—seemed too big a gamble. He didn't want to undermine the lucrative ad sales for his print magazines, either.

"The safe way of doing it was not to risk any brands, because you didn't know what was going to happen with the internet," Udell recalled. "We decided that it would be safer at that moment in time to call it something else."

So Epicurious.com was born. In May 1995, Udell became the founder and president of CondéNet, a new digital publishing arm for the company. (It would be another ten years before Condé Nast deigned to officially absorb CondéNet; until then, it remained a parallel unit under the Newhouses' Advance Publications umbrella.) Udell had a budget—minuscule by Condé standards—and a modest office on East Forty-fifth Street, around the corner from the 350 Madison mothership. Her internet connection had to be beamed in from 350 via radio waves; when the service kept dropping out, Udell discovered that a secretary was blocking the signal with a potted plant on a windowsill. CondéNet's servers were stored in Jersey City, sharing a floor with a local dental office; when the dentist's drill blew a fuse, CondéNet's servers went dead, and any unsaved work was lost. Si had granted Epicurious the rights to digitize five thousand recipes. But in the bizarre, every-tub-on-its-own-bottom culture of Condé Nast, he barred the site from publishing any of the lush photographs from the *Gourmet* archives.

Epicurious's launch, in August 1995, came without the fanfare that usually accompanied a new Condé publication, but it proved a modest success. A database allowed users to plug in specific ingredients—say, what they had sitting around the pantry—and find matching recipes. "Gail's Recipe Swap," a community board feature, attracted hundreds of dedicated commenters, some of whom met up in person for "IRL" dinner parties. This was a breakthrough in digital food media; Eater.com would not exist for another decade. Still, the message from the powers at Condé Nast was one of ambivalence, bordering on contempt. In July 1997, James Truman, Si's editorial director, grew bored during a meeting of editors and executives discussing the future of Epicurious. Less than halfway through the gathering, Truman stood up.

"This is just too interesting for me," Truman said, and left.

SI DID ULTIMATELY INVEST in the 1990s dot-com boom, but it was in the form of his favorite medium: a print magazine. In 1998, Condé Nast paid about $80 million to purchase *Wired* outright. According to Linda Rice, a senior Condé executive who was involved in the deal, Si refused to spend an extra $100,000 to secure the rights to *Wired*'s website and its other digital offshoots. At the time, the *Wired* website was losing money and dragging down the brand's overall finances. Eight years later, Condé Nast would pay $25 million to reunite *Wired* and Wired.com. "Si would not spend the money," Rice recalled, saying that the lawyers advising the deal were "practically crying" that Si could not see the long-term benefit. "When you have a family-owned business, you can do what you want," Rice said, "and sometimes you are going to make mistakes."

The combination of Condé's shimmering Manhattanites with Silicon Valley–based *Wired*, a start-up whose workers ate lunch in an illegal loft kitchen, proved awkward. When Steve Florio flew to San Francisco to welcome the staff, he quipped, "Think of us as your rich uncles in New York." The uncles did not disappoint. *Wired*'s then editor, Katrina Heron, was dumbfounded to be offered a $40,000 annual clothing allowance, an amount considered modest by Condé editor in chief standards. (She barely spent any of it.) Si encouraged Heron to accept an interest-free loan for a down payment on an apartment in San Francisco; when she left Condé Nast in 2001, no one at the company asked for the money back. "This is the worst-run business," Heron remembered thinking to herself. "These people are idiotic." Later, after she sold the apartment, Heron mailed a cashier's check to Condé Nast for the amount she had borrowed. The accounting office called, befuddled, and asked Heron what the money was for. They had no record of it.

Meanwhile, the editors at Condé's print titles in New York were given little incentive to familiarize themselves with the internet. When a features editor joined *Vogue* in 1994, he sent an email to the staff introducing himself. A response arrived from Anna Wintour—in the form of a fax. "This is *Vogue*," Anna wrote. "We don't email. It's so impersonal."

In hindsight, the ambitions of Condé's tiny web team look prescient. One idea at Epicurious, never acted upon, was to post menus from restaurants across the country and allow users to place food orders. Another site, Swoon, featured an online dating section; a travel site called Concierge.com, an arm of *Condé Nast Traveler*, provided hotel suggestions based on users' preferences (beach, city, golf). The basic tenets of Seamless, Tinder, Goop, and other future tech behemoths were there, but Condé's leadership did not grasp the long-term potential. Instead, Si was content with small, minimally funded websites that were essentially cordoned off from his most lucrative magazine brands. By 1997, *Vogue, Vanity Fair, GQ,* and *The New Yorker* still did not have websites. "We are uninterested in making electronic versions of our print titles," Joan Feeney, the editorial director of CondéNet, said that year. "That doesn't make sense to us; it seems more a vanity operation than anything else." She added, "People say, 'Why isn't *Vogue* online?' And I say, 'Why would it be?'"

In 1999, Anna agreed to experiment with a website. Ironically, her efforts, forward-looking and well-intentioned as they were, sowed the seeds of the digital fashion revolution that decades later would leave her and her magazine struggling for relevance.

Vogue.com launched in September 1999, and it became the first internet site to publish photographs of every look from high-fashion runway shows in near real time. Back then, shows in Paris, Milan, and

New York were highly exclusive, and designers put strict limits on which of their looks could be photographed for public consumption; sometimes, fewer than half a dozen images were released. Anna took it upon herself to persuade designers to shed their concerns about piracy and exclusivity. She dispatched Joan Feeney of CondéNet to ateliers in Paris, armed with a laptop to show designers firsthand how their clothes would appear on the site. Many of the designers had never even used the internet; after some initial reluctance, they fell in line. "Because Anna blessed it, it came to pass," Feeney recalled. Readers on Vogue.com were invited to sort photos by individual designers and specific categories, like swimsuits, lamé, and hot pants. ("Choose over 5000 looks from the world's top designers.") Thus Condé Nast pioneered the instantaneous digital coverage that would eventually undo its own authority in the fashion world.

Feeney had pitched her bosses on charging a twelve-dollar annual fee, about the same cost as a print subscription, but the sales executives said no. Their bonuses were based on print ad sales, and anything that threatened that revenue was anathema. Vogue.com would be further undermined a year later, when Condé introduced a new website that combined its magazines' fashion coverage under one roof. Once again, Si set aside the company's globally renowned brand names and instead created a new one: Style.com, a URL that Condé purchased from Leslie Wexner's retail conglomerate, Limited Brands. On launch day, in September 2000, Style.com included a rudimentary revenue-sharing agreement with Neiman Marcus, whereby Condé Nast earned a cut of sales from merchandise purchased on the site. The soon-to-be-multibillion-dollar e-commerce market was in its nascent stages; Net-a-Porter had started just three months before. But in another so-close-yet-so-far moment, Condé let the opportunity pass by. It would be another fifteen years before the company embarked on a belated effort to convert Style.com into a full-blown retail destination. By then, in part because of its own hesitation to embrace the web, Condé Nast was no longer the paramount power in fashion. An entire generation of consumers raised on smartphones trusted the taste of amateur Instagram influencers and upstart retailers like Ssense over the expertise of editors at a single company in New York. Condé Nast invested more than $100 million in the new Style.com, which launched near the end of 2016. The site shut down after nine months.

AGAIN AND AGAIN, EDITORS CAME TO FEEL that Condé—hindered by a combination of caution, arrogance, incuriosity, and incompetence—was years behind where it should be on the digital front. In December 2003, two years after *The New Yorker* launched its website, the magazine's managing editor, Pamela Maffei McCarthy, wanted to post an online conversation between Philip Gourevitch and George Packer about the discovery of the deposed Saddam Hussein in a spider hole in Iraq. This was major breaking news, and McCarthy wanted the audio posted right away—but it was a Sunday, and she discovered that CondéNet did not operate on the weekends. At that time, *The New Yorker* had no capability to publish a story on its website on its own. McCarthy had to dig out a phone book to look up the home number of a CondéNet executive who could help.

As late as October 2009, editors at *GQ* and *Details* could only share "print" articles with Condé's online menswear portal, men.style.com, twice a month. The site had no blog posts, and users couldn't write comments. "We're very 2002 right now," a *GQ* editor quipped at the time. Linda Wells, the editor of *Allure*, recalled how difficult it was to get the attention of CondéNet or to secure a budget for a website. At one point, she pitched a digital "product finder" that would help readers sift through cosmetics products online. "I couldn't get the tech or the support," she said. Internally, magazine websites were often viewed as virtual advertisements that could attract subscribers to the "real deal" in print. In 2008, just 3 percent of Condé's overall ad revenue stemmed from digital sales, less than rivals like Time Inc. Condé Nast did not appoint a chief technology officer until 2010.

"They just felt there was no point in being a leader," recalled Dominique Browning, who edited *House & Garden* until 2007. "They would wait and see how things unfolded. I think that ultimately was a catastrophic decision, in terms of catching up with where the world was going. We were very, very slow."

In Si's defense, virtually no one in publishing at the time could predict the future. James Truman pointed out to me that the dot-com crash in 2000 had reinforced the broader institutional resistance to expanding on the internet. "Si thought [the web] was a giant money pit," Truman recalled. After the late-1990s tech bubble burst, "people like Si looked like they had been right all along."

Ruth Reichl, who became editor of *Gourmet* in 1999, nudged Si to create Gourmet.com for years. She and her staff had watched as online foodie culture blossomed and their magazine, the grande dame of epicurean glossies, was left behind. (*Gourmet* was first published in 1941, and purchased by Condé Nast in 1983.) Because *Gourmet*'s recipes appeared online under the Epicurious banner, Reichl believed she was missing a crucial opportunity to entice the next generation of food enthusiasts to read her magazine. By 2007, Si had relented and agreed to start a website, but he included a proviso that left Reichl dumbstruck: *Gourmet*'s own recipes were off-limits. Now it was Epicurious's success that Si was worried about cannibalizing.

By 2011, Condé had created a new division, Condé Nast Entertainment, to focus on creating online video and bulking up digital revenues. But it could be hard to persuade some editors to pay attention. At one meeting with the division, Graydon Carter became distracted by a pair of ugly leather clogs worn by one of its top executives; afterward, the offending footwear was all he could talk about. "They were really bad shoes, and we had a standard to uphold," recalled Dana Brown, defending his boss. "It *was Vanity Fair* and Condé Nast after all." Around 2015, *Vanity Fair* put up a poster in its office that read, "Think Like a Start-Up."

When James Truman and the editor Kim France founded a magazine in 2000 called *Lucky*, which celebrated shopping and included price tags on every item it featured, Truman saw an easy opportunity to expand into e-commerce. But Condé never took the last logical step and converted it to an online marketplace. Truman faced stern opposition from top sales executives, who believed a Condé-owned shopping site would compete against, and therefore alienate, the department stores that spent tens of millions of dollars on print advertising. (*Lucky* ceased publication in 2015.) A similar fate befell *Domino*, the DIY decoration magazine founded by Deborah Needleman in 2005. *Domino* celebrated a proto-Instagram aesthetic of Lucite coffee tables and eye-popping Jonathan Adler–style prints. Early on, when Needleman asked her Condé Nast bosses to hire a web editor, she was told not to bother: her magazine's budget covered thirty employees, and a web person would be "a waste of a headcount." Undeterred, Needleman developed a business plan for a website where users could collect images from anywhere on the web and store them in folders, creating custom mood boards for decorating ideas that could be shared with friends. The site, called My Deco File, went live in August 2008. Condé Nast was paying Needleman about $500,000 a year, plus a clothing allowance and a free car—but the company refused to hire a Deco Files support staff. "I was on my own," Needleman recalled. "No one cared." *Domino*, along with Deco Files, was abruptly shut down by Condé Nast five months later, and Needleman left the company. (Condé let her keep the car.)

In 2010, a site called Pinterest, remarkably similar to the one Needleman had envisioned, debuted. In 2019, it went public. In January 2025, its market capitalization was $22 billion.

18

The Elephant

The debut cover of *Condé Nast Portfolio*, the blockbuster new business magazine that Si brought to market in May 2007 at a cost estimated between $100 and $150 million, was a nighttime aerial photograph of the Manhattan skyline, skyscrapers aglow with electric light, a romantic vision of American power and hegemony. The lead headline touted an essay by Tom Wolfe, the country's foremost chronicler of status, on "The New Masters of the Universe," the hedge fund kings who had succeeded 1980s corporate specialists as the national avatars of wealth. The issue was a 332-page behemoth, with 185 pages of high-priced ads, the heft itself a conspicuous argument by Condé Nast that, no matter where the magazine industry was headed in the digital age, print remained supreme.

It was the wrong idea at the exact wrong time.

Even before it hit newsstands, *Portfolio*, whose tumultuous and expensive run lasted only two years, had been described as perhaps "the most counterintuitive (not to say craziest) media venture of the decade." Just as online news was devouring the advertising base for print media, and rival magazine publishers were shifting resources to the web, Si decided to bet on the sort of luscious, big-budget print product that, since his father's death in 1979, had driven the growth of his family's influence. He had faced naysayers before: the critics who denounced his revival of *Vanity Fair* as overpriced and superficial, who assumed Tina would be exiled back to London and Si exposed as another failed striver. Now, as Si neared eighty, *Portfolio* offered him a chance to prove the doubters wrong, one more time—maybe the last time before he would be forced to relinquish control of his kingdom to the next generation. After all, hadn't Condé Nast always given readers what they wanted, before they knew they wanted it?

Si had reasons beyond ego to invest in this new venture. When he conceived of *Portfolio*, in 2005, business magazines like *Fortune* and *Forbes* were still posting healthy ad revenues. A new era of Wall Street hedonism was underway, fueled by record banking profits. Ivy League graduates and other rising elites—the core Condé demographic—were choosing Goldman Sachs and Lehman Brothers over law school. And if Tina Brown had managed to sex up suits like Barry Diller and Michael Ovitz, why couldn't another talented young editor do the same for Ken Griffin and Jamie Dimon? Si also believed deeply that luxury advertisers would never accept the gimcrack world of digital banner ads, that they needed the thick pages of a glossy magazine to appropriately showcase their wares. "There was a sense that Condé Nast was in such a unique position that it wouldn't be as vulnerable to the market changes that were coming," Tom Florio recalled.

To enact his vision, Si again turned to an outsider: Joanne Lipman, a financial journalist who had spent her entire twenty-two-year career at *The Wall Street Journal*. She created a pair of lifestyle sections, Weekend Journal and Personal Journal, that modernized the paper's stippled pages and succeeded with readers and advertisers. Lipman was in contention to replace the longtime *Journal* editor Paul Steiger when, in 2005, Si invited her to lunch at his East Side apartment and asked if she thought it was a good idea for Condé Nast to start a business magazine. "Oh my god, yes!" Lipman replied. Later, she said she felt so elated by their discussion that if she had been hit by a truck on the way out, she would have died happy. When she got back to her office, there was an email waiting for her from Si: "Let's do it."

True to his word, Si spared no expense. Lipman was able to hire more than seventy-five journalists, lure stars with salaries in the mid-six figures, and give her team more than a year to develop the magazine without having to produce a single issue. Internet aside, this was still the peak era of Condé, and the staff acted accordingly. "All I did for a year was go to extremely expensive restaurants and woo people to write for us," recalled Jim Impoco, a deputy editor who was eventually ousted after clashing with Lipman. "I put on twenty-five pounds from my expense account." Ambitious cover ideas were commissioned, executed, and abandoned. One early concept involved photographing the Brooklyn Bridge from a helicopter, with the *Portfolio* team arranging for a container ship and a water taxi to sail under the bridge at the exact moment that a fleet of cars crossed its span. The staff pulled it off—but never used the resulting image, which was deemed not dramatic enough for the debut issue. Tom Wolfe's essay was rumored to have cost twelve dollars a word. Its first sentence was a signature Wolfean onomatopoeia—"Not bam bam bam bam bam bam, but *bama bampa barama bam bammity bam bam bammity barampa*"—and a joke flew around the office that the nonsense opening sentence "was two hundred bucks right there." (The full piece ran 7,400 words, netting Wolfe twice the average newspaper reporter's annual salary.) The day that the first issue was published, every staff member received a bottle of Perrier-Jouët Champagne, and Lipman went to the Nasdaq to ring the closing bell.

Inside 4 Times Square, though, there were signs of unease. Lipman had trouble fitting in with the Condé milieu. Part of this was her background in newspapers, which left her unfamiliar with the expectations of a glossy magazine. She turned down a wardrobe allowance—standard-issue for Condé editors in chief—and some of her styling choices raised eyebrows among the staff. "She was a fish out of water," recalled one former colleague. "I don't think she quite understood what the Condé culture was, or what the vibe should be, because it wasn't really her." The notion of Lipman, an accomplished journalist, being judged for her clothes and makeup would be repellent at many professional organizations. And yet Condé Nast was all about perception, and the success of *Portfolio*—its ability to attract high-end readers and high-spending advertisers—hinged in part on Lipman projecting a high-status image. Ugly bits of gossip soon turned up in the trade press, painting Lipman as a rube; *The New York Observer* reported that after being urged to assign an article to the five-time National Magazine Award finalist James Fallows, she had asked to see his clips. (Lipman told me this anecdote "is laughable and invented.")

Then the high-flying economy, the basis of *Portfolio*'s business model, began to collapse. Bear Stearns was sold for a paltry two dollars a share in March 2008; advertising began to dry up. Confident Condé Nast kept spending. In the summer of 2008, the writer Jesse Eisinger filed a story about the credit derivatives desk at JPMorgan Chase. Presciently, Eisinger identified the bank's mutant securities as a lurking risk to the global economy. The *Portfolio* editors settled on a headline—"The $58 Trillion Elephant in the Room"—and commissioned a photograph of a live elephant inside an office building, "to illustrate the notion that these credit derivatives are the huge problem in the room that people are trying to ignore."

It would have been easier and cheaper to create this scene with a stock image of a pachyderm and the magic of Photoshop. But this was Condé Nast. "There wasn't really any hesitation," the photographer, Phillip Toledano, said about the pitch from the editors. "It just made sense. Of *course* it's going to be an elephant."

The shoot at the Brooklyn Navy Yard happened in early September—days before Lehman Brothers collapsed. An elephant was trucked in from Connecticut and led by handlers into the studio through a massive garage door. "I'm just standing there fucking amazed," Toledano recalled. The result was a dramatic and arresting visual, the sort of manufactured fantasy that had long been a Condé calling card: an elephant bellowing beside a water cooler as a white-collar worker cowers in fear. Between the star photographer, studio fees, and rental of a gigantic exotic animal, the image was exorbitantly expensive to produce—$30,000 for the elephant alone, a staffer later told *The New York Times*. And yet the photograph was buried inside the November 2008 issue, the cover of which instead featured Dov Charney, the founder of American Apparel, reclining on a bed and flashing a come-hither look. (Lipman told me that she did not authorize the elephant shoot and was alarmed by the cost. "I assumed it was Photoshop—and was stunned when I found out they hired an elephant!" she wrote in an email. "This was a real 'not in Kansas anymore' moment for me. We never did anything like that again.")

The collapse of Wall Street and the ensuing economic downturn seemed expressly, almost perversely, designed to hurt *Portfolio*. Financial firms, whose advertising was expected to provide a healthy chunk of revenue, pulled their ads en masse; luxury, automotive, and travel advertisers retrenched, too. *Portfolio* reportedly lost close to $35 million in 2008; by the first quarter of 2009, its ad pages were down 40 percent. Lipman had leaned into an elevated form of service journalism, publishing explanatory articles on the basics of fractional private jet ownership and useful tips for truffle hunting. ("Make sure your truffle feels heavy for its size; that means it's fresher, because its natural moisture hasn't yet evaporated.") Such features now looked risibly out of touch.

Something deeper, too, was turning in the culture, a change that boded poorly for Si Newhouse and the elite society his kingdom presided over. It wasn't just consumption that was losing its luster. The Great Recession, and the ensuing bailout for Wall Street's wealthiest, had signaled a larger shift in societal attitudes toward the establishment. The carefree capitalism that had buttressed Condé Nast's fortunes all these years was yielding to wariness, suspicion, even disgust and anger toward the elite. On April 27, 2009, two years after its debut, Si told Lipman that he was shutting down *Portfolio*. The Last Great Magazine Launch had failed.

At the time, Lipman defended her creation as "the right magazine at a very unfortunate time." "Si was generous, and he was truly heartbroken when the magazine closed," she wrote to me sixteen years later. "He loved *Portfolio*. So did readers—our renewal rates were among the best in the building. Condé Nast for me was an entirely different world. I'm a subway girl, so entering a world of car service and first-class travel and wardrobe allowances (which I turned down!) was an eye-opener. Elephant aside, we were not big spenders, especially compared with other magazines in the company."

But in the immediate wake of the closure, it was Tina Brown who grasped the existential significance of the magazine's demise. "All this is so unlike Si," Tina wrote in a post for her relatively new web publication, *The Daily Beast*. "Until now, he was always the media emperor who could live and do as he chose." As familiar as she was with Si's caprice, Tina knew that he loved magazines, relished doting on them, and was willing to sustain enormous losses to preserve them. The death of *Portfolio*, she concluded, amounted to an "unprecedented sight": "The magazine world's last big believer, Si Newhouse, exhibiting what looks like signs of throwing in the towel."

THE SPENDTHRIFT CULTURE OF CONDÉ NAST could not remain immune from the Great Recession. In October 2008, editors were asked to reduce their budgets by 5 percent; five months later, word came down that another 10 percent had to go. *The New York Post* reported that several top editors and executives had even relinquished their chauffeured Mercedes in favor of the subway; among the straphangers were David Remnick and Ruth Reichl of *Gourmet*. "When they gave up the town cars, that was a moment," recalled Jim Impoco. "That was like Marie Antoinette saying, 'No croissants for me this morning!'"

Part of the problem was the erosion of other branches of the Newhouse empire. The family's regional newspapers had once functioned as financial buffers for the big spenders at the magazines; one executive claimed that in the 1990s, *The Staten Island Advance* netted more money than all of the Condé titles combined. The digital revolution had steadily worn away those revenues—and then, in June 2007, the iPhone went on sale. Here was all the power of the internet, with its myriad platforms for information and lifestyle journalism, placed directly in the consumer's pocket. In the ensuing years, billions would be sold. Being privately held, Condé Nast refused to disclose the extent of its pecuniary plight. But while Condé was spared the two-week furloughs that were imposed at the Newhouse newspapers in the spring of 2009, the company's chief executive, Chuck Townsend, was forced to issue an all-staff memo expressing a very un-Condé sentiment: "We'll all have to do more with less."

Townsend was a genteel, mid-Atlantic lockjaw type who favored elegant suits and once served as commodore of the New York Yacht

Club. He had climbed the Condé ranks as a salesman and ascended to the top job in 2004 after Steve Florio stepped down with health issues. (Florio died in 2007.) In an earlier era, Townsend might have been an ideal steward for Condé, adept at glad-handing advertisers and working a cocktail hour. "What Si saw in Chuck was someone who had really good breeding," recalled a person who worked under him. But Townsend had the misfortune to reach the summit just as the mountain began to melt. In July 2009, he hired McKinsey, the white-shoe management consulting firm, to conduct a top-to-bottom review of Condé Nast business practices. The company that once spared no expense in the pursuit of creative excellence was capitulating to cost-cutters who wanted several magazines to slash a quarter of their budgets. And Alex Liberman was no longer around to tear up the budget sheets and banish the suits from his office.

If one had to pinpoint the end of Condé's halcyon era, it might be August 11, 2009, when *The New York Observer*, the paper of record for Manhattan's shapers of the monoculture, ran a devastating story declaring that "the enchanting, mystical era of Condé Nast is pretty much over." Weekly flower deliveries and complimentary Oranginas were gone. The receptionists who greeted guests at each magazine's office—a tradition dating to *Vogue*'s gold-and-lapis antechamber in the Graybar Building—were laid off (although *The New Yorker* managed to transfer its receptionist to the fiction department). Graydon Carter had been spotted waiting in line with the plebes at the Gehry cafeteria's stir-fry station, sending chills through the lower ranks. Condé's zephyrs of old-school civility were wafting into the past.

"In the old days, everyone sent gifts to everyone else," one editor recalled. "If someone had a baby, they might get eight deliveries of flowers from the office. And everyone would expense it. . . . There would be lots of flowers and all sorts of gift bags and you'd try to look at the name tags of the people getting them. But there's not many of those rides on the elevators these days." All these subtle indignities were encapsulated in a detail that could only have mattered in Condé's rigidly hierarchical world. Before 2008, mini-fridges at 4 Times Square were fully stocked with bottles of Fiji water. After the crash, the Fiji turned into Poland Spring. Then, in 2009, the Poland Spring supply dwindled, too.

"We won't have any more after this," an employee complained. "We have to start drinking tap water."

Chuck Townsend took exception to all the focus on potables. "The Red Bulls and Oranginas are maybe no longer there, but what's the difference?" he told the *Observer*. "I don't want to lose the specialty or the quirkiness, but a lot of this stuff that has been part and parcel of it is just meaningless." He added, "You don't need it! You don't need the Orangina!" But Condé *did* need the Orangina, and all the other little luxuries that had made the company a byword for sumptuousness. Without the decadence and the perks, the smugness and the swagger, the entire edifice of Si's creation—the illusion that sustained its excesses all those years—came crashing down.

In October 2009, Condé announced it was closing *Gourmet*, its venerable food magazine, along with three other titles. "In the economics of the '80s, '90s and early 2000s, this would be a business decision balanced by the cultural reticence to part with iconic brands," Townsend said. "This economy is a completely different bag." These concessions may have seemed seismic within 4 Times Square. But in other ways, Condé exceptionalism endured. One marketing executive who joined Condé well after the crash expected to find an organization grudgingly coming to terms with financial reality. Instead, they were shocked by how little seemed to have changed. "All the publishers had car services with a driver that was their driver 100 percent of the time," the executive recalled. "Most of them had clothing budgets." Tom Florio's idea of saving money was to reserve a room at the Paris Ritz that was less expensive than his typical 2,100-euro-a-night suite.

Few on the company's publishing side were incentivized to bet on digital expansion. Internet ads paid pennies on the dollar compared to print ads; the commissions and bonuses that paid for private school and summer homes were not going to materialize from the web. And the executives could scrape together just enough evidence to convince themselves, and persuade their bosses, that the print business remained viable. *Vogue*, for instance, recorded its biggest-ever issue in September

2012: 916 pages, weighing in around five pounds. Even as once-mighty Time Inc. stumbled toward oblivion—it would eventually be sold, in 2017, to a second-tier publisher based in Iowa—Condé Nast, fueled by residual prestige and institutional intransigence, tried to carry on.

In this environment, the act of spending itself took on an elegiac air, as if the denizens of a crumbling palace were throwing a final bacchanalia before the coup. Editors took themselves out for elaborate steakhouse dinners, figuring they should take advantage of expense accounts before they were vaporized. In 2016, well after Condé's fortunes had turned, mid-level New York–based staffers were still flying out to California for ten-day work trips, with rooms booked at luxe hotels in Beverly Hills. In 2017, Condé Nast was reported to have lost more than $120 million.

Eventually, the bottom dropped out. Having moved to sleek new offices at 1 World Trade Center, Condé began squeezing its magazines onto fewer floors, freeing up commercial space that it could sublet. *Vogue* resorted to gimmicky tactics like "Vogue100," where members paid $100,000 a year for perks like breakfasts with Anna and invitations to sponsored parties. In a cost-saving measure that rivals like Hearst had instituted years earlier, Condé consolidated its copy desks, fact-checkers, and photo researchers into a central operation, stripping individual magazines of their proprietary teams. (Si's favorite, *The New Yorker*, was exempt, and its editing staff allowed to continue using Microsoft Word when other magazines were required to switch to Google Docs.) These efficiencies were ultimately not enough to offset the accelerating collapse of the print advertising market. In 2017, *Self*—the magazine that in 1979 had kicked off Si's ambitious reinvention of the company—ended its print edition. *Teen Vogue* went next, followed by the company's onetime revenue leader, *Glamour*, and three years later by the once-innovative *Allure*. Editors who once sweated over typefaces and photo crops were now urged to focus on raising their web traffic and making "snackable" online videos go viral.

In September 2017, Graydon Carter announced that he would leave *Vanity Fair* after twenty-five years at its helm. The digital revolution, he believed, was sapping the magazine business of its old romance. In 2015, though, he pulled off one final print triumph, landing the first photographs of Caitlyn Jenner, formerly Bruce, who had recently revealed her new identity as a woman. The arresting cover—Jenner in a stylish corset, shot by Annie Leibovitz and accompanied by the cheeky headline "Call Me Caitlyn"—was in its own way a milestone, a transgender celebrity looking as glamorous and confident as any Hollywood star. President Barack Obama issued a statement, posting on Twitter that "it takes courage to share your story." *Vanity Fair* published the story on its website well before the physical magazine appeared on newsstands, and the online traffic numbers broke the magazine's prior record. But the success of the Jenner cover masked Graydon's growing discontent. His relationship with Anna, a one-time friend and champion, had soured, particularly after she was promoted in 2013 to the newly created role of artistic director, which granted her Alex Liberman's old powers to oversee nearly every title at Condé Nast. Anna refrained from meddling with *The New Yorker* and *Vanity Fair*, but at one point, over lunch, she told Graydon that she had some advice about the fashion choices in *Vanity Fair*'s photo shoots.

"Can I offer you some advice on *Vogue*'s writing?" Graydon replied. The one-time friends fell into a new period of froideur.

For a while, Graydon staved off the budget and staff cuts that Condé was imposing on other magazines, but in late 2016, Anna conveyed to him that *Vanity Fair* had to acquiesce to the newly centralized structure and give up its longtime fact-checkers, designers, and photo editors. Graydon balked and was granted a reprieve, but he knew it was a matter of time before he could no longer protect *Vanity Fair* from what he believed would be a damaging retrenchment. The following year, Graydon put into motion a plan that his aides wryly dubbed "London Bridge," Buckingham Palace's code word for its playbook in the event of Queen Elizabeth II's death. Not one to wait for a corporate permission slip, he arranged to break the news of his departure with a journalist at *The New York Times* (me) and choreographed the announcement down to the minute to avoid any leaks. Even the Newhouses would be left in the dark. Steven Newhouse, by then a top executive at Advance, was standing in an Apple store on the Upper East Side when he learned of Graydon's exit via a *Times* alert on his iPhone. "You had the scoop before me," he said when we spoke later that day. Steven was quick to say that he had previously scheduled plans to dine that evening with Graydon and his wife, and that he had no interest in missing their date. In fact, he was looking forward to it: "We'll have more to talk about than we had anticipated."

ONE DAY IN THE MID-2010s, Condé Nast staffers were summoned to a series of company-wide seminars on diversity, held by an outside firm. The watchword for the event was *inclusiveness*. During one meeting, an attendee piped up to point out that the entire company had been founded on, and sustained for decades by, the celebration and fostering of exclusivity. An awkward silence filled the room.

The economic damage wrought by the 2008 market crash was one thing; Condé's magazines had weathered recessions in the past. But the company now faced a more existential threat: Condé's métier was privilege, and privilege had become a dirty word. The elites whose lives were romanticized, packaged, and sold to the masses by Condé as exemplars of American success were suddenly being recast as villains amid a populist surge. Wealth porn, long a core appeal of the Condé stable, was no longer sexy—in the immediate aftermath of the crash, it could even be seen as borderline obscene. College students who graduated into the 2008 meltdown had struggled to find work, and economists predicted this early setback would significantly curtail their lifetime earnings. The totems of American success that were fetishized by Condé Nast—designer clothes, beautiful houses—appeared increasingly unobtainable. "America is an aspirational country, and up until recently, when people who were living affluent lives were displayed in magazines, the country was fine with that, because readers had a chance at those lives," reflected Graydon Carter. "The financial crisis in 2008 changed the rules dramatically. The aspirational aspect of American culture has diminished because chances are, you can't achieve affluence the way you could've 25 or 30 years ago."

Vanity Fair's Todd Purdum detected this shift in the early 2010s, when he pitched Betsy Bloomingdale, an LA socialite and Nancy Reagan confidante, on a profile depicting her as the last great hostess-with-the-mostest in Hollywood. Bloomingdale readily agreed; to be profiled in *Vanity Fair* was a kind of lifetime achievement award within her milieu. "Then she called back," Purdum remembered, "and said her son had told her she couldn't do it in the wake of Occupy Wall Street, and that she'd be absolutely pilloried."

Soon, the company ran into another cultural sea change: the rise of identity politics. Too often, Condé's magazines had showcased a thin, white, heteronormative Anglo-American ideal. As heated debates over racial equity coursed through corporate America, employees who felt excluded from or forced to conform with this vision were no longer willing to stay quiet. By decade's end, complaints had grown inside 1 World Trade Center about microaggressions, pay disparities, and a workplace culture that some nonwhite staff members said could be intimidating at best and discriminatory at worst. When the socialite and *Vanity Fair* contributor Reinaldo Herrera visited *VF*'s web department one day in 2013, he noticed several employees of Asian descent. "It's like a visit to the Orient in here!" Herrera mused aloud, according to several people who witnessed or overheard his remark. In June 2020, the editor of *Bon Appétit*, Adam Rapoport, resigned amid accusations of racial insensitivity, prompted in part by the resurfacing of a photograph from years earlier in which Rapoport, who is white, was shown dressed up as Puerto Rican for a Halloween party. *Bon Appétit* had been a digital success story for Condé, thanks to its popular cooking videos featuring a multiethnic group of millennial staffers, but several of them had complained about pay disparities and feeling tokenized, and some later quit.

The history of race and exclusion at Condé Nast was complex and fraught—regressive and progressive by turns. In 1938, Condé Montrose Nast fired Cecil Beaton, the celebrated society photographer, after Beaton smuggled anti-Semitic remarks into an illustration for *Vogue*; hidden in his drawing was the phrase "all the damn kikes in town." After the offending language was highlighted in Walter Winchell's gossip column, Beaton was summoned to Nast's penthouse. "My periodicals have been free of attacks on race and creed and I am determined that they must remain free from such attacks," Nast told the press. "I was particularly distressed that these slurring comments should have been printed in *Vogue*, especially during these days of cruel, vicious, and unreasoning persecution of Jews." At a cost of roughly $800,000 in today's dollars, Nast paid to reprint the offending page in a portion of the month's print run to excise the anti-Semitic language.

Gordon Parks, a Black photographer, was almost broke and living in a YMCA in Harlem in the mid-1940s when his portfolio was sent to the art director of *Harper's Bazaar*, Alexey Brodovitch. When they met, Brodovitch praised Parks's work, but he apologetically explained that the Hearst Corporation forbid the hiring of Black employees, "not even for sweeping floors." Parks recounted the exchange a few days later to Edward Steichen, who nearly choked on his corned beef sandwich. "That son-of-a-bitch," Steichen muttered, and then scrawled a name and address on a sheet of paper. "Go see this man," he instructed Parks. "Tell him I sent you." The address was the Condé Nast office, and the man was Alex Liberman, who told Parks, "We must give you a chance." Soon, Parks was shooting for *Glamour*. Alex became a mentor to Parks, gradually increasing the prestige of his assignments and the size of his paychecks. After six months, Parks received a commission to shoot women's evening wear for *Vogue*—the beginning of a wider recognition of his talents. Parks shot for *Vogue* for five years and went on to a celebrated career at *Life* magazine and in Hollywood, where he directed *Shaft*.

William Norwich, a former *Vogue* editor, recalled his awe at *Vogue*'s decision, in March 1966, to put Barbra Streisand on its cover. "She had been called basically a singing anteater," said Norwich, who grew up Jewish, referring to anti-Semitic comments about the size of Streisand's nose. "Can you imagine the revelation it was for people to see Barbra Streisand? Down in the South, or in Westport, Connecticut, WASP-land? 'Barbra Streisand, that Jewess?' I found that *Vogue*, in its gentle way, declared moments that moved people culturally. It would behoove some people to have a sense of history and of what *Vogue* has contributed."

March 1966 was also the month when Donyale Luna, a Detroit-born model and a member of Andy Warhol's Factory crowd, appeared on the cover of *British Vogue*, becoming the first Black cover model on any version of *Vogue* around the world. Luna almost made the cover of *Vogue Paris* in 1966, too—but according to Alex Liberman's stepdaughter, Francine du Plessix Gray, Sam Newhouse intervened. In her memoir, du Plessix Gray wrote that Sam caught wind of the idea and insisted that Alex arrange for the image of Luna to be replaced. *Vogue Paris*'s editor, Edmonde Charles-Roux, refused to accede, and she was quickly fired. Du Plessix Gray did not speculate on Sam's motivation, only that he was "cautiously conservative." It's possible that Charles-Roux was already on the outs with the powers at Condé Nast, who viewed her edgy version of *Vogue Paris* as too avant-garde for the commercial market. One biographer speculated that Charles-Roux seized on the pretext of American racism as a useful public rationale for her firing.

There is ample evidence, however, that Luna was blocked again at Condé Nast later that year, this time from appearing in American *Vogue*. Richard Avedon had photographed Luna in April 1965 for his previous employer, *Harper's Bazaar*, and the pictures prompted objections from readers and advertisers in the American South and, reportedly, William Randolph Hearst Jr. himself. Avedon later said that "for reasons of racial prejudice and the economics of the fashion business," he "was never permitted to photograph" Luna for *Bazaar* again. The backlash had led, in part, to Avedon's move to Condé Nast in 1966, and the photographer was now planning "The Great Fur Caravan," a lavish fashion shoot in Japan, for *Vogue*. Avedon wanted to cast Luna as the lead model, but he encountered resistance. Alex Liberman called and recommended that he cast Veruschka instead; next was talk of bringing both models on the shoot. Then, as the departure date neared, Diana Vreeland called Avedon into her scarlet office.

"Dick, you can't take Luna to Japan. She's nobody's idea of what anybody wants to look like," Vreeland said, according to Avedon, who described the conversation to the journalist Doon Arbus in 1972.

The photographer recalled feeling sick to his stomach. "Diana, she's extraordinary," Avedon said.

"So was King Kong," Vreeland replied.

Recalling their exchange six years afterward, Avedon said, "That's when I knew I had to get out of that room." Nearly another decade would pass before a Black model, Beverly Johnson, finally made the cover of American *Vogue*.

ANNA WINTOUR'S TRACK RECORD on inclusivity was mixed. In 1989, for her first September issue as editor, Anna insisted on putting Naomi Campbell on the cover. She did so despite the skepticism of Si Newhouse, who had sighed and asked her, "You're going to put an African American model on the September cover of American *Vogue*?" Recalling the experience years later, Anna said that "it never crossed my mind to think that way. I just thought, 'This is a fantastic girl, this is the model of the moment, this is a great image.'" In a July 1997 editor's letter, Anna acknowledged that "black models appear less often than I, and many of you, would like on *Vogue*'s covers," and offered this explanation: "It is a fact of life that the color of a cover model's skin (or hair, for that matter) dramatically affects newsstand sales." Still, the following year, *Vogue* put Oprah Winfrey on its October cover, a decision that generated enormous publicity and newsstand sales. If Winfrey had qualms about appearing in a magazine that historically featured white women, she did not publicly express them. In the *Vogue* article, she conveyed her excitement at receiving the ultimate Condé honor: "I'm a Black woman from Mississippi. Why would I be thinking I was gonna be in *Vogue*? I would never have even thought of it as a possibility. That's why it's so extraordinary."

And yet, over the years, Anna made mistakes. Her editor's letter in the Winfrey issue revealed that the talk-show host had "promised she would lose twenty pounds by our deadline," a comment that would likely be criticized as fat-shaming today. Anna's biographer, Amy Odell, reported an ugly incident from the early 2000s involving André Leon Talley, the gay Black fashion editor who was Anna's longtime consigliere—and, toward the end of his life, would deride her as "a colonial broad." Talley often wrote memos to Anna urging her to feature more Black models in the magazine. According to Odell, after receiving one such missive, Anna said to another editor, "Could somebody tell André that not every month is Black History Month?" (A person close to Anna told me: "Anna does not recall saying that, nor is it language she'd ever use.") A notorious cover shoot in 2008 featured LeBron James, dribbling a basketball and baring his teeth as the model Gisele Bündchen, clad in a slinky dress, holds on to him. This was the first time that a Black man was featured on a *Vogue* cover, and several editors were alarmed: the composition of the image strikingly evoked the classic movie poster of *King Kong*, with James as the ape and Gisele as Fay Wray, the damsel in distress. "There was a lot of, 'Anna, this is not going to go over well,' but she was dismissive," Anna's longtime managing editor Laurie Jones told Odell. "She just didn't see it." The backlash was immediate, with critics accusing *Vogue* of trafficking in ugly stereotypes. Anna was bewildered by the reaction. (A confidant of hers later told me that she had received positive feedback about the image from people who were involved with the shoot.)

In 2016, Anna appointed a Black woman, Elaine Welteroth, as editor in chief of *Teen Vogue*—sort of. Welteroth had made a name for herself as a beauty editor at *Glamour* and *Teen Vogue*, where she advocated for Black representation in the magazine. According to Welteroth, Anna offered her a co-editor-in-chief role where she would split leadership duties with two other editors; the position came with a measly $10,000 raise, and Welteroth was given less than an hour to decide whether to accept. One year later, after Welteroth told Anna that she felt tokenized and disempowered in her role, Condé increased her salary, gave her a corner office, and appointed her sole editor in chief of *Teen Vogue*. (She was only the second Black person to hold the title at Condé, after Keija Minor at *Brides* in 2012.) Within a year, *Teen Vogue*'s print edition was shuttered, and Welteroth left the company.

In 2016, after Graydon announced his plans to depart *Vanity Fair*, Anna made clear that she wanted a new direction for the magazine that wasn't "pale, stale, and male," according to a person who spoke with her at the time. She and David Remnick ultimately urged Condé to hire Radhika Jones as Graydon's successor. Jones was an Indian American journalist with a doctorate in English and comparative literature from Columbia, who had held top editing roles at *The Paris Review* and *Time*, where she oversaw the Time 100 Gala. For her debut issue, Jones chose as her cover star Lena Waithe, a queer Black actress and screenwriter; the accompanying profile opened with a sentence that read like a challenge: "If you haven't heard of Lena Waithe, check yourself for a pulse." Many readers hadn't; Waithe had played a breakout role on the Netflix show *Master of None*, but she was still a relatively niche celebrity at the time. Jones later pointed out that between 1983 and 2017, *Vanity Fair* had featured just seventeen Black people on its covers. Her supporters applauded Jones for elevating a different kind of celebrity than *VF* had promoted in the past, but her choices would also prompt objections from some senior Condé leaders. At a company brand strategy meeting in April 2019, Jones laid out her plans for *VF*'s second half of the year. Two senior executives questioned her editorial vision and declared that advertisers were befuddled by it. Anna, irritated, banged her hand on the conference table to cut the tension and defended Jones, instructing the executives "to get your advertisers to follow along."

By decade's end, the Black Lives Matter movement had reached a crescendo, and the outside pressure on Condé to reckon with its own history regarding race and inequality became too great to ignore. In June 2020, Anna issued an apology for *Vogue*'s past treatment of Black staffers. "I want to say plainly that I know *Vogue* has not found enough ways to elevate and give space to Black editors, writers, photographers, designers and other creators," she wrote to her staff. "We have made mistakes, too, publishing images or stories that have been hurtful or intolerant. I take full responsibility for those mistakes."

19

The Back of the Book

For decades, Condé Nast editors in chief oriented their work lives around the monthly "print order" meeting, where every page of a magazine's forthcoming issue would be laid out end to end on a series of whiteboards, awaiting the scrutiny of Si Newhouse. Si often arrived for these sessions in his usual slouchy sweatshirt and baseball cap, his feet sometimes clad only in socks; his editors wore the chicest outfits from their fashion closets, and some women summoned a full hair-and-makeup crew so they would attend looking their best. A five-star general reviewing his platoon, Si peered at the pages with rapt intensity, examining every headline, caption, and layout, clocking the transitions between words and photographs and ads: proprietor, connoisseur, and critic all at once.

The ritual was an apt expression of Condé's obsessive focus on the art and craft of print magazines—a craft that was inexorably receding into the past.

Si died on October 1, 2017, at eighty-nine. In his final years, his cognitive skills had begun to decline, and he had gradually relinquished his duties as the Medici of Condé Nast. His daily exercises fell off, and, eventually, he lost the ability to speak and walk. His wife, Victoria, took him on visits to the farm of the actress Isabella Rossellini, where he appeared to enjoy the animals. Si's brother, Donald, later shared that Si had been diagnosed in 2014 with a progressive form of dementia. "He knew what was coming," Donald said after Si's death. "We all knew what was coming." At Si's memorial service, the attendees included Ralph Lauren, David Geffen, Leonard Lauder, Jeff Koons, and Diane von Furstenberg. Speakers recounted Si and Victoria's ardent devotion to their dogs—first Nero, and later Cicero—who often flew with them to the classical music festivals in Vienna and Salzburg.

"My father was not an easy man to know," his daughter, Pamela Mensch, said at his funeral. "He was not comfortable with intimacy, or with other people's emotions."

Mensch described Si's favorite play as *Henry V*, Shakespeare's history of an immature and undisciplined prince who feuds with and defies his controlling father, and ultimately inherits the kingdom and leads his country to untold glory. It's easy to see why Si embraced this narrative. The world has produced many billionaire businessmen, but few who were willing to pour a personal fortune into a company of creative eccentrics, to encourage profligacy in the name of beauty, to emphasize the accumulation of status over the accumulation of profits. From his privileged but anxious childhood onward, Si had yearned to find a place in the American establishment, and to prove wrong a hard-driving father disappointed by an eldest son whose tastes ran to finery and restaurants and "women's magazines." And because Alex Liberman took him under his wing, Si absorbed a specific postwar European ideal of social status and aesthetic excellence. At its peak, Condé Nast manifested Alex's mission of bringing continental refinement and sophistication to a prosaic America, propelled by the fortune of a striver.

As early as the mid-1990s, Si predicted that his cousin Jonathan Newhouse "will take my place" atop Condé Nast upon his retirement. Like Si, Jonathan was a magazine purist and aesthete. His father, Norman Newhouse, one of Sam's younger brothers, oversaw *The Times-Picayune*; Jonathan dropped out of Yale to join the family business, starting at Condé Nast when *Vanity Fair* relaunched in 1983. He moved through *The New Yorker*, *Gourmet*, and *Details*, and then transferred to Paris in 1990 to lead Condé's international arm, eventually settling in London. There, Jonathan—easily recognized by his buzz cut, bow tie, and suspenders—became a fixture of the European social scene.

Nicholas Coleridge, the Old Etonian who led Condé Nast in Britain (and was an old *Tatler* chum of Tina Brown), took Jonathan under his wing, introducing him to top designers like Nicolas Ghesquière.

Jonathan's interest in fashion, art, and culture seemed to position him as a natural heir to Si, but it was not to be. By 2017, Condé Nast had to focus as much on cutting costs as creating beautiful magazines. Donald Newhouse's son, Steven, was roughly the same age as Jonathan; he was less of a social butterfly, but he was an early adopter of the internet, and had been trusted to look after more lucrative arms of the family empire. (Jonathan's $100 million e-commerce venture at Style.com, meanwhile, had collapsed after less than a year.) In 2019, Steven was elevated to copresident of Advance, sharing the title with his father. Jonathan was named as Condé Nast's chairman, but the industry view was that Steven was now firmly in charge.

Steven has evinced a protectiveness toward his family's trophy properties; when rumors arose in 2022 that Jay Penske, owner of *Rolling Stone* and *Variety*, wanted to buy *Vanity Fair*, a person close to Steven said he would never sell off a publication that he considered key to the Newhouse family's legacy. Still, Donald Newhouse turned ninety-five in 2024—he no longer holds a title at Advance—and no one is quite sure what his descendants will do after his death. Thanks primarily to investments made by Donald, and later Steven, the Newhouses do not necessarily need to worry about Condé Nast being in the red. In 2015, Advance sold its cable TV business to Charter Communications, the telecom giant, in a $10.4 billion deal, with the Newhouses retaining a significant minority stake in the combined company. The family were also early investors in Discovery Inc., which in 2022 merged with WarnerMedia to create Warner Bros. Discovery, an entertainment conglomerate encompassing HBO, CNN, and the Warner Bros. movie studio. The Newhouses are currently among the company's largest outside shareholders.

Ironically, the family also collected a windfall from a shrewd bet on an internet company whose scruffy egalitarianism was the antithesis of Condé's we-know-best airs. A Condé business executive learned about Reddit a few months after the website's founding in 2005; its creators were just out of college and sharing a cramped apartment near Boston. When an email from Condé corporate arrived out of the blue, the founders had to google the name Condé Nast. Steven Newhouse was impressed with Reddit's user base of young, educated men, an audience that he believed could complement Condé's army of female readers. After a few months of negotiations, Condé Nast acquired Reddit for roughly $10 million in 2006. Steven intentionally kept his purchase at arm's length, allowing its founders to work from California away from Condé's more analog-minded executives in New York. The site's visual quality was barely better than Craigslist. But by 2012, Reddit boasted more than three billion page views each month, and Barack Obama, running for re-election, participated in the site's popular "Ask Me Anything" feature. When Condé spun out Reddit in 2011, Advance Publications retained a roughly one-third stake.

In March 2024, Reddit went public—with the Newhouse family reaping a windfall of roughly $2.1 billion. Steven's $10 million bet had yielded a 210-times return. To the degree that the Newhouses can keep bankrolling *Vogue*, *Vanity Fair*, and *The New Yorker* into the next decade, it may be the success of an anarchic, low-fi social media platform that guarantees it.

FOR ALL THE ELEGIES DIRECTED toward the golden age of Condé Nast, we continue to live in the culture that it made. The iPhone brought the means of glamour production to the masses, and the masses chose to replicate the status markers that Condé Nast popularized. Influencers and TikTok stars bring their followers on house tours that resemble old *Architectural Digest* spreads. Celebrities post provocative photographs and envy-inducing travelogues that would not be out of place in *Vanity Fair* or *Traveler*. Athletes arrive for press conferences in elaborate designer outfits straight from *GQ*. American politics merged with American entertainment—the ultimate expression of Tina's old formula of high/low—and a man with deep ties to the Condé ecosystem, Donald Trump, achieved its biggest starring role.

But the company's diminution is also a loss.

There is no doubt that media benefits from a new diversity of voices, both in the creation of culture and the curation of it. But as a reporter at *The New York Times*, I've seen firsthand the effects of fragmentation in our society. Americans no longer share the same facts, much less the same magazines. Liberation came at the cost of unity; we are suspicious of one another, alienated and apart. It may seem shallow to put Condé Nast in the same group as the information gatekeepers, like newspapers and broadcast networks, that once controlled national debates over politics and public policy. But Condé's waning clout is symptomatic of a broader collapse of community engendered by the fall of our media institutions. For all its faults, Condé brought discernment to the culture. It imported the avant-garde to Midwestern dentists' offices, and brought peerless writing and reporting and arts criticism to mass-circulation publications. Now in the waiting room we read our phones, where an algorithm spits back content based on what we've already seen. We're cosseted by a computer's bloodless taste. Who challenges us? What broadens our tastes, our sense of the world? Who are our gatekeepers?

What if the answer is no one? For all our choices, are we more enlightened or less? With so many voices, who, really, is being heard?

The lavish lifestyles portrayed in Condé magazines were in some ways more benign than the ones depicted on social media, because the magazine version was so self-evidently a fantasy. Few Condé readers believed that the world as portrayed by Helmut Newton or Annie Leibovitz was an attainable goal. One could admire Condé's dream worlds, or use them as inspiration, whereas the images depicted on Instagram are often intended as envy-inducing glimpses into *real life*. Here are people you *know*, or maybe a mutual friend or an old classmate, straining to convince you of the perfection of their vacations, their partners, their clothes, their homes. Glossy magazines never implied that an average person could have *all* of what they portrayed. Condé Nast offered vicarious thrills. But in the post-gatekeeper era, the old elite status fantasies have shifted from aspirations to *expectations*, with all the commensurate pressures that come with that shift.

In late 2024, a leading luxury goods analyst, Luca Solca, published a chilling report on younger consumers and the fashion and retail sector.

Solca argued that the long-term market prospects for luxury goods were bright—because the alienation, insecurity, and nihilism instilled in young people by social media had created an eager base of new consumers. "Exposure on social media is reducing people's self-assurance and magnifying their insecurity," he wrote. "Narcissism is emerging as a defense against these deep-rooted fears." For all the revelry in some quarters that Condé's elitist world has crumbled, the supposedly more egalitarian sphere of social media has found new ways to replicate the striving and status-seeking culture that Condé magazines were often blamed for. Bonnie Morrison, an editor who worked at *Self* and *Men's Vogue*, calls this "the democratization of elitism," and notes that nowadays, Instagram can be "an endless scroll of things to buy, or things to want." Instead of being obsolesced by the culture, the Condé creed was absorbed by it: its values of elite fantasy, sophistication, and social combat now spring forth from the thousands of digital outlets that saturate our daily lives.

The erosion of Condé has also meant the end of hundreds of jobs for writers, editors, journalists, and photographers. Creative work itself is increasingly commodified; the proliferation of DIY media platforms means that essays and photographs are worth less and less. Flawed as it was, Condé offered compensation, apprenticeship, and a platform for creatives to hone their best work. The artist Barbara Kruger, who worked as a designer at *Mademoiselle* early in her career, attributes her success in part to her time at Condé Nast. "I had no education as a designer, so it was really a learning experience for me, and an incredible opportunity," she told me. "The fluencies that I developed in the art department at *Mademoiselle*, in my job as an editorial designer, morphed into my work as an artist."

Another casualty is curation, at a moment where it is desperately needed. "Magazines, in my opinion, once were the chief emissaries of culture from month to month," said Ruth Ansel, an art director for *House & Garden*, *Vanity Fair*, and *Vogue*. "They spoke of a wider world one could enter as a reader and be swept along by the inspiration and information." Now, the algorithms that rank articles online reinforce individual readers' assumptions and biases. The fire hose of digital media has yielded a siloed culture that feels increasingly flattened and incoherent. "What is boring about reading everything online—and it is boring—it's just an uncalibrated list of stories," says Tina Brown. "There's no sense of hierarchy of any kind. You can't splash a headline, you can't splash a picture, and say, '*This* is the important thing today.' You can't create an energy of 'Pay attention to *this*!'" Perhaps unsurprisingly, Tina continues to defend the virtues of cultural gatekeepers. "There is a place, a necessary place in our culture, and without them—whether it's in magazines, TV, movies, theater—the creative talents producing original, sometimes risky, material are orphaned," she told me. "Gatekeepers have the power to say, 'I am publishing it, green-lighting it because I love it, I believe in it and I have the ability to make it happen.'"

I WAS AT A PARTY IN LONDON in 2023 when I ran into Michael Bloomberg, whose New York City mayoralty I had covered for several years at *The New York Times*. He asked which Condé Nast characters I planned to feature in my book. When I told him Tina Brown, Bloomberg looked puzzled.

"I spoke at her funeral," he said to me, matter-of-factly.

I explained that Tina was, in fact, alive.

"Oh!" Bloomberg's face brightened. "I meant Helen Gurley Brown!"

Arguably, Tina never regained the cultural power she wielded during her days at Condé Nast. Her *Talk* magazine, funded by Harvey Weinstein, launched in 1999 with a massive celebrity-packed party beneath the Statue of Liberty and a debut cover that featured a trademark Tina high/low collage of Hillary Clinton, George W. Bush, and Gwyneth Paltrow posing in a bikini. But the magazine failed barely three years later, its bravado sapped by an advertising recession and the post-9/11 cultural malaise. Recently, Tina referred wryly to her exit from *The New Yorker* as "probably the dumbest career move of anybody's life." Tina wrote a popular biography of Princess Diana and then, in 2008, re-emerged as the editor of an online news site, *The Daily Beast*, which was backed by Barry Diller. The *Beast* attempted to translate Tina's spunk to the web, but it was plagued by overspending and an ill-fated merger with *Newsweek*.

Tina left in 2013 and founded an events business called Women in the World; she published her diary from her time at *Vanity Fair* and then created an investigative journalism conference named for her husband, Harry Evans, who died in 2020. Tina likes to stay abreast of the latest delivery systems for news and ideas, and in 2024 she started a Substack, *Fresh Hell*, where she posts semi-regular dispatches about a zeitgeist that still bears the influences of her transformative tenure at Condé Nast.

After his exit from *Vanity Fair*, Graydon Carter took a break in Provence; at one point, he approached the Newhouses about buying his old magazine, but nothing came of it. In 2019, Graydon co-founded *Air Mail*, an upscale online-only newsletter that has gained a dedicated following and spawned stylish brick-and-mortar retail offshoots in New York and London. In 2023, he successfully returned to the high-society trenches with a lavish party at the Hôtel du Cap-Eden-Roc during the Cannes Film Festival; the starry guest list (Leonardo DiCaprio, Martin Scorsese) and subtle touches (custom-made ashtrays) were imported straight from Oscar extravaganzas of the past. His memoir, *When the Going Was Good*, became a bestseller in the spring of 2025, as readers responded to its nostalgic portrait of a lost era of excess. At a grand book party in Lower Manhattan—the kind of lavishly catered media soiree that rarely happens nowadays—Graydon received hosannas from the A-listers who once feared his poison pen. "I've known him when he was in charge of everything and very scary," said the actress Candice Bergen, "and I love him when he is more benign."

In April 2025, Radhika Jones surprised her staff by announcing that she would step down from the editorship of *Vanity Fair*. Forced to contend with shrinking budgets and layoffs, Jones had grown weary of managing decline. The magazine's influence had faded, too: Movie stars (and politicians) now routinely bypass the traditional media to speak directly to fans; when they do appear in a publication like *VF*, they have the power to demand certain photographers and writers, ensuring the coverage is to their liking. Inside Condé, some senior figures acknowledged that Jones had never quite adapted to the public-facing aspect of her role—the impresario "it" factor that her predecessors relished. In 2019, her first year overseeing the magazine's Oscar party, Jones was asked which celebrity she was most excited to meet. She answered Sundar Pichai, the chief executive of Google.

David Remnick has edited *The New Yorker* for more than a quarter century, ably navigating the institution through the convulsions of the media industry's digital transformation. Against expectations, he made *The New Yorker* one of Condé's few digital success stories, installing a paywall that now generates significant income. (According to a person briefed on the numbers, the magazine's circulation revenues more than doubled in the five years after a full-fledged paywall was introduced in 2014.) The New Yorker Festival is an annual staple that attracts thousands of paying attendees and healthy revenues. Since magazines became eligible for the Pulitzer Prize in 2015, Remnick's *New Yorker* has won eight of them, including the public service medal for Ronan Farrow's 2017 investigation into the sexual predations of Tina's old boss, Harvey Weinstein. The magazine celebrates its centennial year in 2025, and a Netflix crew has been invited to make a documentary to mark the occasion. As *The New Yorker* turns one hundred, Remnick is about to turn sixty-seven. He has said that he'd like to avoid the messy succession dramas of earlier eras.

And Anna remains. Decades after she was passed over to succeed Alex Liberman as editorial director, Anna now holds the lofty titles of chief content officer, Condé Nast, and global editorial director, *Vogue*, effectively occupying Alex's old perch as Condé's all-seeing creative force. She further consolidated her power when Condé ousted the editors in chief of many of *Vogue*'s international editions, including tastemakers like *Vogue Paris*'s Emmanuelle Alt. *Vogue*s around the world now carry many of the same photo shoots, cover stars, and articles. Condé management called this a sensible decision, given the increasingly globalized nature of fashion and the arts. It was also an obvious cost-saving measure that resulted in hundreds of layoffs, and critics say the move devalued local voices while contributing to a lamentable homogenization of the magazines' style and taste.

Anna has always had critics, and her oversight of a multitude of Condé titles has yielded mixed editorial and financial results. Yet after more than thirty-five years running American *Vogue*, there is no end in sight to her reign. Her sway with the world's top designers and luxury conglomerates is without rival; in many ways, the ongoing influence of Condé Nast itself hinges on Anna alone. Challengers to her crown have consistently fallen by the wayside. In 2023, Edward Enninful, the celebrated editor of *British Vogue*, announced he would step down in favor of a fuzzy role as "global creative and cultural adviser." Enninful, who is gay and Black, was widely credited for diversifying the models, designers, and photographers who appeared in his magazine, while maintaining a signature Condé edge and style. He had been viewed as Anna's likely successor at American *Vogue*—so much so that at least one member of Condé Nast's corporate board was taken aback when they heard about Enninful's sidelined new role. The board member was concerned that the Newhouses had no clear succession plan in place for when Anna does finally step away, according to a person familiar with their thinking. Enninful's departure was another clear signal that Anna has no plans to abdicate her role as *Vogue*'s editor in chief. "Do not give up the title," she once advised a friend. "You *never* leave your title."

Anna still works long days, tiring out much younger editors with relentless emails and phone calls. Her *Vogue* now includes a podcast, a mobile app, numerous sponsored events, and a revamped, popular website that engaged younger readers with clever ideas like hiring Jack Schlossberg, a Kennedy descendant and cheeky TikTok star, as a political correspondent. Her activism in Democratic politics has only grown; in 2024, Anna hosted a fundraiser for Joe Biden and coordinated a "Designers for Democracy" march in Manhattan, with a cameo from the First Lady. "No one has shaped this industry more than you," Jill Biden told Anna, who was waving a small American flag. "Now you're shaping the world." When Donald Trump recaptured the presidency in November 2024, Anna was openly emotional and her voice cracked as she addressed the election result with her staff. Weeks later, in the final days of his tenure, Biden presented Anna with the Presidential Medal of Freedom, one of the nation's highest civilian honors.

At a time of scarcity and decline in her industry, Anna has retained her taste for spectacle and the public enchantment it can generate. Ahead of the 2024 Summer Olympics, she persuaded the Paris authorities to cordon off the entire Place Vendôme—a virtually unheard-of feat—to stage an elaborate *Vogue*-branded fashion show with Katy Perry, Kendall Jenner, Gigi Hadid, Serena Williams, and Sabrina Carpenter among the models. The local gendarmes were ready to shut down the proceedings if the event stretched past its allotted hour. Unsurprisingly, Anna pulled it off.

The only person at Condé Nast who still effectively outranks Anna is the company's chief executive, Roger Lynch, a former streaming-music bigwig with no previous experience in magazines. Lynch, who was hired in 2019, has joined Anna in proclaiming a bright road ahead, talking up the digital growth of Condé's brands and its efforts to adapt content for film and television. He argues that Condé will thrive as a multipronged entity in which magazines are merely one branch, coexisting with live conferences, membership clubs, and e-commerce tie-ins. The official word from management is that the old world of copious expense accounts and ruthless cultural elitism is an anachronism best forgotten. Even the title of "editor in chief" is being retired in favor of the bloodless "head of editorial content."

"This is no longer a magazine company," Lynch declared in 2022.

It was a rallying cry to embrace the future—and an epitaph for a glorious past.

Acknowledgments

This book was written without the participation of the Condé Nast Publications, which instructed current editors to decline my requests for interviews. Steven Newhouse did not respond to my inquiries; his father, Donald, also declined to speak, citing Steven's decision. Jonathan Newhouse was perfectly polite when I approached him at a dinner party, but he indicated that it was his family's wish that he remain silent. None of this surprised me: the Newhouses have been intensely private for decades. For the proprietors of a media empire, they are wary of journalistic scrutiny. I am, however, deeply grateful to the Newhouse family members who granted me their time, memories, and insight; their generosity was a gift.

I interviewed more than two hundred people in the course of my reporting, including dozens of current and former employees of Condé Nast, close associates of the Newhouses, and longtime observers of the magazine world. Many spoke on the record; others requested anonymity in order to share candid details; some welcomed me into their homes and shared their personal archives. I am indebted to every person who patiently fielded my questions. This book would not exist if not for their many kindnesses.

It also would not exist without David Kuhn and Nate Muscato, my agents at Aevitas Creative, who took a chance on a first-time author and nurtured the germ of an idea that I brought to them. David, your skepticism made me raise my game; Nate, you were a patient listener when I needed it the most. At Aevitas, thank you to Erin Files, Helen Hicks, Liana Raguso, and Allison Warren.

My editor Eamon Dolan was a sage steward of the manuscript. Tzipora Chein wrangled all the nitty-gritty. Thanks also to the eagle-eyed Rachael DeShano, Kyle Kabel for the elegant design, and the entire team at Simon & Schuster, including Ingrid Carabulea, Bri Scharfenberg, Jackie Seow, Priscilla Painton, and Jonathan Karp.

My fact-checker, Sameen Gauhar, is a tireless and exacting collaborator whose contributions were too myriad to catalog here; I don't recommend writing a book without her. Any remaining errors are my own.

The photo insert resulted from the Herculean efforts of the singular Steven Chaiken and Jeff Roth. Elisa Rivlin, Jonathan Lyons, Ryan Fox, and David McCraw meticulously answered my legal queries. Gary He was an all-around cheerleader. My researcher, Beatrice Wingfield, is astoundingly talented at unearthing gems in the archival coal mines. Paul Friedman, at the New York Public Library, was an invaluable resource.

The New York Times has been my professional home for nearly two decades. No institution is more dedicated to journalistic excellence. Over the years, I've benefited from the wisdom and generosity of countless colleagues; to name them all would require a chapter in itself. Carolyn Ryan gave me a career and showed me the joy of newspapering; she is a peerless mentor and a dear friend. Ellen Pollock's love for news is infectious, and she granted me the space and time to finish this book. Joe Plambeck is the best media editor working today, and my colleagues on the *Times* media desk are best-in-class. Jim Windolf provided a gold mine of old interviews and reporting notes. Bill Brink, Michael Paulson, Sarah Lyall, Alexandra Jacobs, Sadie Stein, and Vanessa Friedman made this a better book. Matt Flegenheimer and Rebecca Ruiz sharpened my thinking, and Maureen Dowd encouraged me from the start. John Koblin shared the fruits of his encyclopedic Condé knowledge, and talked me off the ledge too many times to count.

Thanks to my Forlini's gang—Audrey Gelman, Annie Karni, Ilan Zechory, and Ted Mann—for daily serenity. Chloe Malle and Graham

ACKNOWLEDGMENTS

Albert made me laugh until my sides hurt. Aimée Bell and David Kamp spurred me on, and Ben Schrank made the whole thing happen in the first place. David M. Rappaport helped me climb the mountain. Simon Vozick-Levinson officiated my wedding, and then he reviewed my manuscript—that's friendship! Love to you, Sarah, and the D52 crew: Zach Seward, Doug Lieb, and Dan Hemel.

Scoop, Kate, and Bunz Wasserstein were the source of hundreds of hours of merriment and desperately needed distraction throughout this project, and offered wise advice all along the way. I have so much love for them, Tip & Kitty, and Wassersteins far and wide.

To my mom and dad, Joseph and Patricia Grynbaum: Thank you for opening the world to me and for giving me the confidence to pursue the life that I imagined. Every child should be so fortunate. I love you lots and lots.

My cat, Pajama, was not helpful: she pranced across my keyboard, demanded food when I needed to concentrate, and distracted me by looking perfect at all times. I adore her, endlessly.

The idea for this book, like all the best things in my life, came from Juli Weiner, my wife and my closest friend. You read every page, managed my anxieties with wit and cheer, and never stopped believing in me, which often made one of us. Life with you is big and interesting. Every day I feel lucky to be your partner. I love you.

Notes

Introduction Perfect Bound

xii *"Bosses wear Prada"*: At the time, Anna Wintour did not have oversight over *The New Yorker*; a union organizer said Anna's home was chosen as a protest site because she served as a "proxy" for Condé Nast. Katie Robertson and Rachel Abrams, "New Yorker Employees Stage Protest Outside Anna Wintour's Townhouse," *New York Times*, June 8, 2021.

xvi *a space-age cafeteria*: Herbert Muschamp, "Tray Chic," *New York Times*, April 23, 2000.

xvii *"We are the top-end"*: Richard Pérez-Peña, "Can Si Newhouse Keep Condé Nast's Gloss Going?" *New York Times*, July 20, 2008.

xviii *"hurtful or intolerant"*: Sara Nathan, "Anna Wintour Admits to 'Hurtful and Intolerant' Behavior at Vogue," *New York Post*, June 9, 2020.

xviii *"past its prime"*: Katherine Rosman and Brooks Barnes, "It Was the Hottest Oscar Night Party. What Happened?" *New York Times*, February 21, 2019.

xviii *"I miss the black-and-whiteness"*: Michael M. Grynbaum, "Graydon Carter to End 25-Year Run as Vanity Fair's Editor," *New York Times*, September 7, 2017.

Chapter 1 Class, Not Mass

1 *the country's leading publications*: Nast's revamp of *Collier's Weekly* is discussed in Caroline Seebohm, *The Man Who Was Vogue: The Life and Times of Condé Nast* (New York: Viking, 1982), 29–31; Frank Luther Mott, *A History of American Magazines* vol. iv (Cambridge, MA: Belknap Press, 1957), 453–56.

1 *When Nast met Clarisse Coudert*: Susan Ronald, *Condé Nast: The Man and His Empire* (New York: St. Martin's Press, 2019), 53–57.

2 *once forgot to send*: Edna Woolman Chase and Ilka Chase, *Always in Vogue* (Garden City, NY: Doubleday, 1954), 43–44.

2 *"Don't be so violently"*: "The Press: Fifty Years on the Crest," *Time*, November 1, 1954.

2 *"Vogue says"*: Walter G. Robinson, "The First Thirty Years," *Vogue*, January 1, 1923.

3 *"wealthiest and most"*: Condé Nast, "Class Publications," *The Merchants and Manufacturers Journal*, June 1913.

3 *"He didn't want a big circulation"*: Chase and Chase, *Always in Vogue*, 66.
3 *"It is the avowed mission"*: Seebohm, *The Man Who Was Vogue*, 77.
3 *In 1910*: Seebohm, *The Man Who Was Vogue*, 72.
4 *By 1926*: Chase and Chase, *Always in Vogue*, 67.
5 *Boston Brahmin*: For a biographical précis of Crowninshield, see Geoffrey T. Hellman, "Profiles: Last of the Species," *New Yorker*, September 19 and September 26, 1942; and Helen Lawrenson, "The First of the Beautiful People," *Esquire*, March 1973.
5 *"The House Beautiful"*: Dorothy Parker, "The Theatre," *New Yorker*, March 21, 1931.
5 *palatial Park Avenue penthouse*: Christopher Gray, "Streetscapes/1040 Park Avenue, at 86th Street," *New York Times*, November 5, 2000.
5 *"Everybody who was invited"*: Diana Vreeland, "Vreeland Remembers (Sort Of)," *Vanity Fair*, April 1984.
6 *"Probably why I became obsessed"*: Lauren Santo Domingo, comment on LinkedIn: https://www.linkedin.com/feed/update/urn:li:activity:6847969814644838400.
6 *ninety-three dollars a share to two dollars*: Ronald, *Condé Nast: The Man and His Empire*, 235.
7 *"Does the young woman in Fort Smith"*: "Condé Nast," *New York Herald Tribune*, September 21, 1942.
7 *"got most of their ideas"*: "The Press: Condé Nast," *Time*, September 28, 1942.
8 *"A 5-3, kinky-haired"*: "Eye on Vogue," *Women's Wear Daily*, December 5, 1960.
8 *"not-too-successful salesman"*: Collie Small, "Little Publisher, Big Empire," *Collier's*, August 4, 1951.
8 *declined to respond*: Jean R. Hailey, "Publishing Tycoon Samuel I. Newhouse Dies at Age 84," *Washington Post*, August 29, 1979.
8 *"It was a toy for Mitzi"*: "Eyes on Vogue," *Women's Wear Daily*, December 5, 1960.
8 *Solomon Neuhaus was born*: For the most thorough accounts of Sam Newhouse's upbringing, see Richard H. Meeker, *Newspaperman: S. I. Newhouse and the Business of News* (New Haven, CT: Ticknor & Fields, 1983); and S. I. Newhouse, as related to and written by David Jacobs, *A Memo for the Children* (New York: privately printed, 1980).
9 *appeared on the cover of* Time: "The Newspaper Collector," *Time*, July 27, 1962.
9 *tried to bolster*: Meeker, *Newspaperman*, 162.
9 *"I was small, young and poor"*: S. I. Newhouse, *A Memo for the Children*, 130.
9 *"I can't hire you!"*: S. I. Newhouse, *A Memo for the Children*, 16.
10 *Mitzi was the first woman*: Meeker, *Newspaperman*, 40.
10 *"the other fellow"*: S. I. Newhouse, *A Memo for the Children*, 33.
10 *married at the Commodore*: Carol Felsenthal, *Citizen Newhouse: Portrait of a Media Merchant* (New York: Seven Stories Press, 1998), 22–23.
10 *bent into the shape*: Meeker, *Newspaperman*, 57.
11 *a thirteen-room duplex apartment*: "Reports of Activity in Metropolitan Real Estate Market," *New York Times*, May 25, 1940, 31.
11 *730 Park Avenue*: Details from Felsenthal, *Citizen Newhouse*, 24–27; Meeker, *Newspaperman*, 123–24; "730 Park Avenue, Plan of Apartment B," Avery Architectural & Fine Arts Library, Columbia University, New York Real Estate Brochure Collection, https://dlc.library.columbia.edu/nyre/cul:zw3r2281xm.
11 *one of the few Park Avenue addresses*: Michael Gross, *740 Park: The Story of the World's Richest Apartment Building* (New York: Broadway Books, 2005), 57–58.

NOTES

11 *a sprawling estate*: Felsenthal, *Citizen Newhouse*, 26.
12 *"They'd never sell"*: Meeker, *Newspaperman*, 239. According to Meeker, Sam said this to Wesley Clark, a longtime dean of the School of Journalism at Syracuse University.
12 *Newsweek was available*: "Magazine for Sale," *Time*, January 27, 1961; John A. Lent, *Newhouse, Newspapers, Nuisances: Highlights in the Growth of a Communications Empire* (New York: Exposition Press, 1966), 144–45.
13 *"ever-eager"*: Katharine Graham, *Personal History* (New York: Knopf, 1997), 187, 348.
13 *dismissed Sam*: A. J. Liebling, *The Press* (New York: Ballantine Books, 1975), 5.
13 *"journalist chiffonier"*: Liebling, *The Press*, 36.
14 *"My god"*: Jane Franke, interview by author.
14 *"wanted a Park Avenue life"*: Pamela Mensch, interview by author.
14 *"I got the idea that"*: Calvin Trillin, interview by author.
15 *"shrimp"*: "Samuel I. Newhouse, Publisher, Dies at 84," *New York Times*, August 30, 1979.

Chapter 2 Mitzi's Boy

17 *"An interesting city apartment"*: Enid Nemy, "When the Bachelor Goes Home," *New York Times*, April 6, 1966.
19 *"Go home"*: This exchange was described by Jane Franke and Deborah Hart Strober, interviews by author.
19 *"I'm going in now!"*: Arnold Scaasi, *Women I Have Dressed (and Undressed!)* (New York: Scribner, 2004), 89–90.
19 *"seemed very young"*: Scaasi, *Women I Have Dressed*, 87–88.
20 *Sam's idea of quality time*: S. I. Newhouse, *A Memo for the Children* (New York: privately printed, 1980), 35.
21 *entertained thoughts of suicide*: Felsenthal, *Citizen Newhouse*, 35–36, 44; Thomas Maier, *Newhouse: All the Glitter, Power, and Glory of America's Richest Media Empire and the Secretive Man Behind It* (New York: St. Martin's Press, 1994), 28–29.
21 *a left-wing pro-labor newspaper*: Sam's objection to his son reading a left-wing newspaper is also notable because he later described his Russian immigrant father, Meyer, as a socialist who sought "some kind of collective salvation." Sam drew a contrast with his own belief in "individual responsibility and the potentials of the free marketplace." S. I. Newhouse, *A Memo for the Children*, 6–7.
21 *In letters to Lowenstein*: Si's correspondence from 1944 can be found in the Allard K. Lowenstein Papers #4340, Box 192, Southern Historical Collection, University of North Carolina at Chapel Hill.
22 *"Love, Si"*: Box 1, Folder 14, Lowenstein Papers.
22 *"Fantastic"*: Graydon Carter, *When the Going Was Good: An Editor's Adventures During the Last Golden Age of Magazines* (New York: Penguin Press, 2025), 345.
22 *Harvard . . . Cornell . . . "Si Mason"*: Felsenthal, *Citizen Newhouse*, 37–38, 46, 51.
23 *"I didn't feel"*: Franke, interview by author. Details of Si's first marriage and divorce are primarily based on Franke's account. Franke's quotes are taken from interviews with the author.
23 *By the end of 1950*: "Miss Jane Franke Becomes Fiancee," *New York Times*, December 14, 1950.

23 *an ivory-bound Bible*: "Jane Franke Bride of Publisher's Son," *New York Times*, March 12, 1951.
24 *hired a divorce lawyer*: Felsenthal, *Citizen Newhouse*, 73.
24 *"I have to finish"*: Deborah Hart Strober, interview by author.
25 *"If I asked"*: Deborah Hart Strober, interview by author.
25 *eleven dollars' worth of shaving cream*: Daniel Machalaba, "Newhouse Chain Stays with Founder's Ways, and with His Heirs," *Wall Street Journal*, February 12, 1982.
25 *"When you grow up"*: Pamela Mensch, interview by author.
25 *Mitzi employed a personal assistant*: Pamela Mensch, interview by author.
26 *masthead*: "American Vogue," *Vogue*, October 15, 1964.

Chapter 3 The Silver Fox

28 *quashed an effort*: The Harry Winston anecdote was recounted in an interview with Carol Phillips, found in the Dodie Kazanjian and Calvin Tomkins research materials on Alexander Liberman, 1927–1999, box 14, folder 55, Archives of American Art, Smithsonian Institute, Washington, DC (hereafter "Liberman Archives").
29 *"the most meaningful"*: Dodie Kazanjian and Calvin Tomkins, *Alex: The Life of Alexander Liberman* (New York: Knopf, 1993), 6.
29 *"those thousands of female Walter Mittys"*: Gay Talese, "Vogueland," *Esquire*, July 1961.
30 *he was born*: The description of Alexander Liberman's biography and his early relationship with Si Newhouse is based on interviews with their associates and on the detailed accounts found in Francine du Plessix Gray, *Them: A Memoir of Parents* (New York: Penguin Press, 2005); Kazanjian and Tomkins, *Alex*; Charles Churchward, *It's Modern: The Eye and Visual Influence of Alexander Liberman* (New York, Rizzoli, 2013); and Alexander Liberman, *Then: Photographs 1925–1995* (New York: Random House, 1995).
30 *fateful doodle*: An account of Liberman's breakthrough illustration is found in "Art Lover," *New Yorker*, November 26, 1960, 44.
31 *conveyed "some sense of Americana"*: Kazanjian and Tomkins, *Alex*, 160.
31 *"When I took layouts"*: Lucy Sisman and Véronique Vienne, *Alex Liberman: Ways of Thinking About Design* (New York: Lucy Sisman, 2013). I am grateful to Lucy Sisman for providing a copy of this invaluable book, a collection of firsthand accounts of Alex's time at Condé Nast.
31 *"power and publicity"*: du Plessix Gray, *Them*, 476.
32 *he evicted his stepdaughter*: du Plessix Gray, *Them*, 416.
32 *"If Si Newhouse knows"*: Barbara Rose, interview, box 14, folder 60, Liberman Archives.
32 *"little heebs"*: Catherine di Montezemolo, interview, box 14, folder 21, Liberman Archives.
33 *"associate, friend, brother"*: Kazanjian and Tomkins, *Alex*, 5–6.
33 *"He didn't really move"*: Grace Mirabella, *In and Out of Vogue* (New York: Doubleday, 1995), 220.
33 *Krazy Kat*: Tina Brown, *The Vanity Fair Diaries, 1983–1992* (New York: Henry Holt, 2017), 253.
33 *"Si couldn't resist"*: Babs Simpson, interview, box 14, folder 60, Liberman Archives.
33 *"weenie boyness"*: Carol Felsenthal, *Citizen Newhouse: Portrait of a Media Merchant* (New York: Seven Stories Press, 1998), 178.

NOTES

34 *"very at ease"*: Felsenthal, *Citizen Newhouse*, 173.
34 *"a certain dignity"*: Kazanjian and Tomkins, *Alex*, 277.
34 *"We were part of a crusade"*: Alexander Liberman, interview, box 14, Liberman Archives.
34 *"Did you make Si happy"*: Tatiana's nightly query was recalled by another source as "Did you please Si today?" In their biography of Liberman, Kazanjian and Tomkins reported the phrase as "Did you see Si today?" *Alex*, 343.
35 *tin tycoon*: "Party Week Is Ending in Portugal," *New York Times*, September 7, 1968.
35 *a cocktail party*: Kazanjian and Tomkins, *Alex*, 277–79.
35 *Sam reminded him*: Felsenthal, *Citizen Newhouse*, 186.
35 *flying together*: Carol J. Loomis, "The Biggest Private Fortune," *Fortune*, August 17, 1987.
36 *Sam overruled*: S. I. Newhouse, *A Memo for the Children* (New York: privately printed, 1980), 105–6.
37 *By 1988*: Geraldine Fabrikant, "Si Newhouse Tests His Magazine Magic," *New York Times*, September 25, 1988.

Chapter 4 Si Finds His *Self*

40 *"In the late 1970s"*: Graydon Carter, interview by author.
40 *"Your boss wants"*: "Asides: The New Woman," *Wall Street Journal*, January 10, 1979.
41 *belly dancing*: Rochelle Udell, *Adventures of the Baker's Daughter* (self-published memoir fragments), https://adventuresofthebakersdaughter.com/expectations-none.
41 *80 percent of whom worked*: N. R. Kleinfield, "Self: A Surprising Success" *New York Times*, August 17, 1981.
41 *"When I got married"*: Nancy Yoshihara, "Women's Magazine Dilemma: Who Are They For?" *Los Angeles Times*, December 23, 1979.
41 *"You Too Can"*: Paul London, "You Too Can Fly over the Middle-Income Bracket," *Self*, January 1979, 114.
41 *"The Handbook"*: Ellen McCracken, *Decoding Women's Magazines: From Mademoiselle to Ms.* (London: Macmillan, 1993), 154–55.
41 *"Magazines used to teach"*: Milton Moskowitz, "Urge to Merge Is Back in Style," *Insiders' Chronicle*, November 3, 1977.
41 *Circulation nearly doubled*: Circulation data from Philip H. Dougherty, "Condé Nast Celebrates Success of Bride's," *New York Times*, June 12, 1979, and N. R. Kleinfield, "Self: A Surprising Success," *New York Times*, August 17, 1981.
42 *Si was so eager*: Geraldine Fabrikant, "Si Newhouse Tests His Magazine Magic," *New York Times*, September 25, 1988.
42 *printing different versions*: "Magazine Notes from All Over," *New York*, October 10, 1983.
43 *Emily Post*: "Tea Party," *New Yorker*, April 3, 1948.
44 *"Somebody paid $3,500 for this"*: Advertisement, *Vanity Fair*, September 1929.
45 *"When I was a kid"*: Jonathan Becker, interview with Jim Windolf.
45 *"This is only entertainment"*: Amy Fine Collins, "The Cult of Diana," *Vanity Fair*, November 1993.

NOTES

46 *"No, Richard"*: Richard Locke, interview with Jim Windolf. Locke, who died in 2023, rarely discussed his brief tenure at *Vanity Fair*. The transcript of this interview is among his only extant comments on the matter; subsequent quotes from Locke are taken from it, unless otherwise noted. I also draw from an autobiographical statement that Locke wrote in 2004 about his life and career, provided by his wife, Wendy Nicholson.

47 *"We live in a world"*: Craig Unger, "Can Vanity Fair Live Again?" *New York*, April 26, 1982.

48 *"The idea of publishing"*: Elizabeth Pochoda, interview with Jim Windolf.

48 *"This is what they'd done"*: Tina Brown, *The Vanity Fair Diaries, 1983–1992* (New York: Henry Holt, 2017), 20.

48 *three hundred copies*: Bruce Cook, "Vanity Fair's Chaotic Comeback," *Washington Journalism Review*, September 1983.

49 *"the twelve pages"*: Henry Fairlie, "The Vanity of 'Vanity Fair,'" *New Republic*, March 21, 1983.

49 *"incredibly bad"*: Jane Perlez, "Vanity Fair Sparks Sharp Reaction," *New York Times*, March 30, 1983.

49 *"We never believed"*: Perlez, "Vanity Fair Sparks Sharp Reaction."

49 *"This is a disaster"*: Fabrikant, "Si Newhouse Tests His Magazine Magic."

49 *"It is Richard's"*: Perlez, "Vanity Fair Sparks Sharp Reaction." Alex's involvement in selecting the Glaser cover is described by Lloyd Ziff in an interview with Jim Windolf.

49 *"it reminds you of"*: A version of Capote's submission to *Vanity Fair* later appeared in *Esquire* magazine. Truman Capote, "Indelible Exits and Entrances," *Esquire*, March 1983.

49 *"I hope nobody"*: Tom Zito, "Skeletons and Keys: Looking for Capote," *Washington Post*, March 13, 1983. Wayne Lawson described the negative reaction to Capote's column in an interview with Jim Windolf.

49 *"You need to schmooze"*: Lloyd Ziff, interview with Jim Windolf.

49 *"From the beginning"*: "Ex 'Vanity Fair' Editor: Jazzy Layout Wins," *USA Today*, April 28, 1983.

50 *Leo Lerman*: Lerman's diaries offer an invaluable account of Condé Nast's early years. See Stephen Pascal, ed., *The Grand Surprise: The Journals of Leo Lerman* (New York: Knopf, 2007). This account of Lerman also draws from Stephen Pascal, "Obituary: Leo Lerman," *Independent*, August 28, 1994; Holly Brubach, "Leo Lerman; A Movable Salon," *New York Times*, January 1, 1995; William Grimes, "Leo Lerman, 80, Editor at Condé Nast Magazines," *New York Times*, August 23, 1994; Curt Suplee, "Vanity Fair Editor Fired," *Washington Post*, April 27, 1983.

51 *"I'm in a very purple mood"*: James Wolcott, interview with Jim Windolf.

Chapter 5 British Invader

53 *"The construction workers"*: Tina Brown, *Loose Talk* (London: Joseph, 1979), 179.

53 *"Watch out New York"*: Tina Brown, *Happy Yellow*, Bush Theatre archives, London.

54 *"a rising young barrister"*: Tina Brown, *Life as a Party* (London: Andre Deutsch, 1983), 25.

54 *"How do I"*: Tina Brown, *The Vanity Fair Diaries, 1983–1992* (New York: Henry Holt, 2017), 27.

55 *"I've never taken"*: Alexander Liberman, interview, Dodie Kazanjian and Calvin Tomkins research materials on Alexander Liberman, 1927–1999, box 14, Archives of American Art, Smithsonian Institute, Washington, DC.
56 *"It wasn't so much"*: Brown, *Vanity Fair Diaries*, 32.
56 *"minor-league Kennedys"*: Enid Nemy, "Dominick Dunne, Chronicler of Crime, Dies at 83," *New York Times*, August 29, 2009.
57 *"But the timing"*: Brown, *Vanity Fair Diaries*, 45–46.
57 *"If you have the wrong"*: Patrick McCarthy, "Eye," *Women's Wear Daily*, December 12, 1983.
58 calling him *"evil"*: Stephen Pascal, ed., *The Grand Surprise: The Journals of Leo Lerman* (New York: Knopf, 2007), 405.
58 *"remarkably young"*: Graydon Carter, ed., *Vanity Fair 100 Years* (New York: Abrams, 2013), 234.
58 topic of conversation: John Duka, "Notes on Fashion," *New York Times*, January 10, 1984.
59 *"I want to share"*: Charles Leerhsen, "A New Editor for Vanity Fair," *Newsweek*, January 16, 1984.
60 *"No one"*: Stephen Schiff, interview by author.
60 *"all the ladies"*: Brown, *Vanity Fair Diaries*, 99.
61 *"police reporter"*: Eddie Hayes, *Mouthpiece* (New York: Broadway Books, 2005), 128.
61 *"Who are all those"*: "Here Come the Yuppies!" *Time*, January 9, 1984.
61 doubled in size: Geraldine Fabrikant, "Wooing the Wealthy Reader," *New York Times*, October 14, 1987.
61 *"It's almost as though"*: Peter W. Kaplan, "Why the Rich Rule the TV Roost," *New York Times*, April 7, 1985.
61 *"It was the first time"*: Fran Lebowitz, interview by author.
62 a net worth: Philip H. Dougherty, "Advertising," *New York Times*, April 2, 1986.
62 *"Please, please"*: Judy Bachrach, *Tina and Harry Come to America* (New York: The Free Press, 2001), 135.
62 *"pussy-whipped"*: Tina Brown, "The Mouse That Roared," *Vanity Fair*, October 1985.
62 *"I don't even know"*: Jo Thomas, "At Home, the Royal Couple Provoke an Unremitting Demand for Gossip," *New York Times*, November 9, 1985.
63 *"Go to nature"*: Gail Sheehy, "The Hidden Hart," *Vanity Fair*, July 1984.
63 troubled Mondale's aides: Bernard Weinraub, "Ideas for His Speech Led Mondale to Ms. Ferraro," *New York Times*, July 15, 1984.
63 *"terribly inaccurate"*: "Hart Denies Using Spiritual Adviser," *New York Times*, July 4, 1984.
64 *"The story you mention"*: Gary Hart, interview by author.
65 ad revenue: Alex S. Jones, "An Intensely Private Family Empire," *New York Times*, March 9, 1985.
65 *"I love this song"*: Brown, *Vanity Fair Diaries*, 131.
66 *"Fred-and-Gingered"*: William F. Buckley, Jr., "The Way They Are," *Vanity Fair*, June 1985.
67 *"Can you believe this?!"*: Stephen Schiff, interview by author.
67 *"You have to occasionally"*: "Blond Ambition," *60 Minutes*, CBS News, October 21, 1990.
67 *"With* Vanity Fair*"*: Tina Brown, "Editor's Letter," *Vanity Fair*, September 1985.
68 *"hierarchy of hotness"*: John Seabrook, *Nobrow: The Culture of Marketing, The Marketing of Culture* (New York: Vintage Books, 2001), 28.

68 *"I remember"*: Michael Shnayerson, interview by author.
68 *"Image replaced"*: "The 1989 Hall of Fame: Media Decade," *Vanity Fair*, December 1989.
68 *"Why are you reading"*: John Motavalli, "Tina Talks," *Inside Media*, June 24–July 14, 1992.
68 *"For me"*: Pamela Mensch, interview by author.
68 *tripled between*: Albert Scardino, "Big Spender at Vanity Fair Raises the Ante for Writers," *New York Times*, April 17, 1989.
68 *"There are good things"*: "N.Y. Times Magazine: Changes and Signs of Strain," *New York Observer*, February 26, 1990.
69 *two dollars a word*: Scardino, "Big Spender at Vanity Fair."
69 *"I could send"*: Michael Shnayerson, interview by author.
70 *"As I see it"*: "Flattery Will Get You Ten Pages . . . Maybe," *Spy*, August 1990.
71 *advertisers*: Daniel Lazare, "Evans-Brown Team—Or Is It Brown-Evans?" *New York Observer*, May 7, 1990.
71 *"Eddie Murphy"*: Stephen Schiff, interview by author. Tina Brown told me that she reassigned Schiff because film reviews were often out-of-date by the time the monthly magazine reached newsstands.
71 *"Actors shouldn't be"*: Motavalli, "Tina Talks."
71 *60 percent*: Lazare, "Evans-Brown Team."
71 *nine out of twelve*: Geoffrey Stokes, "Queen Tina," *Spy*, May 1992.
72 *"Tina almost created"*: Elizabeth Kolbert, "How Tina Brown Moves Magazines," *New York Times Magazine*, December 5, 1993.
72 *"One's job isn't"*: Tina Brown, *Happy Yellow*, Bush Theatre archives, London.
72 *he raised her salary*: Brown, *Vanity Fair Diaries*, 331, 334.

Chapter 6 Enter Anna

73 *"Two first ladies"*: John Koblin, "Michelle Obama Joins in a Salute to Anna Wintour," *New York Times*, May 5, 2014. See also Marc Karimzadeh, "First Lady Helps Open Wintour Costume Center," *Women's Wear Daily*, May 6, 2014.
74 *The woman who would preside*: For details of Anna's upbringing and early career, I am indebted to a pair of thorough biographies: Jerry Oppenheimer, *Front Row: Anna Wintour: The Cool Life and Hot Times of Vogue's Editor in Chief* (New York: St. Martin's Press, 2005); and Amy Odell, *Anna: The Biography* (New York: Gallery Books, 2022).
75 *a too-short miniskirt*: Georgina Howell, "Two of a Type," *Sunday Times* (London), July 13, 1986.
75 *"I was the one"*: Alice Steinbach, "Always in Vogue," *Baltimore Sun*, May 20, 1990.
76 *"I was told"*: Sam Reed, "Anna Wintour Calls Being Fired as a Stylist a 'Character-Building' Moment," *Hollywood Reporter*, October 26, 2017.
76 *The London tabloids*: Oppenheimer, *Front Row*, 118.
76 *fashion editor of* Viva: Details from Oppenheimer, *Front Row*, 116–50; Odell, *Anna*, 56–65.
76 *Odeon*: Keith McNally, interview by author; Frank DiGiacomo, "Live, from Tribeca!" *Vanity Fair*, November 2005.
77 *her own clothes rack*: "Between the Lines," *New York*, July 6–13, 1981.
77 *daily Windexing*: Oppenheimer, *Front Row*, 176–77.

77 *"She just wanted to know"*: Fran Lebowitz, interview by author.
77 *Lauren apologized*: Edward Kosner, *It's News to Me: The Making and Unmaking of an Editor* (New York: Thunder's Mouth Press, 2008), 215–16.
77 *up-and-coming designers*: "Fashion," *New York*, September 21, 1981.
78 *Andie MacDowell*: Anna Wintour, "In the Heat of the Night," *New York*, July 6–13, 1981; Oppenheimer, *Front Row*, 184–85.
78 *"Yours"*: "Anna Wintour on Leaving London for New York," *Guardian* (London), May 19, 1997.
78 *"I want to"*: Anna Wintour, interview, Dodie Kazanjian and Calvin Tomkins research materials on Alexander Liberman, 1927–1999, box 15, folder 9, Archives of American Art, Smithsonian Institute, Washington, DC (hereafter "Liberman Archives").
78 *"democratic snobbery"*: Mary McCarthy, "Up the Ladder from Charm to Vogue," *Reporter*, July 18 and August 1, 1950.
79 *"un-shined shoes"*: Amanda Mackenzie Stuart, *Empress of Fashion: A Life of Diana Vreeland* (New York, Harper, 2012), 220.
79 *"I have known"*: Dodie Kazanjian and Calvin Tomkins, *Alex: The Life of Alexander Liberman* (New York: Knopf, 1993), 285.
79 *"Famous last gifts"*: Lucy Sisman and Véronique Vienne, *Alex Liberman: Ways of Thinking About Design* (New York: Lucy Sisman, 2013).
79 *"We're going to lose"*: Grace Mirabella, *In and Out of Vogue* (New York: Doubleday, 1995), 153.
80 *"to go middle-class"*: Martha Sherrill Dailey, "Grace Mirabella, The Vagaries of Vogue," *Washington Post*, July 25, 1988. Warhol's line about the firing has been quoted widely, including by Mirabella herself, but it does not appear in his published diaries.
80 *"There was a lot of cashmere"*: William Norwich, interview by author.
80 *"I'm overloaded"*: Alexander Liberman, interview, box 3, folder 12, Liberman Archives.
81 *short skirt*: Dodie Kazanjian and Calvin Tomkins, *Alex: The Life of Alexander Liberman* (New York: Knopf, 1993), 310.
81 *"It's maddening"*: Amy Gross, interview by author. See also Grace Mirabella, *In and Out of Vogue*, 214–16.
82 *long lunch*: Liz Tilberis, *No Time To Die* (London: Weidenfeld & Nicolson, 1998), 136.
82 *"What is this?"*: Lucy Sisman, interview by author.
83 *She considered work trips*: Mirabella, *In and Out of Vogue*, 3, 177–78.
83 *Si chartered a jet*: Christopher S. Wren, "Cairo Gala Draws a Glittering Crowd," *New York Times*, September 28, 1979; Mirabella, *In and Out of Vogue*, 180.
83 *never dream of it*: Mirabella, *In and Out of Vogue*, 222.
84 *losing ground to Elle*: Joan Kron, "Style Setter," *Wall Street Journal*, January 30, 1986.
84 *she was put off*: Mirabella, *In and Out of Vogue*, 173, 191–203. The book also includes Mirabella's account of her firing.
85 *"My god"*: Alexander Liberman, interview, box 12, Liberman Archives.
85 *"After it was on"*: Anna Wintour discusses her experience in the wake of Mirabella's firing in an interview found in box 15, folder 9, Liberman Archives.
85 *"I am very much"*: Liz Smith, "Wintour of Discontent at Condé Nast," *New York Daily News*, August 1, 1988.
86 *"very unstylish"*: Woody Hochswender, "Changes at Vogue," *New York Times*, July 25, 1988.
86 *"makes one feel"*: Tina Brown, *The Vanity Fair Diaries, 1983–1992* (New York: Henry Holt, 2017), 294–95.

86 *"gained a little weight"*: Anna Wintour, "Anna Wintour Shares Her Vogue Story," *Vogue* website, August 14, 2012, https://www.vogue.com/article/anna-wintour-on-her-first-vogue-cover-plus-a-slideshow-of-her-favorite-images-in-vogue.

87 *"I wanted the covers"*: Kazanjian and Tomkins, *Alex*, 321.

87 *from Babe Paley*: Stephen Drucker, interview by author.

87 *Avedon*: Michael Gross, *Focus: The Secret, Sexy, Sometimes Sordid World of Fashion Photographers* (New York: Atria Books, 2016), 253; Odell, *Anna*, 136. Condé Nast agreed to buy out the final two years of Avedon's contract: Philip Gefter, *What Becomes a Legend Most: A Biography of Richard Avedon* (New York: Harper, 2020), 506–7.

88 *"You want to be"*: Geraldine Fabrikant, "The Jury's Out on the Hipper Vogue," *New York Times*, April 30, 1989.

88 *Tina had encouraged*: Kevin Haynes, "Anna's Big Year," *Women's Wear Daily*, November 10, 1989.

89 *"the most important"*: Amy M. Spindler, "The Winner Is . . . Fashion," *New York Times*, October 27, 1996.

90 *"simply offered to sift"*: Degen Pener, "Notes," *New York Times*, February 7, 1993.

90 *refusal to be typecast*: "Vogue's Point of View," *Vogue*, December 1993.

90 *"I would like to be"*: Carl Sferrazza Anthony, "Camera Girl: The Coming of Age of Jackie Bouvier Kennedy" (New York: Gallery Books, 2023), 124.

91 *"was like accepting"*: Stephen Birmingham, quoted in Anthony, "Camera Girl," 128.

91 *"My god"*: Nicholas Haslam, Redeeming Features: A Memoir (London: Jonathan Cape, 2009), 174.

91 *"a dark-haired, pretty woman"*: "Mrs. Lyndon Baines Johnson," *Vogue*, May 1, 1964.

91 *China . . . Nancy Kissinger*: Mirabella, *In and Out of Vogue*, 177; "Fashion: In China Now," *Vogue,* August 1979.

92 *"Although I don't know"*: Anna Wintour, "First Ladies," *Vogue*, June 1997.

92 *"To have one's photo"*: Robin Givhan, "Model Behavior," *Washington Post*, November 15, 1998.

93 *"pretend you're photographing"*: *Today*, NBC News, transcripts, November 19, 1998.

93 *700,000 copies*: Lisa Lockwood, "Agony and Ecstasy," *Women's Wear Daily*, January 29, 1999.

93 *"People have seen it"*: Alex Kuczynski, "The First Lady Strikes a Pose for the Media Elite," *New York Times*, December 7, 1998.

93 *"Oh, I don't need"*: Gail Sheehy, *Hillary's Choice* (London: Pocket Books, 2000), 421.

Chapter 7 A Man's World

96 *"I never posed for any picture"*: Richard Reeves, *President Kennedy: Profile of Power* (New York: Simon & Schuster, 1993), 287–88.

96 *In the 1970s*: David Kamp, "It All Started Here," *GQ*, October 2007. Kamp's essay is a definitive account of *GQ* under Jack Haber.

96 *$9.2 million*: Martha M. Hamilton, "Inside the Newhouse Empire," *Washington Post*, October 16, 1983.

96 *"It wasn't like today"*: Eliot Kaplan, interview by author.

97 *"You want the Marlboro"*: Jack Kliger, interview by author.
97 *Colacello*: Tina Brown, *The Vanity Fair Diaries, 1983–1992* (New York: Henry Holt, 2017), 48.
97 *Arthur Cooper*: Details of Cooper's upbringing and career are derived from author interviews with numerous colleagues, including Robert Draper, Eliot Kaplan, Jack Kliger, Alan Richman, and Kate White; eulogies by Eliot Kaplan and Martin Beiser at Cooper's memorial service in June 2003; and Tina Kelley, "Art Cooper, Who Transformed GQ Magazine, Is Dead at 65," *New York Times*, June 10, 2003.
97 *"We grew up in the middle"*: Eliot Kaplan, interview by author.
98 *"consisted mostly of 300-word"*: Eliot Kaplan, eulogy, "Remembering Art Cooper," June 18, 2003.
98 *Ephron almost laughed*: Kate White, interview by author.
99 *William Hurt*: This episode was recalled by Eliot Kaplan in his eulogy and by Kate White in an interview by author.
99 *"What I wanted to do"*: Nicole Beland, "So What Do You Do, Art Cooper?" Media Bistro, November 19, 2002, https://web.archive.org/web/20040623084542/http://www.mediabistro.com/content/archives/02/11/19/.
99 *Marilyn vos Savant*: David Remnick, "America's Smartest Man . . . and Woman," *GQ*, September 1986.
99 *"Who is this person?"*: Eliot Kaplan, interview by author.
100 *"For men, it had some fantasy"*: Jack Kliger, interview by author.
100 *"The American Male Opinion Index"*: A press release with the survey results is available on LexisNexis. PR Newswire, March 23, 1988.
100 *"It helped make it okay"*: Gary Van Dis, interview by author.
100 *"Now with women"*: Nancy Yoshihara, "Men's Magazine Gets a Facelift," *Los Angeles Times*, September 23, 1980.
100 *circulation*: Gigi Mahon, *The Last Days of The New Yorker* (New York: McGraw-Hill, 1988), 298.
100 *"Men, it seems, read"*: Deirdre Carmody, "In Magazines, It's a Man's World Once Again," *New York Times*, March 26, 1990.
101 *"the first one in his family"*: Bernice Kanner, "Peacock Alley," *New York*, September 26, 1983.
101 *Gerald Murphy*: "The Riviera Story," *GQ*, April 1986.
101 *Phillips Academy*: Paul Hochman, "The Natty Professor," *GQ*, October 1994.
101 *"For $300 apiece"*: Peter Mayle, "Expensive Habits," *GQ*, June 1989.
102 *"Very GQ"*: Jack Kliger described the meeting with Alex Liberman in an interview with the author.
102 *"turned those initials"*: Quintanilla, "Fashion as One Piece of the Puzzle."
102 *from 1986 to 1996*: Robin Pogrebin, "Has Esquire Gone Out of Style?" *New York Times*, July 1, 1996.
102 *"crawl across the desert"*: Eliot Kaplan, eulogy, "Remembering Art Cooper," June 18, 2003.
102 *"I'll buy this"*: Lorne Manly, "Off the Record," *New York Observer*, August 25–September 1, 1997.
103 *The awards were handed out*: Jeff Gremillion, "Live From N.Y., It's 'GQ,'" *Mediaweek*, October 28, 1996.
103 *$1 million*: Joanne Lipman, "Glitzkrieg," *Wall Street Journal*, January 4, 1996.

103 *"It's very nice"*: Arthur Cooper, "The Heidi Chronicles," *GQ*, September 2002.
104 *Art paid models*: Lorne Manly, "The New Esquire Man Pops His GQ Mentor," *New York Observer*, January 12, 1998.
104 *"What's your favorite part of sex?"*: Adrienne Miller described her time at *GQ* in her memoir, *In the Land of Men* (New York: Ecco, 2020), 112.
104 *Niccolini pled guilty*: Matt Stevens et al., "Julian Niccolini, Face of the Four Seasons Restaurant, Is Forced to Resign," *New York Times*, December 17, 2018.
105 *"It was such"*: Adrienne Miller, interview by author.
105 *"I never had any intention"*: Alan Richman's comments are from an interview with the author, unless otherwise noted.
105 *Art dispatched him to Monte Carlo*: Alan Richman, "Too Much Is Never Enough," *GQ*, May 1999.
106 *"That moment at the Milan"*: Robert Draper, interview by author.
106 *"Breasts for Guests"*: Tom Sietsema, "Guy Food," *GQ*, August 2001.
106 *Art got roped into*: David Carr, "MediaTalk," *New York Times*, February 17, 2003; Michael Gross, "The Manly Art of War," *New York Daily News*, February 23, 2003.
106 *"We were making fun"*: Greg Gutfeld, interview by author.
107 *"He was so lost"*: Kate White, interview by author.
107 *"I'm fine. I overdid it a bit"*: Alex von Bidder, interview by author. Additional details from David Zinczenko, interview by author.
107 *"It's as if it was scripted"*: Keith J. Kelly, "GQ Editor Art Cooper Dead at 65," *New York Post*, June 10, 2003.
108 *"GQ is an aspirational"*: Carl Swanson, "The Rise of Maxim Magazine," *New York Observer*, February 1, 1999.

Chapter 8 The Ballad of Donald and Si

109 *"cuff links"*: E. Graydon Carter, "Donald Trump Gets What He Wants," *GQ*, May 1984.
110 *"This Trump fellow"*: Peter Osnos, interview by author.
110 *"was very definitely"*: Jane Mayer, "Trump's Boswell Speaks," *New Yorker*, July 25, 2016.
110 *two great decisions*: Laura Landro and Laurie P. Cohen, "Get Ready World: Donald Trump Wants a Best Seller," *Wall Street Journal*, November 30, 1987.
111 *ski vacation*: Peter L. W. Osnos, *An Especially Good View: Watching History Happen* (New York: Platform, 2021), 241.
111 *"I just don't know"*: Pamela Mensch, interview by author.
111 *Cohn started his comeback*: Thomas Maier, *Newhouse: All the Glitter, Power, and Glory of America's Richest Media Empire and the Secretive Man Behind It* (New York: St. Martin's Press, 1994), 95–97.
112 *"He reached into his drawer"*: Nicholas von Hoffman, *Citizen Cohn: The Life and Times of Roy Cohn* (New York: Doubleday, 1988), 327.
112 *paid Cohn a retainer*: von Hoffman, *Citizen Cohn*, 327–28.
112 *Si sat vigil*: Margot Hornblower, "Si Newhouse, the Talk of The New Yorker," *Washington Post*, May 6, 1985.
112 *Studio 54*: There are numerous accounts of Si and Trump's mutual attendance at Cohn's Studio 54 parties. See for example Wayne Barrett, "The Birthday Boy: Roy

Cohn is 52 at 54," *Village Voice*, March 5, 1979, https://www.villagevoice.com/the-birthday-boy-roy-cohn-is-52-at-54/.

112 *"I didn't see how we could"*: Cohn's memoir was eventually issued by a different publishing house. Thomas Maier, *Newhouse*, 193–94.

112 *"There's no question"*: Peter Osnos, interview by author.

113 *Trump was upset*: Tom Mathews, "High Gloss News," *Newsweek*, May 1, 1989.

113 *"If I had these"*: Marie Brenner, "After the Gold Rush," *Vanity Fair*, September 1990.

113 *"We buried the hatchet"*: Jim Windolf, "Off the Record," *New York Observer*, May 10, 1993.

114 *"I sort of admire him"*: Howard Kurtz, "Spy Magazine to Fold," *Washington Post*, February 18, 1994.

114 *"too tacky"*: Amy Odell, *Anna: The Biography* (New York: Gallery Books, 2022), 145.

114 *"coming out of her nightmare"*: Vicki Woods, "The Real Ivana," *Vogue*, May 1990.

114 *750,000 copies*: Amy Odell, *Anna*, 145.

114 *hundreds of copies*: Ben Kesslen and James Messerschmidt, "Trashed!" *New York Post*, August 24, 2022.

114 *"Ivana was thrilled"*: Alice Steinbach, "Always in Vogue," *Baltimore Sun*, May 20, 1990.

114 *"I should turn"*: Alexander Liberman, interview transcript, Dodie Kazanjian and Calvin Tomkins research materials on Alexander Liberman, 1927–1999, box 14, Archives of American Art, Smithsonian Institute, Washington, DC.

115 *"She is a true beauty"*: Sally Singer, "How to Marry a Billionaire," *Vogue*, February 2005.

115 *"good-natured"*: "Letter from the Editor," *Vogue*, February 2005.

115 *"It was a bit disconcerting"*: "Ivanka's Trump Card," *Good Morning America*, ABC News, transcript, October 13, 2009.

116 *"You never got"*: Juli Weiner, "A Future President's Letter to Vanity Fair," *Vanity Fair* website, April 11, 2011, https://www.vanityfair.com/news/2011/04/donald-trump-letter-201104.

116 *"Every C-SPAN Shot"*: Juli Weiner, "Every C-Span Shot of Donald Trump Looking
116 About Seth Meyers's Donald Trump Jokes," *Vanity Fair* website, May 1, 2011, https://www.vanityfair.com/news/2011/05/every-c-span-shot-of-donald-trump-looking-angry-about-seth-meyerss-donald-trump-jokes.

116 *"This is the only"*: Michael M. Grynbaum, "Graydon Carter to End 25-Year Run as Vanity Fair's Editor," *New York Times*, September 8, 2017.

118 *"Truth Hurts"*: Cover, *Vogue*, November 2021.

118 *her voice quavered*: Amy Odell, *Anna*, 3.

118 *overheard by a British tabloid*: Alan Selby, "Vogue Editor Anna Wintour Apologizes after Rant Against Donald Trump," *Daily Mirror*, December 10, 2016.

118 *"It just shows that"*: Hope Hicks, interview by author. Hicks's quotes are from this interview unless otherwise noted.

118 *"There's a meeting"*: Graydon Carter, interview by author.

119 *"I can't even believe"*: Graydon Carter, interview by author. Trump's meeting at 1 World Trade Center was described to me by numerous participants.

120 *Anna appeared on the late-night show*: Lisa Respers France, "Anna Wintour Names Who She Would Axe from Met Gala," CNN website, October 26, 2017.

120 *"They're biased"*: Kelsey Ables, "Melania Trump Calls Vogue 'Biased' for Not Putting Her on the Cover," *Washington Post*, May 14, 2022. Amy Odell discusses the abandoned *Vogue* shoot in *Anna*, 4.

120 *subscriptions to* Vanity Fair *had soared*: Benjamin Mullin, "Vanity Fair's Subscriptions Soar After Troll-y Trump Tweet," Poynter website, December 16, 2016, https://www.poynter.org/business-work/2016/vanity-fairs-subscriptions-soar-after-troll-y-trump-tweet/.

Chapter 9 Philistine at the Gate

122 *"It didn't last long enough"*: Thomas Maier, *Newhouse: All the Glitter, Power, and Glory of America's Richest Media Empire and the Secretive Man Behind It* (New York: St. Martin's Press, 1994), 272.

123 *Circulation had barely budged*: Eric N. Berg, "Newhouse Makes Offer for The New Yorker," *New York Times*, February 13, 1985.

123 *investing in . . .* Elle: Gigi Mahon, *The Last Days of The New Yorker* (New York: McGraw-Hill, 1988), 146-147.

123 *Jasper Johns*: Carol Felsenthal, *Citizen Newhouse: Portrait of a Media Merchant* (New York: Seven Stories Press, 1998), 294, 296.

123 *Now Si was aggressively*: Mahon, *Last Days*, 234–35; Maier, *Newhouse*, 276–79; Pamela G. Hollie, "Newhouse to Acquire 17% of The New Yorker," *New York Times*, November 14, 1984. See also Gigi Mahon's book-length account of the acquisition.

123 *"He wanted to buy it"*: Thomas Maier, *Newhouse*, 278.

124 *"The decision to buy"*: Pamela Mensch, interview by author.

124 *"a deliberate affront"*: Douglas C. McGill, "Editor Says Staff Did Not Give 'Our Approval,'" *New York Times*, March 9, 1985.

125 *for the past fourteen years*: Margot Hornblower, "New Face at The New Yorker," *Washington Post*, September 18, 1985.

125 *"We don't want anyone"*: Michael Gross, "Tina's Turn," *New York*, July 20, 1992.

125 *"we have never published"*: "Notes and Comment," *New Yorker*, April 22, 1985.

125 *"I've never seen Si"*: Margot Hornblower, "Si Newhouse, the Talk of The New Yorker," *Washington Post*, May 6, 1985.

125 *"You mean you don't want"*: Gigi Mahon, *Last Days*, 290.

126 *Eustace Tilley's head*: Hornblower, "Si Newhouse, the Talk of The New Yorker."

126 *"Si has got himself"*: Stephen Pascal, ed., *The Grand Surprise: The Journals of Leo Lerman* (New York: Knopf, 2007), 536.

126 *"was so careful about"*: Calvin Trillin, interview by author.

126 *"The* New Yorker *people"*: Jonathan Alter, interview by author.

126 *"very much the ravenous"*: Lillian Ross, private notes, April 25, 1985. Courtesy of the Lillian Ross estate.

127 *"like he was an alien"*: John Koblin, "Magazine Honchos Remember Steve Florio," *New York Observer*, January 2, 2008.

127 *"who takes the prisoner"*: Lillian Ross, private notes, April 25, 1985. Courtesy of the Lillian Ross estate.

127 *"We'll tell you whether"*: Geraldine Fabrikant, "Cash vs. Cachet at New Yorker," *New York Times*, June 2, 1986.

127 *"I just blew it out of here"*: Mark N. Vamos, "Change at The New Yorker is the Talk of the Town," *Business Week*, March 10, 1986.

NOTES   311

127 *market survey*: Christopher Hitchens, "American Notes," *Times Literary Supplement*, March 7, 1986.
128 *Shawn once insisted*: Louis Menand, "A Friend Writes," *New Republic*, February 26, 1990.
128 *One spot featured*: "Driver," television advertisement, 1986, posted by 80sCommercialVault, "Best Commercials of 1986," YouTube, September 2, 2019, https://youtu.be/rrTbiZFtscA?feature=shared&t=3634.
128 *"energized by"*: Philip H. Dougherty, "Advertising," *New York Times*, September 25, 1985.
128 *"The New Yorker reader"*: Mark N. Vamos, "Change at The New Yorker is the Talk of the Town," *Business Week*, March 10, 1986.
129 *"Mr. Newhouse, would you"*: Robert Gottlieb, *Avid Reader: A Life* (New York: Picador, 2016), 196.
130 *"The ultra-forceful Newhouse"*: Gottlieb, *Avid Reader*, 196.
130 *The letter*: Gottlieb, *Avid Reader*, 199–200; see also an account by Lillian Ross, *Here but Not Here: A Love Story* (New York: Random House, 1998), 208, 214–20.
130 *"This did not speak well"*: Gottlieb, *Avid Reader*, 200.
130 *an unpleasant exit*: Ross, *Here but Not Here*, 217, 221.
131 *a feature-length screenplay*: Info, screenplay, first revision of original draft. Courtesy of the Lillian Ross estate. The title page, which lists Lorne Michaels as a producer, credits Ross alone as having written the story and screenplay. Ross acknowledges in her memoir that Shawn was her uncredited coauthor: "Bill threw himself into the work with his old energy, concentration, and enthusiasm and was enjoying himself enormously." Ross, *Here but Not Here*, 229.
132 *"He wasn't interested"*: Calvin Trillin, interview by author.
132 *he kept a toaster*: John McPhee, "Editors & Publisher," *New Yorker*, July 2, 2012.
132 *"could never understand"*: Tina Brown, *The Vanity Fair Diaries, 1983–1992* (New York: Henry Holt, 2017), 268.
132 *watching the drama*: Brown, *The Vanity Fair Diaries*, 238.
133 *"It confirmed my"*: Gottlieb, *Avid Reader*, 201.
133 *"I never worked"*: Robert Gottlieb, interview by author.
133 *"merely a magazine"*: Hendrik Hertzberg, "Journals of Opinion," *Gannett Center Journal*, Spring 1989.

Chapter 10 Eustace Tina

136 *"fever is sweeping"*: George Christy, "The Great Life," *Hollywood Reporter*, March 4, 1988.
136 *"was a strategic"*: Michael Gross, "Social Life in a Blender," *New York*, February 2, 1998.
137 *"news and literature combined"*: Tina Brown, *The Vanity Fair Diaries, 1983–1992* (New York: Henry Holt, 2017), 322–23. See also James L. W. West, *William Styron: A Life* (New York: Random House, 1998), 451–55.
137 *"the diabolical discomfort"*: William Styron, "Darkness Visible," *Vanity Fair*, December 1989.
137 *"Out of a great deal"*: Laurel Graeber, "Out of His System," *New York Times*, August 19, 1990.
138 *nearly twenty-one thousand*: Philip M. Boffey, "Reagan Urges Wide AIDS Testing but Does Not Call for Compulsion," *New York Times*, June 1, 1987.

NOTES

138 *"It was bringing"*: Michael Shnayerson, interview by author.
138 *Demi Moore*: Annie Leibovitz, *Annie Leibovitz at Work* (London: Jonathan Cape, 2008), 90–93; Demi Moore, *Inside Out* (New York: HarperLuxe, 2019), 160–70; Tina Brown, *Vanity Fair Diaries*, 399–400; Demi Moore, interview, *The Howard Stern Show*, October 9, 2019, https://www.facebook.com/watch/?v=2458510061135434.
139 *"I don't think so"*: Lucy Sisman, interview by author.
139 *"Why not?"*: Tina Brown, *Vanity Fair Diaries*, 400.
139 *"I guess they want"*: Charles Lewis, "Vanity Bare," *Ottawa Citizen*, July 23, 1991.
139 *"sickening, cheap sensationalism"*: Mark Muro, "Moore's Pregnant Pose: Is It Hip or Hype?" *Boston Globe*, July 12, 1991.
139 *"the ultimate yuppie madonna"*: Roberta Smith, "Through Annie Leibovitz's Lens, a Celebration of the Celebrated," *New York Times*, July 25, 1991.
140 *"Isn't it ironic"*: "Breaking Pregnancy Taboos," *PrimeTime Live*, ABC News, July 18, 1991.
140 *"a young Arabian racehorse"*: Nancy Collins, "Demi's Big Moment," *Vanity Fair*, August 1991.
140 *"A piece on a collection"*: Lou Chapman, "At The New Yorker, the Newhouse Era Brings a New Look," *New York Observer*, April 24, 1989.
141 *"doesn't do celebrities"*: Michael M. Thomas, "Forbes Will Be Missed; Few Mourn Drexel," *New York Observer*, March 5, 1990.
141 *"run pictures"*: N. R. Kleinfield, "Rumors Outpace Changes Under New Yorker's Editor," *New York Times*, December 7, 1988.
141 *still in the red*: Tina Brown, in *The Vanity Fair Diaries* (406), wrote that Si estimated the losses at that point as $19 million a year. Robert Gottlieb, in his memoir, pegged it at $2 million.
143 *"a piece that had"*: Robert Gottlieb, *Avid Reader: A Life* (New York: Picador, 2016), 222.
143 *"but he didn't like"*: Renata Adler, *Gone: The Last Days of The New Yorker* (New York: Simon & Schuster, 1999), 238. See also Gottlieb, *Avid Reader*, 231–33.
143 *"I'm good at putting"*: Michael Gross, "Tina's Turn," *New York*, July 20, 1992.
144 *roughly $350,000*: The exact dollar figure has been estimated as somewhere between $300,000 and $400,000 annually. Gottlieb said in 2020 that the payout was adjusted upward every three years or so to reflect inflation. See Felsenthal, *Citizen Newhouse*, 354; and Ben Smith, "Condé Nast Is Facing an Era's End," *New York Times*, April 26, 2020.
144 *"I'm the happiest"*: Jim Windolf, "Tina Brown's Debut," *New York Observer*, September 14, 1992.
144 *"Did you make up"*: Michael Gross, "Tina's Turn."
145 *redeemed a check*: Julius Lowenthal, "Every Man Has His Price," *Spy*, July 1990.
145 *"his famous aversions"*: "Naked City," *Spy*, December 1990.
145 *"Those Nasty Men"*: James Ledbetter, "Long-Fingered Spy Owners Seek Deep-Pocketed Buyer," *New York Observer*, March 19, 1990.
145 *"We were friends"*: Graydon Carter, interview by author.
145 *"to stave off poverty"*: "Spy Man Taking Newhouse Gold," *New York*, September 19, 1988.
146 *"I figured it was"*: Graydon Carter, interview by author.
146 *"dwarf billionaire" . . . "socialite–war criminal"*: "Little Men," *Spy*, June 1987.
146 *"so I would have known"*: Graydon Carter, interview by author.
147 *"I've got two things"*: Graydon Carter, interview by author.

148 *"It's one of the"*: Tina Brown, interview by author.
149 *"I talked about both"*: Jennifer Senior, "Graydon Rides the Wave," *New York*, December 11, 2000.

Chapter 11 Lapses of Taste

151 *"The rumors are true"*: Michael Gross, "Tina's Turn," *New York*, July 20, 1992. Additional details from Thomas Maier, *Newhouse: All the Glitter, Power, and Glory of America's Richest Media Empire and the Secretive Man Behind It* (New York: St. Martin's Press, 1994), 307–8.
152 *"underbelly of mediocre"*: Tina Brown, podcast interview, *Print Is Dead (Long Live Print!)*, February 2, 2024.
152 *"It was ten years"*: Tina Brown, *Print Is Dead*.
152 *"It's none of"*: Lou Chapman, "At The New Yorker, the Newhouse Era Brings a New Look," *New York Observer*, April 24, 1989.
153 *archives*: Jim Windolf, "Tina at Two," *New York Observer*, October 3, 1994.
153 *sexist barbs*: Michael Gross, "Tina's Turn," *New York*, July 20, 1992.
153 *"a great girl"*: Lorne Manly, "Off the Record," *New York Observer*, May 5, 1997.
153 *"a tarty breathlessness"*: "Annals of The New Yorker," *New York Times*, July 9, 1998.
153 *"A great American"*: Ben Yagoda, *About Town: The New Yorker and the World It Made* (New York: Scribner, 2000), 420.
154 *a conspiracy afoot*: Tina Brown, "Three Weddings and a Funeral," in Victor S. Navasky and Evan Cornog, eds., *The Art of Making Magazines* (New York: Columbia University Press, 2012), 122.
154 *William Shawn once balked*: The Mel Brooks anecdote was recalled by Calvin Tomkins in an interview with Randy Kennedy in *Ursula* (Spring 2020); it also appears in Felsenthal, *Citizen Newhouse*, 361. Kenneth Tynan's profile of Brooks ran in *The New Yorker*, October 30, 1978.
155 *"The important thing"*: Elizabeth Kolbert, "How Tina Brown Moves Magazines," *New York Times*, December 5, 1993.
155 *fact-checking department*: Peter Canby, "Fact-checking at The New Yorker," in Victor S. Navasky and Evan Cornog, eds., *The Art of Making Magazines* (New York: Columbia University Press, 2012), 79–80.
155 *"Joe Mitchell would"*: "David Remnick: Media Prince," *TBD with Tina Brown*, podcast, February 19, 2019.
155 *Tina did try*: Thomas Kunkel, *Man in Profile: Joseph Mitchell of The New Yorker* (New York: Random House, 2015), 319–20.
156 *"the Terminator"*: Elizabeth Kolbert, "How Tina Brown Moves Magazines," *New York Times*, December 5, 1993.
156 *"Tina wanted something"*: Jeffrey Toobin, interview by author.
156 *On his walk to work*: Windolf, "Tina at Two." In his own account of this episode, Chancellor said that he shelved the first draft of his tree article because it came out "rather boring." Later, seeking to substitute two "Talk" items that were rejected by Tina, he showed the article to McGrath, "who agreed that it wasn't quite right." Alexander Chancellor, *Some Times in America* (London: Bloomsbury, 1999), 160–62.
157 *Toobin called Alan Dershowitz*: Jeffrey Toobin recounts his reporting for the Simpson article, and the frenzied media response, in *The Run of His Life: The People v. O. J. Simpson* (New York: Simon & Schuster, 1997), 145–58.

158 *"I want to welcome"*: *Nightline*, ABC News, transcript, July 22, 1994.
158 *"Once I decide"*: Jeffrey Toobin, "An Incendiary Defense," *New Yorker*, July 25, 1994.
159 *"kiss[ing] the ass"*: Joanne Weintraub, "Tina Brown's New Yorker," *American Journalism Review*, April 1995. Also see Felsenthal, *Citizen Newhouse*, 360.
159 *"the great high/low show"*: Tina Brown, "Editor's Letter," *Vanity Fair*, September 1992.
159 *"Don't you get it?"*: David Kuhn, interview by author.
160 *"A porn shoot"*: Susan Faludi, "The Money Shot," *New Yorker*, October 30, 1995.
160 *circulation was up*: Jim Windolf, "Tina at Two."
160 *"gone too far"*: Brown, *Vanity Fair Diaries*, 383.
161 *"suck my dick"*: John Lahr, "Dealing with Roseanne," *New Yorker*, July 17, 1995.
161 *"If the magazine were"*: Associated Press, "'New Yorker' Not Big Enough," *Albany Times Union*, September 9, 1995.
161 *"slaves of the buzz"*: Maureen Dowd, "Eustace Silly," *New York Times*, September 3, 1995.
162 *"Semicolons"*: James Wolcott, "With Respect to Roseanne," *New Yorker*, February 26 and March 4, 1996.
163 *"I froze internally"*: Daphne Merkin, interview by author.
163 *"warmed-over prurience"*: Terry Tang, "The Respite of Reticence Amid a Cyclone of Candor," *Seattle Times*, March 1, 1996.
163 *"SWM seeking"*: "Quickly Quotable," *New York Times*, February 12, 1998.
164 *about $1 million annually*: Yagoda, *About Town*, 423.
164 *"The way Tina"*: Calvin Trillin, interview with author.
165 *"By the time"*: Maurie Perl, interview by author.
165 *"The questions journalists"*: Elizabeth Kolbert, "How Tina Brown Moves Magazines," *New York Times*, December 5, 1993.
165 *"Questions were not"*: Deirdre Carmody, "Tina Brown's Progress at the New New Yorker," *New York Times*, April 12, 1993.
165 *"Too much then"*: John Seabrook, *Nobrow: The Culture of Marketing, The Marketing of Culture* (New York: Vintage Books, 2001), 38.
166 *"Galley five"*: Jonathan Alter, "Ruminating with Calvin Trillin," *Old Goats with Jonathan Alter*, December 18, 2022, https://web.archive.org/web/20221218231228/.
166 *"Is Housman hot?"*: Anthony Lane, "Talk of the Town," *New Yorker*, August 3, 1998.
166 *"My goal"*: Tina Brown, letter to Jim Windolf, September 23, 1994.
166 *"Tina always said"*: Hjärta Smärta and Ika Johannesson, *Hall of Femmes: Ruth Ansel* (Stockholm: Oyster Press, 2010), 43.
166 *"Tina decided"*: Stephen Schiff, interview with author.
167 *nearly 870,000*: Ben Yagoda, *About Town*, 424.

Chapter 12 Life as a Party

169 *"you've got six hours"*: Jon Kelly, interview by author.
170 *"I could hardly"*: Graydon Carter's quotes in this chapter are from interviews with the author, unless otherwise noted.
171 *"I thought"*: Jennifer Senior, "Graydon Rides the Wave," *New York*, December 11, 2000. Senior's portrait is perhaps the definitive profile of Graydon Carter.
171 *Self-invention*: This description of Graydon Carter's early years is based on author interviews with Graydon Carter and papers found in *The Canadian Review* Fonds,

NOTES

Archives and Special Collections, University of Calgary. I also draw from Senior's profile and David Blum, "Who is E. Graydon Carter and How Did He Get Here?" *New York*, April 17, 1989.

171 *"Carter had an understanding"*: Larry Krotz, "Life Before Vanity Fair," *National Post*, January 4, 2003.

171 *"always fluctuated"*: Graydon Carter, untitled article dated October 22, 1975, box 7, folder 6, *The Canadian Review* Fonds, Archives and Special Collections, University of Calgary.

172 *He once showed up*: Carl Swanson, "154 Minutes with Graydon Carter," *New York*, October 11, 2013.

172 TV-Cable Week: Michael Gross, "Tina's Turn," *New York*, July 20, 1992.

172 *"New York bristles"*: David Blum, "Spying on 'Spy,'" *New York*, April 17, 1989.

173 *"now that Tina's gone"*: Linda Stasi, "Inside New York," *Newsday*, July 20, 1992.

174 *"resemble car salesmen"*: "Miramax Brothers Court Headlines Like This One; Business Booms," *New York Observer*, September 16, 1991.

174 mailing list: Thomas Maier, *Newhouse: All the Glitter, Power, and Glory of America's Richest Media Empire and the Secretive Man Behind It* (New York: St. Martin's Press, 1994), 335–36.

174 *"out of the spotlight"*: Deirdre Carmody, "Vanity Fair Is Doing Nicely, but Out of the Spotlight," *New York Times*, January 25, 1993. Ad trends are taken from Geraldine Fabrikant, "Abrupt Departure at Vanity Fair," *New York Times*, May 11, 1993.

174 *"a little bit like"*: Russell Miller, "The Spy Who Came into the Fold," *Sunday Times* (London), October 11, 1992.

175 *"if I'd had my choice"*: Robert Gottlieb recounted this comment in "Remembering Si Newhouse," *Charlie Rose*, PBS, October 23, 2017.

175 *"primogeniture loser"*: James Kaplan, "Mom Always Liked You Best," *Spy*, June 1990.

176 *"he extended to me"*: Jim Windolf, "Quid Pro Quo Settles Graydon's War on Liz," *New York Observer*, March 27, 1995.

176 *"the best argument"*: "I Spy Feud Brewing: Liz Versus Magazine," *Newsday*, November 27, 1989.

176 in Converse sneakers: "Society Grunge," *Vanity Fair*, April 1993.

176 *"the worst moment"*: Jane Sarkin, interview by author.

176 *"If it hadn't been"*: Michael M. Grynbaum, "Graydon Carter to End 25-Year Run as Vanity Fair's Editor," *New York Times*, September 7, 2017.

176 *"Graydon's been"*: Merrie Morris, "Merrie-Go-Round," *Washington Times*, May 3, 1993.

177 drew accusations of racism: "Color Blind?" *Hollywood Reporter*, March 27, 1995.

177 *"I started to scream"*: Claudia Eller, "A Tribute or a Demeaning Reflection?" *Los Angeles Times*, March 16, 1995.

178 *"It's not just"*: Graydon Carter, "The Inside Story Behind the Vanity Fair Party," *Vanity Fair* website, October 10, 2006, https://www.vanityfair.com/culture/2006/10/oscars_graydon200503.

178 *"panorama"*: Frank DiGiacomo, "The Oscars Enter the New Century!" *New York Observer*, April 3, 2000.

178 Regis Philbin: DiGiacomo, "The Oscars Enter the New Century!"

178 *"Everyone's trying"*: Frank DiGiacomo, "Oscars MCMXCVIII," *New York Observer*, March 30, 1998.

178 *"I'm sorry"*: Frank DiGiacomo, "A Tense Best-Picture Victory for the Miramax Mogul Who Stormed Oscar Beach," *New York Observer*, March 29, 1999.

179 *"I need to come in"*: Jane Sarkin, interview by author.
179 *"People needed that"*: Jane Sarkin, interview by author.
180 *at the Dakota*: Lorne Manly, "Off the Record," *New York Observer*, December 16, 1996.
181 *"The basic atmosphere"*: Kathleen Sharp, "Graydon Carter," *Hollywood Reporter*, June 8, 1999.
182 *"Who wants tuna?"*: Dana Brown, *Dilettante: True Tales of Excess, Triumph, and Disaster* (New York: Ballantine Books, 2022), 157.
183 *"getting your own"*: Maureen Dowd, "Feathered and Tarred," *New York Times*, June 10, 1998.
183 *"deprived of her voice"*: "Monica Lewinsky," *Vanity Fair*, December 1998.
184 *"You better call"*: Todd S. Purdum and Jim Rutenberg, "In the Prelude to Publication, Intrigue Worthy of Deep Throat," *New York Times*, June 2, 2005.
184 *Graydon never contacted*: Graydon Carter, "The Checks Are in the Mail," *Vanity Fair*, July 2005.
184 *first pitched the story*: Todd S. Purdum and Jim Rutenberg, "In Final Chapter of Watergate, Intrigue Worthy of Deep Throat," *New York Times*, June 2, 2005. See also Katharine Q. Seelye, "Disclosure by Magazine Catches Post by Surprise," *New York Times*, June 1, 2005.
185 *a $100,000 payment*: David Carr and Sharon Waxman, "Vanity Fair Editor Got $100,000 for Suggesting a Movie," *New York Times*, May 14, 2004.
185 *one out of every three*: Eliza Gray, "Camelot Tales," *New Republic*, April 11, 2011.
186 *"I try not to be"*: Alex Williams, "Graydon Carter, the Last Impresario," *New York Times*, February 28, 2014.

Chapter 13 Age of Empire

187 *"I was sitting there"*: Alexandra Penney's quotes are from interviews with the author, unless otherwise noted.
188 *"Wear this ribbon"*: Alexandra Penney, "Letter from the Editor," *Self*, October 1992.
188 *"pinkwashing"*: See Gina Kolata, "Some Breast Cancer Activists Assail Rampant 'Pinkification' of October," *New York Times*, October 31, 2015.
189 *"Dash! Vitality!"*: Dodie Kazanjian and Calvin Tomkins, *Alex: The Life of Alexander Liberman* (New York: Knopf, 1993), 344.
189 *"I don't want to go there"*: Polly Mellen, interview by author.
189 *"Beauty is news"*: Linda Wells, "Beyond Beauty," *Allure*, March 1991.
190 *"This is going"*: Linda Wells, interview by author.
190 *"a bold"*: Linda Wells, "Our Secret Weapons," *Allure*, October 1996.
191 *"You see those women"*: Jonathan Wingfield, "Portfolio: Ruth Ansel," *System*, Fall/Winter 2016, https://system-magazine.com/issues/issue-8/portfolio-ruth-ansel.
191 *"She was the discoverer"*: Joshua Levine, "Brand Anna," *Wall Street Journal*, March 24, 2011.
191 *"How did I do?"*: Kevin Haynes, "Anna's Big Year," *Women's Wear Daily*, November 10, 1989.
191 *Michael Kors*: Levine, "Brand Anna."
191 *"I just came for"*: Michael Gross, "War of the Poses," *New York*, April 27, 1992.
192 *Edna Woolman Chase*: "Benefit Party for Costume Institute Set," *Women's Wear Daily*, October 18, 1948.

NOTES

193 *"This," Talley declared, "is Anna"*: Frank DiGiacomo, "Careerist Glitzmongers Hijack Bluebloods' Ball," *New York Observer*, December 11, 1995. See also Aileen Mehle, "Suzy," *Women's Wear Daily*, December 6, 1995, and Amy Odell, *Anna: The Biography* (New York: Gallery Books, 2022), 174–77.

193 *"the collective coming-out"*: Frank DiGiacomo, "Careerist Glitzmongers Hijack Bluebloods' Ball," *New York Observer*, December 11, 1995.

193 *"The future is"*: Amy M. Spindler, "When Fashion Marries Music," *New York Times*, December 5, 1995.

193 *had only been created*: "Times Magazine Names Style Editor," *New York Times*, September 8, 1998.

193 *"Fashion needs to"*: Spindler, "When Fashion Marries Music."

194 *"I don't even know"*: Frank DiGiacomo, "Met Life," *New York Observer*, December 15, 1997. Although Madonna was a guest at the event, she did not perform a song; Wrightsman didn't attend, citing a previous dinner engagement.

195 *"Hello, Puff Daddy"*: Frank DiGiacomo, "It's the Last Party of the Century," *New York Observer*, December 13, 1999.

195 *hot-air balloon*: Levine, "Brand Anna."

195 *more than $250 million*: Figure provided by the Metropolitan Museum of Art.

195 *"I just think"*: Frank DiGiacomo, "Back to the Couture," *New York Observer*, April 21, 2003.

196 *"I feel a sense"*: *To Russia with Vogue*, Mary FitzPatrick, producer, *Trouble at the Top*, BBC2, March 3, 1999.

196 *Condé paid $2 million*: "Vogue Cancels Extravaganza in Red Square," *WWD*, September 2, 1998.

196 *"In Russia. At Long Last"*: Michael Idov, *Dressed Up for a Riot: Misadventures in Putin's Moscow* (New York: Farrar, Straus & Giroux, 2018), 13.

197 *800,000 readers*: Fleur Britten, "Vogue Russia Closes," *Guardian* (London), April 20, 2022.

197 *"The Arabs deserve"*: Elizabeth Paton, "A Muslim Fashion Identity," *New York Times*, November 3, 2016.

198 *"We covered our poor"*: Bernd Runge, interview by author.

198 *In the early years*: An early history of Condé's international editions can be found in H. W. Yoxall, "The Story of the Condé Nast Publications" (New York: privately printed, 1951), in Ilka Chase Papers, box 20, folder 15, Billy Rose Theatre Division, New York Public Library.

198 *"Vogue carries to the four corners"*: Paul Géraldy, "Bouquets," *Vogue*, January 1, 1923.

199 *An internal booklet*: Carl Swanson, "Off the Record," *New York Observer*, March 8, 1999.

199 *an estimated $100 million*: Charles V. Bagli, "Condé Nast's Stylish Clan Moves into Times Sq.," *New York Times*, June 20, 1999.

200 *"Sometimes, Brian would"*: Shawn McCreesh, "44 at the Royalton," *New York*, April 8, 2024.

200 *a dozen cappuccinos*: Dana Brown, *Dilettante: True Tales of Excess, Triumph, and Disaster* (New York: Ballantine Books, 2022), 29–30.

200 *had met Gehry at a dinner party*: Paul Goldberger describes Si and Gehry's relationship in *Building Art: The Life and Work of Frank Gehry* (New York: Vintage Books, 2017), 338–41.

201 *"It was a very witty"*: James Truman, interview by author. Truman's quotes are from this interview unless otherwise noted.

318   NOTES

201 *"The company's fashion"*: Herbert Muschamp, "Tray Chic," *New York Times*, April 23, 2000.
202 *"slightly vaginal"*: Alexandra Jacobs, "Condé Nast Employees Get Their Very Own Private Cafeteria," *New York Observer*, April 17, 2000.

Chapter 14 "Do It All Grandly!"

203 *"Si used money far more"*: Katrina Heron, interview by author.
204 *"That was the kind"*: Stephen Drucker, interview by author.
204 *"This is what I failed at"*: Joan Kron, interview by author.
205 *"He drove with reckless"*: Lucy Sisman, interview by author.
205 *"I had to learn how"*: Jennifer Barnett, interview by author.
205 *"No, no. I didn't flee"*: Lucy Sisman and Véronique Vienne, *Alex Liberman: Ways of Thinking About Design* (New York: Lucy Sisman, 2013).
206 *"Darling, I had"*: Véronique Vienne, "Make It Right . . . Then Toss It Away," *Columbia Journalism Review*, July/August 1991.
206 *"This is what"*: Sisman and Vienne, *Alex Liberman*.
207 *"There was a way"*: Linda Wells, interview by author.
207 *"We were in heels"*: Plum Sykes, interview by Liana Satenstein, *Neverworns*, May 16, 2024, https://neverworns.substack.com/p/the-plum-sykes-x-neverworns-live.
207 *"The clothes that people"*: *Boss Women: Anna Wintour*, Christine Hall, dir., BBC1, 2000.
207 *"I was absolutely terrified"*: Lynden Volpe Greenfield, interview by author.
208 *ran an item about it*: Susan Heller Anderson, "The Press," *New York Times*, October 24, 1986.
208 *"possessed no evidence"*: "Editors' Note," *New York Times*, October 25, 1986.
209 *One grandee*: Lauren Waterman, "Manhattan When I Was Young," *The Entertainment Staff*, April 4, 2018, https://lauren.substack.com/p/manhattan-when-i-was-young.
209 *"I had absolutely no qualifications"*: Kate Reardon, interview by author.
209 *"Dearie"*: Linda Wells, interview by author.
210 *twenty-one-page booklet*: Amy Odell, *Anna*, 162.
210 *fifty words a minute*: *Rooms with No View: A Woman's Guide to the Man's World of Media* (New York: Harper & Row, 1974), 88.
210 *employment form*: Condé Nast Publications Inc. application for employment, May 21, 1951. Jacqueline (Kennedy Onassis) Bouvier Vogue Magazine Prix de Paris Papers, box 1, JFK Library.
213 *"We did it as much"*: William Norwich, interview by author. I am grateful to Catherine Hong, who preserved a copy of the list and posted it on her Instagram, where Norwich provided details on its origins.
213 *"When people have"*: Katrina Heron, interview by author.
213 *"I understand"*: Lucy Sisman, interview by author.
213 *"There was a kind of largeness"*: Linda Wells, interview by author.
214 *"You're not in"*: Dominique Browning, interview by author.
214 *"I wasn't that interested"*: John Leland, interview by author.
214 *Edna Woolman Chase*: Edna Woolman Chase and Ilka Chase, *Always in Vogue* (Garden City, NY: Doubleday, 1954), 211, 225; Ilka Chase Papers, Billy Rose Theatre Division, New York Public Library, box 20, folder 7.
214 *Steichen*: Matthew Josephson, "Commander with a Camera-II," *New Yorker*, June 10, 1944.

215 *"one of the great"*: Joan Kron, "Copping a Feel at Vogue," *New York*, May 26, 1975.
215 *"We were always"*: Sisman and Vienne, *Alex Liberman*.
215 *David Bailey*: Grace Mirabella, *In and Out of Vogue* (New York: Doubleday, 1995), 131.
215 *she enlisted him to return*: Norman Parkinson, *Lifework* (London: Weidenfeld & Nicolson, 1983), 112–13.
216 *"Money . . . was not something"*: Polly Mellen, interview by author.
216 *"I believe that money"*: Geoffrey T. Hellman, "Art Lover," *New Yorker*, November 26, 1960.
216 *"Take the Concorde"*: Francine du Plessix Gray, *Them: A Memoir of Parents* (New York: Penguin Press, 2005), 443.
216 *"It was like Vietnam"*: Graydon Carter, interview by author.
217 *"If you're not"*: Eliot Kaplan, interview by author.
217 *a turtle for sale*: Ruth Reichl, *Save Me the Plums* (New York; Random House, 2019), 119.
218 *"There is such truth"*: Stephen Drucker, interview by author.
218 *forty-one thousand air miles*: Tina Brown, "Editor's Letter," *Vanity Fair*, December 1989.
218 *"Don't nickel"*: Graydon Carter, interview by author.
218 *"many many thousands"*: Hamilton South, interview by author.
218 *Big Apple Car*: Details derived from Diana Clemente, interview by author; Alan Feuer, "Bensonhurst Journal," *New York Times*, April 16, 2000; Alan Feuer, "Mob Leader Is Guilty of Ordering 3 Murders," *New York Times*, April 6, 2001; John Marzulli, "Twisted Tale of Mob-Taxi Case," *New York Daily News*, October 12, 2008; Kimberly Stevens, "An Admiral of the Limo Fleet," *New York Times*, August 22, 1999; Charles V. Bagli, "Condé Nast Will Be Anchor of 1 World Trade," *New York Times*, May 17, 2011.
220 *"I shall miss seeing you"*: Diana Clemente, interview by author.
220 *Condé signed on as*: Michael Calderone, "It's Condo Nast," *New York Observer*, April 10, 2006.
221 *"We were expected"*: Dana Brown, *Dilettante: True Tales of Excess, Triumph, and Disaster* (New York: Ballantine Books, 2022), 223.
222 *"you're spending an awful lot"*: Sarah Slavin, interview by author.
223 *"Don't you girls worry"*: Pamela McCarthy, interview by author.
223 *"We would not receive"*: Linda Wells, interview by author.
223 *"What do you want"*: Mirabella, *In and Out of Vogue*, 207.
223 *"Si was extremely secretive"*: Tina Brown, interview by author.
224 *"It is better"*: Rebecca Mead, "The Truman Administration," *New York*, May 23, 1994.
224 *"What is the glass"*: Rochelle Udell, *Adventures of the Baker's Daughter* (self-published memoir fragments), https://adventuresofthebakersdaughter.com/expectations-none.
225 *"Well, you might"*: Sarah Slavin, interview by author.
225 *hired an efficiency engineer*: Edmund Wilson, *The Twenties: From Notebooks and Diaries of the Period* (New York: Farrar, Straus & Giroux, 1975), 39; George H. Douglas, *The Smart Magazines: 50 Years of Literary Revelry and High Jinks at Vanity Fair, The New Yorker, Life, Esquire, and The Smart Set* (New Haven: Archon Books, 1991), 108.
225 *"Typing stifles"*: Sarah Slavin, interview by author.

Chapter 15 Up Is Up

227 *The world's most glamorous*: Joseph Nocera and Peter Elkind, "The Buzz Factory," *Fortune*, July 20, 1998.
229 *"I was not short on"*: David Carr, "The Tell-All Steven Florio Won't Sell," *New York Times*, June 27, 2005.
229 *"Si likes it"*: Edward Hayes, with Susan Lehman, *Mouthpiece: A Life In—And Sometimes Just Outside—The Law* (New York: Broadway Books, 2005), 124.
230 *license plate*: Gigi Mahon, *The Last Days of The New Yorker* (New York: McGraw-Hill, 1988), 310.
230 *"I'm going to keep it"*: Carl Swanson, "Off the Record," *New York Observer*, February 1, 1999.
230 *Ron Galotti*: This portrait is derived from author interviews with Ron Galotti and Jay McInerney, "Goodbye, Mr. Big," *New York*, April 30, 2004.
230 *"I used to tease"*: Tom Florio, interview by author.
231 *"Succeed, succeed, succeed"*: Mitchell Fox, interview by author.
231 *"the dictator"*: Iris Cohen Selinger, "Si Speaks," *Inside Media*, December 4–17, 1991.
231 *More than two dozen*: Joanne Lipman, "Glitzkrieg," *Wall Street Journal*, January 4, 1996.
231 *"Was I a motherfucker?"*: Ron Galotti, interview by author.
232 *pushed their heads*: Keith Kelly, "Muzzle for Mad Dog," *New York Post*, September 22, 1999; Alex Kuczynski, "Condé Nast Pays Woman Injured by Executive," *New York Times*, September 22, 1999.
232 *"wouldn't have thrown down"*: Amy Odell, *Anna: The Biography* (New York: Gallery Books, 2022), 228.
232 *"Charles is not"*: Tina Brown, "A Woman in Earnest," *The New Yorker*, September 15, 1997.
233 *"I was prepping"*: Susan Mercandetti, interview by author.
233 *$80 million*: Robin Pogrebin, "Media," *New York Times*, June 1, 1998.
234 *Edward Sorel sketch*: Warren St. John, "Tina Brown's Contract Negotiations at The New Yorker," *New York Observer*, June 1, 1998.
234 *"nosebleed"*: Keith Kelly, "Red Ink Still Flows at Tina's New Yorker," *New York Daily News*, January 20, 1998; Patrick M. Reilly, "Newhouse Acts to Stem New Yorker's Red Ink," *Wall Street Journal*, January 30, 1998.
234 *When Si called Tina*: This exchange was described by a person familiar with the conversation. See also Janny Scott and Geraldine Fabrikant, "Editor of The New Yorker Leaving for New Venture," *New York Times*, July 9, 1998.
234 *reimbursed by Condé Nast*: David Plotz, "Let Si Get This," *Slate*, December 6, 1997.
235 *"To graft it"*: Jay Stowe, "S. I. Newhouse Lumps New Yorker In with Condé Nast Glossies," *New York Observer*, September 8, 1997.
235 *cut his face shaving*: Lynn Hirschberg, interview with author.
236 *"Washington think tank"*: Warren St. John, "Tina Goes Cheek to Cheek with Miramax," *New York Observer*, July 20, 1998.
236 *"Don't go anywhere"*: Michael Kinsley's quotes are from an interview by the author unless otherwise noted.
236 *Slate on Paper*: Peter H. Lewis, "Print Edition for Journal on Internet," *New York Times*, June 26, 1996.
236 *"You seem reluctant"*: Kinsley composed an account of his interactions with Si in

the immediate aftermath of this conversation, from which this dialogue is drawn. Kinsley emailed his account, that same evening, to members of the *Slate* staff and Bill Gates. The message was widely forwarded and later published in full by one of *Slate*'s digital competitors. Si also independently confirmed the account. Bruce Barcott, "The Last Temptation of Kinsley," *Salon*, July 14, 1998; Robin Pogrebin, "Staff Writer Named Editor at New Yorker," *New York Times*, July 14, 1998.

237 *"Springsteenian"*: Jonathan Sale, "Passed/Failed," *Independent*, October 19, 2006.
238 *"I didn't know how"*: "David Remnick," podcast interview, *Print Is Dead (Long Live Print)*, June 7, 2024.
238 *"That never crossed"*: Ken Ringle, "The New Yorker's Literary Lion Cub," *Washington Post*, August 5, 1998.
238 *an infelicitous phrase*: "Bloquez Cette Métaphore!" *New Yorker*, October 19, 1981.
238 *"Five people tore that"*: Ken Ringle, "The New Yorker's Literary Lion Cub," *Washington Post*, August 5, 1998.
238 *"He said there were no"*: Sally Quinn, interview by author.
239 *"Do I get to make"*: David Remnick, podcast interview, *Print Is Dead (Long Live Print)*, June 7, 2024.
239 *"I had steeled myself"*: Lloyd Grove, "Insider to Succeed Editor Tina Brown at New Yorker," *Washington Post*, July 13, 1998.
240 *"A balance between"*: Kathleen Sharp, "Talk of the Town," *Hollywood Reporter*, July 12, 1999.
240 *"David's mandate"*: Grove, "Insider to Succeed Editor Tina Brown at New Yorker."
240 *"I hate to sound"*: Daniel E. Slotnik, "Gladys Bourdain, Who Helped Her Son Reach an Audience, Dies at 85," *New York Times*, January 14, 2020.
241 *"I have to tell you"*: Ken Ringle, "The New Yorker's Literary Lion Cub," *Washington Post*, August 5, 1998.

Chapter 16 A House Divided

244 *sensible domestic style*: Dominique Browning, *The Well-Lived Life: One Hundred Years of House & Garden* (New York: Assouline, 2003), 7, 45.
244 *an entire reshoot*: Joan Kron, "The House and Garden Blues," *New York*, April 28, 1975.
244 *"I couldn't make it"*: Paige Rense, *Architectural Digest: Autobiography of a Magazine, 1920–2010* (New York: Rizzoli, 2018), 35. This chapter draws details from Rense's coffee table–sized memoir and a definitive profile of Rense by Joan Kron, "Interior Motives," *New York Times*, November 4, 1990. Kron uncovered the untold story of Rense's early life, to Rense's chagrin.
245 *"Sherry believed"*: Paige Rense, "Ciao, Sherry," *Cosmopolitan*, November 1967.
245 *She kept a collection*: Amanda Vaill, "The Only Dame in Town," *New York*, February 21, 1994.
246 *"It's all, 'Look at me!'"*: Vaill, "The Only Dame in Town."
246 *circulation . . . revenue*: Kron, "Interior Motives."
246 *"has the hideousness"*: Martin Filler, "A Gilded Age at Architectural Digest," *New York Review of Books*, November 4, 2018.
246 *"the people who had the palazzo"*: Joan Kron, interview with author.
247 *"It was never discussed"*: Rense, *Architectural Digest: Autobiography of a Magazine*, 294.

247 *Paige once paid*: Beverly Russell, *Deadline Diva: A Journalist's Life: Snubbing Cary Grant and Other Stories* (High Falls, NY: privately published, 2015), 77–78. Russell was the editor in chief of *Interiors* at the time of this incident.

247 *"Lou, have you"*: Carol Felsenthal, *Citizen Newhouse: Portrait of a Media Merchant* (New York: Seven Stories Press, 1998), 281.

248 *"Apparently I am"*: Tina Brown, *Vanity Fair Diaries, 1983–1992* (New York: Henry Holt, 2017), 257.

248 *"I was shocked"*: William Grimes, "The Hearth and Home Wars," *Avenue*, April 1988.

248 *"Look how dramatic"*: Nancy Novogrod, interview by author.

248 *"Decorators would say"*: Joan Kron, interview by author.

248 *"Let's say there are"*: Lorne Manly, "Off the Record," *New York Observer*, November 3, 1997.

249 *"I killed it once"*: Penelope Green, "Margaret Russell Unveils the New Architectural Digest," *New York Times*, February 2, 2011.

249 *"I can't be seen"*: Dominique Browning, interview by author.

249 *"because the competition"*: Graydon Carter, interview by author.

250 *"richly deserved"*: Irin Carmon, "Paige's Curse," *Women's Wear Daily*, January 28, 2008.

Chapter 17 **Technical Difficulties**

251 "Computers!": Linda Rice, interview by author.

251 *"They'll be playing"*: Joan Juliet Buck, *The Price of Illusion* (New York: Atria Books, 2017), 299.

251 *a single computer*: Eric Gillin, "The Oral History of the Launch of Epicurious," *Epicurious*, August 18, 2015, https://www.epicurious.com/about/epicurious-oral-history-article.

251 *"I don't worry"*: "Steven Florio," *Charlie Rose*, PBS, February 3, 1995.

252 *"You're going to have"*: Richard Pérez-Peña, "Can Si Newhouse Keep Condé Nast's Gloss Going?" *New York Times*, July 20, 2008.

252 *"The digital world"*: Deborah Needleman, interview by author.

253 *Steven O. Newhouse*: Some details from Linda Fibich, "A New Era at Newhouse," *American Journalism Review*, November 1994.

253 *"was being shown off"*: Daniel Machalaba, "Newhouse Chain Stays with Founder's Ways, and with His Heirs," *Wall Street Journal*, February 12, 1982.

253 *"No one else"*: John Huey, Martin Nisenholtz, and Paul Sagan, "Riptide: What Really Happened to the News Business," Shorenstein Center Discussion Paper Series 2013.D-81, Harvard University, Cambridge, MA, September 2013.

253 *15 percent stake*: Michael Wolff, *Burn Rate: How I Survived the Gold Rush Years on the Internet* (New York: Simon & Schuster, 1998), 45.

253 *"If I had been"*: John Huey, Martin Nisenholtz, and Paul Sagan, "Riptide: What Really Happened to the News Business."

254 *trouble with a turkey*: The story of Epicurious's origins is derived from author interviews with Rochelle Udell and Joan Feeney; Rochelle Udell, *Adventures of the Baker's Daughter* (self-published memoir fragments), https://adventuresofthebakersdaughter.com/expectations-none; Gillin, "Oral History of the Launch of Epicurious"; Amy Odell, *Anna: The Biography* (New York: Gallery Books, 2022), 172–73; Jeff Jarvis, *Magazine* (New York: Bloomsbury Academic, 2024), 104.

255 *"The safe way"*: Rochelle Udell, podcast interview, *Print Is Dead (Long Live Print!)*, February 16, 2024.
255 *Her internet connection*: Gillin, "The Oral History of the Launch of Epicurious."
256 *"This is just"*: Lorne Manly, "By Newhouse's Decree, James Truman Plays Prince of Condé Nast," *New York Observer*, August 18, 1997.
256 *$80 million*: Amy Harmon, "Digital Culture Pioneer Sold to Condé Nast," *New York Times*, May 11, 1998.
256 *"Si would not spend"*: Linda Rice, interview by author.
256 *"Think of us as"*: Amy Harmon, "Media Talk," *New York Times*, July 27, 1998.
257 *"This is the worst-run"*: Katrina Heron, interview by author
257 *"This is* Vogue*"*: Odell, *Anna: The Biography*, 173.
257 *post menus from restaurants*: Deirdre Carmody, "Condé Nast to Jump into Cyberspace," *New York Times*, May 1, 1995.
257 *"We are uninterested"*: Bob Andelman, "Why Isn't Vogue Online?" *Mr. Media*, March 24, 1997, https://mrmedia.com/2007/08/joan-feeney-condenet-editorial-director-mr-media-interview-classic-1997.
258 *"Because Anna blessed"*: Jeff Jarvis, "Capturing the History of Our Early Web: Vogue.com & Style.com," *BuzzMachine*, September 14, 2015, https://buzzmachine.com/2015/09/14/capturing-history-early-web-vogue-com-style-com.
258 *"Choose over"*: Vogue.com, home page, November 28, 1999, https://web.archive.org/web/19991128123549/http://www.vogue.com/run/SearchCollections/SpecifySearch.
258 *twelve-dollar annual fee*: Amy Odell, *Anna: The Biography*, 200.
258 *Neiman Marcus*: Lisa Lockwood, "Style.com and W Go Live Monday," *Women's Wear Daily*, September 15, 2000.
259 *$100 million*: Elizabeth Paton and Vanessa Friedman, "Condé Nast Closes Style.com Months After Its Debut," *New York Times*, June 13, 2017.
259 *"We're very 2002"*: Gillian Reagan, "More Than Fashionably Late, Condé Nast Hits the Internet," *New York Observer*, October 27, 2009.
259 *"I couldn't get"*: Linda Wells, interview by author.
259 *just 3 percent*: Nat Ives, "Time Inc. Tops List of Digital Earners," *Advertising Age*, January 19, 2009.
259 *"They just felt"*: Dominique Browning, interview by author.
260 *"Si thought [the web] was"*: James Truman, interview by author.
260 *nudged Si to create*: Ruth Reichl, *Save Me the Plums: My Gourmet Memoir* (New York: Random House, 2019), 207–10.
260 *"They were really bad"*: Dana Brown, *Dilettante: True Tales of Excess, Triumph, and Disaster* (New York: Ballantine Books, 2022), 223.
261 *"a waste"*: Deborah Needleman, interview by author.

Chapter 18 The Elephant

263 *"the most counterintuitive"*: Paul Farhi, "A New Portfolio," *American Journalism Review*, April/May 2007.
264 *"There was a sense"*: Tom Florio, interview by author.
264 *"Oh my god, yes!"*: John Koblin, "At Columbia, the Inadvertently Boldface Joanne Lipman Sticks to the Script," *New York Observer*, March 14, 2008.
265 *"All I did"*: Jim Impoco, interview by author.

265 *"Not bam bam"*: Tom Wolfe, "The Pirate Pose," *Portfolio*, May 2007.
265 *Ugly bits of gossip*: Michael Calderone, "Lipman's Legions Leery in Portfolio's Second Sortie," *New York Observer*, August 14, 2007.
266 *"There wasn't really"*: Phillip Toledano, interview by author.
266 *$30,000*: David Carr, "Portfolio Magazine Shut, a Victim of Recession," *New York Times*, April 27, 2009.
267 *luxury, automotive, and travel*: Carr, "Portfolio Magazine Shut, a Victim of Recession."
267 *ad pages*: Jon Fine, "Condé Nast Shutters Portfolio. Why It Failed," *Bloomberg Businessweek*, April 27, 2009.
267 *"Make sure"*: "Eat Sheet: Truffles," *Portfolio*, October 2007.
267 *"the right magazine"*: John Koblin, "At Portfolio, Prehistory Was Prologue," *New York Observer*, April 29, 2009.
267 *"All this is so unlike"*: Tina Brown, "The Quake at Condé Nast," *Daily Beast*, April 27, 2009.
268 *in favor of the subway*: Keith J. Kelly, "Sic Transit Gloria," *New York Post*, March 25, 2009.
268 *"When they gave up"*: Jim Impoco, interview by author.
268 *netted more money*: Reeves Wiedeman, "What's Left of Condé Nast?" *New York*, October 28, 2019.
268 *"We'll all have"*: Peter Kafka, "Condé Nast CEO Chuck Townsend to the Troops: Keep Your Heads Up, and Your Expenses Down," *AllThingsD*, March 5, 2009.
269 *"the enchanting, mystical era"*: John Koblin, "The Gilded Age of Condé Nast Is Over," *New York Observer*, August 11, 2009.
270 *"In the economics"*: Stephanie Clifford, "Condé Nast Closes Gourmet and 3 Other Magazines," *New York Times*, October 5, 2009.
270 *idea of saving money*: Amy Odell, *Anna: The Biography* (New York: Gallery Books, 2022), 267.
271 *$120 million*: Wiedeman, "What's Left of Condé Nast?"
272 *"it takes courage"*: @BarackObama, Twitter, June 1, 2015, https://x.com/BarackObama/status/605487361011544065.
272 *"Can I offer you"*: Dana Brown, *Dilettante: True Tales of Excess, Triumph, and Disaster* (New York: Ballantine Books, 2022), 252.
273 *"America is an aspirational"*: David Marchese, "Graydon Carter," *New York Times*, July 19, 2019.
274 *"Then she called back"*: Todd Purdum, interview by author.
274 *anti-Semitic remarks*: The offending language appeared in Frank Crowninshield, "The New Left Wing in New York Society," *Vogue*, February 1, 1938.
275 *"My periodicals have been"*: "Magazine Artist Out over Slur in Drawing," *New York Times*, January 26, 1938.
275 *paid to reprint*: Allen Ellenzweig, "Antisemitism, Now in Vogue," *Tablet*, January 18, 2022, https://www.tabletmag.com/sections/arts-letters/articles/antisemitism-now-in-vogue.
275 *Gordon Parks . . . Alex Liberman*: Gordon Parks, *Voices in the Mirror: An Autobiography* (New York: Doubleday, 1990), 120–23; Gordon Parks, *A Hungry Heart: A Memoir* (New York: Atria Books, 2005), 95–97.
275 *"She had been called"*: William Norwich, interview by author.
276 *"cautiously conservative"*: Francine du Plessix Gray, *Them: A Memoir of Parents* (New York: Penguin Press, 2005), 408–9.

NOTES

276 *already on the outs*: William Grimes, "Edmonde Charles-Roux, 65, Novelist and Editor of French Vogue, Is Dead," *New York Times*, January 22, 2016; "Fashionable Novelist," *New York Times*, November 22, 1966.

276 *One biographer*: Dominique de Saint Pern, *Edmonde, l'envolée* (Paris: Éditions Stock, 2022), 179. ("Fine mouche, Edmonde saisit le prétexte du racism antinoir des Américains, à mi-mot, habilement, sans s'étendre ni polémiquer.")

276 *the pictures prompted objections*: David Michaelis, "The Now of Avedon," *Vanity Fair*, December 2009; Philip Gefter, *What Becomes a Legend Most: A Biography of Richard Avedon* (New York: Harper, 2020), 285. It's possible that the negative response to the Luna photograph in *Bazaar*—which included canceled subscriptions and advertisers pulling ads, according to Gefter—was a factor in how Condé Nast handled the Charles-Roux episode the following year.

276 *"for reasons of racial"*: Dennis Christopher, "Donyale Luna: Fly or Die," *Andy Warhol's Interview*, October 1974. See also Richard J. Powell, *Cutting a Figure: Fashioning Black Portraiture* (Chicago: University of Chicago Press, 2008), 103.

276 *"Dick, you can't take"*: Doon Arbus, interview with Richard Avedon, March 17, 1972, typed transcript "Dick on Luna," Richard Avedon Foundation, New York. Avedon also recalled Vreeland describing Luna with phrases like, "There's no splendor to her, there's no glory to her. She could be sitting on the side of the road in the Bahamas watching the tourists go by." Avedon was a champion of Luna and her career, although one of his reasons for casting her in the Japan shoot could be read as problematic today: "It seemed to me that that presence in this country—that black presence in this country of yellow people, and in the snow, would be very, very beautiful." I am grateful to Elspeth H. Brown for providing a copy of this transcript, which she cites in her invaluable book, *Work! A Queer History of Modeling* (Durham, NC: Duke University Press, 2019). The dialogue with Vreeland was reported in *Donyale Luna: Supermodel*, Nailah Jefferson dir., HBO, 2023.

277 *"You're going to put"*: Campbell, who was born in Britain, is of Afro Jamaican and Chinese Jamaican descent. "Anna Wintour on Why She Pushed for Naomi's First American Vogue Cover," *No Filter with Naomi*, interview by Naomi Campbell, posted April 22, 2020, by Naomi, YouTube, 26 min., 22 sec., https://www.youtube.com/watch?v=o77-_zV5i-E.

277 *"black models appear"*: Anna Wintour, "Letter from the Editor," *Vogue*, July 1997.

277 *"I'm a Black woman"*: Jonathan Van Meter, "Oprah's Moment," *Vogue*, October 1998.

277 *"promised she would lose"*: Anna Wintour, "Letter from the Editor," *Vogue*, October 1998.

277 *"a colonial broad"*: Veronica Horwell, "Obituary: André Leon Talley," *Guardian*, January 20, 2022.

278 *"Could somebody tell"*: Amy Odell, *Anna: The Biography* (New York: Gallery Books, 2022), 195.

278 *"There was a lot of"*: Odell, *Anna*, 268.

278 *Anna offered her*: Elaine Welteroth, *More than Enough: Claiming Space for Who You Are (No Matter What They Say)* (New York: Penguin, 2020), 227–29, 265–66.

279 *"If you haven't"*: Jacqueline Woodson, "Lena Waithe Is Changing the Game," *Vanity Fair*, April 2018.

279 *Vanity Fair had featured*: Radhika Jones, "Editor's Letter," *Vanity Fair*, July/August 2020.

326 NOTES

279 *"to get your advertisers"*: Chantal Fernandez, "Why It's So Difficult for Condé Nast to Change," *Business of Fashion*, July 1, 2020. Additional details from Edmund Lee, "A Reckoning Rattles Condé Nast," *New York Times*, June 15, 2020.
279 *"I want to say plainly"*: Sara Nathan, "Anna Wintour Admits to 'Hurtful and Intolerant' Behavior at Vogue," *New York Post*, June 9, 2020.

Chapter 19 The Back of the Book

281 *"He knew what"*: "Remembering Si Newhouse," *Charlie Rose*, PBS, October 23, 2017.
282 *"will take my place"*: Jon Fine, "The Advance of Steve Newhouse," *Ad Age*, January 28, 2002.
283 *Steven was elevated*: Keith J. Kelly, "New Blood at Condé," *New York Post*, April 5, 2019.
283 *learned about Reddit*: Details from Christine Lagorio-Chafkin, *We Are the Nerds: The Birth and Tumultuous Life of Reddit, the Internet's Culture Laboratory* (New York: Hachette, 2018); David Carr, "Left Alone by Its Owner, Reddit Soars," *New York Times*, September 2, 2012; Michael M. Grynbaum and Mike Isaac, "Condé Nast's Owners Set to Reap a $1.4 Billion Windfall from Reddit," *New York Times*, March 20, 2024.
286 *"Exposure on social media"*: Luca Solca, "Global Luxury Goods," Bernstein, August 22, 2024.
286 *"the democratization of elitism"*: Bonnie Morrison, interview by author.
286 *"I had no education"*: Barbara Kruger, interview by author.
286 *"Magazines, in my opinion"*: Hjärta Smärta and Ika Johannesson, *Hall of Femmes: Ruth Ansel* (Stockholm: Oyster Press, 2010), 69–70.
287 *"What is boring"*: Tina Brown, podcast interview, *Print Is Dead (Love Live Print!)*, February 2, 2024.
287 *"There is a place"*: Tina Brown, interview by author.
287 *"probably the dumbest"*: Janice Min, "Tea with Tina Brown," *Ankler*, October 20, 2024, https://theankler.com/p/tina-brown-on-trump-harris-and-our.
288 *"I've known him"*: Jada Yuan, "Graydon Carter Can't Help but Wish He'd Gotten That Jeff Goldberg Scoop," *Washington Post*, March 26, 2025.
289 *a Netflix crew*: Charlotte Klein, "The New Yorker's Anxious 100th Birthday Celebration," *New York*, January 23, 2025.
290 *"No one has shaped"*: Rachel Tashjian and Maura Judkis, "Anna Wintour Kicks Off Fashion Week with Jill Biden," *Washington Post*, September 7, 2024.
291 *"This is no longer"*: Kara Swisher, "The C.E.O. of Condé Nast," *Sway* podcast, *New York Times*, May 23, 2022.

Index

Abedin, Huma, 118
Advance Publications
    cable TV business, 124, 141, 228, 283
    CondéNet, 255
    expansion of, 11, 37
    magazine business (*see* Condé Nast Publications)
    newspaper business, xiii, 10–13, 18–19, 21, 23–25, 29, 36, 52, 124, 227–28, 268
    The New Yorker, purchase of, 124, 125
    Random House, purchase of, 42, 110, 129
    Reddit, one-third stake in, 284
advertising
    1980s and increase in disposable income, 61–62
    in *Allure*, 189–90
    in *Architectural Digest*, 248–49
    in *Condé Nast Portfolio*, 263–64, 267
    digital sales and, 259
    e-commerce as threat to, 260–61
    exclusivity of Condé Nast attracting, 231
    in *GQ*, 96–97, 99, 102
    internet vs. print, 270
    Liberman's influence in, 33
    in *The New Yorker*, 121–22, 123, 127–28
    in Russia, 196
    Si's changes at Condé Nast Publishing and, 28

Trump and, 113
    in *Vanity Fair*, 44, 48–49, 51, 65, 68, 71, 113
    in *Vogue*, 3–4, 84, 194
AIDS epidemic, 137
Air Mail, 288
Allen, Woody, 240
Allure
    advertising in, 189–90
    Best of Beauty awards, xii, 189–90
    high/low concept in, 189
    internet and technological advances, 251, 259
    Kron as writer for, 204
    launch of, 189
    Liberman hiring Sisman at, 204–5
    shutdown of, 190, 271
    Wells as editor of, 189–90, 213–14, 223
Als, Hilton, 159
Alt, Emmanuelle, 289
Alter, Jonathan, 126
Andersen, Kurt, 70, 172
Angels in America (play), 20
Aniston, Jennifer, 249
Anna Wintour Costume Center, Metropolitan Museum of Art, New York, 73–74
Ansel, Ruth, 166, 191, 286
anti-Semitism, 32, 274–75
Apparel Arts, 95

INDEX

The Apprentice (TV show), 111
Architectural Digest, 243–50
    AD100 list of designers, 247
    advertising in, 248–49
    cultural importance of, xi, 284
    early years of, 244
    high/low concept in, 247
    House & Garden as competition for, 246–48, 249
    popularity of, 18
    Rense as editor of, 244–50
    Russian editions, 197
    Si's purchase of, 243, 248
Arendt, Hannah, 154
Armani, Giorgio, 88
Armstrong-Jones, Anthony (Lord Snowdon), 32
Arnault, Bernard, 191
Arnold, Tom, 69, 160–61
The Art of the Deal (Trump), xv, 110–12
art world
    art published in *Vanity Fair*, 5, 43–44
    Liberman mentoring Si on, 29
    Liberman's art, 45, 79
    Si's purchase of art, 123
    Vanity Fair, rebranding of, 43–45, 47
Astaire, Fred, 5
Astley, Amy, 205–6
Astor, Brooke, 12
Astor, Caroline Schermerhorn, 1, 4, 12
Astor, Vincent, 12
Auermann, Nadja, 165
Auletta, Ken, 127, 155
Avedon, Richard
    cover of *GQ*, 109
    cover of *Vanity Fair*, 47
    exclusive contract with *Vogue*, 3
    Kinski photograph with snake, 189
    in *The New Yorker*, 165
    portraits for O. J. Simpson trial, 157
    on racial prejudice in fashion, 276–77, 325n276
    Vogue covers, 87–88, 306n87

Bailey, David, 215
Baker, Josephine, 5, 44
Baldwin, Billy, 17
Balmain, Pierre, 83
Bandy, Way, 138
Banks, Tyra, 106
Barkin, Ellen, 194
Barnes, Fred, 158
Barnett, Jennifer, 205
Barr, Roseanne, 69, 160–62
Barsotti, Charles, 121
Barthelme, Frederick, 128
Baryshnikov, Mikhail, 47
Basinger, Kim, 59, 89, 217–18
Beaton, Cecil, 3, 25, 27, 274–75
Beatty, Warren, 173–74
A Beautiful Mind (movie), 185
Becker, Jonathan, 45, 47
Beckman, Richard "Mad Dog," 232
Benchley, Robert, 43
Bening, Annette, 69
Benson, Harry, 64–65
Bercu, Michaela, 86–87
Bernstein, Carl, 184
Bernstein, Robert L., 112
Biden, Jill, 290
Biden, Joe, 290
Big Apple Car Service, 218–20
Bishop, Elizabeth, 48
Black Lives Matter movement, 279
Blahnik, Manolo, 115
Bloomberg, Michael, 249, 287
Bloomingdale, Betsy, 274
Boesky, Ivan, 60
Bon Appétit, xii, 248, 254–55, 274
Bouché, René, 29, 32
Bourdain, Anthony, 240
Bourdain, Gladys, 240
Bouvier, Jacqueline, 210
Bradlee, Ben, 56
Bradshaw, Jon, 76
breast cancer awareness, 187–88
Brenner, Marie, 71, 113, 182
Brides, 278
British Vogue
    beginning of, 4, 198
    Enninful as editor of, 290
    first Black cover model, 276
    training staff of *Vogue Russia*, 196
    Wintour as editor, 81–82
Broadway Video, 130
Brodovitch, Alexey, 275

INDEX

Brooks, Mel, 154
Brown, Dana, 200, 221, 260
Brown, Helen Gurley, 39
Brown, Tina
   advising Wintour at *Vogue*, 88
   background, 53–54, 60–61
   consultancy at *Vanity Fair*, 56–57
   cultural importance of *Vanity Fair* and, 67–69, 135–37
   as editor of *The Daily Beast*, 287
   as editor of *The New Yorker*, 142–44, 148–49, 151–67, 223, 232–34, 287
   as editor of *Vanity Fair*, xiv–xv, 58–72, 135–42, 151, 218, 232–33
   on English royals, 62
   at fifth anniversary party for *Vanity Fair*, 135–36
   Fresh Hell Substack, 288
   on Gottlieb, 132
   hiring process at *The New Yorker* for, 142–44, 148–49
   hiring process at *Vanity Fair* for, 54–59
   The Hot List of *The New Yorker* and, 163–65
   marriage to Harry Evans, 55–56
   Moore's cover of *Vanity Fair* and, 138–40
   on *The New Yorker*, 141–42
   notoriety of, 71–72
   on online content, 287
   on *Portfolio*, 267–68
   Reagans' portrait in *Vanity Fair* and, 64–66
   on rebranded *Vanity Fair*, 48, 57
   resigning from *The New Yorker*, 235
   salary with Condé Nast, 72
   on Si firing Mirabella from *Vogue*, 86
   Talk magazine and, 240, 287
   at *Tatler*, 54, 55
   television show idea, 232–33
   on *Today* show, 66
   Trump and, 113
   von Bülow feature, 66–67
   as writer, 53–54, 287–88
Browning, Dominique, 214, 249–50, 259–60
Buatta, Mario, 248, 249
Buck, Joan Juliet, 251

Buckley, Pat, 192
Buckley, William F., Jr., 66
Bullock, Sandra, 89
Bündchen, Gisele, 278
Bunyan, John, 43
Burrough, Bryan, 174
Bushnell, Candace, 230

Caine, Michael, 100
Calvin Klein, 127, 136
Campbell, Naomi, 88
The Canadian Review, 171–72
cancer fundraising, 187–88
Capote, Truman, 49, 56, 302n49
Carey, David, 234, 241, 249
Carey, Hugh, 35
Carpenter, Sabrina, 291
Carson, Rachel, 154
Carter, Graydon
   background and early career, xiv, 170–72
   career reflections, xviii
   co-founding *Air Mail*, 288
   on competition in industry, 249–50
   at Condé Nast global retreat of 2006, 169–70
   on Condé Nast Publications, 40
   as editor of *Vanity Fair*, 113–14, 147–49, 169–70, 172–86, 271–73
   on expensive photo shoots, 216–17
   GQ article on Trump and, 109
   Great Recession and, 269, 273
   internet and technological advances, 260
   mortgage from Advance Publications, 220
   office of, 180–81
   Oscar parties and, 174–80, 185–86
   restaurants owned by, 116–17, 185
   Spy magazine and, 70, 144–47, 172–73, 175–76
   Trump, feud with, 113–14, 116–20
   Wintour, friendship with, 145–46, 272
   writing for *House & Garden* and *Vogue*, 145–46
Carter, Jimmy, 35, 95
Cartier, 215
Castelli, Leo, 29, 123

Cattrall, Kim, 181–82
Chagall, Marc, 43
Chancellor, Alexander, 156, 313n156
Chanel (company), 190, 192
Chanel, Coco, 31
Charles III (King of England), 62
Charles-Roux, Edmonde, 276, 325n276
Charney, Dov, 266
Charter Communications, 283
Chase, Edna Woolman, 4, 31, 192, 214
China, *Vogue* fashion shoot in, 91
Christian Dior (company), 191
Chronicle of a Death Foretold (García Márquez), 48
Church of Scientology, 240–41
Clemente, Diana, 219–20
Clinton, Bill, 115, 182
Clinton, Hillary Rodham, 90, 92–93, 115, 117–18
Clooney, George and Amal, 195
Coddington, Grace, 82, 189, 220
Cohn, Roy
    sexuality, 20, 22
    Si, friendship and business relationship with, 20–24, 111–13, 126
    Si's divorce and, 23–24
    on Si's purchase of *The New Yorker*, 125
    Trump and, 111–12
Colacello, Bob, 97
Coleridge, Nicholas, 283
Colette, 43
Collier, Robert, 1
Collier's Weekly, 1
Collins, Joan, 62
Collins, Nancy, 140
Combs, Sean "Puff Daddy," 194–95
Condé Nast Entertainment, 260
Condé Nast Portfolio, 263–79
    advertising in, 263–64, 267
    closure of, xvii–xviii, 267–68
    elephant photo shoot, 266–67
    launch of, xvii, 169–70, 263–64
    Lipman as editor of, 264–67
Condé Nast Publications
    in 1960s, 27–28
    in 1970s, 39–40
    accounting system for, 225–26
    Allure, launch of, 189
    Architectural Digest, purchase of, 243, 248
    Bon Appétit, purchase of, 248
    Cohn giving newsstand preference to, 111
    competition among magazines of, 249–50
    Condé Nast Portfolio, launch and closure of, xvii–xviii, 169–70, 263–64, 267–68
    Condé Nast Traveler, launch of, 135, 224–25
    counterculture and industry competition, 39–40
    cultural importance of, xi–xiii, xvii–xviii, 28, 37, 135, 188–89, 284–87
    death of Si and changes at, xviii, 282–83
    discrimination at (*see* racial insensitivity and bias; sexism and misogyny)
    employee perks at, xiv, 34, 58, 103, 105–6, 216–21
    financial losses of, 227–28, 231, 233–34
    folkways and expectations of, 204–8
    global company retreat of 2006, 169–70
    Gourmet, purchase and closure of, 42, 135, 270
    GQ, purchase of, 42, 96
    Great Depression and, 6
    Great Recession and, 266–70, 273
    hiring process at, 54–59, 78, 80–81, 84, 142–49, 204–5, 210–14
    House & Garden, closure of, 248, 250
    international growth of, 195–98
    internet and technological advances, xvii–xviii, 251–61, 290–91
    Liberman's influence in, 28, 32–35
    Nast's purchase and growth of, 2–6
    nepotism and favoritism at, 208–10
    Newhouse Sr.'s purchase of, 7–8, 13–15, 24–26
    The New Yorker, purchase of, 65, 124, 141–43
    offices and cafeteria of, xvi, 27, 198–202, 220, 271
    photo shoot budgets of, 214–18

Reddit, purchase of, 283–84
Self, launch of, 40–43
Si's early changes at, 28
social status of employees at, xi, xiv, 71–72, 82–83, 103, 133, 203–7, 221
Tatler, purchase of, 54
Trump and, xv, 109–20, 284
Wintour as artistic director of, 272
Wintour as chief content officer, 289
Wired, purchase of, 256
See also advertising; *individual publications*
Condé Nast Traveler, xii, 135, 224–25, 257, 284
CondéNet (digital publishing), 255
Conran, Terence, 75
Conway, Kellyanne, 119
Cooper, Arthur "Art"
   background and early career, xiv, 97–98
   on car service, 220
   clothing and image of, 98, 103–4
   death of, 107
   as editor of *GQ*, 98–107
   on expensive photo shoots, 217
   on *GQ*, 108
   Gutfeld, feud with, 106
Corden, James, 120
Cosmopolitan, 39–40, 227
Coward, Noël, 5, 43
Crowninshield, Frank, 5, 30, 43–44, 63, 225
Cruise, Tom, 179
cultural change
   Architectural Digest and, xi, 284
   Condé Nast Publications and, xi–xiii, xvii–xviii, 28, 37, 135, 188–89, 284–87
   Condé Nast Publications interview process and knowledge of, 204–5, 210–14
   Condé Nast Traveler and, 284
   gatekeepers of, xviii, 287
   GQ and men's magazines, xi, 100–102, 106–8, 284
   Great Recession and identity politics, 273–74
   health and fitness revolution, 40–42, 100
   House & Garden and, 243–44

internet and digital revolutions, xvii–xviii, 251–61
Liberman and, 114–15
The New Yorker and, xi, 124–25, 128–29, 133, 239–40
racial insensitivity and bias at Condé Nast Publishing called out, 274–79
Self and fitness revolution, 40–42
Trump and, 109–11
Vanity Fair and, xi, 5, 44, 51–52, 55, 59–61, 67–69, 135–37, 139–40
Vogue and, xi, xix, 84, 88–90, 93
Cummings, E. E., 43

The Daily Beast, 287
Dalí, Salvador, 32
Danes, Claire, 89
Deep Throat, 184
de la Renta, Annette, 192
de la Renta, Oscar, 73, 192
Demarchelier, Patrick, 114
Dershowitz, Alan, 157–58
Details, 135, 214, 224, 259
The Devil Wears Prada (film), xii, 31, 74, 204
de Wolfe, Elsie, 5
Diana (Princess of Wales), 54, 62, 232, 287
Diaz, Cameron, 89
Dietrich, Marlene, 32
DiGiacomo, Frank, 178, 193
Diller, Barry, 60, 176, 185, 193, 287
Dior, Christian, 32
discrimination. *See* racial insensitivity and bias; sexism and misogyny
Doctorow, E. L., 59
Domingo, Lauren Santo, 6
Domino, 252, 261
Donghia, Angelo, 138, 245–46
Doppelt, Gabé, 31, 89, 200
Dowd, Maureen, 161–62, 183
Downie, Leonard, Jr., 183–84
Draper, Robert, 106
Dress & Vanity Fair, 4–5
Drucker, Stephen, 87, 217–18
Drudge, Matt, 178
Duchamp, Marcel, 31
Duke of Marlborough, 19
Dunne, Dominick, 56–57, 59, 66–67
Dunne, Dominique, 56–57, 59

du Plessix, Tatiana, 30, 32–34
du Plessix Gray, Francine
   on first Black cover model, 276
   on Liberman, 31, 34
   recommendation of Locke for *Vanity Fair*, 46
   Vanity Fair cover, 51
   writing for *The New Yorker*, 162
Duquette, Tony, 246
Durst, Douglas, 198–99
Dynasty (soap opera), 62

e-commerce market, 258, 260–61
Eisinger, Jesse, 266
Eisner, Michael, 233
Elgort, Arthur, 76, 91
Elkind, Peter, 227
Elle, 84, 123
Ellis, Perry, 138
Emanuel, Ari, 181
Enninful, Edward, 290
Ephron, Nora, 98
Epicurious.com, 255–57, 260
Epstein, Sam and Judith (grandparents of Si), 10
Ertegun, Ahmet, 60
Esquire, 39, 42–43, 95–96, 101–2
Esteban, Michel, 76
Estée Lauder, 190
Evangelista, Linda, 88
Evans, Harold "Harry," 55–56, 135, 224–25, 288
Evans, Robert, 185

Fairchild (publisher), 97
Fallows, James, 266
Faludi, Susan, 159–60
Family Weekly, 98
Farrow, Ronan, 289
Fashion Fête, Ritz-Carlton (1914), 4
Feeney, Joan, 257–58
Fein, Esther, 240
Feitler, Bea, 47
Felt, W. Mark, 184
feminism, 140, 161–63, 189
Ferraro, Geraldine, 64
Fish, (Mrs.) Stuyvesant, 4
Fisher, Carrie, 161

Fleischmann, Jeanne, 123
Fleischmann, Peter, 122–23, 126
Fleischmann, Raoul, 121–22
Florio, Steven T.
   character of, 228–30
   as chief executive of Condé Nast Publications, 167
   death of, 269
   on electronic publishing, 251–52
   financial losses of Condé Nast and, 228, 231
   firing of brother, xvi
   on *GQ* readers, 101
   on market changes, 264
   as president of Condé Nast Publications, 234
   as president of *The New Yorker*, 126–28, 141
   social status of employees and, 213–14
   Wired purchase and, 256
Florio, Tom, 167, 230–31, 234
Floyd, George, xviii
Flusser, Alan, 102
Fonda, Jane, 40
Ford, Tom, 89, 96
Fortune, on excessive spending at Condé Nast Publications, 227–28, 231
Four Seasons Grill Room, Manhattan, 103
Fox, Mitchell, 231, 249–50
Foxman, Ariel, 221
Foy, Gray, 50
France, Kim, 220, 260–61
Frankenstein, Chester, 23
Frazier, Ian "Sandy," 161
Fresh Hell Substack (Brown), 288
Friedan, Betty, 189
Friedman, Sanford, 22
Friend, Tad, 163
Fuhrman, Mark, 157

Gaitskill, Mary, 163
Galliano, John, xv, 115, 191
Galotti, Ron, xv, 139, 230–31
Gandee, Charles, 211, 213
García Márquez, Gabriel, 48
Garfinkle, Henry, 111
Gauguin, Paul, 5

gay men
   AIDS epidemic and, 137–38
   GQ and, 96–97
   Si's friendships with, 20, 22
Geffen, David, 70, 282
Gehry, Frank, xvi, 200–202
Gentlemen's Quarterly. See GQ
Géraldy, Paul, 198
Gere, Richard, 143, 192
Gershwin, George, 5
Gevinson, Tavi, xviii
Gibson, Charles Dana, 1
Gilded Age in New York, 1–2
Givenchy, 191
Givhan, Robin, 92
Gladwell, Malcolm, 159
Glamour, 6, 29, 141, 197, 271
Glengarry Glen Ross (play), 59
Goldberg, Whoopi, 69
Goldman, Ron, 157
Goldsmith, Barbara, 208
Goldwyn, Samuel, 5
Gopnik, Adam, 220
Gore, Al, 234
Gottlieb, Robert
   as editor of *The New Yorker*, 129–30, 132–34, 140–41, 143–44, 312n141
   at Knopf, 46, 129
   on Si, 175
Gourevitch, Philip, 259
Gourmet
   closure of, 270
   eccentric spending at, 217
   online revolution and missed opportunities for, 254–55, 260
   Si's purchase of, 42, 135
GQ, 95–108
   advertising in, 96–97, 99, 102
   competition for, 106
   Cooper as editor of, 98–107
   cultural importance of, xi, 100–102, 106–8, 284
   expenses of, 105–6
   international editions, 102–3
   internet and technological advances, 257, 259
   Men of the Year Awards, 103
   rebranding, 99–100
   Russian editions, 197
   sexist workplace culture at, 103–5
   Si's purchase of, 42, 96
   Trump, article and cover on, xv, 109–10, 113
Graham, Donald, 184
Graham, Katharine, 12–13
Graves, Michael, 246
Graybar Building, Manhattan, 27
Grazer, Brian, 185
Great Depression, 6
Great Recession, 220, 266–70, 273
Greenberg, Clement, 48, 51
Grinnell, Sun-Hee, 207
Gropp, Louis Oliver, 224–25, 247
Gucci, 89
Guccione, Bob, 76
Gunzburg, Nicholas de, 27
Gutfeld, Greg, 106–7

Haber, Jack, 96, 99
Haden-Guest, Anthony, 77
Hadid, Gigi, 291
Hahn, Emily, 124
Halberstam, David, 98
Haley, Charlotte, 187–88
Hall, Jerry, 125–26
Hamilton, William, 121
Hannah, Daryl, 59
Happy Yellow (Brown), 53, 72
Hardwick, Elizabeth, 47
Harpers & Queen, 75
Harper's Bazaar, 75–76, 84, 198, 276, 325n276
Harris, Kamala, xix
Harry Winston (retailer), 28
Hart, Gary, 63–64
Hayes, Eddie, 229
health and fitness revolution, 40–42, 100
Hearst, William Randolph, Jr., 276
Hearst Corporation
   attempt to hire Brown, 72, 142
   as competition for Condé Nast Publications, 39–40, 226, 227
   refusing to hire Black employees, 275–76
   See also individual publications
Henri Bendel dress shop, New York, 3

Heron, Katrina, 203, 213, 256–57
Herrera, Reinaldo, 274
Hersey, John, 154
Hersh, Seymour M., 155, 240
Hertzberg, Hendrik, 152–53
Hicks, Hope, 118–20
Higgins, Alice, 25
high/low concept
 in *Allure*, 189
 in *Architectural Digest*, 247
 combining politics with entertainment, 284
 in *The New Yorker*, 158–59, 239
 in *Vanity Fair*, 48, 59–60, 68, 159
 in *Vogue*, 87, 191
Hilton, Paris, 182
Hitchens, Christopher, 55, 174, 184
Hitler, Adolf, 63, 113
Hogg, Min, 75
homosexuality. *See* gay men
Honecker, Erich, 165
Hoover, Lou Henry, 90
Hopson, Maury, 138
Horace Mann School for Boys, Bronx, New York, 20–21
Horst, Horst P., 30, 43, 91
HotWired, 253
House & Garden
 Architectural Digest as competition for, 246–48, 249
 Carter as writer for, 145–46
 celebrity homes in, 247–48
 closure of, 248, 250
 cultural changes, reflecting, 243–44
 Marron's apartment featured in, 123
 Nast's purchase of, 4
 revival of, 249
 Si's rebranding of, 42, 246–47
 Wintour as editor at, 82, 200, 247–48
Housman, A. E., 166
Howard, Ron, 185
Hughes, Robert, 47
Hurley, Elizabeth, 89
Hurt, William, 99, 102
Huxley, Aldous, 5

identity politics, 274
Impoco, Jim, 265, 268
Instagram, xviii, 59, 250, 258, 286. *See also* social media
internet and digital revolution, 251–61
 advertising revenue and, 270
 Condé Nast's reduced cultural influence and, xvii–xviii, 285–87
 CondéNet and Epicurious.com, 255–57
 early technological advances and, 251–54
 missed opportunities in, 259–61
 newspaper industry and, 268
 Vogue.com and Style.com, 257–59
 Wired purchased by Condé Nast Publications, 257–58
 See also social media
The Invention of Love (play), 166
Iraq War, 240
Irving, John, 48
Isabell, Robert, 135, 192

Jackson, Michael, 69, 218
Jacobs, Marc, 73, 191, 192–93
James, LeBron, 278
Janklow, Angela, 208
Janklow, Morton, 208
Javits, Jacob, 35
Jenner, Caitlyn, 272
Jenner, Kendall, 291
Jewish people
 anti-Semitism and, 32, 274–75
 Hollywood movie industry and, xiv
 housing restrictions for, 11
 Ivanka Trump converting to Judaism, 119
 "Our Crowd" elite, 12, 20, 35
Johns, Jasper, 123
Johnson, Beverly, 277
Johnson, Lady Bird, 91
Jones, Laurie, 278
Jones, Radhika, 278–79, 288–89

Kahn, E. J., Jr., 125, 140–41
Kaminsky, Howard, 110
Kaplan, Eliot, 97–98, 219
Kaplan, Peter W., 235–36
Karan, Donna, 71, 73
Karr, Mary, 162

INDEX   335

Kawakubo, Rei, 77
Keaton, Alex P., 44
Keillor, Garrison, 153
Keller, Thomas, 180
Kelly, Jon, 169–70
Kelly, Michael, 102
Kempner, Nan, 195
Kennedy, Jacqueline, 90–91
Kennedy, John F., 96
Kennedy, Robert, 96
Kidman, Nicole, 179, 184
The Kid Stays in the Picture (documentary), 185
Kinski, Nastassja, 189
Kinsley, Michael, 236–37, 320–21n236
Kissinger, Henry, 91, 146, 194
Kissinger, Nancy, 91
Klein, Calvin, 71, 73, 192
Kliger, Jack, 97, 100, 101
Knapp, Cleon "Bud," 244–45
Knauss, Melania. *See* Trump, Melania
Knopf, 46, 129
Koch, David, 194–95
Koons, Jeff, 51, 282
Koren, Edward, 47
Kors, Michael, 78, 191
Kosner, Edward, 77, 149
Kravis, Henry, 192
Kron, Joan, 204, 246, 248
Kruger, Barbara, 286
Kuhn, David, 159
Kushner, Jared, 119
Kushner, Tony, 20

Lacroix, Christian, 84, 86–87
Ladies' Home Journal, 3–4
Lagerfeld, Karl, 71, 88, 191–92, 195, 196
La Grenouille, New York, 84
Lahr, John, 160–61
Lane, Anthony, 159, 166
Lange, Jessica, 69
Lansing, Sherry, 177
Lauder, Evelyn, 187–88
Lauder, Leonard, 282
Lauder, Ronald, 71
Lauren, Ralph, 49, 71, 73, 77, 192, 282
Lazar, Irving "Swifty," 174–75
Lazarus, Hyman, 9–10

Leach, Robin, 61
Lebowitz, Fran, 61, 77, 178
Le Cirque, New York, 60, 84
Lehman, Ernest, 179
Leibovitz, Annie
    Caitlyn Jenner photograph, 272
    Demi Moore photograph, 138–40
    celebrity shoots for *Vanity Fair*, 69–70
    exclusive contract with *Vogue*, 3
    expensive photo shoots, 216–18
    Hillary Clinton photographs, 90, 92–93
    John Irving photograph for *Vanity Fair* ads, 48
    Mick Jagger photograph, 47
    at Oscar parties, 176
    salary of, 218
Leland, John, 214
Lenin's Tomb (Remnick), 238–39
Lerman, Leo, 50–51, 56–58, 126
LeRoy, Warner, 208
Leser, Bernard, 209
Letterman, David, 100
Levin, Amy, 98
Lewinsky, Monica, 92, 178, 183
LGBTQ+ people. *See* gay men
Liberman, Alexander Semeonovitch
    on accounting system for Condé Nast Publications, 225–26
    Allure, hiring Sisman for, 204–5
    on *Architectural Digest*, 246
    art and sculpture of, 45, 79
    background, xiv, 30
    on computers, 251
    as editorial director of Condé Nast Publishing, 33
    on firing employees, 206
    GQ and, 97, 99, 101–2
    hiring Parks as photographer, 275
    influence in Condé Nast Publishing, 28, 32–35
    on Ivana Trump *Vogue* article and cover, 114
    on Moore *Vanity Fair* cover, 139
    mortgage from Advance Publications, 34
    retiring from Condé Nast Publishing, 223–24

Liberman, Alexander Semeonovitch (*cont.*)
   as Si's mentor, 28–30, 32–34, 282
   social status and image, 30–32, 55, 114–15, 191, 203–4
   social status of employees and, 213
   on sparing no expense, 214–16
   Vanity Fair, hiring Locke for, 46–47
   Vanity Fair, hiring Brown for, 54–58
   Vanity Fair, rebranding, 43–52
   Vogue, firing Mirabella from, 80, 83–85
   Vogue, firing Vreeland from, 79
   Vogue, hiring Wintour for, 78, 80–81, 84
   as *Vogue* art director, 30–34, 45
Liberman, Tatiana du Plessix, 30, 32–34, 301n34
Liebling, A. J., 13, 134
Lifestyles of the Rich and Famous (TV show), 61
Lindbergh, Peter, 87
Lipman, Joanne, 264–67
Little, James Bradley, 245
Locke, Richard, 46–50, 302n46
Lois, George, 39, 49
London, Jack, 1
Lonstein, Shoshanna, 178
Louis Vuitton, 191
Lowenstein, Allard K., 20–22
Lucky, 260–61
Luna, Donyale, 276, 325n276
Lynch, Roger, xviii, 291

M, 97
MacDowell, Andie, 78
MacNeil, Robert, 68
Mademoiselle, 286
Madonna, 69–70, 88, 194
Mamet, David, 59
Man Ray, 43
Maples, Marla, 114, 115
Margaret, Princess (Countess of Snowdon), 19, 32, 54
Marino, Dan, 99
Marron, Donald, 122–23
Matisse, Henri, 43, 47
Maxim, 106–7
Mayer, Jane, 155
Mayle, Peter, 102

McCallum, Patricia, 22
McCarthy, Joseph, 20
McCarthy, Mary, 78
McCarthy, Pamela Maffei, 222–23, 259
McGrath, Charles, 129, 156
McInerney, Jay, 152
McKinsey & Company, 269
McNally, Brian, 200
McNally, Keith, 76–77
McPhee, John, 151, 238
McQueen, Alexander, xv
Meisel, Steven, 176
Mellen, Polly, 78, 189, 209–10, 216
Menaker, Daniel, 152
Menchicchi, Louis "Red," 219–20
Mengers, Sue, 185
Mensch, Pamela Newhouse (daughter of Si)
   birth of, 23
   criticism of *Vanity Fair*, 68
   at father's memorial service, 282
   on father's purchase of *The New Yorker*, 124
   on Newhouse family, social status of, 14, 25
   on Trump, 111
men's magazines, 100–101, 106. *See also GQ*
Mercandetti, Susan, 232–33
Merkin, Daphne, 162–63
Metropolitan Museum of Art, New York
   Anna Wintour Costume Center at, 73–74
   Met Gala at, xii, xv, 115, 116, 120, 192–95
Metzner, Sheila, 215
Michael (Prince of Greece), 209
Michaels, Lorne, 130, 311n131
Michener, James, 98
Midler, Bette, 185
Milken, Michael, 60
Millay, Edna St. Vincent, 5
Miller, Adrienne, 104
Miller, Arthur, 247
Miller, Beatrix, 81
Miller, Dennis, 153
Miller, Lee, 31
Minor, Keija, 278

INDEX   337

Mirabella, Grace
  on 1980s culture, 84
  as editor of *Vogue*, xv, 79–86, 216,
    222–23
  fashion shoot in China, 91
  meeting Wintour, 78
  on social graces of Si, 33
  on Wintour's *Vogue*, 191
misogyny. *See* sexism and misogyny
Mitchell, Joseph, 155
Mizrahi, Isaac, 139
Mondale, Walter, 35, 63–64
Mondrian, Piet, 31
Monkey Bar, New York, 185
Montana, Joe, 99
Moore, Demi, 138–39
Morrison, Bonnie, 286
Morrison, Susan, 146
Morton's, West Hollywood, 175, 179
Moss, Adam, 149
Moss, Kate, 192–93
Murdoch, Rupert, 55, 218
Murphy, Eddie, 71
Murphy, Gerald, 101
Muschamp, Herbert, 201–2

Nast, Clarisse Coudert, 1–2
Nast, Condé Montrose
  birth of, 1
  cultural authority of, 5–6
  death and eulogies for, 6–7
  firing Beaton for anti-Semitism,
    274–75
  Great Depression and, 6
  hiring efficiency engineer for
    company, 225
  magazine purchases and growth of
    publishing company, 2–6
  marriage to Clarisse Coudert, 1–2
  obelisk monuments of, 6
  shipping *Vogue* internationally, 198
  social status and wealth, 1–6
Nast, Natica, 12
National Magazine Awards, 182
Nazis, 119. *See also* Hitler, Adolf
Needleman, Deborah, 252, 261
Neeson, Liam, 194
Negroponte, Nicholas, 253

Neiman Marcus, 258
Nelson, Jim, 107, 221
Newark Star-Ledger, 29
Newhouse, Donald (brother of Si)
  birth and childhood of, 10–12
  family newspaper business and, xiii,
    18, 21, 52, 124, 227–28
  investments securing Newhouse
    family, 124, 141, 283
  marriage, 24–25
  on Si's dementia and death, 281–82
  on Si's purchase of *The New Yorker*,
    124, 143
Newhouse, Jane Franke (first wife of Si),
  14, 18–19, 23–25
Newhouse, Jonathan (cousin of Si),
  196–98, 282–83
Newhouse, Meyer (grandfather of Si),
  8–9
Newhouse, Mitzi Epstein (mother of Si)
  design and fashion interests, 10–11,
    13–14, 19
  Libermans, friendship with, 32–33
  marriage to Newhouse Sr., 10
  meeting Princess Margaret, 19
  relationship with Si, 18–20, 25
  social status, 11–14, 19, 25, 35
  Vogue and, 8, 13–14, 25
Newhouse, Norman (uncle of Si), 282
Newhouse, Rose Arenfeldt (grandmother
  of Si), 9
Newhouse, Sam, III (son of Si), 23
Newhouse, Samuel I., Sr. (father of Si)
  Advance Publications and, 8, 10–11
  birth and childhood of, 8–9
  Cohn and, 111–12
  Condé Nast Publications, purchase of,
    7–8, 13–15, 24–26
  death of, 15, 35–37
  early career, 9–10
  Libermans, friendship with, 32–33
  marriage to Mitzi Epstein, 10
  newspaper business, 18–19, 36
  The New Yorker, attempt to purchase,
    121–22
  relationship with Si, 18, 20–22, 25–26,
    33, 36, 112, 299n21
  social status, 8, 11–14, 19, 25, 35, 121–22

338   INDEX

Newhouse, Samuel Irving "Si," Jr.
   birth and childhood of, 10–12
   children of, 23
   Cohn, friendship and business relationship, 20–24, 111–13, 126
   death of, xii, xviii, 281–82
   divorce from Jane Franke, 24
   education, 20–23
   family newspaper business and, 19, 23–25, 29
   father, relationship with, 18, 20–22, 25–26, 33, 36, 112, 299n21
   Lowenstein, friendship with, 20–22
   marriage to Jane Franke, 23–24
   marriage to Victoria Carrington Benedict de Ramel, 36
   mother, relationship with, 18–20, 25
   movies, reverence for, 175
   sexuality, 22
   social status and, xiii, 15, 17, 25, 33, 126, 203, 282
Newhouse, Samuel Irving "Si," Jr. at Condé Nast Publishing
   on advertising sales, 231
   Allure and, 189–90
   apartment featured in *The New York Times*, 17–18
   Architectural Digest, purchase of, 243, 248
   Bon Appétit, purchase of, 248
   British Vogue and, 81–82
   Brown's resignation and, 235
   as chairman, 36, 40
   Condé Nast Portfolio, closure of, 267–68
   Condé Nast Portfolio, launch of, xvii, 263–64
   Condé Nast Traveler, launch of, 135, 224–25
   employees' fear of, xv–xvi
   expensive photo shoots and employee perks, 216–21
   at fifth anniversary party of *Vanity Fair*, 136
   financial losses of Condé Nast and, 227–28
   Gourmet, purchase of, 42, 135
   GQ and, 42, 95–108
   hiring Carter for *Vanity Fair*, 144–48
   House & Garden and, 82, 246–48
   internet and technological innovation, 252–61
   Liberman mentoring, 28–30, 32–34, 282
   at Met Gala, 193
   monthly "print order" meetings with, 281
   new offices and cafeteria at 4 Times Square, xvi, 199–202
   The New Yorker and, 28, 65, 122–34, 141–42, 151, 166–67, 235–41
   Oscar parties of *Vanity Fair* and, 177, 179
   Random House, purchase of, 42, 110
   Self and, 40–43, 187
   Tatler, purchase of, 54
   Truman as Liberman's successor, 224
   Trump and, xv, 109–17, 308–9n112
   Vanity Fair and, 43–52, 54–58, 65–66, 68–69, 72, 172–73
   on *Vanity Fair* television show, 232–33
   Vogue and, 26, 28, 83, 85–86
   Wintour and, 82–86
   Wired, purchase of, 256
Newhouse, Steven O. (nephew of Si), 119, 253, 272–73, 283–84
Newhouse, Victoria Carrington Benedict de Ramel (second wife of Si), 36, 200–201, 281
Newhouse, Wynn (son of Si), 23
Newman, Barnett, 29
Newsweek, Newhouse Sr.'s attempt to purchase, 12
Newton, Helmut, 59, 67, 76
Newton-John, Olivia, 40
The New Yorker, 151–67
   advertising in, 121–22, 123, 127–28
   Brown as editor of, 142–44, 148–49, 151–67, 223, 232–34, 287
   Brown resigning from, 235
   criticism of, 153–54, 160–63
   cultural importance of, xi, 124–25, 128–29, 133, 239–40
   financial losses and gains of, 227–28, 233–34, 241
   Florio as president of, 126–28, 141

INDEX

Gottlieb as editor of, 129–30, 132–34, 140–41, 143–44, 312n144
high/low concept in, 158–59, 239
The Hot List of, 163–65
internet and technological advances, 257, 259
Newhouse Sr., Liebling's insults of, 13
Newhouse Sr.'s attempt to purchase, 121–22
New Yorker Festival, 241, 289
Next Conference, 234
on O. J. Simpson trial, 156–59
paywall of website, 289
Pulitzer Prizes of, 160, 289
Remnick as editor of, 163, 238–41, 289
search for new editor of, 236–38
Shawn as editor of, xv, 122–30, 154
"Shouts & Murmurs" feature, 152
Si's purchase and publication of, 28, 65, 122–34, 141–43
"Special Women's Issue," 161–63
"Talk of the Town" feature, 156, 165
on Trump, 119
union employee protests, xii, 295nxii
New York magazine, 77–78
The New York Observer
  Carter as editor at, 146–47, 174
  on Carter-Trump relationship, 113
  on end of Condé Nast era, 269–70
  Met Gala coverage in, 193
  "Sex and the City" column in, 230
The New York Times
  on Brown hired for *The New Yorker*, 144
  on Carter's retirement from *Vanity Fair*, 272
  on Condé Nast cafeteria, xvi, 201–2
  DealBook Summit, 233
  on favoritism at *Vanity Fair*, 208
  on men's magazines, 100–101
  Met Gala coverage in, 195
  on Mirabella fired from *Vogue*, 86
  Newhouse Sr.'s attempt to purchase, 12
  on Oscar parties of *Vanity Fair*, xviii
  Si's apartment featured in, 17–18
  on Si's purchase of *The New Yorker*, 124

Styles section, xv
on Time & Life Building, xvi
Trump and, 117, 118–19
on VH1 Fashion Awards, 89
on Wintour's changes at *Vogue*, 88
Niccolini, Julian, 103, 104
Nicholson, Jack, 69–70
Nixon, Richard, 184
Nocera, Joseph, 227
Norwich, William, 80, 211, 213, 275
Noth, Chris, 230
Novogrod, Nancy, 248

Oates, Joyce Carol, 76, 162
Obama, Barack, 116, 117, 272, 284
Obama, Michelle, 73
O'Connor, John D., 184
Odell, Amy, 232, 277–78
Orlean, Susan, 159
Ormond, Julia, 196
Orth, Maureen, 183
Oscar de la Renta (company), 92
Oscar parties of *Vanity Fair*, xii, xv, xviii, 116, 174–80, 185–86, 288–89
Osnos, Peter, 110, 112
Ovitz, Michael, 70, 165

Packer, George, 259
Paglia, Camille, 140
Paltrow, Gwyneth, 177, 194
Parade, 98
Paramount Hotel, New York, 135
Parker, Dorothy, 5
Parks, Gordon, 275
Passages (Sheehy), 63
Patcévitch, Iva, 32, 35
Patchett, Ann, 217
Penn, Irving
  Vanity Fair photographs, 47, 50–51
  Vogue photographs, 26, 30–31, 191, 215
Penney, Alexandra, 187–88, 221
Penske, Jay, 283
Perl, Maurie, 152, 157, 164–65, 220
Perry, Katy, 291
Pfeiffer, Michelle, 59, 89
Picasso, Pablo, 43, 44
pink ribbon campaign, 187–88
Pinterest, 261

Place Vendôme fashion show, France (2024), 290–91
Playboy, 39, 95
Pochoda, Elizabeth, 48
Pollitt, Katha, 162
Pollock, Jackson, 31
Pool, Mary Jane, 42, 246
Portfolio. See *Condé Nast Portfolio*
Post, Emily, 43
Pulitzer Prize, 160, 289
Purdum, Todd, 182, 216, 274
Putin, Vladimir, 197

Queenan, Joe, 99
Quinn, Sally, 56, 238

racial insensitivity and bias
    at *Bon Appétit*, xii, 274
    at Condé Nast Publishing, 274–79, 325n276
    at Hearst Corporation, 275–76
    in *Vanity Fair*, 177, 274
    at *Vogue*, xviii, 276–79, 325n277
Ralph Lauren, 49
Random House, 42, 110–12, 129
Rapoport, Adam, 274
Rayner, Billy, 221–22
Reagan, Nancy, 64–66, 246
Reagan, Ronald, 64–66, 137–38, 246
Reardon, Kate, 209
Reddit, 283–84
Red Scare, 20
Reichl, Ruth, 260, 268
Remnick, David
    background, xiv, 237–39
    as editor of *The New Yorker*, 163, 238–41, 289
    Great Recession and, 268
    Lenin's Tomb, 238–39
    recommending Toobin for *The New Yorker*, 156
    Trump and, 119
    writing for *GQ*, 99
    writing for *The New Yorker*, 155
Rense, Paige, xiv, 244–50
Revlon, 83
Rice, Donna, 64
Rice, Linda, 225, 256

Richards, Keith, 59
Richardson, John, 248
Richman, Alan, 105–6
Ripken, Cal, Jr., 99
Ritts, Herb, 62, 183
Ritz-Carlton, *Vogue* Fashion Fête (1914), 4
Roberts, Julia, 89
Rolling Stone, 39
Rose, Barbara, 32
Ross, Harold, 121–22, 151
Ross, Lillian, 126–27, 130–32, 311n131
Ross, Steve, 70
Rossellini, Isabella, 281
Royalton Hotel, New York, 136, 200
Rubell, Steve, 135–36
Runge, Bernd, 198
Russian Vogue, 195–97
Russo, Rene, 80
Ryder, Winona, 89

Saint-Laurent, Yves, 83
Salinger, J. D., 130
Salle, David, 78
Sarkin, Jane, 136, 176, 179
Savant, Marilyn vos, 99
Sawyer, Diane, 69
Scaasi, Arnold, 19–20
Schell, Jonathan, 129
Schiff, Stephen, 60, 67, 71, 166, 304n71
Schiffer, Claudia, 192
Schjeldahl, Peter, 240
Schlafly, Phyllis, 139
Schlossberg, Jack, 290
Schnabel, Julian, 78
Schrager, Ian, 135–36
Schumacher, Joel, 140
Schwartz, Tony, 110
Schygulla, Hanna, 51
Scientology, 240–41
Scott, L'Wren, 180
Seabrook, John, 68, 165
Seinfeld, Jerry, 194
Self, 40–42, 187–88, 271
Sendak, Maurice, 47
Sephora, 190
Sertl, William, 217
sex, *The New Yorker* on, 162–63
"Sex and the City" column (Bushnell), 230

INDEX 341

Sex and the Single Girl (H. G. Brown), 39
sexism and misogyny
    Condé Nast Publishing leadership
        and, 222–24, 229, 232
    encountered by Brown at *The New*
        Yorker, 153
    encountered by Wintour at *Vogue*, 210
    at *GQ*, 103–5
    media on alleged affair between Si
        and Wintour, 85
    in *Vanity Fair* "Hollywood Issue," 177
Shaffer, David, 82, 85, 136–37
Shapiro, Robert, 157
Shawn, William
    as editor at Broadway Video, 130
    as editor of *The New Yorker*, xv, 122–30, 154
    screenplay criticism of Condé Nast, 131–32, 311n131
    Si's purchase of *The New Yorker* and, 125–26
Sheehy, Gail, 63–64, 71
Shepherd, Cybill, 69
Shnayerson, Michael, 68–69, 138
Simmons, Richard, 40
Simons, Raf, 73
Simpson, Babs, 33
Simpson, Nicole, 157
Simpson, O. J., 156–59
Sinatra, Frank, 83
Sinclair, Upton, 1
S. I. Newhouse School of Public
    Communications, Syracuse
    University, 22
Sischy, Ingrid, 133, 144
Sisman, Lucy, 82, 204–5, 213
60 Minutes profile on *Vanity Fair*, 67
Slavin, Sarah, 221–22
Smith, Liz, 67, 83–85, 176
Smith, Roberta, 139–40
social media
    amateur influencers and, 258
    dangers of, 285–87
    as depictions of real life, 285
    high/low concept in, 59–60
    house tours on, 250, 284
    Vogue and, 290
    See also internet and digital revolution

Social Register, 2
social status and wealth
    1980s and increase in wealthy people, 61, 84
    clothing and, 98, 101, 207
    Condé Nast cafeteria, eating in, 202
    Condé Nast employees and, xi, xiv, 71–72, 82–83, 103, 133, 203–7, 221
    conspicuous consumption and, xiii–xiv, 2, 3–4, 61–62
    Gilded Age in New York and, 1–2
    hiring process at Condé Nast
        Publications and, 210–14
    influencers and social media, 285–87
    Jewish people and "Our Crowd" elite, 12, 20, 35
    Liberman and, 30–32, 55, 114–15, 191, 203–4
    magazine instruction on, 41–42
    Manhattan's "Four Hundred," 1–2
    Met Gala and, xv, 195
    Nast family and, 1–6
    Newhouse Sr. and Mitzi, 8, 11–14, 19, 25, 35, 121–22
    The New Yorker and, 122, 125
    Oscar parties of *Vanity Fair* and, 178–80, 185–86
    Si and, xiii, 15, 17, 25, 33, 126, 203, 282
    taste as indicator of class, 3, 67–68
    Trump and, 111
    Vanity Fair and, 5, 60–62, 183
    Vogue and, 2–3
Solca, Luca, 285–86
Sorel, Edward, 153
South, Hamilton, 218
Spero, Anthony, 219
Spice Girls, 89
Spy, 70, 144–47, 172–73, 175–76
Stahl, Lesley, 117
Stark, Koo, 54
The Staten Island Advance, 10–11
Steichen, Edward, 3, 43, 214, 275
Stein, Gertrude, 5
Steinberg, Saul, 60
Stone, Sharon, 89
Stoppard, Tom, 166
Streisand, Barbra, 275
Studio 54, 72, 112, 308–9n112

Stuff, 106
Style.com, 258–59
Styron, William, 137
Sutherland, Donald, 100
Sykes, Plum, 207
Syracuse University, 22

Talese, Gay, 29, 159
Talk, 240, 287
Talley, André Leon, 114, 115, 193, 277–78
Tartikoff, Brandon, 102
Tatler, 54, 55, 197
Taylor, Elizabeth, 69
Taylor, Lisa, 80
Teen Vogue, 205–6, 271, 278
Thackeray, William, 43
30 Rock (TV show), 181
Thomas, Isiah, 99
Thompson, Hunter S., 39
TikTok, xviii, 59–60, 250, 284. *See also* social media
Tilberis, Liz, 194
Time & Life Building, New York, xvi, 199–202
Time Inc., 271
Tisch, Lawrence, 146
Tisch, Steve, 175
Toledano, Phillip, 266
Toobin, Jeffrey, 156–58
To Russia with Vogue (documentary), 196–97
Townsend, Charles "Chuck," xvii, 268–70
Trillin, Calvin
　on Gottlieb, 132, 143
　on Hot List of *The New Yorker*, 164
　on Newhouse family, social status of, 14
　on Remnick as editor of *The New Yorker*, 239
　on Si's purchase of *The New Yorker*, 126
Trow, George W. S., 125, 128, 158–59
Truman, James
　cafeteria at 4 Times Square and, 199–202
　as editor of *Details*, 224
　on Epicurious.com, 256
　influence on Liberman's clothing, 114–15
　on internet, 260
　as Liberman's successor at Condé Nast Publishing, 224
　Lucky and, 260–61
Trump, Donald J., 109–20
　The Apprentice TV show and, 111
　The Art of the Deal, xv, 110–12
　Brenner's investigative piece on, 71, 113
　Carter at *Vanity Fair*, feud with, 113–14, 116–20
　Condé Nast Publications and, xv, 113, 284
　GQ article and cover, xv, 109–10, 113
　media relations and presidency, 117–20, 290
　Melania, marriage to, 115
　Si and, xv, 109–17, 308–9n112
　Vanity Fair articles on, 71, 110, 113–14, 116–17, 120
Trump, Ivana, 69, 113, 114
Trump, Ivanka, 115, 119
Trump, Melania, xv, 90, 115–16, 120
Trump University, 116–17
Turner, Kathleen, 69
Turnure, Arthur, 2

Udell, Rochelle, 254–55
Ukraine, Russian invasion of, 197
Updike, John, 153, 247
Urban, Binky, 102

Vadukul, Max, 217
Valentino, 71
Vanity Fair, 53–72
　advertising in, 44, 48–49, 51, 65, 68, 71, 113
　The Art of the Deal excerpt in, 110
　Barr, article and cover on, 160–61
　Brown as editor of, xiv–xv, 58–72, 135–42, 151, 218, 232–33
　Carter as editor of, 113–14, 147–49, 169–70, 172–86, 271–73
　celebrity coverage in, 69–70
　criticism of, 68, 70–71
　Crowninshield as editor of, 5, 43–45, 63
　cultural importance of, xi, 5, 44, 51–52, 55, 59–61, 67–69, 135–37, 139–40, 284
　on Deep Throat, 184

INDEX

on English royals, 62
fifth anniversary party for, 135–36
high/low concept in, 48, 59–60, 68, 159
"Hollywood Issue," 177, 179
hyping upcoming magazine articles to press, xiv–xv, 174
internet and technological advances, 257
Jones as editor of, 278–79, 288
Lerman as editor of, 50–51, 56–58
Locke as editor of, 46–50
Moore, article and cover on, 138–40
Nast's purchase of, 4–5
nepotism and favoritism at, 208
offices of, 180–81
Oscar parties, xii, xv, xviii, 116, 174–80, 185–86, 288
on politics, 63–66
on public health issues, 136–38
racial insensitivity and bias at, 177, 274
Reagans' portrait in, 64–66
sexism and misogyny at, 177
Si's and Liberman's rebranding of, 43–52
60 Minutes profile on, 67
social status and wealth, focus on, 60–62
television show idea, 232–33
Trump, articles on, 71, 110, 113–14, 116–17, 120
"We Nominate for Oblivion" feature in, 43–44, 63
writers' salaries at, 45, 69
van Wyck, Bronson, 178–79
van Zandt, Pamela, 83
Vendler, Helen, 47
Versace, 192
Versace, Donatella, 73, 196
Versace, Gianni, 71, 88, 194
VH1 Fashion Awards, 89
Vidal, Gore, 249
Viva, 76
Vogel, Lucien, 30
Vogue, 73–93
　in 1960s and 1970s, 78–80
　advertising in, 3–4, 84, 194
　anti-Semitism in, 274–75
　beginning of, 2–3
　biggest issue, 270–71
　Carter as writer for, 145–46
　celebrity covers and career boosts, 89–90
　Chase as editor of, 4, 31
　China, fashion shoot in, 91
　counterculture and industry competition, 40
　cultural importance of, xi, xix, 84, 89–90, 93
　designers, shaping careers of, 190–91
　employees and social status, 207–8
　exclusive photographers for, 249
　expensive photo shoots for, 215–17
　Fashion Fête of 1914, 4
　global fashion and, xv
　high/low concept in, 87, 191
　hundredth-birthday party and centennial issue, 191
　international offices and versions of, xvi, xviii, 195–98, 289–90 (*see also British Vogue*; *Vogue Paris*)
　internet and technological advances, 257–58
　Ivana Trump, article and cover on, 114
　Liberman as art director at, 30–34, 45
　Melania Trump, articles on, 115, 120
　Met Gala and, xii, 115, 116, 120, 192–95
　middle-class readers, appeal to, 3–4
　Mirabella as editor at, xv, 79–86, 216, 222–23
　Mitzi Newhouse in, 25
　Nast's purchase of, 2–3
　new era of celebrity coverage in, 88–89
　Newhouse Sr.'s purchase of, 13–14
　overspending on models, 222
　"People Are Talking About . . ." column, 25
　Place Vendôme fashion show, 290–91
　on politics, 63, 90–93, 117–18, 290
　racial insensitivity and bias at, xviii, 276–79
　Russian Vogue, 195–97
　Si appointed as publisher and changes to, 26–28
　social status and wealth, 2–3
　Teen Vogue, 205–6, 271, 278
　VH1 Fashion Awards and, 89
　Vogue100 perks, 271

Vogue (cont.)
  Vogue Paris, 4, 198, 251, 276, 289
  Vreeland as editor at, 34–35, 45, 79, 215–16, 276–77
  Wintour as creative director at, 80–81
  Wintour as editor at, xv, 73–74, 83–93, 114–15, 117–18, 249
  Wintour as global editorial director, 289–90
Vogue.com, 257–58
Vogue Paris, 4, 198, 251, 276, 289
Vogue Russia, 195–97
Volpe, Lynden "Carolyne," 207–8
von Bülow, Claus, 67
von Furstenberg, Diane, 73, 176, 282
Vreeland, Diana
  as editor of Vogue, 34–35, 45, 79, 215–16, 276–77
  luxury design input of, 190–91
  Met Gala and, 192
  on Nast's parties, 5
  in Vanity Fair, 59

Wachenfeld, Haus, 91
Waithe, Lena, 279
Walker, Mike, 158
Wallace, Thomas J., 252
Walters, Barbara, 24
Wang, Alexander, 73
Wang, Vera, 209–10
Warburg, Gerald, 12
Warfield, Rebecca, 79
Warhol, Andy, 80, 83, 305n80
Warner Bros. Discovery, 283
Washington Post, 12–13, 238–39
Wasserstein, Wendy, 162
Waugh, Auberon, 55
Waverly Inn, New York, 116–17, 185
Weaver, Sigourney, 69
Webb, Jonathan, 171
Weber, Bruce, 96, 127
Weiner, Anthony, 118
Weinstein, Harvey, 89–90, 194, 234–35, 240, 287, 289
Wells, Linda
  on CondéNet, 259
  on culture of Condé Nast Publishing, 207

  as editor of Allure, 189–90, 213–14, 223
  Liberman and, 115, 189
Welteroth, Elaine, 278
Wexner, Leslie, 258
White, Kate, 107
White House Correspondents' Dinner, 184–85
Whitney, Ruth, 224
Wickenden, Dorothy, 159
Wigand, Jeffrey, 182
Williams, Serena, 291
Wilson, Phyllis Starr, 40–41, 187
Winchell, Walter, 274–75
Winfrey, Oprah, 277
Wintour, Anna
  Anna Wintour Costume Center, Metropolitan Museum of Art, 73–74
  as artistic director of Condé Nast, 272
  background and early career of, 74–77
  Carter, friendship with, 145–46, 272
  as chief content officer of Condé Nast, 289
  as creative director for Vogue, 80–81
  designers, shaping careers of, 190–91
  as editor of British Vogue, 81–82
  as editor of House & Garden, 82, 200, 247–48
  as editor of Vogue, xv, 73–74, 83–93, 114–15, 117–18, 249
  first Vogue cover, 86–88
  as global editorial director of Vogue, 289–90
  global fashion and, xv
  Hillary Clinton and, 90, 117–18
  as inspiration for The Devil Wears Prada, 74, 204
  internet and technological advances, 257–58
  management style of, 210
  Met Gala and, 192–95
  mortgage from Advance Publications, 220
  Presidential Medal of Freedom, 290
  Princess Diana lunch conversation in The New Yorker, 232
  on racial bias at Vogue, xviii, 277–79
  tribute to husband, 136–37

INDEX

Trump and, 114–15, 117–20, 290
union employees picketing outside home of, xii, 295nxii
VH1 Fashion Awards and, 89
Vogue100 perks and, 271
Wired, 253, 256–57
Wolcott, James, 152, 159, 161–62
Wolfe, Tom, xvii, 39, 263, 265
Women's Wear Daily, xvi
Woodward, Bob, 184
Wright, Lawrence, 240–41

Wrightsman, Jayne, 194
Wurtzel, Elizabeth, 137

Yamamoto, Yohji, 78, 114
A Year in Provence (Mayle), 102
Youngbird, Marilyn, 63–64
"Youth Quake," 79

Zellweger, Renée, 89
Zinczenko, David, 107
Zuckerman, Mort, 60, 233